Social Change in Brazil, 1945–1985

Social Change in Brazil, 1945–1985

The Incomplete Transition

Edited by

Edmar L. Bacha
and
Herbert S. Klein

University of New Mexico Press
Albuquerque

Library of Congress Cataloging-in-Publication Data

Transição incompleta. English.
    Social change in Brazil, 1945–1985 : the incomplete transi-
tion/.
    edited by Edmar L. Bacha and Herbert S. Klein.—1st ed.
        p.   cm.
    Revised translation of: Transição incompleta.
    Includes bibliographies.
    ISBN 0-8263-1111-3 (pbk.)
    1. Brazil—Economic conditions—1945–1964. 2. Brazil—
Economic conditions—1964–1985. 3. Brazil—Social conditions
—1945–1964. 4. Brazil—Social conditions—1964-   I. Bacha,
Edmar Lisboa. II. Klein, Herbert S.   III. Title.
HC187.T7213   1989
303.4'0981—dc19-   88-19895
                              CIP

First English edition

Originally published in 1986 as *A transição incompleta, Brasil
desde 1945*.
Rio de Janeiro: Paz e Terra.

*Dedicated to the Memory of
Carlos F. Díaz Alejandro*

CONTENTS

TABLES

Introduction

Edmar L. Bacha and Herbert S. Klein

The crisis of the external debt is the main economic factor affecting Brazil in the decade of the 1980s. It is the cause of the severe recession of 1981–83, which broke the process of rapid growth that had characterized the Brazilian economy and society since the end of World War II. Although the Brazilian economy appeared to have recovered its capacity for growth after 1984, in fact the economic imbalances directly or indirectly associated with the external debt crisis remained intense. Before this new pause, Brazil had experienced four decades of profound change, from a predominantly agrarian society into an urban and industrial one. Today Brazil is the seventh most industrialized nation of the western world.

So rapidly has this change occurred that its ramifications are little understood. The current generation finds itself living in a modern industrial society, but their parents were born into a different world. Contemporary critics, when viewing their nation from the perspective of an advanced industrial society, cannot understand the anomalies within their own world, which still exhibits many traces of its former rural and slave-bound antecedents. Finally, the overwhelming force of the change has obscured serious problems within the country, and only now are Brazilians realizing that the process of growth and change inevitably leaves discontinuities and disjunctures.

The recession of the early 1980s is giving way to renewed growth, while

1

the long and painful transition to a democratic government is being attempted after twenty-one years of military rule. Now seems an appropriate time to rethink the basic changes that occurred in the past forty years and to analyze their impact for the future evolution of national society.

Our aim is to look at fundamental structural change in a largely quantitative fashion, in an attempt to set the societal changes in the broadest possible context. Thus, we have concentrated in this volume on structures and the broad social and economic conditions in which they developed. We have tried to examine how and why the occupational structure has changed, how cities have grown and rural society has been transformed, and what has occurred in the areas of wealth distribution and the creation of modern educational and welfare systems for the entire population. Clearly this approach underplays the issues of changing ideologies, cultures, and political movements. But we felt that these had already been dealt with in the available literature, just as the more structural questions have been too often ignored.

This ignorance is not caused by any fundamental lack of data. Indeed, Brazil is one of the few societies undergoing rapid urbanization and industrialization which has produced an impressive output of statistics essential to interpreting its social change. In surveys undertaken largely in response to political protests over its unbridled capitalist approach, but also a product of its own technocratic administration, the military regimes of the 1964–84 period have been especially concerned with surveying the national population through some of the most complete samples ever taken of any society. While systematic annual-based, national-level economic and social statistics were not fully developed until the last decade, thus making it difficult to undertake some historical and comparative analyses, the extant survey data, state-level surveys, and national decennial censuses, constitute a body of quantitative materials unprecedented in a society so recently passing through the stages of modernization. The following chapters all explore at a macro-level the impressive national statistical surveys by which Brazil's changes can be measured.

An analysis of these structural changes in the last forty years shows the profound nature of the transformations in Brazilian society as well as their incompleteness. Brazil has now gone through the so-called demographic transition and has achieved mortality and natality rates for a broad sector of its population that are comparable to most of the world's newly industrializing and advanced societies. Yet there still exist rural areas with mortality rates indicative of a traditional backward society experiencing minimal social change. Brazil has provided education for the majority of its population and created the second most advanced university and scientific research system in the Third World. Yet 25 percent of the population remains illiterate, and the public secondary education system is characteristic of a far more backward social system. Health care is now available to almost all Brazilian citizens, yet no unemployment insurance plan has yet evolved for Brazil. The massive expansion of industry and government services has led to a profound structural mobility, massive creation of new jobs, and a level of social mobility among the most rapid in the world; at the same time, the nation has one of the highest indices of inequality of income and wealth, however measured. In too many areas, Brazil remains what we have called elsewhere a "Belindia." That is, a regionally and class defined society comparable in every way to Belgium, but coexisting with poorer, more rural, and more northern part of the country comparable in most respects to India.

That the contrasts can be documented in the midst of all this change can be clearly seen in each chapter. But the meaning of this seeming division is difficult to interpret. Is this a result of incomplete or distorted capitalist growth? Are the upper and middle class urbanites of São Paulo the advanced frontier to which most Brazilians are moving, or are they an enclave that moves farther and farther away from the rest of Brazil? This is the fundamental question that emerges from a study of the recent Brazilian past. Its answer requires an analysis of both the voluntary and involuntary forces that shaped this change. It is particularly important to determine just how important pre- and post-1964 government policies were in influencing this growth pattern. Also, one must try to determine the impact of industrial growth and masssive commercialization of agriculture on the social fabric.

While it is not possible to fully answer these questions, a look at the evolution of the Brazilian economy during this period is essential to place these questions in perspective. The Brazilian economy from the mid-1940s until the mid-1980s experienced accelerated economic growth, marked by a few pauses and readjustments before continued expansion. Such fundamental government policies as import substitution and exchange rate manipulations, which sought to use national resources to turn Brazil into an industrialized and exporting economy, were already in place by the 1950s and would be reinforced in the 1960s and 1970s.

Following the readjustments of the world markets after World War II, the demand for Brazilian commodities led to higher world prices and sustained growth. This rapid growth slowed in the cyclical crisis of 1953–56. Then the coffee industry experienced a structural crisis with falling world prices, forcing the national government both to stockpile coffee and to institute a massive eradication program. This structural crisis and the response of the Kubitschek government led to the definitive end of the dominance of coffee in the Brazilian economy. By 1962, the government adopted a unified exchange rate system for exports that neutralized the taxing impact of the exchange rate system on agriculture and tended to eliminate the traditional forced savings that agriculture had made available to the rest of the economy since World War II. The last regimes prior to the military takeover also instituted policies to promote industrial growth nationally through import substitution and government investments in both infrastructure and production.

Thus the coming to power of the military regimes did not in and of itself lead to any revolutionary change in national economic policies; instead, they tended to reinforce policies that had already been initiated by earlier governments. The costs of these programs were in turn shifted more to the working classes and less toward other sectors in the society through controls over wages. The military inherited an economy going through another of its cyclical balance of payments and growth slowdowns in 1963–67. The decision to continue the export orientation and industrialization policies of the previous regimes led to adoption of a mini-devaluation program beginning in 1968. This was another piece in the neutralization of the anti-export bias inherent in previous policies toward both agriculture and industry. This change went a long way toward helping exports enter the international market. It also began a very successful program of tax incentives to industrial exports beginning in 1966, which gave a major boost to industrial export activity.

Beginning in 1967 and lasting until 1973, an unusual conjuncture of world market conditions helped to sustain a new cycle of growth in the Brazilian economy, which was unique in its lack of the usual foreign exchange constraints. The rise of international commodity prices and the sudden availability of cheap international credit through the growth of the Eurodollar market created a situation in which the economy could sustain growth rates on the order of 11 percent each year for six years in a row. Equally the government's control over wages and increased tax collections due to better administration led to reduced budget deficits and sustained investments in industry and agriculture. Not only was industry expanding at an impressive rate, but also there was a massive shift in the agricultural sector. Thanks to the successful unification of the exchange markets, which ended the traditional bleeding of rural profits into the urban sector, as well as the deliberate government policy of cheap credits, agro-business developments led to the soya revolution and the growth of new agricultural commodities and new world markets for these exports.

But the delayed crisis in the cyclical balance of payments finally overwhelmed the economy, with the twin impact of the two world oil price shocks and the debt crisis. In October 1973 came the first OPEC (Organization of Petroleum Exporting Countries) oil price increases, the general crisis of the international commmodities markets, and the acceleration of inflation. Growth within Brazil dropped from 11 percent to 7 percent per annum, and even this lower rate could only be sustained through heavy borrowings and increasing government deficits. To boost exports the government after 1974 provided cheap credit to agriculture—on the order of 3 percent of the GNP (Gross National Product) by the last years of the decade. Subsidized credit was also extended to industry, and tax incentives were maintained, all at the expense of increasing external debt. But these activities only delayed the inevitable adjustments, which had been the traditional pattern up to this time.

The final jolt came with the drying up of cheap credit from abroad as a result of the combined impact of the second oil price crisis of 1979–80; the rise of international interest rates beginning in 1979 provoked by the policies of U.S. Federal Reserve President Paul Volcker; and the Mexican moratorium of August 1982. These factors led to back-to-back world recessions in 1980 and 1982 and the reimposition of traditional external constraints on the Brazilian economy. The forced march of industrialization, which had been promoted by the government since the mid-1970s, could not be continued now that the government could no longer dispose of the cheap international credit that had permitted the previous boom.

The 1981–83 period of recession, caused by the crisis of the foreign debt, marked a dramatic return to the more traditional experience of growth restrained by the availability of foreign earnings, which had characterized Brazil's experience from the beginning of the twentieth century. In comparison with past experience, the crisis of the 1980s occurs under the threats of an extraordinary high rate of national inflation, extremely large public-sector deficits, and a foreign debt four times greater than the usual exports of the country. In compensation, the increasing sophistication of Brazilian industry allows a more flexible response to fluctuations in the international economy.

The Brazilian economy's temporary return to growth after 1984 was associated on the one hand with the expansion of the international economy caused by record fiscal deficits of the United States resulting in an extraordinary expansion of exports to that country, and on the other hand the maturation of national investments in petroleum exploration initiated in the mid-1970s, which allowed a significant reduction in Brazil's dependence on petroleum imports. The significant devaluation of the real rate of exchange at the beginning of the 1980s permitted Brazil to take advantage of these commercial opportunities.

Between 1984 and 1986, economic growth resumed through a combination of the use of idle capacity created by the 1981–83 recession, and the fruition of earlier investments. In February 1986, the first civilian government in twenty-one years decreed a courageous monetary reform, substituting the *cruzado* for the *cruzeiro*, in an attempt to attack Brazilian inflation by a "heterodox shock." But this reform was frustrated by the unleashing of uncontrolled internal demand. By the end of 1986, the experience of the failed *Plan Cruzado* clearly showed the difficulty of simultaneously maintaining a growing internal demand and producing a commercial surplus sufficient to pay fully the interest on the external debt.

By the beginning of 1987, the conflicts that marked the evolution of the Brazilian economy have been accentuated after the failure of the *Plan Cruzado*: decline of real wages, a growing public deficit, and a moratorium on the external debt. Nevertheless, the transition to democracy is proceeding. Thus, the strong contrasts that have marked the Brazilian experience from the beginning are still in evidence, making Brazil's development an experience with few parallels.

Having examined the growth of the Brazilian economy during this forty-year period, one can ask whether all the results of that growth were inevitable, especially in terms of the social outcomes. To answer this question, it is useful to examine the postwar growth experiences of comparable regimes and societies. Several Asian societies offer interesting comparative perspectives. Some large Asian countries have also undergone postwar periods of high growth, industrialization, modernization of agriculture, and urbanization on the scale of Brazil. But their histories of growth have often been accompanied by different social outcomes that have been influenced by differing government policies and initiatives. For example, several of these nations have carried out agrarian reforms while sustaining growth, just as they have invested more heavily in social services, education, and income transfers to level inequalities. The effect of these differing policies can be seen in the results obtained (Table 1).

When compared to Asian countries of medium and large sizes Brazil's growth rates and creation of an industrial sector are seen to surpass any of these countries. Yet large-scale industrializing Asian countries, which often have had less growth than Brazil and far lower per capita incomes, have achieved far better social results. Countries such as India and China, which are far larger than Brazil and have per capita incomes one seventh of Brazil's relatively high rate, have better distributions of income (India), as well as better levels of health and education (China). Thus size alone cannot explain why Brazil has not achieved better social gains for its population.

Nor is the type of regime and political system a sufficient explanatory variable. Authoritarian regimes such as those of South Korea and Thailand—one with a per capita income the same as Brazil, the other with half the Brazilian rate, and both with comparable growth rates over long periods of time—end up with far better rates of income distribution than Brazil. Moreover, South Korea has three times the percentage of secondary school students enrolled than Brazil and a much lower rate of infant mortality, which is a prime indicator of health and nutrition.

The relative openness of an economy to world market conditions or its

Table 1

Comparative Indices of Growth & Welfare Among Major Industrializing Countries in Asia and Brazil in the mid-1980s

Country	Population (in millions) mid-1984	Income per capita ($US/1984)	Percent growth rate per capita*	Percent of income taken by top 10%**	Percent of income taken by bottom 40%**	Infant Mortality (per 1000) 1984	Percent of Children in Secondary School (1983)
China	1,029.2	310	4.5	—	—	36	35
India	749.2	260	1.6	33.6	16.2	90	34
Indonesia	158.9	540	4.9	34.0	14.4	97	37
Philippines	53.4	660	2.6	38.5	14.2	49	63
Thailand	50.0	860	4.2	34.1	15.2	44	29
South Korea	40.1	2110	6.6	27.5	16.9	28	89
Sri Lanka	15.9	360	2.9	28.2	19.2	37	56
Malaysia	15.3	1980	4.5	39.8	11.2	28	49
BRASIL	132.6	1720	4.6	50.6	7.0	68	42

Source: World Bank, *World Development Report, 1986* (New York: Oxford University Press, 1986), pp. 180ff.
Notes: *Annual average per capita growth rates from 1965–84.
**Of households.

dependence on foreign capital markets is another factor often cited as an explanation for the relative backwardness of social welfare in Brazil. Yet such highly dependent countries as Thailand, South Korea, and Malaysia show that this also is insufficient as an explanation. Dependency and integration into the world market did not prevent these nations from making far better progress than Brazil in crucial areas of welfare and equality.

While different patterns of land tenure at the beginning of industrialization and historical institutions such as slavery have obviously had an impact on wealth distribution and the level of social welfare, the fact that Brazil started out at a much higher level of per capita income than most Asian countries of comparable size with comparable experiences of rapid growth suggests that these historical factors were not decisive.

Policies adopted or rejected by governments during periods of rapid growth have played a crucial role in influencing welfare and wealth distribution in these countries. What Brazil has achieved or failed to do in this area, then, is related directly to its governmental policies. Many of these policies could have been different, and would thus have led to different results. As the experience of both larger and authoritarian Asian states shows, levels of welfare and income were not predetermined because of Brazil's size, rapid rate of growth, authoritarian regimes, or external dependence.

It was on the basis of this analysis that we decided to organize this survey of the structural changes and government policies that have shaped the nature of contemporary Brazilian society. The volume is organized in three sections. The first deals with the macro-social changes that have occurred in this period in population growth, the previously dominant rural sector, and the major growth of urban centers. The next section deals with the consequences of these broad structural changes in terms of the evolution of the occupational structure, the patterns of social mobility, and the distribution of income. The last section examines in detail the history of social welfare, education, and health care—the three major areas of government intervention in the social arena since 1945.

The theme that runs throughout this volume is the enormity of the changes that have taken place and the incompleteness of the process. In his study of population change, for example, Merrick argues for a dual population system. He posits a modern demographic elite passing through the mortality transition and then into controlled natality at a pace commensurate with late-industrializing societies. Coexisting with this largely urban and south central sector is another sector with high fertility and mortality rates at the level of traditional underdeveloped societies. Unlike the elite, this sector is found everywhere in Brazil in the lower classes, the rural areas, and throughout most of the Northeast. This results in national rates of life expectancy that are below comparable late-industrializing nations. Merrick argues that these figures show a severe duality, if not dichotomy. But the question remains as to whether these two patterns instead form a continuum, with the more traditional groups moving toward the more modern. Here, as elsewhere in this volume, the question of continuum versus dichotomy, function versus dysfunction, and lineality versus nonlineality reflects opposing views on both the past performance and future development of Brazilian society.

Merrick also signals some profound structural changes through which the population has clearly passed in the last four decades. Interregional migration, which was so intense during the early part of this period, has declined and is no longer a profoundly important phenomenon. Nevertheless, rural-to-urban migration at the intraregional level continues at a rapid pace and appears likely to do so for many years to come. Finally, Merrick investigates the causes of the changing relationship of women to the workforce and shows its profound impact on fertility decline in the absence of changes in other proximate determinants of fertility.

In his survey of the complex evolution of agriculture and rural society in the last four decades, Goodman notes profound and often contradictory changes. There has been both a relative and absolute decline of rural population, which has deeply influenced the social evolution of Brazilian society. This exodus is due to deep structural changes in rural production. These changes essentially relate to the capitalization of agriculture and the creation of a new "industrialized" agriculture well beyond the traditional coffee model. For the first two decades of this period, an extensive model of growth was dominant, and the opening up of western and southern lands provided the major avenue for expansion. But since the late 1960s a true agricultural revolution has occurred in Brazil, with major inputs of subsidized credit leading to a new intensive model of growth. Mechanization, new seeds and fertilizers, and the establishment of a storage and transportation infrastructure have led to significant growth in older nonfrontier areas, especially in the central and southern agricultural zones. The result: new crops, increasing transfers of capital into agriculture, improved yields, and a decline in rural labor requirements. Alongside the new agro-industrial *latifundias* and the older and low production *minifundias* there have also arisen capitalized family farms, especially in the South. The complexity of these multiple transitions has entailed profound changes in labor relations as well as in production and, as Goodman shows, there is an intense debate as to the causes and consequences of this proletarianization of rural labor.

The massive changes in the rural world have been the major force behind the tremendous urbanization of Brazil in the last forty years. By any standards, Brazil since 1940 has evolved from a predominantly rural to a predominantly urban society. This has led to basic changes in everything from occupation and social mobility to fertility and health standards. Clearly, life is better in the cities, and is so perceived by the majority of the rural population. As Katzman stress, it is the "push factor" of rural change that best explains this rapid growth. In contrast to some of the other essays, Katzman sees this growth as more harmonious and less dysfunctional. All cities, large and small, have grown, and cities in all regions have increased their relative shares of population. This means that the process of hyperurbanization found in other societies has not occurred in Brazil, and the relative importance of the two major cities, São Paulo and Rio de Janeiro, has changed little over the four decades. While urban employment has not smoothly kept up with in-migration, especially in the early part of the period, there now seems to be a rough balance between urban employment and population, indicating that the urban service and industrial sectors have enough dynamism to meet increased employment demands. The fact that problems of urban services exist, and that severe problems of adjustment are still to be made, does not mar what Katzman sees as the essentially harmonious growth of urban centers over this period.

Examining these spatial and structural changes at the level of employment, mobility, and income is the concern of the three essays in the second section. Faria in his discussion of employment shows the immensity of the shift of workers from unskilled and semi-skilled agricultural and extractive occupations into service and manufacturing jobs in the period since 1940. This has been accompanied by a change in the quality of labor, resulting in a more highly skilled and better educated workforce. The driving force behind this change has been the industrial sector, which has had extremely high annual growth rates throughout the period. But despite these changes, great poverty still exists throughout Brazil, and the country's level of social well-being is still below that of comparable Asian societies. Critics have laid the blame for this continued poverty on the employment structure created in the last four decades. It is argued that industry has not kept pace with the workers leaving agriculture, the youths entering the job market for the first time, and the workers displaced from more traditional occupations by industrialization. The result has been the excessive expansion of a dysfunctional service sector and the creation of ever-larger pockets of urban poverty. But in an original and extremely important exercise, Faria shows that the industrial sector has grown at a rate sufficient to meet the increased demand for employment, especially during the 1970s. He does admit, however, that industrial growth has been cyclical rather than linear, with periodic crisis and adjustments. On the other hand, steady growth in the government sector has been important in creating jobs. The greatest growth in new employment, in fact, has been in the service sector and especially in government employment. Rather than viewing these jobs as dysfunctional, Faria sees them as closely related to the expanded delivery of basic social services to the population.

This opening up of a new world of industrial occupations and government service has profoundly changed the patterns of social mobility, as described in the essay of Pastore. Brazil is still passing through an early stage of advanced industrialization, with the increase in new and more skilled jobs structurally creating a great amount of upward social and occupational mobility. So rapid has been the growth of new occupations that Brazilians are by and large less educated for their occupational positions than would normally be the case in older industrial societies. In such post-industrial worlds, education is more closely related to job status and mobility is more circular than structural, with upward and downward mobility more evenly matched.

As could be expected, most of this mobility in Brazilian society has occurred at the borders of each class and occupational status. Most people have moved only a small way up the ladder. But there is little question that the overwhelming majority of Brazilians are in higher status jobs than their parents held. Moreover, the highest rates of mobility have occurred in the lowest social and economic strata. The recession of the early 1980s has created a pause in this process, and Pastore asks if we have not moved into a new, less mobile period. Most of the transfers from rural to urban life had occurred by 1985; with the industrial sector slowing its rate of growth, there appears to be a shift toward higher rates of immobility and increased downward mobility. In contrast to Faria, Pastore seems to feel that the growth of an informal labor sector and urban services may not be such a positive phenomenon for continued high rates of intergenerational mobility.

Changes in income distribution have been few in this period, despite the high rates of occupational mobility and the tremendous increase in resources available to all sectors of society, according to Hoffmann. If anything, she argues, inequality has probably been on the increase for most of the period. These levels of resource distribution, however measured, mark Brazil as an unusually unequal society, even for a late-industrializing nation. Hoffmann sees the increasing inequality of resources differing from decade to decade, growing more rapidly in the 1960s than in the 1970s. There have been some positive results nationally, such as reductions in regional disparities and increasing levels of equality in the more advanced regions. The increasing entrance of married women into the workforce, discussed in several essays, also had a positive impact on increasing equality of family income distribution. In fact, a major decline in the levels of poverty has occurred in the last two decades as a result of increasing family income at the lower end of the class structure. But conversely the regions of more recent settlement, such as the North frontier and the Middle-West regions, have experienced increasing rates of inequality, while the new capital entering agriculture in the last two decades has accentuated rural inequalities. As one moves from considering income to measuring the distributions of fixed assets and land, the levels of inequality are even more pronounced. The level of inequality in land ownership is extremely high and has been that way over long periods, well beyond the time limit of this volume. There also seem to be very high levels of concentration in manufacturing and business enterprises in general. Thus, despite mobility, new occupations, and increasing family incomes, Brazil still possesses one of the highest degrees of income concentration in the world today.

The last section of the book is concerned with the changing delivery of government services and their impact on the population of Brazil since 1945. All three essays in this section show profound changes, just as they detail surprising continuities. They also reveal levels of inequality and rates of social welfare that often are worse than those of comparable industralizing societies in other areas of the Third World.

As Coutinho and Salm show, the government provision of social welfare has come late to Brazil, long after comparable stages of growth in Europe and even North America. Moreover the growth of the welfare system has been slow, spreading from the more privileged sectors of the working classes to the rest of the population. It is only in the last two decades that a national approach has been attempted, and even then it has concentrated on the more easily taxed and controlled formal labor sector. Yet this concentration has still meant that 54 percent of the economically active population was contributing to the welfare system by 1980—a rather impressive statistic given the late start of Brazil in all social welfare areas. While the list of services now available to workers and their families over a large part of Brazil is quite substantial even by advanced industrial standards, Coutinho and Salm stress that Brazil still lacks one fundamental feature of modern industrial systems: unemployment insurance. By the standards of Latin America, however, Brazil compares favorably with the wealthiest and most advanced countries in its coverage and benefits. For all the changes that have occurred, the low quality of benefits granted, the difficulties of admininstration and financing, and the still large numbers of rural and informal market workers excluded, combine to create grave inequalities in the system. These find expression in the still relatively low indices of health, education, and welfare measured in the population.

As profoundly revolutionary as the delivery of social services in Brazil in the last four decades has been the delivery of education at all levels. Moura Castro shows that by any indices Brazil has experienced major growth in the delivery of education to its population; this has resulted in a major change in the rates of literacy and of persons completing formal schooling. By 1980, three quarters of the population was literate, and the traditional sexual differences in literacy had all but disappeared. The growth in elementary education was massive, and the government in this period began to support secondary education on a major scale, finally enabling the lower middle class and the privileged sectors of the working class to gain access to secondary schools for the first time. But it was probably at the university level that the most striking change occurred, in terms of both quantity and quality. Since 1945, Brazil has been able to create a modern system of higher education, one of the best in the newly industrializing world. But this growth has not been uniform in terms of the quality or delivery of education. Profound differences in primary and secondary education are still apparent even at the intra-urban level, as well as across regions. Thus the quality of education delivered at the tertiary level has not been matched by anything similar at the primary or secondary level, and public secondary education, despite change, still blocks access to more advanced education for those from the less privileged classes. Even the truly extraordinary university system is not free from serious conflicts as the new research parts find themselves in conflict with the teaching institutions.

Some of the most innovative changes in delivery of social services in the past forty years have occurred in the area of health care. As the study of McGreevey, Piola and Magalhães Vianna shows, Brazil expends a high share of its GNP on health care and now delivers emergency health services at government expense to the overwhelming majority of its citizens. But despite this growth in expenditures, over 80 percent of the monies went for curative rather than primary or preventive care and thus had little impact on national mortality rates. In fact, the share of funds going to primary care has declined progressively in the last three decades as the middle and upper classes have paid for and received ever more curative support. Thus in health, as in many other social areas, a duality, if not dichotomy, exists in which essentially competitive groups with differing aims vie for control over national resources. Nevertheless, the dichotomy is not complete, for the wealthy sector has been taxed to pay for the growth of curative services in the poorer regions. The authors argue that INAMPS (Instituto Nacional de Assistência Médica e Providência Social) transferred more resources from rich to poor than any other part of the social welfare system.

The essays in this volume thus stress the really significant ruptures with past society that have occurred in the last forty years, probably the most momentous in terms of basic structural change of any in Brazilian history. They also portray the continuities with an older order that seem impervious to reform or express themselves under new forms in a changed environment. Although there is a general consensus among the authors as to the basic nature of the changes that have occurred, they also emphasize the biased nature of government interventions in the social sphere, which partly explains the incompleteness of the transformation of Brazilian society since 1945.

The making of this book owes much to the support of Dean Alfred Stepan of Columbia University who helped sponsor the conference on "Brazilian Social Change since 1945" held in New York in December 1984. With generous financial assistance provided by the Ford and Inter-American Foundations, we were able to revise the original papers into this final published form. We would also like to thank Denise Jackson for her outstanding administrative effort and Terry Seymour for her translations of the original Portuguese texts.

1

Population Since 1945

Thomas J. Merrick

INTRODUCTION

Since the end of World War II, Brazil has experienced profound social and economic changes. Almost all of these changes have affected, or been affected by, collateral variations in the size, composition, and geographic distribution of Brazil's population. Highlighted in Table 1.1 are some of the main demographic trends in Brazil during the period under study. The years 1950 and 1980 are used as benchmarks because population censuses were taken in those years.

During the three decades between those two censuses, total population more than doubled. By 1985, it will be triple the total population of 1945. The main reason for this growth is that death rate declines accelerated during the late 1940s and early 1950s, while birth rates remained high until the mid-1960s. As a consequence, a dramatic rise occurred in Brazil's rate of natural increase, which was the main demographic component of population change in this period; international migration, which had played an important role before World War II, was comparatively less important after.

The birth rate has declined since 1965, so that population is growing more slowly during the 1980s than in the three preceding decades. However, the rate of growth remains high by international standards because declines in the death rate have offset declines in birth rates. Brazil's annual rate of growth in the early 1980s (2.3 percent) was close to the average for less developed

15

Table 1.1
Post-War Population Trends in Brazil

	1950	1980
Total population (millions)	51.9	119.1
Birth rate (per 1000 population)	44	31
Death rate (per 1000 population)	15	8
Natural increase (per 1000 population)	29	23
Youth (under age 15, as percent of total population)	42	38
Urban population (percent of total)	36	68
Nonagricultural employment (percent of total economically active population)	40	71
Working women (economically active 30–39-year-old women as percent of all women in age category)	11	34

Sources: Brazilian census data; birth and death rates are averages for years centered on census year from UN.

countries (2.4 percent) and nearly four times the average level for more developed countries (0.6 percent). Since Brazil's death rate is not likely to decline much further, future declines in the birth rate will bring more marked reductions in the rate of natural increase.

Trends in the composition and geographic distribution of the population reflect both demographic and socio-economic changes. Because of recent declines in the birth rate, the percentage of the population under age 15 declined from 42 percent in 1950 to 38 percent in 1980—a figure that is still high in comparison with levels of 20–22 percent found in populations that have lower birth rates.

Most of the population increase that Brazil experienced between 1950 and 1980 occurred in urban areas. The officially designated urban share of total population rose from 36 percent in 1950 to 68 percent in 1980.[1] Rural population continued to grow during the 1950s and 1960s, but at a much slower rate. During the 1970s, rural population declined in absolute as well as relative terms.

Urban population increase reflects the growth of nonagricultural employment, which increased from 40 to 71 percent of the economically active population between 1950 and 1980. Industrial employment accounted for much of the increase in nonagricultural employment between 1950 and 1980, though services continued to account for the largest percentage share of the total.

Industry (manufacturing, construction, mining, and utilities) increased from 14 to 33 percent of total employment, while services increased from 26 to 38 percent. Brazil's level of urbanization is approaching that of Europe and North America (where the averages are 72 and 74 percent), though the share of agriculture in total employment in Brazil is still well above the level of more industrialized countries (in the United States, for example, agriculture accounts for only 3 percent of total employment).

The continued growth of services may reflect some labor-saving bias in Brazilian manufacturing technology, but it is also related to other social, economic, and demographic trends, including the demand for services created by a larger urban population. One trend that is particularly noteworthy in relation to rising service employment is the significant increase in the rate of female labor force participation that occurred between 1950 and 1980 (with most of it coming after 1970), since a large proportion of women are employed in services.

Taking women aged 30–39 as an example, the female labor force participation rate increased from 11 percent to 34 percent for those ages. Some of this increase reflects a wider definition of economic activity in the 1980 census, but most of it represents an increase in female wage labor that reverses a trend which started with declines in agricultural employment, where most women worked as unpaid family workers. The rise in economic activity rates for females reflects increases in the educational attainments of women and has important implications for declines in fertility that will be examined later in this essay.

Since other chapters in this volume touch on topics that relate to demography in the broader sense (education, labor force, and urbanization, to name three), the focus here will be on aspects that are central to the dynamics of population change, including fertility, mortality, and migration, and on their implications for policy.

MORTALITY TRENDS

At the end of World War II, Brazilian mortality rates were high by international standards. The crude death rate was over 20 per thousand and life expectancy at birth was probably less than 45 years. Moreover, the national average masked major regional and socioeconomic differentials. Life expectancy in the more prosperous Southern states was eight years higher than the national average, and sixteen years more than in poorer Northeastern states.

Mortality has declined substantially since 1945. Table 1.2 presents trend data on life expectancy for Brazil and the major regions of the country. Data on infant mortality, another key mortality measure, are also shown. Between

Table 1.2

Estimates of Life Expectancy at Birth and Infant Mortality,
Brazil and PNAD Regions, 1950–1980

Brazil and PNAD Regions	YEAR* OF CENSUS			
	1950	1960	1970	1980
	Life Expectancy at Birth			
BRAZIL	48.9	52.4	57.5	62.6
1. Rio de Janeiro	53.0	57.6	62.6	66.5
2. São Paulo	53.2	58.3	62.5	67.7
3. Southern states	56.8	60.4	62.1	68.1
4. Minas Gerais/Esp. Santo	51.8	55.4	59.4	63.8
5. Northeastern states	40.8	42.8	47.3	53.9
6. Brasília	—	54.6	61.6	67.1
7. Amazon states	51.5	56.1	60.1	66.1
	Infant Mortality Rate			
BRAZIL	130	119	98	86
1. Rio de Janeiro	114	99	79	70
2. São Paulo	112	97	79	64
3. Southern states	100	90	75	63
4. Minas Gerais/Esp. Santo	118	107	91	79
5. Northeastern states	164	157	137	116
6. Brasília	—	110	83	67
7. Amazon states	119	105	88	72

Sources: NAS (1979) and 1980 Census (Tabulações Avançadas).
*The year given is the date of the census; estimates refer to years just prior to the census.

1950 and 1980, expectation of life at birth increased by about fourteen years. Regional differentials, measured either by the ratio of life expectancy in the Southern states to the average for the Northeastern states or by the difference in the number of years lived between the two regions, increased slightly during the 1950s, but have narrowed since 1960.

The pace of mortality decline in Brazil has been more rapid than the declines experienced by currently industrialized countries during the nineteenth century, but less than in certain countries (Sri Lanka and Mauritius, for example) where medical interventions played a more dramatic role in mortality reduction. Brazil also contrasts with other countries, including several in Latin America, in having a lower level of life expectancy at a given level of income per capita than one would expect on the basis of international comparisons involving mortality levels and the level of economic development.

Regional and socioeconomic class differentials in mortality account for a large part of this discrepancy. These differentials are more pronounced in the case of infant mortality rates, which provide a more telling index of the impact of living standards on health conditions than do rates for other age groups. This is because they reflect deaths due to causes such as diarrhea and respiratory infection, which are more difficult to treat in poorly nourished infants than in adults. Infant mortality rates in Northeastern Brazil were 50 percent greater than in Southern states according to 1980 census data. Further, while Brazil and Mexico are about equal in terms of their per capita income levels, life expectancy in Mexico is about five years higher than in Brazil, and infant mortality rates in Brazil are fully one-third higher than in Mexico.

The fact that these reports are based on the census reveals one of the problems encountered in studying vital rates in Brazil: the vital statistics system is still incomplete in terms of timely recording of births, deaths, and other events. National-level recording of vital statistics did not begin until the mid-1970s, and a significant proportion of events go unrecorded or are not recorded at the time they occur. This is particularly true of infant deaths. For this reason, demographers still prefer to rely on retrospective questions in census and survey interviews when estimating vital rates for Brazil. Since these techniques require the use of model life tables, the discrepancy between infant mortality patterns in Brazil and those in standard model life tables could lead to erroneous conclusions about overall mortality levels estimated on the basis of survival of children, and some caution is required in interpreting Brazilian mortality data.

In terms of causes of death, mortality decline in Brazil has followed a pattern that is typical of countries that are experiencing a mortality transition. This consists of a decline in the proportion of deaths attributable to infectious diseases, which have greater impact on infants and young children, and an increase in the proportion of deaths attributable to neoplasms (cancer) and diseases of the circulatory system. In part, the latter trend reflects a "survival effect," in that individuals who have avoided death from infectious causes live long enough to be exposed to the risk of mortality from degenerative causes.

The persistence of high mortality from infectious diseases is an important dimension of regional and class differentials in mortality in Brazil. It is also one of the reasons why Brazilian infant mortality rates are comparatively high. Table 1.3 shows the interrelation between causes of death, age patterns of mortality, and regional mortality differences. Although cause of death data are available only for state capitals, they show substantially higher proportions of deaths attributable to infectious diseases in regions with high mortality, along with a higher proportion of deaths of children under age 5. These

Table 1.3

Age-specific and Cause-specific Proportional Mortality,
by Region, 1970 (Percent of Total Deaths)

	Northeast	Southeast	Frontier	Brazil
Age at death				
Less than 5 years	47.3	26.2	44.7	33.1
55 years and older	25.7	43.8	21.8	37.5
Cause of death				
Infections/parasitic				
diseases	24.5	11.2	26.6	15.8
Neoplasms/circulatory				
diseases	21.1	42.1	19.1	34.9
Accidents, violent				
causes	6.7	9.3	8.2	8.5
Other causes	47.7	36.8	46.1	40.8

Source: World Bank, *Brazil, Human Resources Special Report,* Annex 3, I, Table 2.
Data refer to state capitals.

Table 1.4

Estimated Probability of Death by Age Two (2q0)
of Children Born to Urban Mothers, by Mother's
Household Income Decile and Rural or Urban Residence,
1970 and 1976

Mother's household income decile	1970	1976	Percent Decline
Urban			
1–3	.191	.137	28
3–6	.143	.104	27
7–10	.097	.066	32
Rural			
1–3	.154	.138	10
4–10	.131	.106	19
Total	.133	099	26

Source: Tabulations of 1970 census and 1976 PNAD, reported in Merrick
(1985).

patterns suggest that the Brazilian mortality transition represents a wide spectrum of experiences. Part of the population has already arrived at a post-transition mortality regime, in which circulatory and degenerative diseases are the principal causes of death. The remainder of the population, mainly the poor, continue to suffer from high mortality rates that relate to infectious diseases.

Similar patterns show up in socioeconomic class differentials in mortality, though these are difficult to ascertain from census and survey measures since many of the assumptions underlying indirect estimation are violated when data are broken down into population subgroups. With certain caveats, measures that can be derived reveal major socioeconomic class differentials in child survival rates. Table 1.4 reports the probability of an infant dying before the age of 2 for mothers according to their household income decile and rural or urban residence.

For urban mothers, the probability of an infant dying before age 2 was nearly twice as high for women in the bottom three household income deciles as for women in the top three deciles. In the bottom three deciles, rates for rural women were actually lower than those for urban women. There were across-the-board declines in rates between 1970 and 1976, but declines were slower for lower income mothers, so that class differentials widened in the interim.

Both regional and class differentials in infant and child mortality are the consequence of a variety of interrelated causal factors that reflect living conditions as well as access to health care. Nutritional status is a key variable in the mortality of infants suffering from infectious diseases. Calculations based on the 1974–75 ENDEF (Estudo Nacional de Despesâ Familiar) nutrition survey indicate extensive malnutrition among children in Brazil. At the national level, only 42 percent of children through the age of 17 could be considered adequately nourished according to the survey data, and the figure dropped to 32 percent for the Northeastern states and even less for low income groups in a number of the regions (The World Bank, *Brazil, Human Resources Special Report*, Annex 3, Tables 16–19). Closely associated with infant nutrition levels is the practice of breastfeeding. While evidence on the prevalence of breastfeeding in Brazil is limited, the data that are available suggest that the average duration is very short by international standards (Merrick and Berquo, 1983). This may in part have to do with the popularization of manufactured infant formula, but it may also reflect time pressures on working women as well as cultural prejudices against the practice in urban areas.

Other household-level living conditions, including the quality of shelter and the availability of piped water and sanitation facilities, also affect mortality differentials. Among other things, unsafe water increases the health risk associated with substitution of formula for breast milk, since low income mothers tend to use formula at less than full strength, and mix it with impure water, thus exposing a poorly nourished child to risk of infection with less resistance to fight the infection.

Analysis of infant mortality differentials by household income level, as well as the effects of changes in living standards on those differentials between 1970 and 1976, reveals important differences in the probability of children surviving early infancy depending on whether the household in which their mothers resided had access to internal piped water (Merrick 1983). Efforts by Brazilian authorities to increase access to water and sanitation during the 1970s paid off in terms of reductions in infant and child mortality.

The program did not, however, have an appreciable effect on mortality differentials between income classes. One reason for this is that other variables, particularly maternal education, had an even greater effect on mortality levels. Using census-type questions, it proved difficult to disentangle the multiple effects of education on mortality, since they include the effects of education on income generation, the capacity to purchase and prepare the food required for a better diet, and child care know-how that might manifest itself in practices such as boiling water that is known to be impure. Given the important relationship between educational level and income, it is not surprising that mortality differentials associated with these two variables overshadowed the potential impact of increased access to piped water in reducing them.

The census and survey data on which this analysis of the relation between household income, education, water supply, and infant mortality differentials is based did not include questions about access to health care, which is another potentially important variable in the explanation of mortality differentials. The PNAD (Pesquisa Nacional por Amostra de Domicilia) survey taken in 1981 included a health supplement, but did not include questions on child survivorship that would have enabled an extension of this analysis to include that variable.

The range of experiences in the Brazilian mortality transition alluded to earlier is reflected in what the 1981 PNAD survey reveals about the structure of the Brazilian health system. Urban middle and higher income classes wield greater influence over the formulation of national health policy and the allocation of resources to health care. As a result, the health system has evolved in the direction of services that cater to the needs of that segment of the population which has already completed the mortality transition, rather than to those of groups that are still subject to high risk of mortality from infectious disease.

Over the past three decades, most Brazilian health expenditures have been channeled to the more expensive curative, hospital-based health service system rather than to preventive and primary health care. The medical-hospital component of public expenditures on health increased from 13 percent in 1949 to 85 percent in 1980 (McGreevey, 1982). The resulting distortions and their potential impact on differential infant and child health are illustrated by data from the PNAD survey on access to prenatal care and on use of health facilities for discretionary caesarean section births. The former is an example of preventive care that has a strong impact on child survival, while the latter illustrates a hospital-based, medically oriented procedure that is warranted in a small proportion of cases, but whose use far exceeds normal levels in the case of upper income groups in Brazil.

The 1981 PNAD data show that 3 out of 10 women who reported births in the survey had had no prenatal care. At the same time, 3 out of 10 who did have such care also had caesarean section births (Merrick, 1984). The Brazilian caesarean section (CS) rate is nearly double the U.S. level, where a CS rate of 16 percent is being viewed with alarm. The CS rate for women in lower income and education categories is comparatively low in Brazil; rates for women in upper income and education classes, however, exceeds 60 percent. Moreover, a substantial proportion of the costs of these women's CS deliveries was paid by the public social insurance system, thereby channeling resources to a procedure that had very questionable medical value (though in all likelihood one that was highly valued by consumers) and away from uses that might have contributed to reduction in mortality from basic infectious causes among infants born to mothers who are still subject to Brazil's "other" mortality regime.

Although it is tempting to attribute the persistence of regional and class differentials in mortality in Brazil to a single variable such as differential access to health service, it is important to recognize the synergistic relationship between these differentials and a variety of household and societal variables, including nutritional status, education, safe water and sanitation, and housing conditions. It is also important to recognize one variable that has not been mentioned so far—the interrelation between child health and fertility. While there has been little study of this relationship in Brazil, research in other countries has revealed reduced survival chances for infants born to younger mothers, and for higher parity infants and infants born after a relatively short birth interval. The recent rapid decline in fertility rates in Brazil may also have an effect on infant survival chances, though socioeconomic class differentials in fertility decline may also act to accentuate existing infant mortality differentials.

FERTILITY TRENDS

The most significant demographic event in Brazil during the 1970s was the rapid acceleration of fertility decline. Until the mid-1960s, the Brazilian birth rate had declined only slightly from the peak level of about 44 per thousand that it had maintained since the mid-1940s. This, in combination with a rapidly declining death rate, accounted for the acceleration in population growth that Brazil experienced during the 1950s. Since 1965, the birth rate has declined very rapidly, so that by the early 1980s it was approaching the level of 30 per thousand, a decline of about 30 percent from the 1960s.

The exact path of Brazilian fertility trends is difficult to track because of the incomplete reporting of vital statistics. Until the mid-1970s, the only data that were available were reports from the capital cities. Since then the government has attempted to establish a national system to record and publish vital statistics, but coverage is still not considered complete in the sense of providing both timely and comprehensive recording of events at the national level. As a consequence, most research on national- and regional- level trends and differences is based on indirect estimates derived from census and survey questions about women's reproductive experiences. Brazilian censuses pioneered in the collection of such data, and both census and PNAD national sample survey data have been utilized by Brazilian and other analysts (see U.S. National Academy of Sciences, 1983).

In considering fertility trends in Brazil, it is important to remember that the national-level trend masks substantial regional and socioeconomic class differentials. These can be seen in Table 1.5, which presents estimates of the total fertility rate derived from 1950 to 1980 census data for Brazil, urban and rural areas in Brazil, and the seven regions into which Brazil has been divided in PNAD surveys.

At the national level, the total fertility rate—which is a more refined fertility measure than the crude birth rate because it relates births to women of childbearing age rather than to the entire population and controls for changes in age structure—was close to 6 births per woman until the late 1960s, when it also began to decline rapidly. During the 1970s, total fertility declined by about one-quarter. Data on rural-urban differences in fertility, which are also shown in Table 1.5, suggest that most of the limited decline that occurred before 1970 resulted from redistribution of population from rural to urban areas rather than from declines *within* either rural or urban areas, where little change is observed in rates between 1950 and 1970. During that period, rural-to-urban migration may have dampened fertility decline in urban areas because migrants brought higher rural fertility norms with them and took time to adapt to urban norms. Their adaptation appears to have been rapid, however, because urban fertility declined substantially during the 1970s.

Examination of regional fertility differentials reveals similar patterns. Total fertility rates were well below the national average in the more urbanized and industrialized Southeast (Rio de Janeiro and São Paulo) even in the 1950s.

Table 1.5
Total Fertility Rate, Brazil,
Urban-Rural Residence, and PNAD Regions, 1950–80

| | YEAR* OF CENSUS | | | |
	1950	1960	1970	1980
BRAZIL	6.32	6.18	5.83	4.33
RESIDENCE				
Urban	4.68	—	4.61	3.64
Rural	7.70	—	7.71	6.31
PNAD REGION				
1. Rio de Janeiro	4.42	4.34	3.91	2.65
2. São Paulo	4.52	4.49	4.07	3.13
3. Southern states	5.96	5.75	5.48	3.47
4. Minas Gerais/Esp. Santo	6.90	6.98	6.31	4.11
5. Northeastern states	7.52	7.50	7.58	5.71
6. Brasília	—	—	5.52	3.63
7. Amazon states	7.14	7.32	7.08	5.07

Source: Revised estimates for Report of the Panel on Brazil, Committee on Population and Demography, U.S. National Academy of Sciences, 1983.
*The year given is the date of the census; estimates refer to years just prior to the census.

Rates were also lower in the Southern region. These regions experienced very gradual decline in fertility during the 1950–1970 period, but their impact on the national average was dampened by the continuation of high or even increasing rates in the Northeast, Minas Gerais/Espirito Santo, and Amazon regions.

The 1970s brought acceleration of declines in the Southeastern and Southern regions; more importantly, fertility decline spread to regions that had not experienced declines during previous decades. At the national level, the earlier dampening effect was replaced by accelerated decline. During the 1970s, the pace of decline appears to have been more rapid in the first half of the decade than in the second. Data from the 1976 PNAD survey suggest a national-level total fertility rate in the 4.4 to 4.5 range, compared to 5.8 in the 1970 census and 4.3 in the 1980 census.[2]

Two explanations are possible for this slowing of the decline in the late 1970s. One is that the decline has slowed in the South and Southeast, where rates had already reached comparatively low levels by the mid-1970s. The second is that the censuses and PNAD are representing in their coverage some-

Table 1.6

Total Fertility Rate and Mean Age at First Birth
by Family Income Deciles,
Brazil, Urban, and Rural, 1970–76

Residence, Income deciles	Total Fertility		Percent Decline	Mean Age	
	1970	1976		1970	1976
Total	5.81	4.42	23.9	23.3	23.8
Urban					
Low (1–3)	5.99	4.37	27.0	22.0	21.3
Middle (4–6)	5.82	4.52	22.3	21.5	21.5
High (7–10)	3.88	3.02	22.2	25.2	26.3
Rural					
Low (1–3)	8.00	6.70	16.3	20.5	20.5
High (4–10)	7.66	5.86	22.2	24.3	24.7

Source: Derived from Merrick and Berquó (1983).

what different "Brazils." While the quality of PNAD interviewing is generally better than in the census, the distribution of the population according to education and other characteristics in the 1976 PNAD survey suggests that it represents a population with somewhat higher socioeconomic status than one obtains by interpolating between the 1970 and 1980 censuses.

Socioeconomic class differentials in fertility also need to be considered in the acceleration in Brazil's decline in fertility. Availability of public-use data files for the 1970 census and later PNAD surveys made it possible to tabulate fertility questions according to such measures of socioeconomic status as income and education. However, considerable caution is required in interpreting indirect fertility estimates because the tabulations violate several assumptions about mobility between different groups (see Merrick and Berquó, 1983).

What such tabulations show is that the spread of fertility decline to lower income groups, particularly in urban areas, also contributed to the acceleration of overall declines. Table 1.6 summarizes results of an analysis of trends in total fertility by household income decile and rural or urban residence between 1970 and 1976. Until 1970, lower fertility was limited to upper income deciles in the urban population. After 1970, decline was most rapid among the lower income urban population, though declines of more than 20 percent were recorded for the entire urban population and for upper income deciles in rural areas.

More detailed analysis of these declines, also reported in Merrick and Berquó

(1983), indicates that declines were more rapid for lower and middle income socioeconomic groups in middle income regions. Minas Gerais/Espirito Santo offers a good example of where this phenomenon was occurring. This adds weight to the conclusion that the acceleration of fertility decline around 1970 was the result of continued decline in areas where declines had been occurring gradually since the 1950s combined with the spread of decline to regions and groups that had not participated in earlier declines.

Table 1.6 also presents data on the average age at which women reported their first birth. These reveal important differentials between rural and urban areas and lower and higher income groups. One of the reasons for fertility differentials is that upper income urban women begin childbearing when they are older. This is probably a reflection of their greater educational attainment. Tabulations of total fertility by levels of education reveal differential fertility patterns that are similar to the ones shown here for income.

The question of *why* the acceleration occurred when and as it did involves addressing two sets of analytical questions that demographers and other social scientists have identified as important for the understanding of fertility trends and their relationship to social and economic change. The first set relates to demographic and physiological factors that have a direct effect on fertility rates and are at the same time affected by socioeconomic variables that are generally identified as being important fertility determinants. The second set of questions relates to the social and economic variables themselves.

The reason for distinguishing between the two sets of questions is that the first set of variables generally plays a mediating role in the impact of the second on fertility rates as actually observed. For this reason, the first set of questions has been labeled *intermediate variables* and, more recently, as *proximate determinants* of fertility. Marriage patterns and contraceptive practices represent two important proximate determinants. Important socioeconomic determinants of fertility such as female educational attainment and labor force participation generally achieve their impact on fertility through their effect on one or more of the proximate determinants.

For this reason, the first step toward understanding major changes in fertility patterns such as the acceleration of declines in Brazil is to examine changes in the proximate determinants of fertility. It is now generally recognized that four proximate determinants—marriage rates, contraceptive use, abortion, and post-partum amenorrhea associated with the duration of breast feeding—account for most of the variation in fertility rates that can be explained at this level. Bongaarts (1980) has devised a set of indices that permit decomposition of the difference between a woman's full reproductive potential (sometimes called *natural fertility* and here *total marital fecundity*) and observed total fertility rates into the contribution of each of the proximate determinants.

Table 1.7
Estimates of Proximate Determinants of Total Fertility,
Brazil, 1970 and 1980

Measure and variant*	1970		1980	
	A	B	A	B
ASSUMPTIONS				
Percent of women using contraceptives	32	25	50	44
Contraceptive effectiveness rate	0.80	0.80	0.88	0.88
Months of post-partum infecundity	4	4	3	3
Abortions between ages 15–49 per woman	0.5	1.5	0.5	1.5
RESULTS				
Total births per woman without any of the factors	15.3	15.3	15.3	15.3
Infecundity factor	0.89	0.89	0.93	0.93
Abortion factor	0.96	0.88	0.93	0.83
Contraception factor	0.72	0.78	0.51	0.56
Births per woman adjusted for infecundity, abortion, and contraception	9.34	9.39	6.73	6.60
Nonmarriage factor	0.63	0.63	0.65	0.65
Total fertility rate	5.89	5.92	4.37	4.29

Source: Derived from data presented in Merrick and Berquó (1983).
*Variant A differs from variant B in the relative weights assigned to abortion and contraception. The results reflect the application of the fertility reduction factors to initial fertility levels in the absence of the factor. See Bongaarts (1980) for an explanation of the way in which factors are derived from the various assumptions.

This procedure also shows which of the proximate determinants has contributed most to fertility decline when observations for two points in time are considered.

Since Brazil has not yet conducted a national-level fertility survey along the lines of the World Fertility Survey, which was designed specifically for analysis of the proximate determinants, the best that can be done is to piece together information from a variety of sources and attempt to approximate nationally representative values for the various indices in the proximate determinants framework. Such an approximation is described in Merrick and Berquó (1983), and the results are summarized in Table 1.7.

Data in Table 1.7 are divided into two sections. The first describes the assumptions underlying the decomposition. The first assumptions concern contraceptive use rates, which probably ranged between 25 and 30 percent of married women in reproductive ages around 1970. To translate contraceptive use into a measure of the effect of contraception on fertility, account has to be taken of contraceptive effectiveness, which is also shown in the table. The other two sets of assumptions relate to the duration of breast feeding and abortion. Marriage rates enter directly in the second panel of the table.

Data from state-level surveys suggest that contraceptive use increased substantially during the 1970s, so that the national average reached between 45 and 50 percent at the end of the decade. The practice of breast feeding has been limited in Brazil when compared to other parts of the world, and hence the impact of post-partum amenorrhea is also limited. The data suggests that the average duration of breast feeding declined during the 1970s, which inhibited this effect even more.

As will be seen in the next section, marriage rates changed very little in Brazil during the 1970s. A rise in the rate of reported consensual unions, along with increased contraceptive use, suggests that the mean age of first exposure to the risk of conception (which the age at marriage seeks to measure) may actually have declined during the 1970s.

The main unknown in the analysis of proximate fertility determinants in Brazil is the practice of abortion. Though illegal, it is alleged to be widespread. Extrapolations based on cases of complications arising from aseptic abortions suggest that the annual number exceeds 1 million (compared to about 4 million live births each year). Since data limitations do not allow for exact estimation of the proximate determinants, two sets of assumptions about contraception and abortion are employed. One set assumes a lower abortion rate and a higher level of contraceptive use; the other assumes higher abortion and correspondingly lower contraceptive use.[3]

The resulting approximation of changes in the proximate determinants is shown in the lower panel of Table 1.7. The last row shows the total fertility rates produced by the combined action of the four variables. The ranges of two variants actually come quite close to the estimated levels reported earlier for 1970 (5.8) and 1980 (4.3). The calculations indicate that some combination of increased contraceptive use, increased contraceptive effectiveness, and abortion (possibly declining as contraception was substituted for abortion) contributed most to observed declines in total fertility between 1970 and 1980.

Increases in contraceptive use reflect both increased production and sales of contraceptives in the private sector (commercial sales through pharmacies and distribution by private physicians) and a limited amount of intervention at the state level, particularly in the Northeast, where the Brazilian IPPF (International Planned Parenthood Federation) affiliate BEMFAM (Sociedade Civil de Bem-Estar Familiar) distributed pills under *convenios* with several state governments in the region. Again, the data on which to base generalizations about trends during the 1970s are limited, but summary data from state-level contraceptive prevalence surveys taken between 1978 and 1980 reveal some of the important patterns that have been observed. These are shown in Table 1.8.

Table 1.8 presents contraceptive use rates for three states in which survey data were collected: São Paulo, where private sector distribution played a principal role in access to contraceptives; Rio Grande do Norte, one of the BEMFAM *convenio* states, which had the highest total fertility rate in Brazil in 1970 and then experienced substantial decline during the decade; and Bahia, a state in which neither the private sector nor BEMFAM has had a substantial impact. The table presents rates for the states as a whole and for the women grouped by multiples of the monthly minimum salary within each state, and includes a breakdown by the principal method categories (pill, sterilization, and other).

Contraceptive use rates were highest in São Paulo at 64 percent, a level that approximates those found in low fertility industrialized countries. Bahia had the lowest average rate, 31 percent, or about the level of Brazil in 1970. Rio Grande do Norte's rate was close to the national average level for 1980. Income class differentials are observable in all three states, but are more pronounced in Bahia, where no BEMFAM programs operated, than in Rio Grande do Norte, where the rate for the lowest income category was a full 20 percentage points higher than for the same group in Bahia. This suggests that BEMFAM programs played an important role in increasing access of low income women to contraceptives, manily the pill.

The pill and surgical sterilization were the two most popular methods generally. Sterilization was even more popular than the pill among upper income women in Bahia and Rio Grande do Norte. There is probably a correlation between the high rates of a caesarean section births reported in the preceding section and the high prevalence of sterilization among upper income women reported in these data. Further analysis of these data by Janowitz *et al.* (1982) suggest that this is the case.

Increases in contraceptive use in Brazil during the 1970s also correspond closely to increased local production of contraceptives. Data on the manufacture of contraceptive pills suggest a tenfold increase in production between 1965 and 1980, and the opening of limited regional markets in the Northeast and Amazon states, though the bulk of the distribution is still in the South

Table 1.8
Percentage Distribution of Married Women Aged 15–44,
by Contraceptive Use Status, According to Household Income,
São Paulo, Rio Grande do Norte, and Bahia States

State, year, contraceptive use status	Multiples of minimum salary				
	Total	<1	1–2	3–4	>=5
SÃO PAULO (1978)					
Currently using	63.9	47.4	57.4	67.4	68.5
Pill	27.8	6.4	28.9	34.0	22.0
Sterilization	16.1	5.4	11.0	15.2	22.0
Other	20.0	35.6	27.5	18.2	24.5
Not using	36.1	53.6	42.6	32.6	31.5
RIO GRANDE DO NORTE (1980)					
Currently using	47.0	37.0	46.6	53.4	72.9
Pill	17.9	15.9	18.2	20.9	22.9
Sterilization	17.4	8.4	17.3	23.1	34.4
Other	11.7	12.7	11.1	9.4	15.6
Not using	53.0	63.0	53.4	46.6	27.1
BAHIA (1980)					
Currently using	31.1	18.7	28.4	42.8	65.9
Pill	11.7	6.9	13.5	15.3	15.7
Sterilization	9.6	7.1	7.4	13.2	26.3
Other	9.8	5.7	7.5	14.3	23.8
Not using	68.9	81.3	71.6	57.2	34.1

Source: Tabulations based on state-level contraceptive prevalence surveys, as reported in Merrick (1983).

and Southeast. The data suggest that where contraceptive use remains low, motivation and access to methods, rather than availability, may be critical.

Turning from the proximate determinants of fertility to the social, economic, and political forces that may have been behind these increases in contraceptive use, it is important to recall that Brazil is one of the few countries in the world that did not adopt a national policy during the 1970s to reduce birth rates by subsidizing the distribution of contraceptives (though it did permit foreign agencies to operate through local nongovernmental organizations like BEMFAM). Nonetheless, Brazil experienced a rate of fertility decline that was similar to those of other countries in Latin America at similar levels of development—for example, Mexico and Colombia—which did have such national policies. This raises the questions of what led to decline in Brazil in the absence of a national policy, and what difference it made for Brazil not to have a policy when Colombia and Mexico did.

Detailed analysis of social and economic changes underlying the acceleration of fertility decline in Brazil is beyond the scope of this essay, and has been presented elsewhere (Merrick and Berquó, 1983; Merrick, 1984). Several important points from those studies will be summarized here. Although no single variable or line of argument provides an adequate explanation of Brazilian declines, at least two factors are important.

The first is the increased availability of contraceptives, either through private channels or through the organized family planning agencies that were operating in Brazil during the 1970s. But increased availability does not guarantee increased use. An explanation of the forces that motivated use is also required.

These include a group of variables known as "forces leading to the modernization of reproductive attitudes," where *modernization* describes the adoption of measures to control reproductive outcomes rather than leave them to chance or providence. Among these are increased educational attainment, particularly of women, and increased exposure to mass media and materialistic values communicated by the media. The latter leads to increased sensitivity to alternatives to large family values, such as the desire to have fewer but better educated children or the desire to substitute other forms of consumption—defined broadly enough to encompass use of time and psychic satisfactions as well as material goods—for children. Economists have used the label *tastes* to describe such influences, while sociologists and anthropologists have classified them in terms of norms and values. Brazil has experienced profound changes with respect to them over the past decade and a half.

The forces motivating contraceptive use also encompass variables that affect the capacity of individual couples to realize their reproductive and other aspirations. These operate at two levels: that of the individuals making choices (the *micro* level) and that of social, political, and economic forces that constrain the options open to these individuals (the *macro* level). There is evidence of important changes at both levels in Brazil after 1965.

At the macro level, the lower income urban population experienced both increased economic options and increased difficulty in exercising them during the late 1960s and early 1970s. Consumption of consumer durables, from blenders and television sets to automobiles and housing, increased significantly during the period, particularly among the middle and lower middle income deciles of the urban population. Much of the increase was secured through expanded consumer credit, which was indexed for inflation. A problem for many was that the indexed value of earnings did not keep pace with inflation, while the indexed values of their payments did, which created an economic squeeze.

A strategy for economic survival that many households adopted in order to maintain their standard of living during the period when fertility decline accelerated (1965–75) was to increase economic activity by family members other than the head, principally spouses, often through employment in the so–called urban informal sector. Evidence of increased female labor force participation during the 1970s supports this hypothesis (see Hoffmann, this volume). Further, the greatest increases in female participation occurred among less educated and lower income women. To the extent that work outside the home placed greater demands on these women's time, leaving them less time for child rearing, a major motivation for delay or earlier termination of childbearing emerges. This, in combination with changing attitudes, more accessible and comparatively inexpensive contraceptives, represents a strong working hypothesis for the explanation of the spread of fertility decline to lower income urban women.

A parallel story may be unfolding in rural areas. In addition to the forces already described, rural Brazil has experienced increased consolidation of land into large commercial holdings as a consequence of economic policies aimed at increasing production of nonfood staples needed to generate foreign exchange or to substitute alcohol for imported oil. An increasing proportion of rural workers are being employed as wage laborers rather than as independent smallholders or family labor (some have labeled this process *rural proletarianization*; see Paiva, 1982). These structural changes have the effect of accelerating exposure of the rural population to social and economic forces that might have been delayed until they had shifted to wage labor status via the rural-urban migration process. While fertility decline in rural areas contributed only fractionally to overall decline, the spillover effect of this process on urban areas via migration was probably more significant.

MARRIAGE AND FAMILY TRENDS

Changes in marriage patterns and age structure are always prime suspects in declining birth rates. However, the available evidence indicates that changes in the distribution of women by marital status, either through changes in the mean age of marriage or through increases in the proportion of women remaining single, were not a major factor in Brazil's accelerated fertility decline during the 1970s. Table 1.9 presents data on the distribution of women by marital status and age for 1950 and 1980. There has been very little change over the three decades.

Table 1.9

Reported Percent Distribution of Women by Marital Status
by Age, 1950 and 1980, Brazil

Age	Single		Married		Other*	
	1950	1980	1950	1980	1950	1980
15–19	85.1	83.2	14.8	16.3	0.1	0.5
20–24	47.4	44.5	51.9	53.2	0.7	2.3
25–29	27.7	23.5	70.4	72.6	1.9	3.9
30–39	18.4	13.3	76.3	79.9	5.3	6.8
40–49	14.4	9.0	71.2	77.0	14.4	14.0

Source: Merrick and Berguó (1983).
*"Other" includes widowed, separated, and divorced.

Calculations of the singulate mean age at marriage (based on the proportions of women reported as single at each age) from census data indicate a rise
of about 0.8 years from 1950 to 1970 (22.1 years to 22.9 years), followed by
a decline of 0.3 years from 1970 to 1980. Thus declining marital fertility
(with marriage defined as including both formal and informal unions) rather
than changes in marital patterns accounted for most of the recent fertility
decline.

Two important caveats should be attached to this conclusion. First, while
marriage patterns did not have much impact on global fertility trends, they
play an important role in fertility differentials. Better educated women do
delay entry into marriage both because they work longer before marrying and
because they continue the education process longer. The fact that changing
marriage patterns did not affect fertility declines during the 1970s does not
mean they will have no influence on future declines, or on narrowing of fertility differentials that are associated with differences in the age of entry into
unions.

Second, possible distortions in the measurement of the proportion of wom-
en classified as "married," particularly among women under age 30, can arise
from inadequacies in the reporting of consensual unions. Births to women in
consensual unions account for an important share of total births in Brazil,
which warrants the inclusion of consensual unions in the calculation of marital fertility measures. The problem arises with women who report themselves
as "single" but have had a birth. Accurate calculation of rates such as the
marital feritility rate requires that all women who are "at risk" be included in
the denominator.

In all likelihood, there have been distortions in the Brazilian data arising from women who changed their reporting from "single" to consensual unions after their first birth, even though they were living in consensual unions prior to that birth. The lack of any trend toward increased average age of entry into unions may arise in part from improved reporting of consensual unions, which would bias more recent estimates of the age at marriage downward. Further complications arise from changes in the proportion of women reported as separated and divorced. With changes in the legal strictures on divorce, the proportion of women, particularly those between the ages of 25 and 40, reported as neither married nor single increased from 1950 to 1980.

A related phenomenon is the apparent increase in the proportion of females reported as heads of families. Overall, female headship increased from 12 percent of all families in 1950 to nearly 16 percent in 1980. Female headship rates reflect various underlying processes: among older women, the incidence of widowhood; among younger women, increased rates of separation, divorce, and abandonment. Most of the increase in female headship rates in Brazil between 1950 and 1980 occurred among women between the ages of 20 and 50.

The size of the average family in Brazil decreased from 5.1 person per family to 4.4 between 1950 and 1980. This was partly the result of declining fertility, which led to a reduction in the number of children per family unit from 2.75 to 2.31. But there was also a reduction (from 0.65 to 0.31) in the average number of other relatives per family unit, reflecting some decline in the proportion of extended co-residential family units. The proportion of family units with both spouses present increased slightly (from 0.7 to 0.8), most probably due to the contribution of lower mortality to increased survival of marriage partners. Since census data on family units are based on co-residential units, information about family-level economic and social relationships that reach beyond the reporting residence is missed.

GEOGRAPHIC REDISTRIBUTION OF THE POPULATION

Despite important interstate and interregional migration flows over the past three decades, Brazil's geographic population distribution has remained comparatively stable at the macroregional level. The most populous region of Brazil is the Southeast, which accounts for only 11 percent of the land area but whose percentage share of total population has hovered around 43 percent for the last four censuses (Table 1.10).

The Southeast is also the most densely populated region of Brazil: its average density of 56 persons per square kilometer is four times the national average of 14. The second most densely populated region is the Southern region, with 34 persons per square kilometer. Density in the Northeast is also greater than the national average, though less than either the South or Southeast.

Table 1.10
Percentage Distribution of Brazil's Population by Region
1950 to 1980

Region	Percent of Area	Density (persons/ sq. km.)	Percent of Population 1950	1960	1970	1980
North	42.0	1.7	3.5	3.6	3.9	4.9
Northeast	18.2	22.6	34.6	31.7	30.2	29.3
Southeast	10.9	56.3	43.4	43.7	42.8	43.5
South	6.7	33.9	15.1	16.8	17.7	16.0
Central-West	22.2	4.0	3.4	4.2	5.4	6.3
BRAZIL	100	14.1	100	100	100	100

Source: Population censuses, 1950 to 1980.

In all three cases regional averages are somewhat misleading, since much of their population is concentrated along the coast.

The population share of the Southern region was less than one percentage point higher in 1980 than in 1950, but earlier it had increased by nearly three percentage points from 1950 to 1970, and then declined by two points during the 1970s. In large part, this reflects the experience of the state of Paraná, which attracted many migrants during the 1950s and 1960s, and then lost them during the 1970s.

The only losing region in terms of net percentage changes from 1950 to 1980 was the Northeast, which accounted for nearly 35 percent of total population three decades ago and now holds less than 30 percent. Net redistribution of population away from the Northeast masks much larger net out-migration from that region, since its rate of natural population increase was higher than the national average and migration much more than offset that differential in terms of net total population change. This is the opposite of what happened in the Southeast, where natural increase has been lower than the national average and net in-migration has operated to maintain its percentage share in the total population.

The two remaining regions, the North and Central-West, account for most of the net gains in the precentage distribution. These regions have nearly 65 percent of Brazil's land area. In 1950, they held less than 7 percent of total population. By 1980, their share of total population had increased to just over 11 percent. They are still very sparsely populated. The vast North has an average density of only 1.7 persons per square kilometer—again a misleading figure because more than half of the region's population is concentrated in urban centers.

While the overall regional population pattern remained comparatively stable, the distribution of population by rural and urban residence within regions
changed substantially. The officially designated urban share of total population increased from 36.2 percent in 1950 to 67.6 percent in 1980. For the
Southeast, the 1980 figure reached 83 percent for the region as a whole and
about 90 percent in the states of São Paulo and Rio de Janeiro. Even the
Central-West, the agricultural frontier of the 1960s, is now more than
two-thirds urban. No region had less than 50 percent of its population classified as urban, though Brazil's administrative formula for designating an urban
place tends to overstate the urban share, particularly in areas where there are
many administrative small centers, as in the state of Minas Gerais.

These changes reflect differential patterns of rural and urban population
increase in each region, as shown in Table 1.11. During the 1950s and 1960s
urban population inncreased by about 66 percent nationally, and more rapidly in the South and Central-West. The percentage increase was less during
the 1970s because of the overall decline in population growth. Rural population increased during the 1950s and 1960s, but at only a fraction of the level
of urban increase. During the 1970s, rural population actually declined in
absolute terms.

This shift toward decline in the rural population at the national level during the 1970s was already under way during the 1960s in the Southeast,
where rural population has declined by 17 to 18 percent in each of the last
two decades. During the 1970s rural population declined even in the former
agricultural frontier region, the Central-West. Another former agricultural
frontier, Paraná state in the Southern region, experienced a 29 percent decline
in its rural population during the 1970s; this contrasts with its 87 percent
increase during the 1950s.

Even during its period of most rapid population growth as an agricultural
frontier, the Central-West experienced more rapid urban than rural population increase. During the 1960s, urban population in that region grew four
times as fast as rural population. This pattern appears to be repeating itself in
the Northern region, which has become the agricultural frontier of the 1970s
and 1980s. While its rural population increase was 44 percent over the 1970s,
its urban growth was nearly double that.

While the frontier regions experienced the highest percentage increases in
urban population during the 1970s, the more highly urbanized Southeast
accounted for about half of the absolute growth. A significant proportion of
Brazil's urban population, and of the urban population increase experienced
during the 1970s, was concentrated in the country's nine metropolitan areas,
the three largest of which are located in the Southeast. Approximately 38
percent of urban population growth occurred in metro areas.

Comparison of the metro/non-metro distribution of urban population in

Table 1.11
Population Increase by Region and Rural-Urban Residence
1950–60 to 1970–80

	Percentage Population Increase					
	1950–60		1960–70		1970–80	
Region	Urban	Rural	Urban	Rural	Urban	Rural
North	64.9	26.9	69.8	23.3	87.3	44.0
Northeast	58.2	10.9	56.4	11.6	49.6	5.6
Southeast	62.9	11.4	65.9	-17.3	47.9	-18.2
South	88.5	33.7	67.5	24.4	62.7	-22.2
Central-West	137.8	47.4	142.0	36.2	110.0	-7.6
BRAZIL	66.7	16.9	66.4	6.9	54.5	-5.9

Source: Brazil, Fundação IBGE, undated but after 1980.

1950 and 1980 shows little change over the three decades; the metro share was close to 57 percent at both dates (Table 1.12). The trend was not smooth, however, since the metro areas experienced a surge during the 1960s, followed by a decline during the 1970s. Moreover, there was a shift in the relative importance of the "national" metro areas (Rio de Janeiro and São Paulo) vis-á-vis the others, with the latter experiencing a steady increase in their share in urban population over all three decades.

Population redistribution patterns reflect the combined effects of differential natural increase and internal migration. As noted earlier, internal migration has offset regional differentials in natural increase, so that total population in the Northeast grew less rapidly than if there had not been net out-migration, while the Southeast maintained its population share in spite of lower natural increase because of net in-migration. In the Northern and Central-West regions, part of the reason for gains in the overall percentage distribution was the fact that they experienced both higher than average rates of natural increase and net in-migration.

Brazil has experienced significant internal migration over the last three decades. Identification of migration streams depends on the geographic units being considered and the availability of information for such units. In the case of Brazil, movements have been measured across regional, state, and municipality boundaries, as well as rural and urban shifts whithin and between these units. The decennial censuses are the main source of information about migration in Brazil, but they provide only a partial account of the overall migration picture.

Cross tabulation of the population by place of birth and present residence,

Table 1.12

Distribution of Urban Population by Metro and Nonmetro Areas
1950 to 1980

	Total Population (millions)		Percent Distribution			
	1950	1980	1950	1960	1970	1980
National Metro Areas (SP & RJ)	5.4	21.6	28.7	26.7	28.6	26.8
Regional Metro Areas	2.6	12.9	13.8	14.2	14.8	16.0
Other Urban	10.8	46.0	57.5	59.1	56.6	57.1
Total Urban	18.8	80.5	100	31.8	52.1	100

Source: Merrick and Graham 1979; Brazil, Fundação IBGE, undated.

and more recently also by the place of the most recent prior residence, gives some indication of the volume of movement. In both the 1970 and 1980 censuses, 22 percent of adult (ages 15 and over) Brazilians resided in states other than the one in which they were born. The proportion of individuals who were no longer residents of their native municipality increased from 45 percent in 1970 to 51 percent in 1980, suggesting that while the proportion of interstate moves remained stable, shorter distance moves increased from the 1960s to the 1970s.

Data on the duration of residence and indirect estimates based on an accounting for the components of population change between two censuses provide an indication of the volume and direction of movements during a specific time period. During the 1970s, the only states other than the frontier regions (the North and Central-West) to experience positive net migration balances were Rio de Janeiro and São Paulo (Traschner and Bogus, 1984). Former agricultural frontier states, Goias and Paraná, had net out-migration, in contrast to previous decades in which they experienced net in-migration. Paraná also overtook Minas Gerais in being the state with the largest absolute loss of net migrants, a position that the latter had held for several decades.

Regionally, the largest relative net in-migration during the 1970s occurred in the Northern region, a flow equal to 14 percent of its 1970 population base during the decade. The Southeast had the largest absolute inflow, 1.7 million, but this amounted to only 4 percent of its 1979 base population. The Northeast lost 1.8 million population through net out-migration during the decade, which was the largest flow in both absolute and relative terms.

It should be noted that the flows described are estimates of the net contribution of migration to population change. These estimates generally understate the true volume of migration, since they measure only the difference between in-migration and out-migration. Return flows and onward moves to another destination will be recorded only if they happen to be caught in the census net and included as a previous residence.

Rural to urban migration has intensified over the last three decades. During the 1950s, net rural-urban migration amounted to about 8 million, or 24 percent of the 1950 rural population. During the 1960s, these figures reached 13.8 million (36 percent of the rural population base), and in the 1970s the rural exodus exceeded 17 million, or 42.2 percent of the 1970 rural population (Wood and Carvalho, Table VII-1). Because of their large population bases, the states of Minas Gerais and São Paulo have provided the largest numbers of rural-to-urban migrants. During the 1960s, São Paulo led in both the absolute and relative rate of rural out-migration. During the 1970s, Minas Gerais had the largest number of out-migrants; however, it was the areas that had been the principal agricultural frontiers of the 1950s and 1960s

(Paraná and the Central-West) that led in percentage rates of rural out-migration during the latter decade (see Wood and Carvalho, Table VII-2).

While rural-to-urban migration played an important role in population redistribution, other flows (particularly urban-to-urban) figure significantly in interregional, interstate, and intermunicipality migration. This is particularly true when attention is focused on the last step in the migration process rather than overall lifetime moves. Carvalho (1984) has calculated that 48 percent of intermunicipality moves during the 1960s were urban-to-urban flows, with the percentage rising to 50 percent during the 1970s. Rural-to-urban flows accounted for 28 percent in the 1960s and declined to 26 percent in the 1970s, while rural-to-rural moves increased from 17 to 18 percent between the two decades.

Explanations of the volume and direction of internal migration vary according to the theoretical perspective from which the process is viewed. Theories grounded in neoclassical economic theory focus on the role of differences in economic opportunities (particularly the prospects for employment and increased earnings) in sending and receiving regions, and on the individual migrant's response to these difference in terms of the perceived costs and benefits of moving or not moving. Empirical studies of the migration flows and migrant-native earnings differences in urban destinations suggest that Brazilian migrants have been responsive to economic incentives (as reflected in flows from the poorer Northeast to the more prosperous Southeast) and that they have succeeded in improving their living standards compared with their prospects had they not moved (Graham, 1970; Yap, 1972). While a significant number of migrants have incomes at or below the poverty level, they are not more highly represented in poverty groups than they are in the populations of urban destinations as a whole.

Critics of the economic approach point out its reliance on information about migrants at destinations, which limits the attention it gives to return movers who did not succeed and to conditions in sending regions. Martine and Peliano (1977) found significant return migration after applying an indirect estimating technique to data on migration to several larger urban destinations. They have questioned optimistic interpretations of the migration process in Brazil. Wood (1982) has called for balancing the interpretation of migration in terms of the economically motivated decisions of individual migrants with a broader structural view of the conditions under which those decisions are made. Wood is critical of approaches which suggest that migration results in an increase in welfare when the move is made in response to a deterioration of living conditions in sending areas that were beyond the control of the individuals living there.

Wood and Carvalho (1984) attribute rural out-migration to a variety of factors that have undermined the viability of small-scale agriculture: concentration of land ownership, commercialization and mechanization of agriculture, credit policies, and land prices in an inflationary environment. A major dimension of the resulting proletarianization of rural labor is the emergence of a large contingent of landless laborers known as *boias-frias*, who live in urban areas and travel to work in the countryside during periods of peak agricultural labor demand while seeking employment in the urban informal sector at other times (see Goodman, this volume). The existence of this class of worker further complicates the analysis of rural-urban migration as well as other aspects of demographic and social change that are linked to urban and rural residence patterns.

POPULATION POLICY

Brazil has not yet articulated an explicit population policy, either comprehensive—encompassing a full range of demographic, economic, social, and political interactions including population size and growth rates, internal population distribution, and immigration—or with a more narrow reference to the population growth rate and its main determinant, fertility. Neither is there a mechanism in the Brazilian economic planning system for assessing the impact of population growth at the individual and societal level.

International population conferences, the first in Bucharest in 1974 and the next in 1984 in Mexico City, provide useful benchmarks for describing the evolution of Brazilian views on population policy. Before 1974, Brazil did have elements of a population policy in its laws. For example, the "law of the two-thirds," enacted during the 1930s, specified the proportion of native Brazilians who should be hired by firms subject to the law. However, the Brazilian position on the question of overall population increase and the birth rate in that period could best be classified as implicity pronatalist.

That position reflected several interests: (1) opposition by the Church to government intervention in an area that infringed on its moral teachings about reproduction and the family; (2) nationalist sentiment about the importance of population size in Brazilian aspirations for status as a political and economic power; (3) traditional views of Brazil as underpopulated in relation to its territory and natural resource base; (4) distrust about an issue that was being promoted vigorously by the United States and other industrialized aid donors as "in Brazil's interest" when many Brazilians didn't see it that way; and (5) during the late 1960s and early 1970s, a heady optimism that discounted concerns about rapid population growth on the ground that with the Gross National Product growing at more than 10 percent each year, one really ly did not need to worry about a point or two in the rate of population growth.[4]

Officially, the Brazilian position was mute, except when there were real or apparent attempts at foreign intervention. At the same time, Brazilian views were hardly monolithic, even within the governing technocracy, where figures such as Rubens Vaz da Costa and Mario Henrique Simonsen were speaking out about possible adverse effects of rapid population growth on economic and social development in Brazil.

The 1974 World Population Conference at Bucharest proved to be a catalyst for some important changes, at least in the way in which Brazilian views were articulated. Brazilian representatives at the conference stated most of the traditional Brazilian concerns that underlay its earlier pronatalist position. At the close of their statement, however, the Brazilian representatives noted that it was also the Brazilian view that individual couples had the right to make reproductive choices whithout government interference, and that it was the government's responsibility to ensure that couples with limited income had access to the means of control. Also, the Second National Development Plan included a section on population that stated that Brazil sought a rate of population growth that was consistent with national development goals, and that the then-current rate indeed fulfilled this expectation.

At the national level, very little was done during the 1970s to implement these "policies," even assuming that they truly represented official Brazilian views. No real effort was mounted to determine what population growth and distribution patterns might be more or less consistent with Brazilian development goals. At the same time, some important changes were occurring in the environment in which population action programs operated. These changes in many ways set the stage for policy developments that are occurring during the 1980s. In shifting from a pronatalist to a laissez-faire position on population issues in general during the mid-1970s, the Brazilian government also shifted to a laissez-faire position in its stance on foreign assistance to private organized family planning efforts in Brazil. This set the stage for organizations such as Brazil's IPPF affiliate, BEMFAM, to expand its activities and enter into *convenios* with state governments, including several in the Northeast, to develop its so-called community-based system of subsidized distribution of contraceptives to low income groups.

Another change is a growing recognition of the fact that even though fertility is declining rapidly, population increase is by no means over in Brazil. Demographic momentum will in all likelihood double Brazil's 1980 population of 120 million before eventual population stabilization occurs sometime in the next century. Concern about the increased numbers and their implications for individual and societal welfare appears to have been important in motivating the organization of such entities as the Brazilian Parliamentarians Group and in the commissioning of studies that appeared in *O Segundo Brasil*, which look at the long-run implications of future Brazilian population growth (Costa, 1983).

These and similar expressions of concern about the implications of Brazil's current rate of population growth, along with questions about the role of the government vis-a-vis private nongovernmental family planning agencies in the distribution of family planning services to low income groups, served to focus increased public attention on population policy issues. A parliamentary commission was established to address these questions, and discussion was stimulated as Brazil began to prepare its position paper for the 1984 International Population Conference in Mexico City.

As in 1974, the 1984 meeting appears to have been a catalyst in the evolution of the next stage of Brazilian population policy. In his speech at the conference, the head of Brazil's delegation, Health Minister Waldyr Arcoverde, reiterated the principles stated at the 1974 meeting about the rights of individuals to reproductive choice and the responsibility of the state to ensure they have access to the means of family planning. He went on to say that family planning ought to be an integral part of public health services. At the same time, he allowed that private organizations should continue to operate in the private sector, but stipulated that their activities need to be monitored by the public sector to ensure that they serve the best interests of their clients.

While there is every indication that Brazil is now formulating a national population policy and the mechanisms to implement it, the *form* that the policy and its implementation will take do not yet appear to be fully resolved, and are not likely to be until after a new presidential administration is in place. Brazil does not appear to be moving in the direction of a comprehensive population law such as the one that underpins Mexico's national policy. Rather, Brazilian policy is likely to focus more specifically on the question of family planning.

Practical questions still need to be resolved about how best to incorporate family planning services into a national health system that still has major gaps in the provision of general as well as maternal and child health services. Those gaps affect precisely the low income groups that have least access to contraceptives through the channels that contributed to the rapid increase in contraceptive use during the 1970s by middle and upper income groups. While there is support on all sides for "democratizing" access to family planning in Brazil, it is still too early to tell the path that will be followed.

This brings us back to a question posed earlier about what difference it has made for Brazil not to have had an official population policy and official support of family planning, in contrast to such neighbors as Colombia and Mexico, which had both. In terms of overall trends in fertility, it is difficult to discern differences among the three countries (see Merrick, 1984). Colombia's policy and programs probably contributed to its experience of more rapid declines than Brazil during the same period, and Mexico's policy and program allowed it to catch up with Colombia and Brazil during the late 1970s. All three had total fertility rates of around 4 in the early 1980s.

One difference could be in the extent to which regional and social class inequality in fertility is likely to persist. The Mexican and Colombian programs appear to be reducing such differentials. On the other hand, there is no magic in centralized efforts to remedy such inequality in Brazil. Much of the inequality in access to health services in Brazil can be traced to its centralized health delivery system. Brazil might learn from Mexico, which is now attempting to decentralize its health and family planning system after concluding that too large a proportion of the resources in a centralized system were being channeled to the Federal District, both in terms of administrative costs and in relation to the actual amount spent on the delivery of services.

Another difference could be in the time taken to go from a total fertility rate of four to a rate of two, the level at which population growth would finally stabilize. The decline in fertility noted earlier could be related to the persistence of fertility differentials among lower income groups and regions. It is difficult to prescribe the combination of increased access to fertility control and other social and economic changes that would be needed to reduce such differences, but it is clear that their persistence has important implications for the future growth of the population of Brazil and for the relative size of the population in lower income classes.

NOTES

1. The official definition of urban residence in Brazil is based on the administrative status of localities (as *sedes* of municipalities and districts) rather than population size or urban function. As a consequence, the percentage of population reported as urban is greater than one would find had a definition based on population size been used. For further discussion, see Merrick and Graham (1979), p. 191.

2. The only source of information on fertility rates during the early 1980s is the vital statistics system, whose coverage is still incomplete at the national level. There is some indication, based on data from states with more reliable vital statistics (São Paulo, for example) that the birth rate started to decline again after 1983 after remaining comparatively stable for several years. See Fundação Sistema Estadual de Analise de Dados, Indicadores Demograficos para o Estado de São Paulo, No. 54.

3. The abortion rates in Table 1.7 correspond to a range estimate of the annual number of abortions that runs from about 460,000 to 1.3 million.

4. The best-known spokesman on the last point was Delfim Neto during his term as Minister of *Fazenda* in the early 1970s. See Merrick and Graham, chapter

11. For a review of the influence of elite groups on population policy, see McDonough and DeSouza (1981).

REFERENCES

Albuquerque, Roberto P. de C.A., Marcia Martins, and Vera R. de S. Dias (1981), Padrões e tendências de nupcialidade e algunas características da fecundidade. *Boletim Demográfico* 12 (2):15−81.

Altmann, Ana Maria G., and Laura L.R. Wong (1981), Padrões e tendências da nupcialidade no Brasil. *Anais: Segundo Encontro Nacional*. São Paulo: Associação Brasileira de Estudos Populacionais (ABEP), p. 343−415.

Altman, Ana Maria G., and Carlos E. Ferreira (1979), Evolução do censo demográfico e registro civil como fontes de dados para a análise da fecundidade e mortalidade no Brasil. *Boletim Demográfico* 10 (2):1−85.

Associação Brasileiro de Estudos Populacionais, ABEP (1978), *Anais: Primerio Encontro Nacional*, Campos de Jordão-SP.

————, (1980) *Anais: Segundo Encontro Nacional*, Aguas de São Pedro-SP.

————, (1982). *Anais: Terceiro Encontro Nacional*, Vitoria-ES.

Berquó, Elza *et al.* (1977), *A Fecundidade em São Paulo: Características Demográficas, Biológicas e Sócio-economicas*, São Paulo: Editora Brasileira de Ciências.

Berquo, Elza S. (1980), Algumas Indagacões sobre a recente queda da fecundidade no Brasil. Teresópolis: VI Reunião do Grupo de trabalho sobre o Processo de Reproduçao da População, CLACSO.

Bongaarts, J. (1980). *"The fertility inhibiting effects of the intermediate fertility values"*. *Working Paper n.º 57*, Center for Policy Studies, New York Population Council.

Brasil, Fundaçao IBGE. *Contribuições para o estudo da demografia do Brasil*. Rio de Janeiro, Fundação IBGE, 2.ª ed., 1970.

Brasil, Fundaçao IBGE, Departamento de Documentação e Referência. "Bibliografia sobre recenseamento no Brasil". *Revista Brasileira de Estatística* 41 (jul./set. 1980): 451−82.

Brasil, Fundaçao IBGE (sem data). *Crescimento e distribuição da população brasileira: 1940−1980*. Rio de Janeiro, Fundação IBGE.

Carvalho, J.A.M. de. "Regional Trends in Fertility and Mortality in Brazil", *Population Studies* 28 (dez. 1984): 402−22.

Carvalho, J.A.M. de (1984). "Estimativas indiretas e dados sobre migrações internas no Brasil: uma avaliação conceitual e metodológica das informações censitárias recentes". Belo Horizonte, DECEPLAR/UFMG.

Carvalho, J.A.M. de; PAIVA, Paulo de T.A. e Sawyer, Donald R. (1981). *The Recent Sharp Decline in Fertility in Brazil: Economic Boom, Social Inequality, and Baby Bust*. Documento de trabalho n.º 8. Cidade do México, Conselho Populacional, Representação Regional para América Latina e Caribe.

Carvalho, J.A.M. de e Paiva, Paulo de T.A. (1976). "Estrutura de renda e padrões de fecundidade no Brasil". *In* Manoel A. Costa (organizador), *Fecundidade: padrões brasileiros*. Rio de Janeiro, Altiva Gráfica e Editora Ltda.

Castro, Cláudio de M.; Martine, George e Camargo, Liscio (1984). "O planejamento familiar no Brasil após a conferência do México". Brasília, Centro Nacional de Recursos Humanos/IPEA.

Costa, Manoel Augusto (organizador). O segundo Brasil: perspectivas sócio-demográficas. Rio de Janeiro, Ébano Gráfica e Editora, 1983.

Frias, Luiz A. de M., Mello, Luiz F. R. de e Limeira, Jarbas C. (1982). "Uma estimativa da cobertura do registro de nascimentos para o período 1974–77". Boletim Demográfico 13 (2): 33–46.

Graham, Douglas H. (1970). "Divergent and convergent regional economic growth and internal migration in Brazil 1940–1960". Economic Development and Cultural Change 18:362–382.

Henriques, Maria Helena F. T. (1980). "Uniões legais e consensuais: incidência e fecundidade na América Latina". Boletim Demográfico 10:23–62.

Janowitz, Bárbara et al. (1982). "Cesarian section in Brazil". Social Science and Medicine 15:19–25.

Knight, Peter T. e Moran, Ricardo (1981). Brazil: Poverty and Basic Needs Series. Washington, D.C., The World Bank.

Leite, Valéria da M. (1981). "Níveis e tendências da mortalidade e da fecundidade no Brasil a partir de 1940". Anais: Segundo Encontro Nacional. São Paulo, Associação Brasileira de Estudos Populacionais (ABEP), p. 581–609.

Martine, George e Peliano, José Carlos (1977). "Migração, estrutura ocupacional e renda nas áreas metropolitanas". In M.A. Costa (organizador), Estudos de demografia urbana. Rio de Janeiro, IPEA/INPES, p. 161–96.

Martine, George e Camargo, Liscio (1984). "Crescimento e distribuição da população brasileira: tendências recentes". Revista Brasileira de Estudos Populacionais 1:99–144.

McDonough, Peter e Souza, Amaury de (1984). A política de populaçao no Brasil, Rio de Janeiro, Paz e Terra, 1984.

Merrick, Thomas W. e Graham, Douglas H. (1979). Population and Economic Development in Brazil: 1800 to the Present. Baltimore, the Johns Hopkins University Press.

Merrick, Thomas W. e Berquó, Elza (1983). The Determinants of Brazil's Recent Rapid Decline in Fertility. Washington, The National Academy Press.

Merrick, Thomas W. (1983). "Fertility and family planning in Brasil". International Family Planning Perspectives 9:110–119.

———. (1984a). "Financial implications of Brazil's high rate of cesarian section deliveries". Washington, D. C., Documento de trabalho para o Banco Mundial.

———. (1984b). "Recent fertility declines in Brazil, Colombia, and Mexico". Estudo apresentado na reunião anual da Population Association of America, Minneapolis, 3 maio 1984.

———. (1985). "The effect of piped water on early childhood mortality in urban Brazil, 1970 to 1976". Demography 22:1–24.

Morley, Samuel A. Labor Markets and Inequitable Growth: the Case of Authoritarian Capitalism in Brazil. Cambridge, Cambridge University Press, 1982.

Oliveira, Juarez de C., Vianna, Márcia C. de S. e Oliveira, Zuleica L.C. de (1981). "O perfil da força de trabalho feminino no Estado de São Paulo—1950 a 1976". *Boletim Demográfico* 12 (2):84–119.

Paiva, Paulo de T. A. (1982). "O processo de proletarização como fator de desestabilização dos níveis de fecundidade no Brasil". Estudo apresentado na VII Reunião da CLACSO, Grupo de Trabalho sobre os Processos de Reprodução da População. Cuernavaca, México.

Rodrigues, Walter *et al.* (1981). "Contraceptive practice and community-based distribution program impact in Northeast Brazil". Estudo apresentado na reunião anual da American Public Health Association, Los Angeles.

Silva, Nelson do V. (1979). "Padrões de nupcialidade no Brasil (1940–1970)". *Boletim Demográfico* 9 (4):5–25.

Taschner, Suzana P. e Bogus, Lúcia Maria M. (1984). "Redistribuição espacial e fluxos migratórios nos anos setenta". Estudo apresentado no 4.º Encontro Nacional, Associação Brasileira de Estudos Populacionais, Águas de São Pedro, SP.

Thomé, Antônio M.T. *et al.* (1982). "Prática contraceptiva atual em alguns Estados brasileiros". *In Anais: Terceiro Encontro Nacional*. São Paulo, Associação Brasileira de Estudos Populacionais, ABEP, p. 145–84.

United States, National Academy of Sciences, Committee on Population and Demography. *Levels and Recent Trends in Fertility and Mortality in Brazil*. Washington, The National Academy Press, 1983.

Vetter, David H. e Simões, Celso C. da S. (1980). "Acesso à infra-estrutura de saneamento básico e mortalidade". *Boletim Demográfico* 10 (4):4–29.

Wood, Charles (1982). "Equilibrium and historico-structural perspectives on migration". *International Migration Review* 16:298–319.

Wood, Charles e Carvalho, José Alberto M. de (1984). *The Demography of Inequality in Brazil*. Gainesville, Center for Latin American Studies.

World Bank (1979). *Brazil: Human Resources Special Report*. Washington, D.C., Banco Mundial.

Yap, Lorene (1972). "Internal migration and economic development in Brazil". Ph.D. thesis, Dept. of Economics, Harvard University.

Yunes, João e Ronchexel, Versa S. "Evolução da mortalidade geral, infantil e proporcional no Brasil". *Revista de Saúde Pública* 8 (junho 1974, Suplemento): 3–48.

2

Rural Economy and Society

David Goodman

INTRODUCTION

It is a commonplace to observe that Brazil in the postwar period has changed from an essentially rural economy into a heavily urbanised, diversified industrial society. In 1940, 67 percent of the labour force was in primary sector, and this share had fallen to almost one-third by 1980. Indeed, Brazil's rural population declined in absolute terms by 2.4 million in the 1970s. Many "stylised facts" could be presented to illustrate structural change of this magnitude and intensity, but Brazil's rise into the ranks of the world's largest industrial producers arguably is the most eloquent. Certainly industrial accumulation is the main dynamic element in the rapid postwar economic growth. The consolidation of the industrial sector in the 1950's and its subsequent internationalisation have gradually transformed the terms on which the agrarian question is posed. In the initial phase of postwar import substitution, in addition to the mobilisation of domestic commodity surpluses, agriculture was an important source of net resource transfers to finance industrialisation, and particularly to transform internal savings into industrial capital goods through imports. Subsequently, the imperatives of industrial capital accumulation have emphasised agriculture's role in reducing domestic inflationary pressures and the imbalance in external payments.

Although the foundations of Brazilian industrialisation were well-established by 1930, the export sectors only slowly relinquished their hegemonic position to the urban industrial bourgeoisie.[1] The gradual transition to a mode of accumulation dominated by industrial capital, and their increasing control of the institutional machinery of the state, perhaps is best exemplified by the maintenance of the highly overvalued 1939 exchange rate until 1953 and the introduction of other discriminatory policies against the export sector. Yet, despite the rapid expansion and diversification of the urban industrial sectors in the 1950s and 1960s, agricultural output growth continued to be achieved by the extensive incorporation of land and labour and the reproduction of noncapitalist forms of production. These production relations came under increasing strain as rising urban demand accelerated the development of commodity production, intensifying local conflicts over access to land and employment rights. In the 1950s, these local currents of protest and struggle coalesced into rural labour movements and the agrarian question achieved brief political prominence on the national stage. The articulation of rural-urban relationships in this period of extensive agricultural development, which corresponds roughly to the postwar years until the 1960s, is the unifying theme of Part I.

Differing formulations of this articulation are examined in section I-A on the basis of the seminal contribution by Oliveira (1972). Although noncapitalist agrarian structures met the requirements of urban growth and industrialisation satisfactorily, the contradictions exacerbated by the intensification of commodity production mobilised rural workers and led in the early 1960s to the organisation of rural unions. The origins and recent history of these labour movements are examined briefly in section I-B. The extensive model of agricultural development is considered in greater detail in section I-C, which focuses on the generation of the agricultural surplus, the sources of growth of output, and policy changes. The final section, I-D, provides a bridge between the extensive model and the subsequent industrialisation of agriculture by examining the uneven pattern of technical innovation and the pronounced productivity differentials between export crops and staple foodstuffs.

The central theme of Part II is the redefinition of agriculture's integration with industrial capital from the 1960s onwards under the stimulus of conservative modernisation strategies, discussed in section II-A. This re-articulation is broadly characterised by the transition from extensive sources of output growth to the exploitation of the intensive margin, which has provoked major transformations in rural production relations. These changes, which include the proletarianisation of the "internal peasantries" or resident labour force on large estates and the capitalisation of family labour forms of production in certain crop sectors, are discussed at length in sections II-B to II-D. The new model of industrialised agriculture exhibits important continuities with the previous articulation, notably the macro-economic significance of commodity surpluses. However, the vantage point of the mid-1980s reveals a decisive structural break, with the emergence of agro-industry as the critical element in rural social change.

A pervading theme of this second period, then, is the expansion of a large domestic agro-industrial complex, which signifies the direct incorporation of agriculture into the process of capitalist accumulation in Brazil. That is, the capitalisation of the rural labour process, sustained by massive resource transfers through the institutional credit system, provides an increasing array of industrial and finance capitals with opportunities for surplus appropriation and realisation in agricultural and agro-industrial activities. By the early 1980s, when the rapidly deepening economic crisis finally compelled drastic reductions in agricultural subsidies, Brazil's food and fibre sectors were dominated by large agro-industrial capitals, national and international. It is argued below, however, that this penetration of different capitals, allied to its unevenness and conditioned by the varying historical development of commodity production, has created diverse patterns of social change in Brazilian agrarian structures.

The major structural changes in postwar Brazilian agriculture, such as the demise of the extensive model articulated through the *latifundio-minifundio* complex and merchant-usurer capitals, are examined by a select review of the literature. These debates, reinforced by case study material, not only illustrate recent trends and changing views of the dominant tendency in the social division of labour but also regional differences in rural social structures.

I. EXTENSIVE GROWTH AND THE AGRARIAN QUESTION

Neoclassical and neo-Marxist writers in Brazil have drawn heavily on the formulation of the agrarian question in classical political economy to analyse the relationships between agriculture and industry in the process of economic growth (Mitra, 1977). This approach encourages broadly functionalist perspectives, ascribing agriculture a subordinate, reflexive position in its adjustment to the demands of industrial accumulation. The analysis turns on the intersectoral relationships between the terms of transfer of the agricultural surplus and industrial capital accumulation, which operate through the real price of food, urban wage rates, and the rate of profit. The State occupies a strategic position in this analysis since the intersectoral terms of trade, within certain limits, can be manipulated to promote industrial accumulation and effect real income transfers to the urban sectors. In Brazil, this framework has been widely used to assess the contribution of traditional agriculture to industrial growth in the postwar period before 1970.

A substantial body of literature, with the considerable benefit of hindsight, suggests that the extensive model of agricultural growth successfully discharged its developmental function in mobilising the agricultural surplus in the 1950s and 1960s.[2] The transition from export-led growth to the "new mode of accumulation" was accomplished without root-and-branch State intervention to transform inherited rural social structures, whether to sweep away "feudal" landed oligarchies and precapitalist production relations or to modernise agricultural technology. This view of surplus mobilisation contrasts with the pessimistic diagnoses prevalent in the 1950s and formalised in the dualist, stagnationist positions of the feudalism vs. capitalism debates (Prado, 1960, 1962; Guimaraes, 1963; and Rangel, 1962) and ECLA (Economic Commission for Latin America)—inspired structuralist perspectives (Furtado, 1961, 1964).[3] These diagnoses, which found expression in the Plano Trienal of 1962 and the 1964 PAEG (Programma de AÇAÕ Econômica do Governo) programme introduced after the military coup, maintained that accelerated industrial growth would be blocked by agricultural supply rigidities associated with inherited agrarian social structures, variously characterised as "feudal," "semi-feudal," or "archaic." Industrial capital accumulation would be severely inhibited by adverse movements in the terms of trade as urbanisation exacerbated food supply bottleneceks and inflationary pressures. Furthermore, the development of the home market for manufactures would be restricted by the persistence of noncapitalist social relations of production.

A. The Articulation Model

Within the Marxist tradition, the main attack on these dualist, stagnationist views came from Oliveira (1972) in his celebrated articulation model of the reproduction of noncapitalist relations of production.[4] Rather than a sterile dualism, Oliveira argues, the expansion of "primitive" agriculture has contributed decisively towards the consolidation of an urban industrial pattern of accumulation by generating marketed food surpluses, thereby offsetting long-term tendencies for the terms of trade to move against industry. This model emphasises the extensive incorporation of new agricultural frontiers by the reproduction of the noncapitalist relations of production embedded in the *latifundio-minifundio* complex. Such "archaic" structures are reproduced on the frontier by manipulation of the State apparatus, extending the latifundist monopoly of the land and denying rural workers permanent access to the means of production. The historical process of frontier settlement, or growth by the elaboration of peripheries, ensures the flexibility of agricultural supply for it constantly recreates conditions for permanent primitive accumulation due to the transitory, itinerant pattern of peasant settlement. Primitive accumulation, grounded in the appropriation of peasant surpluses by extra-economic means, is the principal mechanism linking frontier expansion and industrial accumulation. Thus "the majority of the vegetable food crops (such as rice, beans, and corn) supplied to the great urban markets come from zones of recent settlement" (Oliveira, 1972, 16–17).

Conditions for permanent primitive accumulation are not confined to the external agricultural frontier, but also are reproduced on the internal frontier of *latifundia*, through the rotation of uncultivated land, in such long-settled areas as the Northeast. In this model, noncapitalist agrarian structures contribute directly to urban capital accumulation by reducing the reproduction cost of labour employed in commercial agriculture and urban industry. The use-values produced by noncapitalist forms of production represent a subsidy to urban capital accumulation since they depress the level of rural real wages and so exert downward pressure on the real price of foodstuffs, the principal urban wage good. The production of use-values confers a similar subsidy on seasonal and temporary out-migration from the rural sector. More generally, the industrial reserve army is continuously replenished by the absolute surplus labour arising in peasant agriculture, again depressing urban real wages. This model of articulation between rural petty commodity production and peasant family labour agriculture and capitalist industry represented the prevailing orthodoxy among neo-Marxist writers until the later 1970s. By that time, evidence of the rapidly accelerating pace of rural proletarianisation and the capitalisation of the production process has prompted new characterisations of rural social structures and their integration in the accumulation process (D'Incao e Mello, 1976; Brant, 1977; Sorj, 1980).

B. Rural Labour Movements

However, before this transition to an industrialised rural labour process and the exploitation of the intensive margin, the resilience of the traditional, extensive model of output growth "permitted the system to leave the agrarian bases of production untouched, bypassing the problems of landownership . . ." (Oliveira, 1972, 18). This articulation of noncapitalist rural structures and urban capitals was the basis of the structural pact between the rural landed classes and the ascendant urban bourgeoisie. The antagonisms between these classes inherent in the agrarian question thus were attenuated, effectively blocking land reform measures which were proposed with increasing frequency from the mid-1950s (Camargo, 1981). Only at the close of the populist period, when internal divisions had seriously weakened the hegemonic pact, were rural labour movements able to profit from the gathering crisis of legitimacy of the Goulart regime and secure the right to establish unions. This was conceded by the Ministry of Labour in 1962, when the necessary regulations (*portarias*) were issued, and consolidated the following year with the passage of the Rural Labour Statute (*Estatuto do Trabalhador Rural*).

The structural conditions which transformed rural labour movements from sporadic, atomistic responses to local grievances into mobilisations of national political prominence in the late 1950s are inadequately examined in the literature. Forman (1971) attributes the emergence of "mass political participation in rural Brazil" to the intensification of commodity production as pressures increased to mobilise the agricultural surplus. The growing demand of urban consumption and rising prices induced urban commercial capitals to modernise marketing systems, bypassing the peasant marketplace and redefining the role and economic integration of the peasantry in the provision of urban food supplies. These commercial pressures on agricultural production systems, it is argued, led to adjustments in land tenure and land use as rising prices and the modernisation of distribution systems accentuated the competitive advantages of larger production units. This process reinforced tendencies towards the concentration of land ownership, threatening the livelihood and reproduction of small peasant producers. "What we are seeing today is the increasing commercialisation of agriculture, which alters the role of the peasantry—from small-scale producers to rural proletariat" (Forman and Reigelhaupt, 1970, 115). Other accounts, examining the rise of peasant leagues in the Northeast, focus on the expulsion and proletarianisation of *foreiros* and *moradores* in the sugar cane plantations in the mid-1950s and the subsequent expansion of the *ligas* under the leadership of Francisco Juliao into the *agreste* zone of sharecroppers, *arrendatarios* and small *minifundio* owners (Palmeira, 1979; Medeiros, 1981).[5]

The literature provides more extensive analysis of the emergence of land reform and labour rights as national political issues, although the Northeast has received by far the most attention (Camargo, 1973, 1981; Calazans, 1969, 1983; Azevedo, 1982). The origins of rural unions are a vital element in these accounts, which typically begin with the organisational efforts of the Communist Party to establish associations of rural workers, leading to the formation in 1954 of the Brazilian Agricultural Workers and Farmers Union (ULTAB: *União dos Lavradores e Trabalhadores do Brasil*).[6] Although the Fourth Congress of the Communist Party called for a "radical land reform" its later proposals and those of ULTAB gradually adopted a more moderate tone as the Party sought to consolidate a united, anti-imperialist front. The leadership of the Peasant Leagues rejected this moderate line and the underlying political strategy, including a tactical alliance with the populist State, declaring its faith in the revolutionary potential of the peasantry (Medeiros, 1981). This position and the demand for a radical land reform carried the day at the Belo Horizonte Congress called by ULTAB in 1961.[7] These currents were joined around 1960 by a third, the Catholic Church, which became actively involved in the organisation of rural unions.[8] This struggle for hegemony in the peasant movement was intensified in 1962, when the Ministry of Labour declared that legal recognition would be extended to only one union in each *municipio* and one federation in each state.[9]

This initiative drew some of the heat from the land reform issue, which was mired in an interminable legislative impasse and, at the same time, co-opted rural unions into the corporativist institutional framework of the populist State. Thus, despite the indisputable advances made with the passage of the Rural Labour Statute and related legislation in 1962–63, these measures "also linked [rural workers'] organisations to the State, binding rural unionism within the same limits as those that had imprisoned urban trade unionism" (Medeiros, 1981, 37).

Rural unionism quickly became the dominant form of rural labour mobilisation, eclipsing the Peasant Leagues, and in 1963 the National Confederation of Agricultural Workers (CONTAG) was established. According to Medeiros and Soriano (1984), its composition reflected three competing currents: ULTAB, the *Ação Popular*, a movement of so-called radical Catholics, and a second Church group involved in the organisation of Christian unionism (*sindicalismo cristão*), mainly in Pernambuco and Rio Grande do Norte. The land reform proposal passed at the 1961 ULTAB Congress in Belo Horizonte was adopted by CONTAG as its main demand, but the military coup of April 1964 led to the overthrow and persecution of its officers, as well as those of affiliated federations and many unions. However, the intervention in CONTAG was undertaken within the legal norms of the Consolidated Labour Legislation (CLT). "This meant that, although the officers of the entity were removed, the most active leaders persecuted and peasant struggles harshly repressed, the same union structure was maintained . . ." (Medeiros and Soriano, 1984, 5).

The direction of CONTAG following the military intervention was transferred to conservative elements of the Church associated with the Christian Workers Circles (*Circulos Operarios Cristãos*). With the repression of the Leagues and Communist activists, opposition to this conservative line came mainly from liberal groups within the Church, which supported independent unionism. These included the Service of Rural Orientation of Pernambuco (SORPE), whose supporters won the 1966 elections for control of the state federation (FETAPE). This opposition current, supported by more combative federations in Rio Grande do Norte, Paraiba, Minas Gerais, and Rio Grande do Sul, then secured a narrow victory for the leadership of CONTAG in 1967.

In the period 1965–79, CONTAG pursued an essentially legalistic strategy, affirming the primacy of the rule of law, partly to ensure its own survival and also as a tactic to "manage the political retreat" (*administrar o recuo politi-co*) imposed by the increasing severity of the repression, particularly following the Institutional Act No. 5 in 1968 (Azevedo, 1984). CONTAG accordingly focused on achieving fuller recognition and legal enforcement through the courts of the rights granted under the 1963 Labour Statute and the conservative Land Statute (*Estatuto da Terra*), which governs relations between landlords and sharecroppers and tenants (*arrendatarios*). CONTAG also campaigned for other basic rights of citizenship, including extension of social security legislation to rural workers and implementation of land reform provisions of the Land Statute. Among the internal organisational strategies (*para dentro*) pursued by CONTAG, emphasis was given to educational work, practical union administration, and the extension of union representation throughout the countryside. Despite its intrinsic threat to authentic, non-*pelego* leadership, the federal decision to administer the rural social programme (FUNRURAL) through the union network assisted in this organisational aim. As a result of these activities, undertaken in extremely difficult circumstances, CONTAG consolidated the legal gains achieved in the populist period and greatly strengthened its organizational structures.[10] This grassroots work provided the foundation for the increasingly prominent role CONTAG assumed in the Brazilian labour movement during the *abertura* of the Figueiredo administration.

CONTAG's Third Congress held in 1979 marks the major divide between the defensive posture dictated by the repression, with its emphasis on internal organisation and the formal, legalistic pursuit of basic rights, and more outward-looking (*para fora*) strategies, which would involve CONTAG more directly in land and labour conflicts and require wider political initiatives. Resolutions were carried calling for the more vigorous conduct of rural struggle, including collective action, as in the Pernambuco sugar cane workers' strikes of 1979 and 1980, and mass mobilisations (Azevedo, 1984). These activities, reinforced in some cases by other institutions, such as the Pastoral Land Commission (CPT), have brought rural labour questions and the demand for land reform closer to the forefront of public discussion. However, the continuing growth and diversification of Brazilian society since the early 1960s, as well as proletarianisation tendencies within agriculture, have robbed the agrarian question of its former political significance. While it retains a place on the agenda of political and social reform, it no longer poses a threat to the foundations of capitalist accumulation in Brazil.

C. The Extensive Model

The favourable evaluation of the extensive model by neoclassical writers is drawn from analysis of the behaviour of agricultural real prices and estimated long-term trend rates of growth of rural output (Nicholls, 1972; Paiva *et al*. 1973). Despite adverse price trends in some product categories, the mobilisation of commodity surpluses for domestic consumption was achieved, it is argued, on terms broadly favourable to the urban sectors, avoiding the erosion of industrial profit margins from the side of real wages and raw material costs. This position receives further support from econometric estimates of long-term output trends and agricultural supply functions. Mendonca *et al*. (1977) indicate that agricultural output grew significantly faster than per capita income, increasing at an average annual rate of 4–5 percent in the period 1932–73. It is suggested that "the rates of growth of output closely accompanied the macroperformance of the economy as a whole, revealing the positive response of agricultural supply", (Mendonca *et al*., 1977, 109). Studies by Delfim Netto *et al*. (1965), Pastore (1971), and Smith (1969) dealt a further blow to dualist characterisations of "primitive" agriculture, revealing that producers' output decisions were responsive to changes in relative commodity prices and factor costs.

In addition to this positive supply response to internal requirements, agriculture also is deemed to have mobilised export surpluses and released involuntary savings to finance industrialisation. A complex array of discriminatory trade and exchange policies effectively taxed export sector incomes and transferred these resources to selected import substitution activities by means of subsidised exchange allocations. The implicit taxation of the export sector imposed by overvalued exchange rates arising from exchange controls, tariff policy, and other discriminatory measures has been widely discussed (Bergsman, 1970; Pastore, 1979).[11] For example, during the spectacular rise in world coffee prices from the late 1940s to the Korean War boom, these instruments permitted the industrial sectors to appropriate a significant share of the real income gains which otherwise would have accrued to coffee producers. The coffee sector "between 1947 and 1954 furnished the exchange revenue base necessary for the expansion and modernisation of the industrial capital stock in the first phase of the post-war process of import substitution" (Bacha, 1976, 157). Quantitative estimates of resource transfers from export agriculture effected by discriminatory trade and exchange policies are provided for differing sub-periods between the late 1940s and 1970 by Gudin (1969), Fishlow (1972), Veiga (1975), and Bacha (1976). The subsidies conferred on domestic consumption by export quotas, determined by the "exportable surplus" strategy applied to staple crops (Leff, 1967), are estimated in the case of maize by Thompson and Schuh (1978) for the period 1947–70.

The successful performance of the extensive model has been overstated, particularly by those accounts which ignore the urban food supply crises of the early 1950s and early 1960s (Smith, 1969). The tensions within this model became abundantly clear in the early 1970s as agriculture's terms of trade improved sharply and rising real food prices emerged as an important factor in the resurgence of inflation. The origins of these recent domestic supply imbalances can be discerned in quantitative analyses of long-term output growth, which reveal the overwhelming importance of the extension of the cultivated area. The westward movement of the agricultural frontier accelerated after 1940, when the incorporation of new crop land became a major objective of agricultural development policy, promoted by federal infrastructural investment programmes. The successive expansion of new frontiers—Paraná in the 1940s and 1950s and the Central-West and Amazonia since the 1960s—undoubtedly explains the longevity of the extensive model, and the secondary importance policy makers attributed to programmes to accelerate productivity growth. Thus the incorporation of new crop land accounted for 92 percent of aggregate output growth in the period 1948–69 (Patrick, 1975). However, expansion of the cultivated area also is the principal component of growth in twenty-two major crop sectors and in all states, except Rio de Janeiro and São Paulo. The extensive model, in short, characterised long-settled areas in the Northeast and Southeast.

Changes in this pervasive pattern of stagnant or slowly rising yields per hectare can be detected after the mid-1950s. However, productivity growth caused by technological innovation, rather than the occupation of more fertile land, as in the case of coffee in Paraná, is restricted to selected industrial raw materials and export crops. These examples, in turn, are concentrated in São Paulo, with its relatively long tradition of agricultural research and extension services (Smith, 1969).[12] Thus the increase in the rate of productivity growth in industrial raw materials in 1945–60 is attributed by Mendonca de Barros et al. (1977) to the diffusion in São Paulo and neighbouring states of improved, disease-resistant varieties of cotton (Ayer and Schuh, 1974). Yet, even in São Paulo, food crops were relatively neglected in agricultural research programmes as in other, more rudimentary state research systems. In his review of the period 1948–69, Patrick (1975, 103) states, "In a general way, the yield-effect is important for crops of high value per hectare, that are cultivated in limited areas or that have been of modest importance for crops widely cultivated in Brazil and it is not evident that its importance has increased over time."

This view, and particularly the explanatory importance of agricultural research, is supported by Mendonca de Barros et al. (1976, 766). In the Northeast, apart from two sub-periods, the contribution of technological innovation to productivity growth in the years 1935–68 is "almost absent or strongly negative." Moreover, in São Paulo and the Centre-South, "coffee and cotton always account for more than 60 percent of the total gains of productivity;

other products appear [only] sporadically. . . ." In addition to these two crops, agricultural research, again concentrated in São Paulo, is identified as the cause of rising yields per hectare for sugar cane, corn, and soya.[13]

The perceptible, though modest, increase in the contribution of technological innovation to rising crop yields from the mid-1950s coincided with a gradual change in the direction of agricultural development policy towards the active promotion of productivity growth. Transportation and crop storage programmes continued to dominate federal investment in agriculture, as in the Target Plan period of 1956–61. However, policies to accelerate technological innovation were introduced in the early 1950s and assumed increasing importance in the course of the decade, foreshadowing their dominant role in agricultural development policy in the 1960s and 1970s. Given the priority attached to the control of urban food prices, these policies acted on the supply side, subsidising modern inputs, particularly fertilisers and machinery, mainly by granting preferential exchange rates, tariff exemptions, and fiscal incentives. In the early 1960s, these instruments diminished in importance following the gradual unification of the exchange rate system and the introduction of import substitution programmes for fertilisers and agricultural machinery. They were superseded by special rural credit programmes, with low, often highly negative, real interest rates as the principal mechanism to subsidise current output and capital costs in agriculture.[14] Institutional sources of rural credit expanded rapidly throughout the 1950s, and official bank credit to agriculture almost doubled in real terms in 1953–64 (Smith, 1969).

From these relatively small beginnings, official credit programmes by the 1970s had become the linchpin of modernisation policy, effecting massive resource transfers to the rural sector by means of subsidised lending. Reviewing the earlier period, Smith (1969, 261) concludes that "reliance on the market mechanism and selective traditional incentives has characterised the style of agricultural policy in Brazil from 1950 to 1967. The policies . . . attempted to raise agricultural output by increasing profitability without raising consumer prices (marketing investment, subsidised credit), to increase productivity through subsidies on modern inputs, and to stimulate production by reducing uncertainty about agricultural prices."

It is interesting to speculate on the rapid ascendancy of agriculture in the priority ranking of economic policy, as revealed by the huge net resource flows channelled through the National System of Rural Credit created in 1964–65. Rising real food prices and the acute urban supply crises of the early 1960s undoubtedly alerted the new military regime to the economic and political dangers of continued exclusive reliance on the extensive model. The mobilisation of rural labour, although suppressed and politically disarticulated, also threw into prominence the contradictions between "archaic" agrarian structures and modern industry. Indeed, fears that "backward" agriculture would severely constrain economic development were voiced in the PAEG programme introduced after the coup of 1964. However, for the regime's supporters in the rural oligarchy and urban bourgeoisie, the industrialisation of agriculture was infinitely preferable to land reform as a solution to low productivity. The Green Revolution package of biological and chemical innovations was being actively promoted by the international scientific establishment and U.S. agro-industrial capitalists anxious to extend their overseas operations. Furthermore, the modernisation approach to rural development and models of "induced innovation" enjoyed considerable vogue among agricultural economists and advisers to bilateral and multilateral aid organisations. The establishment of EMBRAPA (Empresa Brasileira de Pesquisa Agropecuária) and EMBRATER (Empresa Brasileira de Assistência Tecnica e Estensão Rural) in the early 1970s owes much to the force of these ideological and intellectual currents. Finally, the belief that structural problems are more effectively overcome by free markets and economic incentives rather that reformist solutions also informed the decisions of the post-1964 economic policy-making technocracy. It is exemplified by the internationalist *abertura* strategy introduced in the mid-1960s, which conferred significant gains on agricultural export sectors. We now turn to consider the further distortions these policies brought in their train.

D. Productivity Differentials and Market Segmentation

As domestic agricultural supply imbalances became more pronounced in the 1970s, the uneven pattern of productivity growth and technical innovation attracted greater analytical attention. These productivity differentials and the overt policy discrimination against staple foodstuffs have provided ammunition for orthodox critiques of modernisation policies. Doubts have been rekindled concerning agriculture's role in the accumulation process—not as a source of net savings, but over its capacity to meet the simultaneous demands of domestic supply requirements and export surpluses to relieve the external payments crisis. The improvment in agriculture's terms of trade, stimulated initially by the recovery of world commodity prices, is discernible from 1968, with the real prices of staple foodstuffs rising particularly sharply after 1971 (Mendonca de Barros and Graham, 1978; Homem de Melo, 1979). This evidence of inflationary pressures emanating from agriculture is confirmed by Bacha (1979), who argues that these real price increases were an important source of upward pressure on the urban real wage rate in the 1970s.

Several studies have attempted to quantify these pressures more precisely by analysing trends in food supply and the domestic availability of calories and proteins for human consumption. With due qualifications for the nature of the data,[15] Mendonca de Barros and Graham (1978, 716) conclude that in the period 1962–76 "per capita food supply from domestic sources grew slightly until 1971, while the real price per million calories declined slightly. This tendency is rapidly inverted from 1971 onwards, domestic [food] supply falling between 10 and 20 percent and the real cost per calorie almost doubling. . . ." Homem de Melo (1983, 222) undertakes a similar exercise using an aggregate basket of rice, beans, corn, manioc, and potatoes. His findings are virtually identical, indicating "a fall of 19–21 percent in daily per capita availability between 1967 and 1979. . . ." As the author points out, this decline in calorie and protein availability was moderated slightly by rising wheat imports and the introduction of price subsidies for domestic wheat consumption.

The marked productivity differentials found by crop and region, and rising real prices of staple foodstuffs, are widely attributed to the discriminatory effects of rural modernisation programmes. These differences have been accentuated by domestic price controls and other marketing restrictions and the vigorous export promotion policies adopted in the mid-1960s. The incentives created by these *abertura* policies, including the mini-devaluation system introduced in 1968, were greatly enhanced by the international commodity boom of 1968–73. These policy interventions and international market trends combined to increase the relative profitability and reduce risk in the export sectors. These competitive advantages with regard to staple foodstuffs are compounded by preferential access to the subsidies conferred by modernisation programmes. Conversely, these intersectoral differences in profitability and risk have cause significantly slower rates of technological innovation in the production of staple foodstuffs.[16] Crop substitution in favour of the export sectors has been reinforced, diverting resources away from those sectors catering for internal consumption and aggravating domestic inflationary pressures (Homem de Melo and Zockun, 1977). The market segmentation thesis is clearly stated by Mendonca de Barros and Graham (1978, 720): "there is now a domestic sub-sector and an export sub-sector. Economic policy, by controlling domestic products and permitting price increases to be transmitted to producers (even if partially) strengthens this pattern of segmentation."

However, this is not just a simple dichotomy defined by the market destination of different crops. On this criterion, segmentation undoubtedly has diminished in recent decades. Rather, it is defined by "the existence of two groups of products with different processes of price formation, different levels of supply of technology and which thus present different profitability" (Mendonca de Barros, 1979, 21). This author also stresses the competitive displacement of food crops as export production expands.[17] "The greater profitability of the export sector compresses the production of foodstuffs, generating inflationary pressures; this seems to be, singly, the greatest cost that has been associated with the *abertura* to world markets" (*Ibid.* 23–24). These crop substitution effects are particularly associated with the rapid expansion of soybeans from the mid-1960s, and attention has been drawn to the increasing specialisation and monocultural characteristics of production systems in the Centre-South. In contrast to earlier periods, domestic food crops have failed to accompany the expansion of export production, particularly in São Paulo and Rio Grande do Sul, enhancing the importance of such regions as the Northeast in the supply of staple foodstuffs (Homem de Melo, 1983).

Several contributors place rather greater emphasis on the long-term factors which explain sectoral differences in the rate of innovation. It is suggested that these "technological disequilibria," although heightened by recent agricultural growth and policy, are rooted in the historical institutional bias of agricultural research towards export crops and industrial raw materials (Pastore *et al.*, 1982; Homem de Melo, 1981). "Export crops have been relatively privileged, virtually throughout this century, by the generation of technological innovations in public sector agricultural research centres. Among domestic food crops, it was possible to distinguish only irrigated rice in Rio Grande do Sul and corn, based on the work of the Agronomic Institute of Campinas, São Paulo" (Homem de Melo, 1983, 224). Although this theme is not pursued further here, Homem de Melo (1983) provides a comprehensive historical analysis of the uneven incidence by crop and region of agricultural research in the public sector since 1930.

Segmentation by markets, productivity, and production techniques also has a long pedigree in neo-Marxist analyses. For the recent period, it is suggested that modernisation and *abertura* policies have accentuated the traditional concentration of noncapitalist family labour farms of production in the staple food crop sectors (Graziano da Silva *et al.*, 1977). Such producers, it is argued, can better resist the downward pressure on rates of return exerted by low relative prices and price controls by virtue of their production of use-values. Although at odds with observed trends in agricultural real prices in the 1970s, this sectoral concentration of noncapitalist production allegedly contributes to the maintenance of cheap urban food supplies and the low cost of reproduction of the urban labour force.[18] The view that small family labour peasant producers account for a significant proportion of the net marketed supply of foodstuffs recently has suffered a telling attack by Silva (1984). Special tabulations from the 1975 Agricultural Census reveal that for almost 3 million farms, 63.2 percent of all units, the value of annual gross output is below the level of two annual minimum wages, equivalent to $1,420. These establishments occupy 24 percent of the cultivated area and contribute only 10 percent to total output. Even if it is accepted that urban food supply involves the mobilisation of "innumerable small surpluses," the vast majority of these small farms would nevertheless appear to be essentially consumption units.[19] Consequently, "in analysing the structure of agricultural production, we must conclude that the greater part of the so-called agricultural establishments in Brazil conceal an enormous mass of rural workers unable to find conditions to use their capacity to work, neither as small producers nor as wage workers. An enormous mass of workers is found, thanks to the Brazilian miracle, under-employed or marginalised" (Silva, 1984, 11).

Finally, the segmentation thesis also appears in recent analyses of rural and urban labour markets, especially with reference to their integration and the determinants of the rural wage rate. Bacha (1979) suggests that this integration is restricted, contending that wages in capitalist agriculture are determined by the level of real income per capita, defined in agricultural products, prevailing in the peasant family labour sector. At this level, which varies with the agricultural terms of trade, there is an "unlimited supply of labour" to capitalist agriculture. This "modified Lewis model" has been attacked by Rezende (1984), not in terms of the segmented capitalist-peasant framework, but rather because Bacha (1979) relies on a single index of farm-gate prices, thus neglecting differences in product mix between the two sectors. Rezende (1984) presents empirical evidence to show that rural and urban labour markets for unskilled workers are closely integrated, as exemplified by the intersectoral mobility of the *boia-fria*. On this view, the wage rate in capitalist agriculture is not determined by per capita real income in petty commodity production, as Bacha maintains, but by demand conditions in urban labour markets, and hence by the general level of economic activity. In broader terms, Rezende's point of departure is the fundamental changes in the social relations of production provoked by the capitalisation of the agricultural production process since the 1960s. The ensuing proletarianisation of the farm labour force has greatly enhanced the intersectoral mobility of unskilled workers and so transformed wage determination in rural labour markets. For an increasing proportion of the rural labour force, it is argued, petty commodity production no longer offers alternative rural employment. Clarification of these issues requires further empirical analysis in order to establish the validity of the segmented capitalist-peasant dichotomy and take more adequate account of regional differences in rural labour markets and agrarian social structures.

Despite some chronological overlap, the preceding sections set the stage for the transition from the extensive model to the exploitation of the intensive frontier based on industrial inputs. This transition is characterised by the accelerated capitalisation of the rural labour process under the aegis of conservative modernisation policies which assign a central, privileged r(the *latifundio*. It is accompanied by the emergence of a modern, h internationalised, agro-industrial complex as the strategic factor in rural social change. In Part II, we review first the principal instruments of this modernisation strategy, focusing particularly on the selective expansion of subsidised institutional credit, in section II-A. Our main concern, however, is to analyse recent trends in rural social structures, drawing whenever possible on case study material. We begin in section II-B with analyses of the proletarianisation of the resident labour force on large estates, notably in the Southeast, although similar trends are evident in the sugar cane plantations of the Northeast. This regional perspective is retained in the discussion of small-scale family labour agriculture in section II-C, which examines the rise of capitalised family farms in the wheat-soybean areas of the south and the enclave characteristics of such units in other regions. The decomposition of traditional peasant agriculture is considered briefly in section II-C and recent patterns of frontier settlement in Amazônia are discussed in section II-D.

At this point, however, between the extensive model and the vigorous prosecution of the post-1964 modernisation strategy, it is convenient to review macro-level trends in rural population, the growth of the area in farms and cropland, and the distribution of access to the land. In an essay in this volume, Thomas Merrick has drawn attention to the declining annual rate of rural population growth, which fell from the fairly stable level of 1.6 percent in 1940–60 to 0.6 percent in the 1960s and minus-0.6 percent in the 1970s. Only two of Brazil's macro-regions, the North and Northeast, had positive rates of rural population growth in the 1970s, and absolute numbers declined by 2.4 million during this decade. Thus, despite continuing high rates of net out-migration from the Northeast, we have the cruel paradox that the share of this impoverished, resource-poor region in the total rural population increased from 38 percent in 1960 to 45 percent in 1980. The decline in the absolute size of the rural population first became apparent in the Southeast after 1960 and in the South from 1970; the combined loss in the 1970s exceeded 4 million. This massive rural exodus is graphically illustrated by the case of Paraná, the agricultural frontier of the 1940s and 1950s and still a major target for rural migrants in the 1960s, which lost 1.2 million rural inhabitants or 29 percent of its total in the following decade. Even the more recent frontier region of the Centre-West suffered an absolute loss of rural population in the 1970s. Trends in the interregional distribution of the rural population and intercensual growth rates arising from the rural-urban exodus and rural-rural migration to successive agricultural frontiers can be seen in Tables 2.1 and 2.2.

These data are complemented by trends in the expansion and regional distribution of the area in farms (Table 2.3) and in crops (Table 2.4). The sustained expansion of farm land in the Centre-West and the increasing contribution after 1970 of the North, notably of Pará, emerges clearly, re-

Table 2.1
Distribution of the Rural Population by Macro-Region, 1940–80[1,2]

Macro-Region	1940		1950		1960		1970		1980	
	Absolute (millions)	% Share	Absolute	% Share	Absolute	% Share	Absolute	% Share	Absolute	% Share
North	1.0	3.7	1.3	3.8	1.6	4.1	2.0	4.8	2.8	7.4
Northeast	11.0	39.0	13.2	39.9	14.7	37.8	16.4	39.8	17.3	44.7
Southeast	11.1	39.2	11.8	35.7	13.2	34.0	10.9	26.5	8.9	23.1
South	4.1	14.6	5.5	16.7	7.4	19.1	9.2	22.4	7.2	18.5
Centre-West	1.0	3.5	1.3	4.0	1.9	5.0	2.6	6.4	2.4	6.3
TOTAL	28,356,133	100.0	33,161,506	100.0	38,767,423	100.0	41,054,053	100.0	38,619,797	100.0

[1] In 1960, the census definition changed from actual population to resident population.
[2] Percentage totals may not sum due to rounding.
Source: FIBGE.

Table 2.2

Absolute Change and Annual Growth Rates of the Rural Population, 1940–80[1]

Macro-Region	I. Absolute Change				II. Annual Average Growth Rates (%)			
	1940–50	1950–60	1960–70	1970–80	1940–50	1950–60	1960–70	1970–80
North	207,160	340,276	373,196	869,747	1.81	2.41	2.11	3.71
Northeast	2,175,698	1,436,775	1,693,570	917,339	1.81	1.04	1.10	0.55
Southeast	713,834	1,342,071	−2,280,934	−1,985,069	0.62	1.08	−1.88	−1.99
South	1,383,055	1,864,499	1,800,682	−2,037,170	2.92	2.95	2.20	−2.47
Centre-West	325,626	622,296	700,116	−199,103	2.89	3.95	3.14	−0.78
TOTAL	4,805,373	5,605,917	2,286,630	−2,434,256	1.58	1.57	0.57	−0.61

[1]See Table 2.1

Source: FIBGE.

Table 2.3

Distribution of the Area in Farms and Relative Contribution to its Expansion, 1940–80[1,2]

Macro-Region	I. Percentage Distribution						II. Percentage Contribution to the Expansion of Farm Land				
	1940	1950	1960	1970	1975	1980	1940–50	1950–60	1960–70	1970–75	1975–80
North	12.9	10.0	9.4	7.9	10.1	11.5	–6.9	2.0	–0.6	31.7	21.7
Northeast	21.7	25.1	25.2	25.3	24.3	24.2	44.8	26.3	25.5	14.8	23.8
Southeast	29.1	26.6	25.8	23.6	22.4	20.0	12.4	15.3	11.4	10.0	3.3
South	16.0	15.3	15.6	15.5	14.3	13.0	11.2	20.2	14.6	2.4	4.4
Centre-West	20.4	23.1	23.8	27.8	29.0	31.2	38.5	36.2	49.0	41.2	46.8
TOTAL[2]	197.7	232.2	249.9	294.1	323.9	369.6	34.5	17.7	44.3	29.7	45.7

[1]Percentage totals may not sum due to rounding.
[2]The totals for both I and II are given in millions of hectares.
Source: FIBGE.

Table 2.4
Absolute Change and Growth Rates of the Area
in Crops by Region, 1940–80[1][2]

| Macro-Region | I. Area in Crops: Absolute Change | | | | II. Area in Crops: Annual Average Growth Rates (%) | | | |
	1940–50	1950–60	1960–70	1970–75	1975–80	1940–50	1950–60	1960–70	1970–75	1975–80
North	−687.1	197.8	184.8	578.2	568.1	−12.79	6.31	3.62	14.14	8.09
Northeast	−495.1	3,453.9	1,595.2	710.4	3,249.1	−0.89	5.17	1.69	1.34	5.30
Southeast	−34.3	1,594.3	−429.8	819.2	1,687.6	−0.04	1.74	−0.44	1.65	3.04
South	1,594.8	3,613.5	2,884.4	1,963.0	1,548.7	4.43	6.04	3.08	3.33	2.28
Centre-West	−118.7	757.6	1,037.0	1,946.8	2,130.4	−1.77	8.43	5.81	12.60	8.30
TOTAL	259.6	9,617.2	5,271.6	6,017.6	9,183.9	0.14	4.16	1.70	3.31	4.22

[1]The absolute changes by region, given in thousands of hectares, may not sum to the national total due to rounding.
[2]Area in temporary and permanent crops.
Source: FIBGE.

flecting in part the powerful stimulus of fiscal incentives to extensive cattle ranching. These two regions account for a much lower share of the 15.2 million hectare increase in cropland during the 1970s (see Table 2.4). Indeed, there is a fivefold difference in this decade between the growth of land in farms and of cropland. It is apparent also that relatively long-settled areas in the Northeast, Southeast, and South continue to make significant contributions to the expansion of cropland. Aggregation problems preclude analysis of the changing regional distribution of agricultural production, although Tables 2.3 and 2.4 do provide indirect evidence. We may observe, however, that the Centre-West and North, despite their combined 42 percent share of the area in farms, accounted for only 13.2 percent and 3.6 percent respectively of the land devoted to crops in 1980.

The census data on farm establishments reveal the marked inequality of access to land which characterises Brazilian tenure structures (see Table 2.5). The concentration of land ownership which underlies this inequality is demonstrated unequivocally by recent analyses of the INCRA (Instituto Nacional de Colonização e Reforma Agrária) Cadastral Surveys for 1965–78 (Hoffmann and Graziano da Silva, 1980). The Agricultural Census also provides data on the tenure categories of owner, tenant, sharecropper, and squatter, as well as estimates of the rural labour force. However, due to frequent and confusing changes in their conceptual definition and measurement, these categories provide an unsatisfactory basis for an empirical analysis of recent historical trends in rural social relations.

II. AGRO-INDUSTRIALISATION AND THE INTENSIVE FRONTIER

As we observed earlier, the expansion of rural credit at low or negative real interest rates emerged in the 1960s as the principal instrument to promote farm capital formation and the diffusion of modern inputs.[20] The large estate has been the privileged target and beneficiary of this modernisation strategy, which has been highly discriminatory by size of borrower, crop, and region. The cost of technical innovation, both modern inputs and investment expenditures, has been very heavily subsidised, and programme design and administrative eligibility criteria *de facto* have given large-scale enterprises preferential access to these massive flows of subsidised resources and direct gains accruing from capitalisation. This strategy to capitalise the agricultural production process within the inherited structure of highly concentrated land ownership has become widely known as "conservative modernisation." Its primordial purpose is to transform the "feudal" *latifundio* into a large modern enterprise (CPDA, 1979).

Table 2.5

Distribution of Farm Establishments by Number and Area, 1940–80[1]

Size of Farm Establishment (hectares)	I. Percentage Distribution by Number					II. Percentage Share of Total Area				
	1940	1950	1960	1970	1980	1940	1950	1960	1970	1980
Less than 10	34.4	34.4	44.8	51.2	50.4	1.5	1.3	2.4	3.1	2.5
10–100	51.2	51.0	44.7	39.3	39.1	16.7	15.3	19.0	20.4	17.7
100–1,000	12.8	13.0	9.4	8.4	9.5	33.5	32.5	34.4	37.0	34.8
1,000–10,000	1.4	1.5	0.9	0.7	0.9	31.4	31.5	28.6	27.2	28.7
10,000 and over	0.1	0.1	0.1	0.1	0.1	16.9	19.4	15.6	12.3	16.4
TOTAL	1,904.6	2,064.6	3,337.8	4,924.0	5,159.8	197.7	232.2	249.9	294.1	364.9

[1]The totals are in thousands of farm establishments in I and millions of hectares in II.

Source: FIBGE.

By undertaking an immense re-allocation of resources to agriculture, the State, in effect, subsidised the demand for industrial inputs, consolidating and extending the interdependence between modernising agricultural producers and the agro-industrial sectors. These linkages have been reinforced by credit and fiscal incentives to promote investment in processing industries and marketing systems and accelerate import substitution in agricultural implements, machinery, fertilisers, and biocides. "Insofar as the recent credit expansion is channelled through special credit lines and 'tied' to specific industrialised inputs, it can be seen as a policy to stimulate and diversify investment in the agro-industrial complex" (Goodman and Redclift, 1981, 147). Correspondingly, modernisation strategy has become virtually synonymous with the industrialisation of the rural production process, through mechanisation and increased use of fertilisers and biocides.[21] So much so that Mendonca de Barros (1979) maintains that modernisation has only been "partial" due to the relative neglect of agricultural research and the dissemination of improved crop varieties.

Nevertheless, the post-1964 strategy of conservative modernisation, and the concomitant expansion of the agro-industrial complex, represents the principal watershed in postwar Brazilian agricultural development.[22] The institutional bases of this strategy, notably retention of the highly unequal structure of land ownership, were given by the new balance of class forces which emerged from the crisis of populism. Within this framework, however, the constant, underlying thread of State policy has been to stimulate the entry of large productive capitals, national and multinational, into all sectors of the food and fibre system.[23] The capitalisation of the rural labour process on large estates and, more recently, programmes to intensify commodity production in small family labour agriculture, as in the Northeast, simultaneously reflect and reinforce this penetration of rural social structures. Agro-industrial capitals, with subsidised institutional credit as the catalyst, are the agents of the transition from "primitive," extensive patterns of output growth to industrialised agricultural production. This fundamental re-articulation of the dynamics of capitalist development in agriculture is marked by the emergence of new areas of accumulation for different fractions of productive capital. As we have observed elsewhere, "in the Brazilian case, the *direct* integration of agriculture into the process of reproduction of an increasing array of capitals has rightly been emphasised" (Goodman and Redclift, 1981, 181).

A. The Selective Expansion of Rural Credit

Institutional or formal rural credit grew rapidly throughout the 1960s but accelerated sharply after 1965, increasing more than three fold in real terms in the years 1965–70 (Adams, 1975). The share of rural credit in total bank credit rose from 11 to 25 percent during the 1960s and, perhaps more significantly, the ratio of rural credit to net agricultural production increased from between 12 and 15 percent to over 50 percent. Nevertheless, the marked selectivity of this expansion was already evident, and Araujo (1983) estimates that in 1970 only 410,000 farm establishments had access to institutional sources of credit.

Even this very substantial reallocation of resources to the rural sector was surpassed by the huge resource mobilisation undertaken in the following decade, when total agricultural credit increased *fivefold in real terms*, rising at an average annual rate of 17 percent in the years 1969–79. After 1975, rural credit roughly equalled the net value of agricultural production, and implicit subsidies represented 30 percent of this total. The World Bank further has estimated that the subsidy on this lending in 1978, for example, was US $5–6 billion, approximately 3–4 percent of gross domestic product[24] (IBRD, 1979). According to Araujo (1983), the "social cost" or subsidy element conferred by the negative real interest rates on this rising real volume of credit increased by almost 200 percent between 1975 and 1979, when the subsidy on each cruzeiro of credit was Cr.$0.16. In relation to agricultural production, Araujo (1983) estimates that the credit subsidy was Cr.$0.14 for each cruzeiro of output.

Despite the expanding magnitude of subsidised credit flows to agriculture, their allocation remained highly concentrated and selective. According to the World Bank, only 20–25 percent of all producers had access to credit in 1978, and Agricultural Census data for 1975 provide an even lower estimate of 718,000 establishments, or 14.4 percent of the total (Araujo, 1983). The distributive implications of such unequal institutional access and its impact on rural social structures can be inferred from the fact that "the farmers taking credit (a minority) have had their total, not just their marginal, production subsidised" (IBRD, 1979, 64–65). Even within this small minority, moreover, there is evidence of marked inequality in the distribution of credit by size of establishment. Agricultural Census data for 1975 indicate that the ratio of rural credit to the value of agricultural output was Cr.$0.06 for small establishments under 10 hectares, whereas larger establishments had ratios from 3 to 12 times greater (Araujo, 1983). The highly skewed distribution of rural credit also is revealed by available data on loans by size of contract.[25] The share of small contracts in total credit declined dramatically in 1969–76, receiving only 5 percent of the enormous increase in credit which occurred in these years. On the other hand, large contracts absorbed 61 percent of this increase and more than doubled their share of total credit. The volume of credit allocated to large contracts rose tenfold in this period, whereas the flow to small contracts less than doubled (IBRD, 1979).

In addition to its unequal distribution by size of farm establishment and loan contract, rural credit in the 1970s was heavily concentrated by crop and region. The allocation of operating credit (*custeio*) shows the crop bias towards export commodities, industrial raw materials, and wheat production, which has been subsidised as an import substitution activity since the late 1950s. Six crops—coffee, sugar, rice, corn, soybeans, and wheat—dominate the allocation of *custeio* credit, their combined share easily exceeding 50 percent throughout the 1970s. This selectivity is revealed more sharply by the ratio of *custeio* to the gross value of production (Gomes Paiva, 1982). Policy efforts to stimulate domestic food supply and reduce imports can be detected in the increasing *custeio*/production ratio for beans in the later 1970s.[26] More generally, insofar as staple food crops are produced mainly on smaller establishments, the bias evident in rural credit allocation by crop and size of borrower has been doubly discriminatory. As might be expected, regional differences in output composition and crop bias have led to the spatial concentration of rural credit. Agricultural Census data for 1975 give the following distribution of rural credit: North (1%), Northeast (14%), Southeast (36%), South (36%) and Central-West (13%). These regional shares in total credit broadly coincide with participation in the gross value of agricultural output.

B. Recent Trends in Rural Social Structures

In the preceding section, we stressed that agro-industrial capitals have been the main agents of modernisation and capitalist penetration of agrarian social structures since the 1960s. Yet it would be mistaken to conclude that agro-industrialisation has imposed a uniform pattern on the social division of labour. On the contrary, the very selectivity of the modernisation process, conditioned by regional differences in the historical development of commodity production, has accentuated the diversity of rural social structures. This heterogeneity is likely to remain the distinguishing feature in the medium term, even if one accepts the capitalist/proletarian dichotomy as the dominant tendency in the Southeast, Brazil's economic heartland. This general observation recommends that we adopt a broadly regional perspective in reviewing recent trends in rural social change, although such a division necessarily must be highly schematic.

The Capitalisation of Large Estates

In regions where large estates dominate the agrarian structure, the internal reorganisation of the production process to incorporate labour-saving innovations has brought radical changes in rural labour markets. Mechanisation and the use of herbicides have reduced permanent year-round labour requirements and accentuated their seasonality (Graziano da Silva, 1981, 1984). These tendencies have been reinforced by changes in land use and cropping patterns arising from institutional reforms and the closer integration of certain sub-sectors, notably soybeans and oranges, with expanding international markets. Such institutional changes as the rural labour legislation and the Land Statute introduced in 1963–64 are widely regarded as important factors in the proletarianisation and casualisation of the rural labour force. Similarly, the official coffee tree eradication programme launched in the mid-1960s stimulated the substitution for this labour-intensive crop of mechanised, short-cycle crops, such as soybeans, or permanent pasture. In 1975–77, for example, coffee required 83 man-days per hectare, whereas soybeans needed only 3 man-days. Data cited by Goodman and Redclift (1981) indicate that, with mechanised cultivation but manual harvesting, the ratio of seasonal to permanent labour requirements ranges from 44:1 (cotton) to 8:1 (oranges) and 2:1 (coffee).

In areas of large estates in the Southeast, the conjuncture in the 1960s of subsidised modernisation, institutional changes in labour relations, and rising international demand led to the formation of a capitalist labour market. The internal resident labour force was expelled and replaced by casual temporary wage workers (*volantes*) and specialised, semi-skilled labour. Some writers believe the rising importance of wage labour in agriculture heralds the unification of the rural and urban labour markets and the generalisation of capitalist relations of production (Brant, 1977). In addition to the expulsion of resident workers (*colonos, moradores, agregados*), technological modernisation has been accompanied by greater centralisation of control over internal holdings at the expense of such peasant or noncapitalist forms of production as sharecropping and *arrendamento* tenancies (Gasques, 1980; Graziano da Silva *et al.*, 1982). This expulsion of resident workers and internal peasantries associated with the capitalisation of the labour process on large properties represents the "purification" of wage relations previously concealed by various nonmonetary forms of remuneration. The mixed labour control systems for so long characteristic of large estates, including coffee and sugar cane plantations, finally succumbed under the combined weight of rural labour legislation, the lure of new export crops, and heavily subsidised credit for capital investment and industrial inputs.[27]

The demise of these traditional systems is seen by some writers as the "historical affirmation" of the capitalist mode of production in agriculture. A seminal statement of the "Junker road" thesis is given by D'Incao e Mello (1976) in her study of the formation of a casual rural labour force of *boias-frias* in the Alto Sorocabana region of São Paulo. It is suggested that the growing concentration of land ownership, land speculation, and the increasing utilisation of machinery and industrialised inputs is generalising the capitalist wage relation in agriculture. D'Incao e Mello (1976) also observes that the capitalisation and centralisation of production which characterises the modernisation of large estates is depriving external family labour units of opportunities to extend their operational control over land through short-term tenancies. Changes in land use—notably the process of *pecuarização*, involving the substitution of annual crops by permanent pasture, which increasingly is being renewed by tractorised seeding—similarly are reducing the supply of land available for rent on short leases, again augmenting the "reproduction squeeze" on external peasantries.

These contingents of rural workers, proletarianised as temporary *volante* labour and excluded from the production process, depress wages in rural and urban labour markets. Accordingly, they represent an industrial reserve army as Marx defined it, "whether in terms of its structural causes or the form of its participation in the overall production process of the regional rural economy" (*Ibid.*, 31).

Brant in his case study of the region of Assis in southwestern São Paulo similarly regards the increasing importance of temporary wage labour as marking "the transformation of agriculture into industry and the formation of an industrial reserve army" (1977, 81). The emergence of the *boia-fria* as a consequence of the capitalisation of the production process on large estates thus foreshadows the unification of rural and urban labour markets. Conditions of accumulation in the two sectors gradually will be equalised, paving the way for the further industrialisation of agriculture. For Brant (1977), the strategy of conservative modernisation is consolidating a new model of accumulation based on the expansion of the agro-industrial complex and the penetration of capitalist relations of production. The concomitant growth of a landless free labour force is eroding inherited labour control systems, predicated on labour scarcity and the advantages of maintaining an internal reserve of fixed, resident workers and tenants. The tendencies observed in Assis and other developed regions represent "an advance indication of a new type of urban-rural relations" characterised by agro-industrial expansion and the formation of a capitalist rural labour market. This new articulation of rural-urban relations will supersede the earlier model formulated by Oliveira "in which high rates of industrial accumulation were based on a primitive agriculture" (1972, 87).

The contributions of D'Incao e Mello and Brant, as well as the growth on the periphery of small rural towns of *favela* settlements—a phenomenon hitherto associated with the large metropolitan centres—led to a veritable torrent of literature on *volante* labour and its incidence in other states and regions.[28] While these contributions are too numerous to review here, the emergence of a landless, casual rural labour force typically is taken as *prima facie* evidence of the intensification of capitalist relations of production in the countryside.

However, the view that this large rural proletariat represents the most advanced expression of capitalist relations recently has been challenged. Thus Graziano (1981) suggest that, on the contrary, the new rural proletariat reflects the relatively limited development of the productive forces in Brazilian agriculture, notably in harvest operations, where there are few technological barriers to mechanisation.[29] In similar vein, Goodman *et al.* argue that "the true face of modernisation on these large properties . . . is the relatively small number of permanent, semi-skilled machine operators. The *volante* proletariat, although the product of modernisation, exists only to the extent that this process is incomplete" (1984, 199). The limited mechanisation of harvesting operations for crops typically produced on large estates, such as coffee, sugar cane, cotton, and oranges, thus may be determined by the past conjuncture of rural labour surplus and the repressive institutional context of labour relations.

Since harvest mechanisation would spell the end of *volante* labour as a mass phenomenon, the structural permanence of this large rural proletariat clearly must be in doubt. Whether or not tendencies in the short term operate towards the consolidation or the dissolution of this proletariat,[30] "it is essential to recognise that the *boia-fria* is not the rural variant of urban wage labour, whose condition will be consolidated by the development of capitalist relations in the countryside. The typical expression of modernisation on large properties is the replacement of large numbers of unskilled manual workers by a handful of semi-skilled labour. . . . Large-scale production is not immutably associated with large-scale wage labour employment. The rural proletariat in the form of the *volante* or *boia-fria* thus cannot be seen as a necessarily permanent feature of rural social relations" (Goodman *et al.*, 1984, 200).

C. Small-Scale Family Labour Agriculture

Capitalised Family Farms

The recent literature on rural social change in Brazil has devoted considerable attention to the emergence of capitalised family labour farms.[31] Perhaps not surprisingly, given the internationalisation of the world economy and agro-industrial capitals, these recent debates reflect those currently under way in Europe and the United States (Goodman *et al.*, 1984). Controversy centres on the conflicting conceptualisations of this form of production, and whether it represents a transitional or permanent social category. Both questions concern the way in which capitalised family farms are integrated with agro-industrial capitals and the wider process of capitalist accumulation. Although sharply contrasting perspectives can be distinguished, they share a common analytical focus insofar as agro-industrial capitals are considered to be of strategic importance in determining rural social relations. The expansion of these capitals is treated as an integral part of the post-1964 industrialisation process, the growth of the internal market, and the internationalisation of the Brazilian economy.

For some writers, such as Muller (1982) and Sandroni (1980), the modernised family farm is a small capitalist enterprise, arising within a generalised process of capitalist penetration of Brazilian agriculture, which cuts across different size strata. In contrast, Wanderley (1979), reflecting recent French formulations,[32] conceptualises the capitalised family farm as a specific form of the worker/capitalist relation, rejecting classical notions of social differentiation and subordination to capital. This characterisation of o novo campones on modernised family labour farms as "a worker for capital" is supported by Graziano da Silva (1982), who warns against the adoption of an unnecessarily restrictive concept of proletarianisation. A third formulation turns on the proposition that the distinctive characteristics of the rural labour process depress the rate of profit and so discourage the entry of large capitalist enterprises (Dickinson and Mann, 1976). In these conditions, the modernised family farm is seen as the privileged partner of agro-industrial capitals, and hence as a permanent category in rural social structures (Aidar and Perosa, 1981).

The locus of analytical interest in peasant, family labour forms of production thus has moved from the articulation model of Oliveira (1972) to perspectives which emphasise the generalisation of capitalist production relations and identify agro-industrial capitals as the agent of change in rural social structures. At bottom, however, these recent formulations display a functionalist approach to rural change. They posit the industrialisation of agriculture as a process in which the development of agro-industry leads to the maintenance and reproduction of appropriate rural structures. This hypothesis of an alliance between agro-industrial capitals and privileged forms of production is examined critically in Goodman et al. (1984).

Case Studies from Southern Brazil

The major concentration of capitalised family farms occurs in the wheat-soybean sector of Southern and Southeastern Brazil, reflecting historical specificities of the development of commodity production and regional land settlement patterns. This includes the areas of the Colonias Velhas and Novas settled by European immigrants and their descendants in Rio Grande do Sul, Santa Caterina, and Paraná.[33] Special incentives to stimulate mechanised wheat production as an import substitution activity were introduced in the late 1950s, including price support and credit programmes. This capitalisation process gained further impetus from the general expansion of selective rural credit as part of the conservative modernisation strategy in the 1960s, and the world boom in soybean prices in the early 1970s. However, the wheat-soybean sector constitutes a unique case of the early capitalisation of family labour farming. Elsewhere, this process has followed very much in the wake of the modernisation of the large estate as a secondary and later priority of agricultural development policy.

In regions of small family labour production, a central question is to determine whether the capitalisation of family units is a transitional stage, accentuating the pace of social differentiation and the concentration of land ownership. Alternatively, capitalised family farms may become a stable component of the rural social structure, resisting vertical differentiation tendencies by articulating strategies with institutional finance capital, public agencies, cooperatives and agro-industry which allow them to keep abreast of technical innovation. Evidence can be found for both views, and far more case studies are required before firm conclusions can be drawn. [34]

Peixoto *et al*. (1979), for example, suggest that in the *municipio* of Cruzeiro do Sul in the *Colonias Velhas* region of Rio Grande do Sul, integration with international commodity markets—notably for soybeans—promoted by selective credit policies, has led to the "disarticulation" of the productive base of diversified family agriculture and its traditional labour process. The horizontal process of capitalisation and specialisation, stimulated by access to subsidised resources for the cultivation of wheat and soybeans, has been followed by classic vertical differentiation trends and the emergence of a capitalist/proletarian dichotomy. [35] Peixoto *et al*. (1979) emphasise that these tendencies are crucially influenced by size, which confers better access to subsidised institutional credit, allowing larger proprietors to extend their control over the local resource base by purchasing and renting land. In short, initial size differences are the source of unequal advantages in the capitalisation process and are likely to become structural.

The capitalisation of small-scale agriculture illustrates the parallel, mutually reinforcing action of agro-industrial and institutional finance capitals. Most observers readily acknowledge the major role of institutional credit in the capitalisation—and, many would add, survival—of the small family farm. However, there are remarkably few quantitative studies of farm indebtedness in Brazil and its implications for rural social structures. Are capitalised family farmers caught in a reproduction squeeze between increasing reliance on institutional credit and the attainment of competitive survival thresholds of productivity and net returns per unit of output, which are continuously redefined by technical innovation? Where internal sources of accumulation are inadequate to accompany the ongoing capitalisation process, rising levels of indebtedness may be the prelude to the renting out of land, forced land sales, foreclosure, and eventual proletarianisation. Such a cycle of chronic indebtedness is widely regarded as a central mechanism in the social differentiation of modernised small producers (Strachan, 1982), but this contention is rarely demonstrated empirically.[36]

Soybean production by small family labour farms also is investigated by Lovisolo (1982) in the *municipio* of Candido Godoi in northwestern Rio Grande do Sul. This study finds only limited evidence of a capitalist/proletarian dichotomy developing between small and larger farms as the result of the initial horizontal process of capitalisation. Incipient tendencies towards vertical differentiation have been arrested or even reversed, Lovisolo (1982) argues, as the result of capitalised diversification strategies into commercial milk or pork production. These strategies, adopted by units with land topographically less well-suited to mechanised wheat and soybean production, have fully employed those family members released by the capitalisation of the traditional labour process of diversified subsistence agriculture based on the ox plough and hoe, and the concomitant introduction of soybeans. In this respect, Lovisolo (1982) gives welcome and overdue attention to the internal organisation of capitalised farm enterprises and their adaptation to the new labour process.

Although capitalised diversification strategies have attenuated trends towards the concentration of land ownership and control, mechanisation and the use of modern inputs have raised the minimum size of the economically viable production unit, restricting the scope for the customary subdivision of land between secondary family members. Proletarianisation thus is evident in the increasing practice of making monetary settlements (*ajuste de contas*) in lieu of hereditary property claims to the family holding. Furthermore, the capitalised labour process has undermined the rationale of multifamily occupancy. Under present conditions and with the high price of land in Candido Godoi, this can be maintained only by purchasing a substantially larger holding outside the region.[37] These strategems to avoid subdivision clearly indicate the economic constraints and pressures on the reproduction of capitalised, entrepreneurial family enterprises. Land purchase in other regions also presupposes a capacity to accumulate capital beyond that required to renew the means of production. In regions of small-scale agriculture, therefore, a central issue is the difficulty of "reproducing" dependent family members as free farmers in the *colono* tradition. The minimum size constraints and new family labour requirements associated with capitalisation thus can give rise to proletarianisation as out-migration and off-farm employment.

Capitalised, small family labour enterprises in regions such as Candido Godoi are reproduced in close articulation with agro-industrial capitals, finance capitals, and State institutions. The cooperative movement, consolidated by the wheat import substitution programmes of the late 1950s, is the preferred instrument of State modernisation policy, mediating between these capitals and the heterogeneous cooperative membership (Benetti, 1982). The international market boom in soybean prices from the late 1960s accelerated the transformation of producer cooperatives into large, quasi-capitalist, agro-industrial enterprises supplying a wide range of production, financial, and marketing services. Analyses are needed of these changing patterns of mediation and their effects on local agrarian structures, including the interrelations between small *colonos* and the large-scale capitalist farmers, the *granjeiros*, who established the cooperatives in Rio Grande do Sul. Several recent contributions (Coradini, 1979; Benetti, 1982) and the historical case study of COTRIJUI (Cooperativa Regional Triticola Serrana, Ltd.) by Frantz (1982) show the way forward.

Integration with agro-industrial capitals and State institutions also is imparting a more corporativist character to rural mobilisation in southern Brazil as capitalised family farmers increasingly define their aims within the structures of modernisation. "Capitalisation, which can produce a layer of petty bourgeoisie in the country, at the same time, produces the conditions for its organisation. . . . Given the scale of production, given the investments that must be paid, the only alternative when prices are uneconomic (*não compensadores*), is collective action to put pressure on the government, as recent movements have demonstrated" (Lovisolo, 1982, 90–91). Demands revolve around the conditions of their integration in the wider process of capitalist accumulation and concern credit, input costs, prices, and access to the institutional mechanisms of modernisation. This marks a shift away from a "rural politics," which has access to land as the focus of struggle, and towards an urban definition of power relations (Goodman et al., 1984). It is illustrated by the emerging pattern of mobilisations of capitalised family farmers, such as the "tractorcade" through the state capital, the use of roadblocks, and the withholding of production, which are reminiscent of the tactics employed by their European counterparts. The main demands of this category are losing their classic peasant character, although land remains an issue given the difficulty of maintaining sons in the tradition of "free producers."[38] Nevertheless, the corporativist and specific demands of capitalised farmers are in sharp contrast to the rural encampments—with Ronda Alta as the outstanding recent example—which characterise the mobilisation of marginal peasants and landless workers in the South whose struggle continues to centre on the basic demand for land and agrarian reform.[39]

Capitalised Family Farms: Further Cases

Outside southern Brazil, capitalised family labour farms occur as enclaves in agrarian structures dominated by large properties and a mass of small *minifundio* units on the margin of the modernisation process. Again, this structure reflects the historical antecedents of commodity production and the pervasive *latifundio-minifundio* complex, with its roots in the colonial land grant system. Of course, independent peasant production did arise in these regions, whether within the interstices of the *latifundio*-large mercantile enterprise structure or when the secular decline of export staples led to economic involution and the internal fragmentation of estate holdings.[40] In the Northeast, capitalised enclaves have emerged in areas of external peasant production, which originally were established in articulation with the regional plantation export economy as sources of staple foodstuffs and seasonal labour supply. Since the mid-1970s, selected areas have been incorporated in integrated rural development programmes, such as the Northeast Development Commission (POLONORDESTE) and *Projeto Sertanejo*, which provide access to special credit lines and investment incentives (Sampaio *et al.*, 1980; Wilkinson, 1982; Ferreira Irmao, 1983). Such areas as the northeastern *agreste* constitute important secondary concentrations of capitalised family farm agriculture, without as yet exhibiting the level of technological advance and pervasiveness found in southern Brazil.

Capitalised family farms also occur elsewhere in the Northeast, notably in public irrigation schemes and, to a lesser extent, in public and private settlement projects in northern frontier areas. The "enclave" characterisation of modernisation is particularly pertinent for the production of high-value crops, including grapes and citrus fruit, in the capital-intensive irrigation schemes administered by the São Francisco River Valley Commission (CODEVASF) and the National Department of Works Against the Drought (DNOCS). Agro-industrial capitals attracted by regional fiscal incentives, such as CICA (Companhia Industrial de Conservas Alimentícias) and Maguary, also have created enclaves of "technified" family labour farms. However, these units correspond more closely to out-grower forms of production. That is, although the direct producers may retain ownership of the land, state settlement agencies and agro-industrial capitals exert significant control over the technical basis of production and marketing decisions.[41]

Out-grower arrangements with varying degrees of capitalisation also characterise important crop sectors in Southern Brazil, including tobacco (Leidke, 1977) and viticulture (Santos, 1978), which are dominated by large, mainly multinational, agro-industrial enterprises. The close technical and mercantile control of these monopsonistic firms also is evident in the production of pigs and poultry (Sorj *et al.*, 1982). The so-called *camponeses integrados* retain formal control of the means of production but the entrepreneurial activities of these owner-operators is severely constrained. In these cases, ownership of the land is the basis of their exploitation insofar as the production of use-values for domestic consumption subsidises the cost of family labour, enabling agro-industrial capitals to exert their monopsonistic power and depress the price paid for the commercial crop (Leidke, 1977). With such vertical integration, "the production process is 'technified' and even capitalised but, since productive capital appropriates surplus value through its mercantile control, the transformation of these units into capitalist firms is blocked" (Goodman and Redclift, 1981, 168). The particular circumstances of their subordination to agro-industrial capitals lends distinctive characteristics to peasant mobilisation, with struggles revolving around the control of the immediate labour process, input costs, and marketing margins. Illustrative recent examples include the mobilisation of pig producers in October–November 1980 in Paraná and western Santa Caterina, and the continuing struggle of small family producers against the oligopsonistic control of the Rio Grande do Sul wine industry by multinational capitals (CONTAG, Confederação Nacional dos Trabalhadores na Agricultura, 1981).

Traditional Family Farms: The Northeast

In regions outside Southern Brazil, where capitalised family farming assumes an enclave character, we have already emphasised the threat to the reproduction of traditional external peasantries presented by the modernisation of large estates. This disarticulation of small-scale agriculture operates through local land and labour markets as modernisation reduces the supply of land on large estates available for short annual leases and opportunities for temporary wage employment. These collateral effects reflect changes in land use and crop mix, which, in turn, are determined by many factors, including trends in relative prices, export promotion policies, rural labour legislation, special investment programmes, and property speculation. Among the tendencies in land use promoted by modernisation, the capitalisation of cattle ranching has attracted particular attention because of its pervasive influence throughout Brazil in undermining the reproduction of both internal and external peasantries (D'Incao e Mello, 1976; CPDA-NE, 1978; Moura, 1979). This process of *pecuarização*, stimulated by subsidised official credit for livestock production and rising land values, involves the conversion of cropland to grazing and of natural grassland to permanent, improved pasture.[42] In regions such as the *agreste* zone of the Northeast, where the reproduction of small *minifundio* proprietors traditionally was articulated through wage labour and tenure relations with large properties, *pecuarização* is assigned an important role in the decline of the *latifundio-minifundio complex*. Here, it "has eliminated the greater part of the seasonal employment that was provided by the large properties. Proletarianisation in this specific case, assumes the form of a rural exodus, since it is impossible for the small proprietor to survive with the output of his land" (CPDA-NE, 1978, 19).

The erosion of the conditions of existence of these external *minifundia* thus is intensifying the process of social differentiation and proletarianisation. The evidence suggests, however, that this process and the subsequent consolidation of these small holdings will be protracted. According to special tabulations of the 1975 Agricultural Census, the gross value of output on 1,636,000 establishments, representing 70 percent of all farm establishments in the Northeast, was under one minimum wage (Silva, 1984). In effect, these establishments are essentially consumption units, with a residual but declining role as a labour reserve, given the adverse effects of modernisation on rural employment opportunities and the proletarianisation tendencies at work elsewhere in Brazilian agriculture. In the Northeast, therefore, rural structures will continue to hold large concentrations of impoverished family labour units, which further emphasises the enclave character of small farm capitalisation.

The modernisation process, with its radical changes in land use and management, has aroused increased peasant militancy in response to the expulsion of long-established tenant families. These mobilisations, which revolve around the question of access to the land and the struggle for a livelihood as farmers or *lavradores*, also have led to land invasions (Henfrey, 1984). Operationally, particularly in the more favourable institutional climate created by political *abertura*, the struggle is to secure the tenure and employment rights conferred by the Land Statute and labour legislation. There have been some notably successful mobilisations by small tenants, which have provoked State intervention to expropriate and redistribute land, as in the case of the Alagamar ranch in Paraiba. "Conversely, there are countless instances of the expulsion of *posseiros* and other tenants without due legal compensation by recourse to fraudulent practices (*grilagem*), intimidation, and violence" (Goodman *et al.*, 1984, 206). The accelerated implementation of PROALCOOL since the late 1970s and the corresponding extension of sugar cane into areas of the Northeast traditionally dominated by mixed farming and peasant forms of production, has intensified pressures to expel tenant farm families, increasing peasant militancy and the incidence of violent land conflicts (CONTAG, 1981; Santos Filho and Porto, 1984).

D. Recent Frontier Settlement in Amazonia

Although a detailed review of the evolution of rural structures in Amazonia is beyond the scope of this paper, several alternative interpretations of frontier settlement provide insights into the recent transformation of this process.[43] As we observed earlier, Oliveira's analysis of the mobilisation of the agricultural surplus and the reproduction of the *latifundio* on successive agricultural frontiers is based on the mechanism of primitive accumulation and the exclusion of labour from permanent access to the land. This "growth by the elaboration of peripheries," impelled by the spontaneous frontier settlement of migrant *posseiros*, also has been characterised as a historical process which reproduces the conditions of existence of peasant economy. Thus for Velho (1976), frontier expansion is seen as the reproduction of a peasant mode of production, which is subordinated to the capitalist mode in a permanent process of surplus appropriation.[44] This closed form of frontier occupation, in contrast to the settlement of the American West, creates an undifferentiated peasantry rather than land-owning pioneer farmers. This type of frontier social structure, according to Velho (1976), is explained by the authoritarian antecedents and contemporary character of the State and capitalism in Brazil.

The persistence of the internal dynamic of frontier settlement and its economic determinants also is defended by Foweraker (1981), who argues that the occupation of pioneer frontiers in contemporary Amazonia is achieved principally by the expansion of the "sub-capitalist environment." The reproduction of noncapitalist social relations is explained by the mechanism of primitive accumulation and its continuing significance in sustaining capitalist accumulation at the centre through the mobilisation of a marketed surplus of staple foodstuffs. Indeed, in the Brazilian case, the cycle of frontier development and primitive accumulation is not a historical stage of capitalist development but a "hybrid mode of accumulation" subordinated to capitalism.

Furthermore, Foweraker (1981) contends that the frontier cycle, marked by the transition from the pioneer, noncapitalist stage to capitalist social structures, plays a central role in the reproduction of the conditions of accumulation in Brazilian agriculture. This transition, characterised by violence and the manipulation of administrative-juridical mechanisms by different capitals to achieve monopoly control of the land, culminates in the expulsion of *posseiro* families, instituting private property and a capitalist land market. In short, the cycle of pioneer settlement and primitive accumulation gives way to the monopoly structure of land ownership, reproducing the social relations of the *latifundio-minifundio* complex found in long-settled regions.

This formulation of the "double mill" of primitive accumulation and private property in land in mobilising commodity surpluses on successive new frontiers applies with particular force to the 1940s and 1950s. However, several writers have questioned Foweraker's extension of this analysis to the contemporary occupation of Amazonia and the central role assigned to frontier settlement in the recent dynamics of Brazilian growth (Goodman, 1983; Sorj and Pompermayer, 1983). These authors reject the argument that the surpluses mobilised by *posseiro* families on the pioneer frontier and appropriated by merchant capitals are still of decisive importance to urban food supply. This position "ignores the new bases of agricultural expansion and the re-articulation of relations between agriculture and the urban sectors achieved under the aegis of the agro-industrial complex. The view that primitive accumulation on the pioneer frontier is still essential, in any fundamental sense, to capitalist development in Brazil can no longer be sustained" (Goodman, 1983, 269).

Moreover, as Sorj and Pompermayer (1983) suggest, frontier settlement responds increasingly to the dynamic of agro-industrial accumulation, and not to merchant capitals, which imparts distinctive new characteristics to the process. In analysing this change, Pompermayer (1982) gives weight to the SUDAM (Superintendência do Desenvolvimento da Amazônia) fiscal incentives introduced in the mid-1960s, and to the Programme of National Integration (PIN) and the special regional development programmes of the 1970s.[45] These institutional innovations have given "new rhythm and specificity to the large agricultural undertaking in Amazonia" by attracting modern industrial and agro-industrial capitals. These corporate capitals have used heavily subsidised investment credits to purchase huge tracts of public land at nominal prices for cattle ranching and private land settlement schemes. For such capitals, as Sawyer (1979) also recognises, the presence of *posseiros* is an unnecessary complication, if not an entirely negative factor, due to the attendant depletion of soil fertility. Such capitals typically need not resort to the violence and *grileiro* stratagems used to establish monopoly ownership of the land by merchant capitals, following in the wake of frontier settlers. Modern corporate capitals with access to subsidised credit for land purchase, and the further support of State development agencies prepared to countenance the preemptive enclosure of hitherto unsettled land to ensure "orderly settlement," do not have primitive accumulation as their *modus operandi*.[46]

Consequently, with the State-mediated entry of large corporate capitals, the articulation between frontier settlement and capitalist accumulation is no longer fully specified by permanent primitive accumulation, extension of the "subcapitalist economic environment," and reproduction of the *latifundio-minifundio* social structure. As modern corporate capitals assume control of the settlement process, frontier regions are becoming more directly integrated into the reproduction of agro-industry as sources of supply for meat packing and food processing and markets for modern inputs. Similarly, private settlement companies, such as SINOP (Sociedade Imobiliária Noroeste do Paraná, Ltda.) in northern Mato Grosso, have introduced out-grower arrangements with settlers or *colonos* in order to supply their processing plants (Pompermayer, 1982). Subordination of the rural labour process to institutional finance capital and its technical agronomic criteria also characterises recent public settlement programmes, as in Rondonia. Selective credit programmes are promoting more specialised commodity production of export and industrial crops, including coffee, cocoa (CEPLAC—Comissão do Mano da Lavoura Cacaveira), manioc (PROALCOOL), and rubber (PROBORRACHA). The social structures which characterised the traditional, moving pioneer frontier and subordination to merchant capitals thus are being transformed as patterns of frontier settlement become increasingly determined by the dynamic of agro-industrial capitals.

The more direct participation of modern corporate capitals in frontier settlement will bring changes in the forms of representation and struggle of rural workers. For the present, however, rural conflicts will focus preeminently on the struggle of *posseiros* for permanent access to the land. The intensity and violence of these conflicts between *posseiros*, land-grabbers (*grileiros*), and indigenous peoples, which are already widespread (Martins, 1980; 1981), will be exacerbated as the settlement process falls increasingly under the control of corporate capitals. This control, reinforced by the financial capacity to preempt settlement of large areas, is accelerating the enclosure of the open, pioneer frontier, reducing the opportunities for migrant farm families to gain access, even temporarily, to land. As the frontier is incorporated in the generalised process of capitalist penetration of agriculture, these families are again threatened by mechanisms similar to those that led to their earlier expulsion (Ozorio de Almeida *et al.*, 1981). The capitalist closure of the frontier also is reflected in pessimistic evaluations of the future contribution of State settlement programmes: "Settlement no longer offers a significant alternative to alleviate the general problem of land distribution in Brazil, since the form in which this question is posed in Amazonia today is already similar to its manifestation in the rest of the country" (Ozorio de Almeida and Albuquerque David, 1983, 16).

Marginalised in their region of origin, migrants are fighting a desperate rearguard action to avoid a similar fate in Amazonia. Although supported by progressive sections of the Church and civil society, they lack effective channels of representation and participation. The organisation of *posseiros* and other rural workers, despite recent efforts to strengthen rural unions in Amazonia, remains localised and spontaneous (Azevedo, 1984). This weakness stands in stark contrast to the sweeping exceptional powers to intervene in land conflicts enjoyed by state agencies under national security legislation. These powers are being applied in huge areas of Amazonia following the creation in 1980 of two Executive Groups to control the outbreak of violent land disputes in the Araguaia–Tocantins region (GETAT) and Lower Amazonia (GEBAM). These agencies are now subordinated to the Extraordinary Ministry of Land Affairs, established in 1982, which has wide responsibility for land tenure questions. A preliminary evaluation of GEBAM's land titling and settlement activities suggests that they favour the better endowed, more commercially integrated peasantry, rather than poor, itinerant, or "spontaneous" settlers (Almeida, 1984). Finally, the juridico-political marginalisation of *posseiros* is graphically emphasised by the powerful corporativist representation of large capitals and landed interests achieved through the Businessmen's Association of Amazonia (Pompermayer, 1982). *Posseiro* conflicts will continue to figure prominently in rural labour movements in Brazil but, in the absence of sweeping political and institutional change, this rearguard action by marginalised, poor peasants is likely to achieve only isolated successes.

CONCLUSION

This survey of Brazilian agrarian debates has emphasised the changing formulations of agrarian social structures and their integration in the postwar process of capitalist accumulation. These analyses include the articulation model, the classic internal differentiation process of the "Junker road," and differing conceptualisations of the capitalised family farm and the nature of its subordination to agro-industrial capitals. These prespectives elucidate postwar structural change in rural economy and society, particularly the transformations set in train by the industrialisation of the agricultural production process under the aegis of conservative modernisation strategies. The proletarianisation of internal peasantries, disarticulation of *latifundio-minifundio* interdependence, and capitalisation of small family labour farms have as their common denominator the expansion of agro-industrial capitals and the complementary institutional framework of State policy. Agriculture increasingly is incorporated directly into the capitalist accumulation process or, more specifically, into the reproduction of different fractions of industrial and finance capital.[47] Although the transition to the new model of industrialised agriculture is now widely accepted as the point of departure for analyses of rural social change, the structural permanence of two characteristic manifestations, the capitalised family farm and the mass proletariat of *volantes*, continues to arouse controversy. This essay also has suggested that agro-industrialisation is not identified with a single, unifying dominant tendency in the emerging social division of labour. Indeed, the penetration of agriculture by differen capitals and the varying intensity of this process, allied to historical differences in the development of commodity production, will maintain the present diversity of rural social relations.

As we have argued elsewhere, "the counterpart of the increasingly complex integration of Brazilian agriculture with agro-industrial and institutional finance capitals is the emergence of different forms of representation and struggle among direct rural producers. These processes of integration are rapidly differentiating the perceptions and demands of rural workers, militating against the unification of class struggle" (Goodman *et al.*, 1984, 210). The present account has emphasised the increasingly narrow, corporativist interests and demands of capitalised family farmers whose reproduction is articulated with agro-industrial capitals and State institutions. Similarly, with the further capitalisation of large estates and plantations, particularly the mechanisation of harvesting, the struggles of the *volante* labour force will become more akin to those of an industrial proletariat. However, the classic peasant demand for access to land will remain the rallying cry for the mass of impoverished producers and frontier *posseiros* excluded from the structures of modernisation. This marginalisation is emphasised by the fact that in 1975 some 3.64 million farm establishments, 73 percent of the total, cultivated the land without the use of a plough, whether machine- of animal-drawn. The same proportion of rural families had monetary earnings per capita of one half the minimum wage or less in 1980 (Hoffman, 1984). The struggle of these marginalised producers to eke out a rural livelihood is threatened by the continuing capitalisation of the rural production process and the "enclosure" of Amazônia. They face a dismal and uncertain future unless there are radical changes in the trajectory of the sociopolitical process and class control of the State.

These struggles in the form of land conflicts and invasions to retain access to the land have characterised the modernisation of agrarian structures throughout Brazil, from Rio Grande do Sul to Acre. However, the recent "geography of violence" reveals a relative concentration in the North, particularly in Para and Maranhão, and the Northeast, notably in Bahia. For example, of the 197 deaths recorded in land conflicts in 1980 and 1981, 170 occurred in the area of Amazonia Legal (Santos Filho and Porto, 1984). The rising intensity and much greater incidence of these conflicts is eloquent testimony to the "reproduction squeeze" on marginalised family units and frontier *posseiros* exerted by the accelerating commercialisation and capitalisation of agriculture in these relatively backward, more traditional regions. The violence of land conflicts and peasant resistance is one of the continuities in change which has marked postwar rural economy and society in Brazil, although this history only now is beginning to be told.

NOTES

1. The protracted nature of this transition is emphasised by recent work on industrial investment by Suzigan (1984), who questions the extension of the "export staple" analysis to industrial accumulation in the period after 1914.

2. See, for example, Paiva (1966), Paiva *et al.* (1973), Schuh (1970), Nicholls (1972), and Oliveira (1972).

3. For reviews of this literature, see Castro (1969) and CPDA (1979).

4. See also the contributions by Sa (1973) and Brandao Lopes (1973).

5. Palmeira (1979), citing Camargo (1973), observes that the first attempts to organise peasant leagues in the Northeast occurred with the return to democracy in 1945. These efforts lost their momentum after 1948 when the Brazilian Communist Party (PCB) was declared illegal.

6. In the absence of appropriate labour legislation, rural workers formed associations and *ligas* whose organisational structure and norms were established under the Civil Code.

7. For a detailed treatment, see especially Medeiros (1982).

8. For accounts of the different groups and movements active within the Church, see Calazans (1969), de Kadt (1970), and Cruz (1982).

9. The limitations on the practice of independent unionism imposed by this vertical structure and the politico-institutional control of the State, and the tactical orientations it has engendered in the recent experience of CONTAG, are considered by Azevedo (1984).

10. In 1980, CONTAG claimed to represent 6.8 million members organised in 2,500 local unions, with 21 state federations and one regional office (*delegacia*) for Acre-Rondonia (CONTAG, 1981).

11. Homem de Melo (1981) emphasises that the implicit taxation thesis of exchange rate overvaluation does not apply to agriculture as a whole, and specifically not to rice, beans, potatoes, and onions. The ratio between producers' prices and international prices for these products exceeds unity throughout the period 1948–65, suggesting an implicit tax on domestic consumers and not producers.

12. Research to improve cotton yields began in São Paulo in the 1920s and was followed by hybrid corn research in the 1930s.

13. The limitations of agricultural research and extension systems before 1970 are discussed by Smith (1969), Schuh (1970), and Paiva *et al.* (1973). For further details and additional references, see Homem de Melo (1983).

14. Following the 1962 food supply crises, efforts were made to improve the operation of minimum price programmes for basic commodities. For an evaluation of their effectiveness in the 1960s, see Smith (1969).

15. The basket of food crops comprises rice, beans, manioc, potatoes, and wheat, and imports are excluded from the estimates of domestic supply. These foodstuffs account for 55.4 percent of the calorie intake of low income families in the municipality of São Paulo.

16. Some implications of market segmentation in terms of the risk arising from

institutional- and market-determined differences in the stability of final prices and yields are examined by Homem de Melo (1979) using data for São Paulo.

17. The competitive displacement of foodstuffs by sugar cane also has attracted increasing attention since the introduction of PROALCOOL in 1975, and particularly following the decision taken in 1979 to raise the alcohol production target to 10.7 billion litres by 1985. For further discussion, see IBRD (International Bank for Reconstruction and Development) (1981), Homem de Melo and Gianetti da Fonseca (1981), and Mendonça de Barros *et al.* (1980).

18. An earlier version of this segmentation argument is presented by Lopes (1973) in his analysis of northeastern agriculture and the survival of noncapitalist producers in the sector producing foodstuffs.

19. Silva (1984) estimates that around 2.2 million establishments, 44.2 percent of all units, have an annual gross output of below one annual minimum wage. Such units account for 4.4 percent of total production and their average output is less than one-half the value of the annual minimum wage.

20. Space does not allow more comprehensive discussion of important, complementary elements of recent modernisation strategy. These include special regional development programmes, the reform and expansion of agricultural research and extension services, infrastructure investment programmes, and marketing and distribution policies.

21. For data on trends in the production and utilisation of these industrial inputs, tractors, and other equipment, see Graziano da Silva *et al.* (1977), Gomes Paiva (1982), and especially Contador and Rocha Ferreira (1984).

22. Moreira (1982) has emphasised that import substitution policies, and notably the expansion of intermediate and capital goods sectors under the Target Plan of 1956–61, provided the industrial foundation for modernisation strategies.

23. On the internationalisation of the agro-industrial complex and agro-food chains, see Muller (1979) and Sorj (1980).

24. Several writers, including Sayad (1977) and Rezende (1982), have examined the impact of this rural credit expansion on the observed increase in the real price of rural land, and its effects in aggravating the unequal distribution of land ownership. For a wider discussion of these trends and evidence of the increasing concentration of land ownership in the 1970s, see Graziano da Silva and Hoffman in Graziano da Silva (1982).

25. Before 1973, small contracts were defined as those below 50 times the value of the official minimum wage, and large contracts as those over 500 times this value. Contract size was related to a measure of annual production value in 1974. Small contracts in the later 1970s had an upper limit of roughly US $2,500, while large contracts exceeded US $25,000. (IBRD, 197).

26. Other aspects of the selective incidence of *custeio* credit are examined by Gomes Paiva (1982), including evidence that, for a *given* crop, the more highly capitalised producers receive a disportionate share of the total credit allocated to that crop. Operational criteria introduced in May 1979 made this explicit by relating the amount of *custeio* credit per hectare directly to classes of output per hectare.

27. Ianni (1976) provides an interesting historical case study of production relations in sugar cane cultivation in the Ribeirao Preto region of São Paulo. He also observes the adverse effects of increasing monocultural specialisation on external peasant forms of production.

28. The annual conference papers on *volante* workers published by the Department of Rural Economics, Botucatu, São Paulo, since 1975 are an indispensable source and also reveal the changing focus of interest in this debate. Selected papers from the Botucatu meetings are collected in CNPC-UNESP (Conselho Nacional de Pesquisa-Universidade Estadual de São Paulo) (1982). Reviews of the literature on *volante* labour can be found in Goodman and Redclift (1977) and Saint (1981).

29. Casual observation suggests that at present roughly one third of the São Paulo sugar cane output is harvested mechanically. The ratio of man-days for manual and mechanical harvesting is approximately 10:1. Land preparation and cropping practices already are adapted to mechanised methods.

30. Increasing levels of mobilisation of *volante* labour could significantly accelerate the mechanisation of harvest operations. Until recently, the organisation of temporary rural workers was most successful in the sugar cane zone of Pernambuco. (Sigaud, 1980; 1983). However, the mobilisation of *volante* sugar cane workers in Guariba and the Ribeirao Preto region of São Paulo in May, 1984 may mark the beginning of a sustained improvement in real wages and conditions of work in the most advanced and efficient segment of this industry.

31. The following dicussion draws heavily on Goodman (1984) and Goodman *et al.* (1984).

32. See Faure (1978) and Vergopoulos (1974; 1978).

33. According to Lovisolo (1982), geopolitical considerations were important factors in the extension of small farmer settlement in the frontier areas of western Rio Grande do Sul in the early twentieth century. Although not explored here, the case of Paraná also suggests relationships between the historical development of commodity production and patterns of land settlement which, at a later conjucture, were conducive to the rise of capitalised family labour farming. In this state, which was the principal agricultural frontier in Brazil between the 1930s and 1960s, huge tracts of land were acquired by land development companies and subdivided for sale into family-sized small holdings. For further details, see Foweraker (1981) and Strachan (1982).

34. For a recent review of the case material on the capitalisation of family labour farms in the wheat-soybean areas of southern Brazil, see Goodman (1984).

35. The view that the modernisation of small-scale agriculture has intensified social differentiation and proletarianisation is supported by Sorj (1980) on the basis of case material for the Ijui region of Rio Grande do Sul presented by Coradini (1979).

36. Indeed, there is a surprising lack of empirical studies of farm capital formation and the sources of finance, with the notable exception of Adams *et al.* (1975).

37. Strachan (1982) reports similar problems of extended family labour organisation following the substitution of mechanised wheat-soybean for coffee production in north-western Paraná.

38. This question has created a certain identity of interest between the marginalised

landless workers and the sons of capitalised farmers for whom further subdivision of the family holding will not create economically viable farms. *O Movimento dos Sem Terra* provides one channel for these demands for the expropriation and redistribution of large-scale properties.

39. The significance of Ronda Alta in the context of recent rural mobilisation in southern Brazil is discussed by Grzybowski (1982).

40. Lopes (1976) distinguishes between regions of "unified" and "decadent" *latifundia*. In the latter, "the fragmented production of sharecroppers or small tenants (*arrendatarios*) becomes the basic form, the *latifundio* gives way to peasant economy" (1976, 48, n.7). A classic study of economic involution is Antonio Candido (1964).

41. Sampaio *et al.* (1978) emphasise the close technical supervision imposed on *colonos* in CODEVASF settlement schemes.

42. Whether productive or speculative investment motives are uppermost, *pecuarização* has emerged as a preferred means of achieving centralised control of the production process on arable and mixed farming properties. The eviction of permanent workers and small tenants also simplifies labour relations and removes possible claimants to the property.

43. The literature on recent frontier settlement in Amazonia is too extensive to review here. Apart from numerous case studies, two major contributions are those by CEDEPLAR (Centro de Desenvolvimento e Planejamento Regional) (1979) and the study coordinated by Anna Luiza Ozorio de Almeida at IPEA/INPES (Instituto de Planejamento Econômico e Social/Instituto de Pesquisas).

44. Sawyer (1979) adopts a similar approach, although the concept of "form of production" is substituted for that of "mode."

45. These include the Trans-Amazonian Highway and other long-distance penetration roads, hydroelectric power projects and rural electrification, and the rural infrastructure investments incorporated in the various regional development programmes of the 1970s, such as PRODOESTE, POLAMAZONIA, and POLOCENTRO.

46. At the Columbia conference, Anna Luiza Ozorio de Almeida suggested that this point requires qualification. In her view, based on recent field research, the scarcity of labour during the pioneer stage of land clearance and settlement compels all capitals to behave as merchant capital and adopt noncapitalist forms of production. Labour control practices include indentured migrant workers and variants on the traditional Amazonian *aviamento* system of debt peonage. The thesis that modern corporate capitals can bypass or leapfrog the pioneer stage of frontier settlement thus may require further empirical examination.

47. As segmentation approaches to recent agricultural trends indicate, this integration also has brought greater internationalisation of the resource base and associated agro-food chains. Brazil currently is the second largest agricultural exporter in the world.

REFERENCES

Adams, D.W., *et al.*, *Farm Growth in Brazil* (Columbus, Ohio, The Ohio State University, 1975).

Adams, D.W., "Rural Financial Markets, Farm Level Growth and Capital Formation in Brazil," in Adams, D. W., *et al.*, *Farm Growth in Brazil*.

Aidar, A.C.K., and R.M. Perosa Junior, "Espaços e Limites da Empresa Capitalista na Agricultura," *Revista de Economia Política*, Vol. 1(2), 1981.

Almeida, A.W.B. de, "O Gebam, As Empresas Agropecuárias e a Expansão Camponesa," in IBASE, *Os Donos da Terra e a luta pela Reforma Agrária* (Rio de Janeiro, CODECRI, 1984).

Araujo, P.F. Cidade de, "O Crédito Rural e sua Distribuição no Brasil," *Estudos Economicos*, Vol. 13(2), 1983.

Ayer, H.W., and G.E. Schuh, "Taxas de retorno social e outros aspectos da pesquisa agrícola: o caso do algodão em São Paulo, Brazil" in *Agricultura em São Paulo*, Vol. 21, 1974.

Azevedo, F.A., *As Ligas Camponesas* (Rio de Janeiro, Paz e Terra, 1982).

———, "Unicidade Sindical e Autonomia no Movimento Social Rural," *Presenca*, No. 2., February, 1984.

Bacha, E.L., *Os mitos de uma década: ensaios de economia brasileira* (Rio de Janeiro, Paz e Terra, 1976).

———, "Crescimento Econômico, Salários Urbanos e Rurais: O Caso do Brasil," *Pesquisa e Planejamento Econômico*, Vol. 9(3), December, 1979.

Benetti, M.D., *Origem e Formação do Cooperativismo Empresarial no Rio Grande do Sul* (Porto Alegre, FEE, 1982).

Bergsman, J., *Brazil: Industrialisation and Trade Policies* (London, Oxford University Press, 1980).

Brant, V.C., "Do colono ao bóia-fria," *Estudos CEBRAP*, Vol. 19, 1977.

Calazans, M.J.C., *Le Syndicat Paysan comme instrument institutionel de participation: le cas du Nordest du Brésil* (Paris, Ecole Pratique des Hautes Etudes, 1969).

———, *Os Trabalhadores Rurais e a Sindicalização—Uma Práctica* (Mimeo, Rio de Janeiro, 1983).

Camargo, A. de Alcantra, *Brésil Nord-Est: Mouvements Paysans et Crise Populiste*. These 3 Cycle (Paris, Ecole Pratique des Hautes Etudes, 1974).

———, "A Questão Agrária: Crise de Poder e Reformas de Base" in Fausto, B. (ed.), *O Brasil Republicano, Vol. 3: Sociedade e Política (1930–64)*, História Geral de Civilização Brasileira, *Tomo III* (São Paulo, Difel, 1981).

Candido, A., *Os Parceiros do Rio Bonito* (São Paulo, duas Cidades, 1964).

Castro, A. de B., *7 ensaios sobre a economia brasileira* (Rio de Janeiro, Forense, 1969).

CEDEPLAR, *Ocupação Agricola da Amazonia* (Belo Horizonte, 1979), mimeo, various volumes.

CNPq/UNESP, *A Mão-de-Obra Volante na Agricultura* (São Paulo, Polis, 1982).

Contador, C.R., and L. de Rocha Ferreira, *Insumos Modernos na Agricultura Brasileira* (Rio de Janeiro, IPEA/INPES, 1984, mimeo).

CONTAG, *As Lutas Camponesas No Brasil, 1980* (Rio de Janeiro, Marco Zero, 1981).

Coradini, O.L., *Estrutura agrária, agroindústria e cooperativismo no sul do Brasil*, unpublished ms., Ijui, Rio Grande do Sul, 1979.

CPDA (Centro de Pós-Graduação em Desenvolvimento Agrícola), *Evolução recente e situação atual da agricultura brasileira* (Brasília, BINAGRI, 1979).

CPNA-NE, *Relatório Regional-Região Nordeste* (Rio de Janeiro, EIAP/CPDA/FGV, 1978, mimeo).

Cruz, D. da Silva, *A Redenção Necessária: Igreja Católica e Sindicalismo Rural, 1960–64*, unpublished ms., Campina Grande, Paraiba, 1982.

Delfim Netto, A. *et al.*, *Agricultura e desenvolvimento econômico no Brasil*, Estudos ANPEC, No. 5, 1965.

Dickinson, J.M., and S.A. Mann, "Obstacles to the Development of a Capitalist Agriculture," *Journal of Peasant Studies*, Vol. 5(4), 1978.

D'Incao e Mello, M. da C., *Bóia-fria—acumulação e miséria* (Petrópolis, R. J., Vozes, 1976).

Faure, C., *Agriculture et Capitalisme* (Paris, Anthropos, 1978).

Ferreira Irmao, J., *Agricultural Policy and Capitalist Development in Northeast Brazil*, Ph.D. thesis, University of London, 1983.

Fishlow, A., "Origins and Consequences of Import Substitution in Brazil," in L. di Marco (ed.), *Essays in Honor of Raul Prebisch* (New York, Academic Press, 1972).

Forman, S., "Disunity and Discontent: A Study of Peasant Political Movements in Brazil," *Journal of Latin American Studies*, Vol. 3(1), 1971.

———and J.F. Reigelhaupt, "Bodo Was Never Brazilian: Economic Integration and Rural Development among a Contemporary Peasantry," *Journal of Economic History*, Vol. 30(1), 1970.

Foweraker, J., *The Struggle for Land* (Cambridge Latin American Studies 39, Cambridge University Press, 1981).

Frantz, T.R., *Cooperativismo Empresarial e Desenvolvimento Agrícola: O Caso do COTRIJUÍ* (Ijuí, Rio Grande do Sul, FIDENE, 1982).

Furtado, C., *A pré-revolução brasileira* (Rio de Janeiro, Fundo de Cultura, 1961).

———, *Dialética do Desenvolvimento* (Rio de Janeiro, Fundo de Cultura, 1964).

Gasques, J.G., "Crescimento Econômico, Salários Urbanos e Rurais: O Caso do Brasil—Comentário," *Pesquisa e Planejamento Economico*, Vol. 10(2), August 1980.

Gomes Paiva, S.M., *Crédito Rural e Acumulação de Capital* (Tese de Mestrado, PIMES/UFPe, 1982).

Goodman, D.E., "*Review of Joe Foweraker: The Struggle for Land*," *The Journal of Development Studies*, Vol. 9(2), January, 1983, pp. 268–69.

———, " '*João Yeoman': Capitalised Family Farm Enterprises in Brazilian Agriculture*," (paper presented at the conference on Capitalist Agriculture in Latin America, September 1984).

———, B. Sorj, and J. Wilkinson, "Agro-Industry, State Policy and Rural Social Structures: Recent Analyses of Proletarianisation in Brazilian Agriculture," in Finch, H. and B. Munslow, *Proletarianisation in the Third World* (London, Croom Helm, 1984).

——— and M.R. Redclift, "The 'Boias-Frias'—rural proletarianisation and urban marginality in Brazil," *International Journal of Urban and Regional Research*, Vol. 1(2), 1977.

―――― and M.R. Redclift, *From Peasant to Proletarian* (Oxford, Basil Blackwell, 1981).

Graziano da Silva, J., *Progresso Técnico e Relações de Trabalho na Agricultura* (São Paulo, HUCITEC, 1981).

――――, *A Modernização Dolorosa: Estrutura agrária, fronteira agrícola e trabalhadores rurais no Brasil* (Rio de Janeiro, Zahar, 1982).

――――, "Capitalist 'Modernisation' and Employment in Brazilian Agriculture, 1960–75," *Latin American Perspectives*, Vol. 11(1), Winter, 1984.

―――― *et al.*, *Estrutura agrária e produção de subsistência na agricultura brasileira* (mimeo., Botucatu, São Paulo, 1977).

―――― *et al.*, *Emprego e Relações de Trabalho na Agricultura Paulista, 1960–75*. Texto para Discussão No. 15., IFCH/DEPE/UNICAMP, 1982.

Grzybowski, C., "Os Colonos Sem-Terra de Ronda Alta," *Cadernos do CEAS*, No. 82(1982).

Gudin, E., "The Chief Characteristics of the Post-war Economic Development of Brazil," in H.S. Ellis (ed.), *The Economy of Brazil* (Berkeley and Los Angeles, University of California Press, 1969).

Guimaraes, A. de Passos, *Quatro séculos de latifundia* (Rio de Janeiro, Fulgor, 1963).

Henfrey, C., *Jaguar's Den: The Making of a Brazilian Peasantry and Its Political Implications*, mimeo, 1984.

Hoffman, R., "A pobreza rural no Brasil," *Reforma Agrária*, Vol. 14(1), 1984.

――――, and Graziano da Silva, "A Reconcentração Fundiária," *Reforma Agrária*, Vol. 10(6), 1980.

Homem de Melo, F.B., "Padrões de Instabilidade entre Culturas da Agricultura Brasileira," *Pesquisa e Planejamento Economico*, Vol. 9(3), 1979.

――――, "Política comercial, tecnologia e preços de alimentos no Brasil," *Estudos Econômicos*, Vol. 11(2), 1981.

―――― and Zockun, M.H.G.P., "Exportações agrícolas, balanço de pagamentos, e abastecimento do mercado interno," *Estudos Econômicos*, Vol. 7(2), 1977.

――――, *O Problema Alimentar No Brasil* (Rio de Janeiro, Paz e Terra, 1983).

――――, "A Agricultura nos Anos 80: Perspectivas e Conflitos Entre Objetivos de Política," *Estudos Economicos*, Vol. 10(2), 1980.

Ianni, O., *A classe operária vai o campo*, Caderno CEBRAP 24, 1976, São Paulo.

IBRD (International Bank for Reconstruction and Development), *Capital Markets Study*, (Washington, D.C., mimeo, 1979).

IBRD, *Staff Appraisal Report: Brazil Alcohol and Biomass Energy Development Project* (Washington, D.C., mimeo, 1981).

Kadt, E. de, *Catholic Radicals in Brazil* (London, Oxford University Press, 1970).

Leff, N.H., "Export Stagnation and Autarkic Development in Brazil, 1947–62," *Quarterly Journal of Economics*, Vol. 81, 1967.

Leidke, E.R., *Capitalismo e camponeses: relações entre indústria e agricultura na produção de fumo no RGS* (University of Brasilia, 1977, unpublished ms.).

Lopes, J.R.B., "Desenvolvimento e migrações: uma abordagem histórico-estrutural," Estudos CEBRAP, Vol. 6, 1973.

————, De latifúndio a empresa (Caderno CEBRAP 26, 1976).

Lovisolo, H.R., Terra, Trabalho e Capital: Produção Familiar e Acumulação (Tese de Mestrado, PPGAS/UFRJ, 1982).

Martins, J. de Souza, Expropriação e Violencia: A Questão Política no Campo (São Paulo, HUCITEC, 1980).

————, Os Camponeses e A Política no Brasil (Petrópolis, Vozes, 1981).

Medeiros, L.S. de, "Movimento Camponês e Reforma Agrária," Revista de Cultura e Política, No. 4, 1981.

————, A questão de Reforma Agrária no Brasil, 1955–64 (Tese de Mestrado, FFLCH/USP, 1982).

————, and J.C. Soriano, Reflexões sobre o Sindicalismo Rural: a CONTAG (Rio de Janeiro, 1984, mimeo).

Mendonca de Barros, J.R., "Política e desenvolvimento agrícola no Brasil," in A. Veiga (ed.), Ensaios Sobre Política Agrícola Brasileira (São Paulo, Secretaria da Agricultura, 1979).

————, and D.H. Graham, "A Agricultura brasileira e o problema da produção de alimentos," Pesquisa e Planejamento Econômico, Vol. 8(3), 1978.

———— et al., "Participação dos índices de productividade de terra entre os componentes tecnológicos e alocativo," Pesquisa e Planejamento Econômico, Vol. 6(3), 1976.

———— et al., "A Evolução Recente da Agricultura Brasileira" in J. R. Mendonca de Barros and D.H. Graham (eds.), Estudos sobre a Modernização da Agricultura Brasileira (São Paulo, USP/IPE, 1977).

———— et al., Agricultura e Produção de Energia: Avaliação do Custo da Matéria-Prima para Produção de Álcool (IPEA/INPES, Grupo de Energia, Documento Preliminar No. 3, 1982).

Mitra, A., Terms of Trade and Class Relations (London, Frank Cass, 1977).

Moreira, R.J., "A agricultura brasileira: os interesses em jogo no início dos anos 80," Reforma Agrária, Vol. 12(6), 1982.

Moura, M.M., Estudo de pequena propriedade em duas áreas de Minas Gerais (Rio de Janeiro, CPDA/EIAP/FGV, 1978).

Muller, G., Penetração das empresas transnacionais nos complexos agroindustriais de pecúaria de carne, pecuaria leiteira, cereais, oleaginosas e fumos (São Paulo, CEBRAP/ILET, 1979).

————, "Agricultura e Industrialização do Campo no Brasil," Revista de Economia Política, Vol. 2/2, No. 6, 1982.

Nicholls, W.H., "The Brazilian Agricultural Economy: Recent Performance and Policy" in R. Roett (ed.), Brazil in the Sixties (Nashville, Vanderbilt University Press, 1972).

Oliveira, F. de, "A economia brasileira: crítica da razão dualista," Estudos CEBRAP, Vol. 2, 1972.

Ozorio de Almeida, A.L., et al., The Closing Frontier: Internal Migrations, Family Farming and Colonisation Policies in the Brazilian Amazon (Rio de Janeiro, IPEA/INPES, 1981, mimeo).

————, and M.B. de Albuquerque David, *Escassez de Terras Aptas para Colonização na Amazônia* (Rio de Janeiro, IPEA/INPES, 1983, mimeo).

Paiva, R.M., "Reflexões sobre as tendências da produção, da produtividade e dos preços do setor agrícola," *Revista Brasileira de Economia*, Vol. 20(2/3), 1966.

———— *et al.*, *Brazil's Agriculture Sector* (São Paulo, 1973, XV International Conference of Agricultural Economists).

Palmeira, M., "Demobilização e conflito: relações entre trabalhadores e patrões na agro-indústria pernambucana," *Revista de Cultura e Política*, Ano 1, no. 1., 1979.

Pastore, A.C., "A oferta de produtos agrícolas no Brasil," *Estudos Econômicos*, Vol. 1(3), 1971.

————, "Exportações Agrícolas e Desenvolvimento Econômico" in A. Veiga (ed.), *En saios Sobre Política Agrícola Brasileira* (São Paulo, Secretaria da Agricultura, 1979).

Pastore, J., *et al.*, "Condicionantes da Produtividade da Pesquisa Agrícola no Brasil," in J.R. Mendonca de Barros *et al.*, *Economia Agrícola: Ensaios* (São Paulo, IPE, 1982).

Patrick, G., "Fontes de crescimento na agricultura brasileira: o setor de culturas," in C.R. Contador (ed.), *Tecnologia e desenvolvimento agrícola* (Rio de Janeiro, IPEA, 1975).

Peixoto *et al.*, *A soja na pequena agricultura: um estudo de caso no Rio Grande do Sul* (Brasília, BINAGRI, 1979).

Pompermayer, M.J., "Estratégia de Grande Capital na Fronteira Amazônica Brasileira," *Estudos PECLA*, Vol. 1(3), 1982.

————, and B. Sorj, *Sociedade e Política(s) na Fronteira Amazônica: Interpretações e Argumentos* (Belo Horizonte, 1983, mimeo).

Prado Jr., C., "Contribuição para a analise da questão agrária no Brasil," *Revista Brasiliense*, No. 28, 1960.

————, "Nova contribuição para a análise da questão agrária no Brasil," *Revista Brasiliense*, No. 43, 1962.

Rangel, I., *A questão agrária brasileira* (Recife, CONDEPE, 1962).

Rezende, G.C. de, "Crédito rural subsidiado e preço de terra no Brazil," *Estudos Econômicos*, Vol. 12(2), 1982.

————, *Mercado de trabalho, crescimento econômico e salários rurais no Brasil* (paper presented to the ANPEC Conference, São Paulo, 1984, mimeo).

Sa Jr., F., "O desenvolvimento da agricultura nordestina e a função das atividades de subsistência," *Estudos CEBRAP* 3, 1973.

Saint, W.S., "The Wages of Modernisation: A Review of the Literature on Temporary Wage Arrangements in Brazilian Agriculture," *Latin American Research Review*, Vol. 16(3), 1981.

Sampaio, Y., *et al.*, *Política agrícola no Nordeste: intenções e resultados* (Recife, CME/PIMES/UFPE, 1978).

————, *Desenvolvimento rural no Nordeste: a expêriencia do Polonordeste* (Recife: CME/PIMES/UFPE, 1980).

Sandroni, P., *Questão Agrária e Campesinato* (São Paulo, Polis, 1980).

Santos Filho, J. dos Reis, and M.Y. Porto, "A geografia da violência e algumas presenças em conflitos pela posse de terra," *Reforma Agrária*, Vol. 14(1), 1984.

Sawyer, D.R., *Peasants and Capitalism on the Amazon Frontier* (Ph.d. thesis, Harvard University, 1979).

Sayad, J., "Preço da Terra e Mercados Financeiros," *Pesquisa e Planejamento Econômico*, Vol. 7(3), 1977.

Sigaud, L., *Greve nos engenhos* (Rio de Janeiro, Paz e Terra, 1980).

————, "Luta Política e Luta Pela Terra no Nordeste," *DADOS*, Vol. 26(1), 1983.

Silva, S.S., *Estudos sobre a estrutura de produção e a questão agrária*, Cadernos IFCH/ UNICAMP, No. 11, 1984.

Smith, G.W., "Brazilian Agricultural Policy, 1950–67" in H. S. Ellis (ed.), *Essays on the Economy of Brazil* (Berkeley, University of California Press, 1969).

Sorj, B., *Estado e Classes Sociais na Agricultura Brasileira* (Rio de Janeiro, Zahar, 1980).

Sorj, B., M.J. Pompermayer, and O.L. Coradini, *Camponeses e Agroindústria* (Rio de Janeiro, Zahar, 1982).

Strachan, L.W., *Capitalism and the Peasant: Northwest Paraná, Brazil* (Ph.d. thesis, University of Wisconsin-Madison, 1981, mimeo).

Suzigan, W., *Investment in Manufacturing Industry in Brazil, 1869–1939* (Ph.d. thesis, University of London, 1984).

Thompson, R.L., and G.E. Schuh, "Política comercial e exportação: o caso do milho no Brasil," *Pesquisa e Planejamento Econômico*, Vol. 8(3), 1978.

Veiga, A., "Efeitos da política comercial brasileira no setor agrícola" in C.R. Contador (ed.), *Tecnologia e desenvolvimento agrícola* (Rio de Janeiro, IPEA, 1975).

Velho, O., *Capitalismo autoritário e campesinato* (São Paulo, DIFEL, 1976).

Vergopoulos, K., *La Question Paysanne et le Capitalisme* (Paris, Anthropos, 1974).

————, "Capitalism and Peasant Productivity," *The Journal of Peasant Studies*, Vol. 5(4), 1978.

Wanderley, M. de N.B., *O Camponês: Um Trabalhador Para O Capital* (Texto para discussão no. 2, Campinas, UNICAMP/IFCH/DEPE, 1981, mimeo).

Wilkinson, J., *The State, Agroindustry, and Small Farmer Modernisation: Case Studies from the Brazilian Northeast* (Ph.d. thesis, University of Liverpool, 1982).

3

Urbanization Since 1945

Martin T. Katzman

The concept of an urban problem is one of the most obscure in the whole realm of public policymaking. Unlike other areas of public concern, such as inflation, energy, or unemployment, it is not clear what an "urban problem" is. In Brazil, policymakers have enumerated such items as inadequate housing and infrastructure, rural-urban population imbalance, inordinate growth of large cities, lack of growth poles in lagging areas, disorderly land use, excessive central-city densities, fragmentation of governmental authority, and poverty (Katzman, 1977, chap. 11). While social scientists would be the first to claim that all social phenomena are interrelated, casting one's net so widely inhibits a proper understanding of urbanization, urban problems, and urban policymaking.

Urban studies in Brazil are in their infancy, but the growth in the quantity and quality of the literature has been impressive. Several Brazilian institutes have established a respectable track record of urban research. In addition to updating earlier reviews of the literature (Morse, 1966; Morse, 1971; Katzman, 1977, chaps. 9–11), this essay attempts to present a fruitful way of thinking about urbanization that can guide both researchers and policymakers.

The process of urbanization can be fully appreciated by adopting at least three perspectives. First, urbanization can be viewed as a spatial expression of socio-economic change; that is, as an epiphenomenon. Second, urbanization can be viewed as a casual influence on economic, social, and political change. Third, the dense agglomeration of nonagricultural populations in social systems we call cities poses problems that are essentially different from those in rural social systems. The interrelationships between urbanization and other aspects of social change have evolved during the postwar period as have the perceptions of urban problems and their remedies.

Many scholars of Latin America are inclined to interpret the experience of Brazil as the epitome of dependent (even authoritarian) capitalism. Undoubtedly, there are overwhelming similarities among Latin American countries in their relationship to advanced, capitalist democracies that invite such generalizations. Indeed, the emergence of structuralism, the Latin American version of dependency theory, after World War II was an attempt to explain the commonality of the region's underdevelopment and to prescribe common solutions (Prebisch, 1950; Frank, 1967; Katzman, 1977, chap. 6). These common problems include: low rates of industrial labor absorption, poor performance of raw-material exports, the stagnation of the latifundia-minifundia complex, inequalities in income, and spatial imbalances. But it is important to recognize that there are other dependent, authoritarian, capitalist economies that have had radically different experiences. Particularly instructive are the experiences of authoritarian capitalism in Taiwan, Korea, and Malaysia, where per capita incomes were 90 percent, 85 percent, and 83 percent of Brazil's in 1983 (World Bank, 1984, table 1). From a broader comparative perspective, aspects of Brazilian social change that have been viewed by both apologists on the right and critics on the left as virtually the inevitable consequences of authoritarian capitalism are reinterpreted as only one set of possible policy outcomes.

In any society, policy options in all spheres are narrowed by political, economic, and social institutions and interests that emerge from its historical experience. Policies reflecting the configuration of these forces are often rationalized as being the only "technically feasible" policies. Narrow options, however, may also reflecting tunnel vision. Sharing Keynes's perspective on the role of ideas in shaping action, this essay presumes that modes of thinking about urban problems in Brazil have an independent influence on policy and that misguided thinking about some of these problems has resulted in ineffective policy or unintended consequences.

IMPACT OF SOCIAL CHANGE ON URBANIZATION

As noted by Faria (1985, table 1), Brazil has been transformed from an "essentially agricultural country" to a significant industrial nation. One of the most striking indicators of social change in Brazil has been the urbanization of the population. Prior to World War II, only about one sixth of the population lived in cities of over 20,000 inhabitants. By 1980, nearly one half of the population lived in such cities. When smaller communities are included as "urban," then the urban share of the population rose from one quarter to more than two thirds in the 1940–80 period. By any measure the growth of the urban population was most rapid in the 1950s and 1960s (Table 3.1).

In historical perspective, Brazil's urban transition during the past forty years has been extremely rapid. For comparison, the urban share of the population in the United States rose from 25 percent to 64 percent over the eighty-year period of 1870–1950 (Lampard, 1968, table 2). Today, the 52 percent of Brazilians living in cities with more than 20,000 inhabitants closely approximates the 61 percent of Americans in urbanized areas.[1]

Urbanization began in the major industrial centers of the Center-South, but the process rapidly diffused throughout the nation. In the 1940–70 period, the proportion of population in cities of more than 2,000 inhabitants doubled in virtually every state (Katzman, 1977, table 22). By 1980, more than one third of the population of each region lived in cities with more than 20,000 inhabitants (Faria, 1983, table 2).

Urbanization and Sectoral Change

The dominant conceptual scheme for explaining urbanization is the "dualistic" model of economic development (Fei and Ranis, 1964). This model describes the process by which the economy's center of gravity shifts from the agricultural sector to the industrial/service sector. Participants in the agricultural, rural sector are generally viewed as having traditional patterns of fertility, savings, and technology. Participants in the industrial/service sector are generally viewed as modern in these respects. Moreover, government may treat these sectors differently. It may be simpler to tax industrial/service sectors, and, in turn, public investments may be biased in favor of these sectors, although this need not necessarily be the case.

In the course of economic development, the center of gravity shifts from the agricultural to the industrial/service sector for several reasons: First, as their incomes rise, consumers demand a decreasing proportion of agriculturally based food and clothing. Second, rapid technological change in the industrial sector raises the productivity of industrial labor and capital, which, in turn, lowers the cost of manufactures vis-a-vis food and rural handicrafts. Third, the bulk of savings is generated by industrialists, who tend to reinvest in their own enterprises.

Table 3.1
Urban Population of Brazil, 1940–80, as Percent of Brazilian Population

	official* definition	cities > 2,000	cities > 10,000	cities > 20,000
1940	31.2	25.2	18.5	16.0
1950	36.2	30.8	23.4	21.1
1960	45.1	40.4	32.3	28.8
1970	56.0	52.0	44.5	38.8
1980	67.7	64.8	56.6	51.5

*Defined as the seat of a municipio.
Sources: Merrick and Graham (1979), table VIII-2, through 1970; Katzman (1977), table 21, through 1970; Sinopse Preliminar do Censo Demografico, IX Recenseamento Geral do Brasil, 1980, state volumes, tables 3 and 4.

The dualistic model has successfully explained sectoral changes in the nineteenth-century Japanese and American economies (Kelley and Williamson, 1974; Williamson, 1974). Yap (1976) modified the model by disaggregating the industrial sector into modern and traditional subsectors and successfully explained Brazilian macroeconomic performance in the 1950–65 period.

In the period 1940–60, the share of the labor force employed in manufacturing remained fairly stable at about 9 percent. The manufacturing share reached 11 percent by 1970 and nearly 16 percent by 1980. The share of employment in the remaining industrial subsectors (construction, mining, and utilities), which are not necessarily urban, grew substantially after 1960. The bulk of nonagricultural employment, however, has been provided by the services sector. This conglomerate sector provided about one quarter of the jobs in the labor force in both 1940 and 1950, but nearly half of the jobs by 1980 (Table 3.2).

If the industrial/service sector is assumed to be urban, then the dualistic model becomes a theory of urbanization (cf. Kelley and Williamson, 1983). By recognizing the relatively high fertility and low growth of demand for labor in the rural areas, the dualistic model also becomes a theory of rural-urban migration.

The dualistic model is not a complete theory of urbanization because it does not explain why industrial/service activities are not scattered among agricultural activities, Indeed, in the early stages of economic development, significant industrial activity does occur in rural areas. For example, in 1940 nearly half of all sugar was processed on farms, but by 1970 only 4 percent

Table 3.2
Sectoral Employment Distribution (Nonagricultural), 1940–80,
as Percent of Labor Force

	1940	1950	1960	1970	1980
Total industrial	10.1	13.7	12.9	18.0	24.4
Manufacturing	7.1	9.4	8.6	11.1	15.7
Construction	1.9	3.4	3.4	5.9	7.2
Mining/utilities	1.1	0.9	0.9	1.1	1.5
Total services	25.9	26.4	33.1	37.3	45.7

Sources: Merrick and Graham (1979), table VII-3, through 1970; Faria (1983)
for 1980.

(Katzman, 1977, table 24). In 1960, fully 15 percent of all operatives worked in rural areas (Katzman, 1974, table 3). In order to explain urbanization, the concept of agglomeration economies—economies of scale achieved by concentrating productive activities in space—must be invoked.

The most commonplace and least important advantage of agglomeration is the internal economies of scale in the firm. Economies of scale help explain why agricultural enterprises slough off handicraft activities and purchase manufactures in the course of economic development. If internal economies of scale are significant enough, a factory town, like the Volta Redonda or Cubatão steel complexes, may emerge.

A more important source of agglomeration is the advantages that many small firms in the same industry can gain by common localization. These may include access to a labor pool with industry-specific skills, to common customers, to common suppliers of customized capital equipment and spare parts, and to financial and business services specialized in this industry. Thus, one observes Blumenau specializing in textiles and Belo Horizonte specializing in steel products (Singer, 1968).

The one-industry towns which are created by these "localization economies" are hardly the germ of self-generating growth. This germ can be found in the highly diversified mix of functions servicing a wide range of industries. These "urbanization economies" include municipal infrastructure (water supply, electricity, port and rail facilities), adaptable financial institutions, and a large number of little shops that produce small lots of highly specialized intermediate and capital goods. Urbanization economies such as transportation-communication infrastructure, government offices, and diversified business services may induce the agglomeration of a whole range of tertiary and quarternary activities. Cities that offer such diversity are likely to provide a propitious incubator for self-generating growth.

Hyperurbanization

In the postwar period, population in Brazilian cities did not invariably grow at the same rate as industrial/service employment. In the 1940s, urban population generally kept pace with the growth of manufacturing employment and exceeded the growth of service employment (Table 3.3). What these crude categories miss is the deruralization of some industrial activities that were formerly provided by country craftsmen. About one third of urban employment growth, at least through 1970, can be attributed to the agglomeration of existing industrial and service activities in cities (Katzman, 1977, p. 159).

As noted by Faria (1985), urbanization was faster than growth in employment in manufacturing, and, to a lesser extent, in services during the 1950s, the period of capital-intensive import substitution. This process raised concerns about the "labor absorption problem," "hyperurbanization," and the "bloated" services sector. These concepts were derived from the classical view that the services sector was basically unproductive, and that cities full of service workers were bloated with marginalized workers.

With the exception of São Paulo, most Brazilian metropolises are indeed largely commercial and service centers. In the 1940–80 period, industry employed about 35–40 percent of the labor force in metropolitan São Paulo. Among the remaining twenty largest cities, none approached 30 percent of their labor forces in the industrial sector before 1970. Rio, the second largest industrial city, has had at most only 25 percent of its employment in industry. This level of industrial employment is far below that of cities in the United States at a comparable level of urbanization.[2]

The poor labor-absorption record of Brazilian industrialization resulted in substantial controversy between the neoclassical and structuralist schools. Neoclassical economists could point to distortions in factor markets, created by labor institutions, such as minimum wages and social security taxes and by substantial subsidies to borrowers of capital. Structuralists could point to inappropriate factor proportions in imported technology and to biases in sectoral patterns of consumer demand resulting from post-1964 incomes-distribution policy (Taylor and Bacha, 1976). Limited employment opportunities in the modern industry created a segmented urban labor market, in which a marginalized labor pool engage in relatively unremunerative tasks while awaiting openings in the modern industrial sector (Harris and Todaro, 1970).

The perceptions of both hyperurbanization and the labor absorption problem have diminished as a result of the improved labor-absorption record of

Table 3.3
Annual Percentage Growth of Employment in Manufacturing and Services, and Urban Population, by Decade, 1940–80

	1940–50	1950–60	1960–70	1970–80
Total manuf./services	2.9	4.5	4.1	6.6
Manufacturing	4.9	2.0	5.2	7.8
Services	2.2	5.2	3.8	6.2
Urban				
Official	3.9	5.3	5.0	4.6
Cities>2,000	4.4	5.9	5.3	5.2
Cities>10,000	4.8	6.4	6.0	5.3
Cities>20,000	5.2	6.3	5.8	5.9

Sources: Merrick and Graham (1979), table VII-3; Katzman (1977), table 21; Sinopse Preliminar do Censo Demografico, 1980.

Brazilian industry in the 1960s and especially in the 1970s. Although there has been an increased appreciation of the productivity of the services sector (Baer and Samuelson, 1981), the growth of manufacturing employment has exceeded the growth in service employment in the past two decades. Improved labor absorption has been accompanied by deceleration of the growth rate of large cities.

The dualistic model can explain improved labor absorption and decelerating urbanization by the containment of the real minimum wage, which affects the modern industrial and services sector. During the late 1960s, the minimum wage fell while rural wages rose. By 1973, the minimum wage converged with the average rural wage in most regions (Bacha, 1979; Morley, 1982, table 8.8). Perhaps this was a turning point signaling the end to hyperurbanization.

Influences of Brazilian Policies on Urbanization

Urban migration in the dualistic model is driven by rural-urban welfare differentials. These differentials are not determined solely by such abstractions as "technology" or "factor endowments," but also by politically determined social relations of production and citizenship entitlements.

It is clear that opportunities for a decent standard of living under Brazilian agrarian conditions are poor relative to those available to the rural masses in the nineteenth-century frontier period in the United States and Canada and in the postwar period in East Asia. The inaccessibility of farm land to these masses is due less to Malthusian overcrowding on scarce land than to the limited access of population to abundant land. Brazil never had the equivalent of Pre-emption or the Homestead Act, which provided relatively open access to freeholds for American farmers. Historians can explain the current structure of land tenure in the Northeast or Southeast by the political forces which have influenced much of rural Brazil despite several changes in regimes since 1930 (Dean, 1971; Forman, 1975, chap. 4). Brazil, however, has sufficient resources on the Central-Western frontier to provide land to the landless without land reform in the Northeast or Southeast. Tragically, the post-1964 regime lacked the political will to create conditions for successful settlement schemes or to protect squatters who have worked frontier land for generations. Pathetic squatters in frontier areas from Amazonia to Paraná have been brutally expelled by the *jagunços* of large landowners (Katzman, 1977, chap. 2; Foweraker, 1981; Flynn, 1979, chap. 10; Goodman, 1985).

Lacking access to land, the rural masses have suffered further deterioration of opportunities as a result of subsidized credit for modern inputs like fertilizers and tractors (Sanders, 1973; Sorj and Wilkinson, 1983). Because small holders have been unable to compete with larger farmers for subsidized credit, the celebrated "rural democracy" of Paraná is in the process of decay (Margolis, 1973; Adams and Nehman, 1979).

There is persuasive evidence that an agrarian reform which would include clear title, extension services, and access to credit could substantially improve the condition of the rural masses, especially in the Northeast (Cline, 1970; Kutcher and Scandizzo, 1981). The myth that large farms are necessary to insure the prosperity of smallholders is dispelled by the examples of the peasantry in infertile Taiwan, where 5 hectares is a *large* holding (Fei, Ranis, and Kuo, 1979, table 2.2); in land-rich Malaysia, where the successful settlement schemes allot 4 hectares per holding (Fisk and Osman-Rani, 1981, chap. 10); and in intensely cultivated Korea, where 3 hectares is the maximum permissible holding (Mason *et al.*, 1983, chap. 12).

As elaborated below, a major contributor to rural welfare is the opportunity for nonfarm employment. Indeed, in Taiwan about 70 percent of the farmers engage in industrial and service activities in small-scale enterprises (Fei, Ranis, and Kuo, 1979, table 2.12 and 2.13). However, the viability of these decentralized activities depends critically upon the development of rural infrastructure—electrification, telephones, and feeder roads—as well as on policies that provide small enterprises with as much access to credit as larger enterprises. Brazil is making significant progress in the extension of infrastructure to rural areas, and this should spur the decentralization of industrial and service activities. Countries like Korea and Taiwan have fomented small-scale industrialization by the establishment of specialized development banks (Mason *et al.*, 1980, chaps. 7 & 9).

Another factor weighing in favor of urban opportunities is the poor distribution of public services in rural Brazil. The urban population has far greater access to treated drinking water, electricity, hospitals, and public schools than does the rural population. There may be technological reasons why drinking water and electricity can be provided more cheaply in the city than in the countryside, but the experience of East Asia suggests that the lack of educational and health facilities is more a matter of policy choice than of technological necessity (Fei, Ranis, and Kuo, 1979; Meerman, 1979). This suggests that an improvement in rural conditions through a combination of agrarian reform, encouragement of small-scale rural industrialization, and improved public services would undoubtedly reduce the pressures for rural-urban migration (World Bank, 1979, chap. 6). Indeed, the impressive improvements in access to health care and schooling in rural Brazil in the past decade may well have contributed to the slowdown in urbanization (Salm, 1985).

IMPACT OF SOCIAL CHANGE ON THE URBAN SYSTEM

The concept of an urban system connotes a functional and spatial division of labor among cities. Because individual cities compete for manufacturing and service functions, the growth rates of cities are interrelated.

Until recently there has been relatively little analytic research on urban systems in Brazil. Early research, mostly undertaken by geographers, described hierarchies of urban functions and delineated areas of urban dominance with little analysis of how such hierarchies originate and what forces account for their changes over time. One accomplishment of this approach has been the regionalization of Brazilian space on the basis of counties oriented around urban centers. The results have been incorporated into census definitions of "homogeneous microregions" (IBG, 1968).

The Network of Central Places

In virtually all Brazilian cities, most of the labor force performs services rather than manufacturing functions. The evolution of a system of service centers can be explained by the "central place theory" (see Appendix). A key tenet of this theory is the existence of economies of scale in the production of goods and services. The importance of scale economies differs among various commodities, but they reduce the advantages of farm households engaging in their production. By assumption, farm households are uniformly distributed within each region. To consume a nonfarm commodity, these households must travel to the closest urban center providing the good or service. Each commodity absorbs a different share of household income. Since each commodity faces different cost and demand conditions, the market areas for various commodities vary in size. The more significant the economies of scale and the smaller the demand per household, the larger the market area. In fact, a continuum of commodities by market area can be identified, from the ubiquitous to the unique. In rural São Paulo state, for example, the lowest order (most ubiquitous) commodity was the bar followed by the general store (Leme, 1965, p. 212).

There are great pressures for commodities with market areas of similar size to be produced at the same point. These agglomeration economies include the desire of the consumer to economize on the number of trips; the nodality of the transportation system; and other external economies of production. Individual centers compete for these functions, and a hierarchy of cities or central places emerges. In this hierarchy, each urban place has a hinterland of rural areas and smaller cities which it serves.

The size and market areas of urban places in southeastern Brazil exhibit a central place hierarchy (Suarez-Villa, 1980). In São Paulo state, for example, larger cities tend to offer a larger number of commodities, and the number and size of establishments offering more ubiquitous commodities are greater than in smaller cities. As predicted, the larger towns on the railroad from Campinas to the capital tend to be farther apart from each other than are the smaller towns (Leme, 1965). Even though central place theory was not developed to explain the distribution of industrial towns, the foundations of metropolitan São Paulo's industrial preeminence can be plausibly traced to its origin as the premier market center of the coffee frontier (Singer, 1968, chap. 2; Katzman, 1977, chap. 7; Katzman, 1978a).

What is the impact of rural development on the size and spatial distribution of service centers? In general, the market area for a given product will vary inversely with population density, per capita income, and intra-regional transportation costs. An increase in rural density, perhaps due to the shift toward a more labor-intensive crop (e.g., from cattle to rice), raises the density of demand for all commodities. An increase in agricultural productivity will have the same result via the income effect. Consequently, excess profits are earned by central places, and more firms squeeze into the market, raising the number of centers for each size grouping. A fortiori, the number of people living in these centers increases. An improvement in the intra-regional transportation network has an opposite effect. At a given commodity price, the market area expands, leading to a reduction in the number of enterprises and an increase in the scale of output of the surviving enterprises. Consequently, there are fewer and more widely spaced centers, with the smallest

market centers being somewhat larger than before. Because of scale economies, the concentration of production in fewer enterprises implies the saving
of some labor, and thus the number of people living in these places may
decrease.

The relevance of central place theory to Brazilian urbanization is tested by
a cross-sectional regression analysis of state urban systems for the census years,
1940–1980. To avoid complications introduced by large industrial cities, which
may have multistate hinterlands, attention is focused on towns of from 2,000
to 20,000 inhabitants. These towns included about 40 percent of the nation's
urban population in 1940, but only about 20 percent in 1980. Excluded from
the analysis are Acre, Amazonas, and the territories, which are virtually emp-
ty. To facilitate interstate comparisons, variables are divided by total state
area. The two dependent variables are the number of towns per thousand square
kilometer (of state area) and town population per square kilometer.

The explanatory variables are agricultural productivity, rural density, and
the quality of the state highway network. In 1940–1970, agricultural productivity equals state agricultural income divided by the total farm labor force;
in 1980, the value of cropland per hectare. Rural density equals the farm
labor force divided by the state area. The quality of the highway network is
the number of kilometers of federal, state, and municipal roads divided by
total state area.

As predicted by central place theory, these three factors explain virtually
all of the interstate variance in the number and population of small towns in
Brazil during the 1940–1980 period. As indicated by the standardized regression coefficients, the relative importance of the explanatory variables is remarkably stable throughout 1940–1970 (Table 3.4). Rural population density has
the greatest influence on the number of towns and their population. Except
for 1980, the number and population of towns varies directly with agricultural productivity, although the relationship is significant only in 1960 and
1970. In the 1940–1970 period, the number and population of small towns
tends to vary inversely with the quality of the highway network, but the
relationships are not statistically significant. In 1980, the highway quality
variable had the wrong sign, although not statistically significant.

Throughout the 1940–1980 period, the mean number of towns per thousand rural inhabitants remained invariant at 0.1. The ratio of towns to rural
populations remained stable as well, at about 500 per thousand. This stability suggests that the major forces for urbanization were related to developments in communities larger than 20,000.

The number of towns per area converged in this period, as the interstate
coefficient of variation fell from .91 to .68. The population of the towns per
area converged as well, the coefficient falling from .99 to .71. The coefficient

Table 3.4
Determinants of Small Towns and Their Populations, 1940–80:
Standardized Regression Coefficients.

	Dependent variables		Explanatory variables			
	mean	coeff. var.	rural density	agricult. product	road density	R^2
1940						
number of towns	.34	.92	.987*	.114	−.099	.82*
pop. of towns	1.52	.99	1.057*	.228*	−.170	.85*
1950						
number of towns	.40	.80	.977*	.227	−.178	.81*
pop. of towns	2.02	.82	.944*	.280*	−.129	.82*
1960						
number of towns	.60	.75	.914*	.466*	−.115	.86*
pop. of towns	3.27	.77	.845*	.431*	.008	.88*
1970						
number of towns	.77	.67	.932*	.459*	−.119	.85*
pop. of towns	4.18	.66	.808*	.513*	.004	.86*
1980						
number of towns	.99	.68	.823*	.063	.199	.90*
pop. of towns	5.76	.71	.743*	.181	.232	.88*

*Significance .05 (one-tail).
Sources: Number and population of towns: Sinopse Preliminar do Censo Demografico, 1980, tables 3 and 4. Agricultural output till 1970: Conjuntura Economica, 24 (Junho 1970):89–106; for 1980, use value of cropland per acre. Kilometers of highway: Anuario Estatistico, various years.
Note: Number of towns, population of towns, rural density, and road density are expressed as a ratio to state area. Also, n = 19; Amazônas, Acre, Guanabara (former Federal District), and territories are excluded.

of variation in agricultural productivity remained virtually constant, but those for rural densities converged (from .74 to .65) and those for road density converged as well (from .73 to .59). This reflects the diffusion of innovation observed for larger cities (Merrick and Graham, 1979).

Size Distribution of Cities

In many nations, a large primate city overwhelms the whole urban network. In Latin America, about 52 percent of the Uruguayans, 45 percent of the Argentines and Chileans, 39 percent of the Peruvians, and 32 percent of the Mexicans live in their nation's largest city, invariably the capital. The phenomenon of primacy is not restricted to developing nations, for 48 percent of the Irish, 30 percent of the Danes and New Zealanders, 24 percent of the Australians, and 20 percent of the British and Japanese live in their nations' largest city (World Bank, 1984, table 22).

In Brazil, economic and political power are not monopolized by a single city, and since 1940 urban primacy has been shared by two metropolitan areas of nearly equal size. As a percentage of the national total, the combined population of metropolitan São Paulo and Rio de Janeiro rose slowly, from 3 percent to 4.5 percent during the 50-year period from 1872 to 1920. Since 1920, the growth of these cities has been relatively rapid, and by 1980 metropolitan São Paulo held about 10 percent of the national population; while metropolitan Rio held about 7 percent (Table 3.5). A rarity in the urban history of the modern world, primacy shifted from the traditional leader Rio de Janeiro to the upstart São Paulo in the mid-1950s.

Because the total urban system has been expanding, at least since 1920, the concentration of population in the two primate cities is best gauged with respect to the total urban population. Compared to the population of cities of more than 20,000, there was a substantial increase of population in the two primates in the 1920–1940 period. In the 1940–1960 period, the relative population of the two primates decreased substantially. Since 1960 the relative population of the two primates has remained about the same at 35 percent. Since 1950, however, the metropolitan population of the two primates has decreased with respect to that of the other 11 largest cities (Faria, 1983, table 9).

Although population does not seem to be extraordinarily concentrated in São Paulo and Rio, "hyperconcentration" has been used to justify the transfer of the national capital to Brasília and also to justify discussions of "interiorization" of development in states like São Paulo.[3] In fact, Brazil's urbanization is spread widely throughout the nation.

In the 1940–1950 period, the most rapidly growing cities were in the initial population classes of 10,000 to 20,000 people, and in the cities of over 1 million. In the next decade, these size classes grew the slowest. In the decade 1960–1970, the fastest growing cities were in the size class of 100,000 to 250,000 people (Table 3.6).

Given "random" influences on city size, it can be shown that a central place system generates a rank-size distribution of cities (Beckmann, 1958). According to the rank-size rule, the population of any city of rank r (P_r) is equal to the population of the largest city P_1), divided by its own rank r. If

Table 3.5
Concentration of the Brazilian Population in Metropolitan
São Paulo and Rio, by Decade, 1920–80

	1920	1940	1950	1960	1970	1980
Population of Rio and S.P. (thous.)	1,370	3,198	5,141	7,559	12,389	21,009
As % of nat. pop.	4.5	7.8	9.9	10.6	13.4	17.3
As % of urban pop., cities>2,000	n.a.	30.8	32.1	26.4	25.8	26.8
As % of urban pop., cities>20,000	30.1	51.5	49.7	35.9	36.2	34.3

Sources: Brasil, Censo Demografico, 1940–1970; Tolosa (1973); Sinopse Preliminar do Censo Demografico, 1980.

Table 3.6
Distribution of Urban Population and Growth
by City Sizes, in Thousands, 1940–70.

A. Percent distribution

	urban size classes (thousands)					
	2–10	10–20	20–100	100–500	500–1000	>1000
1940	27.9	11.4	18.3	15.7	0.0	26.7
1950	24.2	10.5	22.6	12.7	3.1	26.9
1960	20.1	10.8	23.0	14.8	9.3	22.3
1970	15.6	9.4	20.6	14.2	10.2	32.0
1980	12.7	7.9	n.a.	n.a.	n.a.	n.a.

B. Annual growth rate (percent), by base-year population

1940–50	3.2	3.6	3.5	3.4	n.a.	3.9
1950–60	3.7	6.0	5.9	5.1	5.1	3.9
1960–70	n.a.	n.a.	5.0	6.0	6.6	5.1
1970–80	n.a.	n.a.	n.a.	n.a.	n.a.	n.a.

Sources: Costa (1970), table V; Brasil, Censo Demografico, 1940-1980.
Note: n. a. = not available

the rule holds, then plotting city size on a logarithmic scale against rank produces a downward-sloping straight line.

At the initial stages of economic development, the level of interregional integration is generally low and cities may belong to separate regional systems. Since economic development is associated with regional integration, a national system of cities is expected to emerge. Consequently, regional systems of cities may adhere to the rank-size rule at all stages of development, but the national system may adhere to the rule only in the later phases of development.

Excluding Rio de Janeiro and São Paulo from his calculations, Costa (1970) examined urban systems in five Brazilian census regions (Amazônia, Northeast, Southeast, Central-West, South). In each region, city-size distributions adhered to the rank-size rule in 1940, 1950, and 1960. Moreover, when all Brazilian cities were considered together, they also fitted the rule equally well in all three periods. Including all cities with populations above 20,000, Faria (1983) found that Brazil has had a rank-size system in the period 1950–1980. Suarez-Villa (1980) found that 1,000 southeastern cities fitted a rank-size distribution in 1970.

A more detailed analysis indicates some interesting anomalies in the rank-size relationship when the *metropolitan* populations of the 125 largest cities are considered. For the census years 1940, 1950, and 1960, the rank-size rule fits the metropolitan network fairly well, although there are substantial deviations. The exponent of the rank is significantly lower than unity, and the constant term consistently lower than the population of the largest city. These deviations are probably explained by the fact that the two largest metropolitan areas, São Paulo and Rio, were nearly the same size.[4]

In a nation where urbanization rates are uneven among states, where new frontier towns are born, and where new towns are planned, one might expect a highly unstable urban hierarchy. Despite these upheavals, the ranking of the 125 largest cities has been remarkably stable in recent decades. The correlation between the 1940 and 1960 ranks of the largest Brazilian cities is .86, compared to .67 for 122 Venezuelan cities and .92 for 157 Spanish cities in the same period (Lasuen, 1972).

In the 1970s, the phenomenon of "polarization reversal" was first noticed around the world. In the context of advanced economies, the phenomenon refers to the deceleration or even stagnation of growth of large metropolitan areas and acceleration of growth in small towns and rural areas. In Brazil, the decline in the growth of metropolitan São Paulo relative to middle-sized cities in its hinterland has been called "polarization reversal" as well (Keen and Townrowe, 1981). As indicated above, the relative population of the two metropolitan primates has been declining since 1950, so this phenomenon is not new. Brazil has yet to join the countries where metropolitan population growth has virtually stopped.

Normative Issues of Urban System Development

A perennial normative issue in urban economic geography is discovering the "optimum" city size. Since cities form a system, there is no theoretical reason to believe that there is a unique optimum city size, although there may be an optimum size distribution.

Research on optimum city size has generally focused upon productivity differentials among cities of different sizes. For example, Boisier *et al.* (1973) found that output per worker was insensitive to city size up to 200,000 population, but varied directly in larger cities. Output per worker, however, varies with capital per worker, which was not controlled in this study. A better measure of worker efficiency, *salary*, was found to be invariant with city size, except for São Paulo and Rio, where living costs, minimum salaries, and average wage were higher. A study of middle-sized cities (population 50,000–250,000) found that output per worker was higher in cities that are part of an urban network, like a satellite city, than in isolated self-standing cities (Andrade and Lodder, 1979).

These results suggest that agglomeration economies tend to increase monotonically with urban size. Because agglomeration diseconomies, such as congestion, pollution, municipal service costs, etc., are not measured, they do not indicate that cities will tend to increase without limit, with all the national population concentrating in the largest cities (Tolosa, 1973). Indeed, this has not happened in Brazil or anywhere else.

One is left with the impression that most research on the size-distribution of Brazilian cities is fruitless numerology, without normative content. Neither theory nor empirical research provides much guidance in identifying an optimum distribution of city size. While there is a tacit dogma among many urban planners, including Brazilians, that a rank-size distribution is optimal, theory lends no foundation to this belief. There is little reason to contend that a rank-size distribution of cities is superior to distributions characterized by greater primacy or greater uniformity in city size.

A more fruitful research program on urban systems would focus on the development of central place hierarchy. In particular, attention should be devoted to identifying policies that could flatten the urban hierarchy and hence diffuse urban functions to the countryside. Such policies may involve improvements in telecommunications, electrification, and transportation.

IMPACT OF URBANIZATION ON SOCIAL CHANGE

Impacts on Industrial Development

Cities in the developing world have often been characterized as "parasitic" (Hoselitz, 1960). Indeed, as the locus of consumption of surplus value or rents by the ruling class (the landowners, the military, and their minions), cities of the "cartorial state" invited this image. In the prewar period, very little productive labor (in Adam Smith's terms) could be observed in the Brazilian cities, outside of the São Paulo–Belo–Rio de Janeiro industrial triangle.

In the postwar period, appreciation of the "generative" role of cities in economic development has increased. Cities arise from the economies of scale that can be realized by agglomerating economic activities. As indicated previously, these are economies internal to the firm, external to the firm but internal to the industry (localization economies), and external to the industry but internal to the city (urbanization economies). Cities are now viewed as the locus of the most intense division of labor, competition, and innovation.

The experience of currently advanced economies suggests that the cities capable of the most persistent self-generating growth, such as nineteenth-century Manchester, or modern New York City and São Paulo, are not characterized by any particular dominant activity (Katzman, 1978a). Such cities appear capable of generating innovative activities, while losing the routinized ones to small peripheral cities. In Brazil, for example, the larger cities tend to have more diversified industrial mixes and less dependence upon "traditional" industries than do smaller cities (Tolosa, 1973, table 4; Smolka and Lodder, 1973, table 4). Furthermore, among middle-sized cities, industrial suburbs in metropolitan areas are far less specialized in "traditional" sectors than are satellite cities and isolated centers (Andrade and Lodder, 1979, table III.5).

How can policymakers create and exploit urbanization economies in a deliberate manner? The "growth pole" paradigm has provided a highly influential theory of urban and regional development planning. According to this theory, economic development tends to begin in a few cities or poles. These poles are dominated by a large-scale, technically advanced, capital-intensive industry that has significant input-output linkages. The growth of this pole spreads development to the rest of the nation (Tolosa, 1971 and 1972).

This misguided theory has encouraged the establishment of iron-steel, petrochemical, and other heavy industrial complexes in hopes of generating growth. Unfortunately, like latifundia, large integrated complexes create few external economies for other firms, since most supply relationships are internalized within the complex. The worldwide track record of planned growth pole and in "natural" cities developed around such complexes (autos in Detroit, steel in Pittsburgh, and perhaps petrochemicals in Houston) has been extremely poor.[5]

The bulk of Brazilian research on growth poles concentrates on site selection. One technique utilizes "gravity models," which generally identify sites that already have good access; *i.e.*, existing metropolises (Ferreira, 1971). Integer programming techniques produce considerably less conservative results (Tolosa and Reiner, 1970).

Brazil has invested greatly in several growth poles, but there has been surprisingly little evaluation of their performance. Goiânia and Brasília were expected to stimulate regional development in the Central-West. The evidence suggests that Goiânia has grown as a central place rather than as a stimulus to the development of the surrounding area. Brasília has had relatively few stimulative linkages with the surrounding region (Katzman, 1977, chap. 3).

Similarly, the Bahian petrochemical complex and the Aratu industrial park have had relatively little stimulative effect on the Northeastern economy, since most of the backward linkages have been to the Southeast (Goodman and Albuquerque, 1971; Reboucas, 1974). There have been virtually no evaluations of earlier growth poles, like the Volta Redonda steel complex.

Unfortunately, the literature on urbanization economies has never articulated a policy-oriented alternative to growth-pole theory. Nevertheless some lessons can be drawn from the historical experience of resilient cities. First, a city dominated by a single industry tends to develop specialized support services and suppliers that are unadaptable to new markets. Thus, growth in a one-industry complex, based on localization economies may be self-limiting rather than self-generating. Second, innovation appears to be proportional to the number of businesses and hence number of entrepreneurs in a city. Cities dominated by big business appear less likely to support entrepreneurship than cities characterized by small business.

Macroeconomic policies that remove distortions in labor costs and financial policies that remove distortions in capital costs will tend to favor smaller businesses. This analysis does imply that "small is beautiful" under all circumstances, but the recognition of the advantages of smallness is a good antidote to the gigantomania that plagues Brazilian planning and policymaking (Katzman, 1977, chap. 7).

Impacts on Rural Development

Dependency theorists tend to view urban-rural relationships as relatively parasitic. A more positive view of urban-rural relationships has emerged from Theodore Schultz's "industrial-urban hypothesis." The hypothesis is based upon the observation that agriculture appears more modern and prosperous in the environs of industrial centers. The industrial center is hypothesized to improve the market for rural labor, capital, intermediate inputs, and outputs. This improvement occurs because of the greater competitiveness and diversification of factor and product markets in larger industrial cities. An important channel for the industrial-urban impact is through the provision of part-time and seasonal nonagricultural job opportunities for secondary workers in farm families. This part-time worker effect has been noted in places as diverse as Tennessee and Taiwan (Fei et al., 1979, chap. 2).

There is some empirical evidence for the industrial-urban hypothesis in Brazil. Nicholls found a positive effect of industrial-urbanism on São Paulo agriculture, a result replicated by Katzman (1977, chap. 3) in Goiás. The normative implication of this finding is that the growth of small and middle-sized cities, the so-called "polarization reversal" effect, can have a stimulative effect on Brazilian agriculture.

Cities have also played an important role in frontier settlement. Brazil's

most successful case of planned frontier settlement included major investments in a system of central places (Katzman, 1977, chap. 4). Today, on the
Amazonian frontier, urban entrepots are essential in importing consumer goods,
capital equipment, and implements, and in exporting the frontier staple.

Impacts on the Family

As in other developing countries, the traditional extended family has
played an important role in lubricating the process of urbanization in Brazil
(Wilkening, Pinto, and Pastore, 1968). Migrants often follow the well-worn
path of a pioneering relative who moves to the city. Once established, a new
migrant brings his own immediate kin. By pooling resources, the migrant is
able to re-establish his immediate family in the city and to serve as a magnet
for extended relatives.

In the long run, urbanization has a significant reciprocal impact on the
family. The urban labor market alters the potential roles available for children vis-à-vis adults and for males vis-à-vis females. The value of children as
producers is less in the urban labor force than in the farm labor force, partly
because of the greater skills required for well-remunerated urban jobs. The
value of children as old age security is less for workers who have access to
national pension schemes, mainly urban workers. In addition to lower economic benefit for having children, females have greater opportunities for part-
time and full-time market employment in the city than they have in the
countryside.

Indeed, evidence on urban-rural fertility differentials substantiates this theory for Brazil. Since 1950, the total fertility rate of rural women has been
more than 60 percent higher than that of urban women. Fertility rates in both
urban and rural areas are lowest in the more advanced and urbanized states,
those which are completing the demographic transition (Merrick, 1985, table
5). These findings hold within regions. For example, among women aged
45–49 who were surveyed in 1965 in municipal São Paulo, lifetime fertility
for the urban born was 5.4 children; for the rural born, 7.35, nearly 50 percent more (Berquo et al., 1968). Parallel results were obtained in Belo
Horizonte, where age-specific fertility varies inversely with duration of residence in the city (Merrick and Graham, 1979, tables X–1 & X–7).

An indirect mechanism that influences fertility is education, which is more
readily available in urban than in rural areas. There is a striking difference in
age-specific fertility between women who have completed primary school and
those who have not (Camargo and Berquo, 1970, table 13). Urbanization,
then, would appear to provide a braking mechanism for population growth
in Brazil.

Impacts on Civic Life

In advanced capitalist societies such as the United States or Western Europe, where opportunities are evenly distributed in space, rural inhabitants have traditionally been active in voluntary associations, like churches and civic groups, and in agrarian political movements. In Brazil, however, there is a vast difference between the opportunities available for civic life in the cities and in the countryside. In addition to offering competitive labor market opportunities, Brazilian cities offer a wider range of sources of information, associations, and potential objects of political allegiance.

Until the 1970s, scholars viewed urban migrants as a source of political instability. According to the argument, new urban migrants were marginalized, or not integrated into society. Either they or their children would easily become disaffected with the established social order and thus prey to radical political leaders.

Careful research has shattered the "myth of marginality" (Nelson, 1969). As in other developing countries, *favelados* have been shown to be highly integrated into the urban economy and generally supportive of the existing social order (Perlman, 1976). When abused by this order, often brutally, their response has been to endeavor to redress grievances by peaceful means, such as protest marches and strikes, rather than through violence.

After two decades of repression in Brazil, voluntary associations of the urban poor are beginning to mobilize for political action. In particular, community organizations have successfully influenced the placement of municipal infrastructure (Cardoso, 1983). The successful flexing of political muscle at the local level will undoubtedly have national repercussions as authoritarian pressures are lifted.

URBAN PROBLEMS AND POLICYMAKING

In evaluating urbanization, it is useful to distinguish problems that are inherent to dense, nonagricultural agglomerations from the problems that are merely more visable in cities—that is, problems *of* cities should be distinguished from problems *in* cities. Problems in cities, such as poverty, are in fact more amenable to sectoral or macroeconomic solutions at the national level than to solutions targeted to specific locations. Attempts to solve essentially national problems at the local level, say by job creation, often exacerbate the problem, for example by inducing more immigration (Harris and Todaro, 1970).

Problems of cities had relatively little salience for Brazilian policymakers in the early postwar years. Politicians and technocrats were obviously aware of the slow growth of industrial employment in the rapidly growing cities, with their putrid slums and other symptoms of marginality. These were viewed as problems of cities that could be solved outside the context of city planning. By the late 1960s, however, the urban housing problem was recognized and attacked by the establishment of the National Housing Bank (BNH), which also assumed major responsibility for financing water supply, sewerage, and urban renewal. As traffic congestion became worse in the 1970s, major urban transportation projects consumed a large share of national investment funds. Today, crime is viewed as a major urban problem.

Urban Problems and the Internal Structure of Cities

From the telescopic perspective of the nation, a city is a point which assembles raw materials from a hinterland and semifinished goods from other cities, transforms this raw material into useful commodities, and distributes these commodities within the city, to other cities, and to the hinterland. From the microscopic perspective, the city is a highly structured system.

There have been relatively few studies of the internal structure of Brazilian cities. The earlier studies, undertaken by geographers, were merely descriptive, with little analytic content. There were exceptions such as Geiger's (1956) study of land use in Guanabara and Keller's (1969) study of development in Campinas.

More recent studies by geographers have swung to an extreme of quantification (replete with that nemesis "factor analysis") minimally linked to theory testing or policy application. There remains a strong descriptive tradition in urban geography, as exemplified by studies of the impact of Rio's Metro (da Silva, 1981). Some geographers, however, have moved to testing and measuring policy-relevant hypotheses, particularly with respect to impacts of infrastructure investments on urban form (e.g. Vetter et al., 1979).

Many studies of the past two decades have emerged as by-products of planning documents and transportation studies (Governo, 1968; Prefeitura, 1968; Secretaria, 1969; GERM, 1973). These multidisciplinary studies invariably follow a cookbook formula which involves the enumeration of data on natural resources, economic base, employment structure, and social services. Offering the clearest picture of the internal structure of a Brazilian city is the Metro Study for São Paulo (Prefeitura, 1969). This examines the origins and destinations of urban traffic flows, which are used to define commuting ranges of neighborhoods and "labor sheds" of firms in different locations.

Aimed at *planning* the development of the city, these transportation studies forecast changes in land use and transportation on the basis of past trends. Since they lack causal models linking such important factors as transportation improvements and industrial location, these studies provide little insight as to how government can shape urban development. Nevertheless, they invariably attempt to justify more infrastructure investments and call for more planning and co-ordination.

Albeit fragmentary and inadequate to illuminate policy recommendations, these planning studies do provide some rudimentary descriptions of the internal structure of Brazilian cities. These descriptions show that Brazilian cities are undergoing internal changes common to cities throughout the world.

Brazilian cities tend to obey Clark's Law: land values, population density, and employment densities decline at an exponential rate from the central business district. As in most cities around the world, these gradients tend to flatten, as internal transportation improves over time (Leme, 1965, fig. 4.35; Prefeitura, 1968, vol. 1, pp. 66ff; Secretaria, 1969, vol. 2, p. 309).

Peripheral expansion—the subdivision and sale of land, the construction of housing, and the extension of municipal services—have been described by Morse (1958), Wilheim (1969), and Rio (1971). As in North America, direction from city center is a good predictor of neighborhood social status. In most cities, lower-status neighborhoods expand in sectors along railroad lines or polluted waterways. Higher-status neighborhoods expand near amenities, such as the least polluted beaches, as in Rio, Salvador, and Recife.

There are few studies of land-use succession and the "filtration" of housing from higher to lower income groups in established neighborhoods. The *Lei do Inquilino*, which gives tenants rent guarantees and tenure, might foster a higher degree of neighborhood stability and rigidity of land uses than in North America. For example, the average Paulista family remains in a residence for nine years as opposed to a North American mean of five years (Prefeitura, 1969, vol. 3). Is the enforcement of this law responsible for the spectacular rise in homeownership from 27 percent in 1940 to 66 percent in the late 1960s in São Paulo (Prefeitura, 1969, vol. 3)? Does this institution affect the ability of Brazilian cities to redevelop decaying areas? Answers to such questions await further research.

Like cities elsewhere, Brazilian cities have well-differentiated sectors, where specific types of commercial and industrial activities agglomerate. For example, smaller workshops tend to congregate in older industrial areas, while large modern factories tend to concentrate on trunk or circumferential highways around the larger cities (Secretaria, 1969, vol. 2, pp. 187–98; Ribeiro and de Almeida, 1980). Near the downtown of large cities like São Paulo, districts specialize in the distribution of such producer goods as tools (Rua Florêncio de Abreu) or extruded metals (Rua Piratininga). Shops in these districts specialize in a few items. The juxtaposition of these shops facilitates the servicing of craftsmen and small manufacturers, who travel by foot or public transit. The extreme concentration of such shops in a single district reflects the low levels of aggregate demand for specialty items, all of which might be found in any department store in North America.

The most interesting differences between Brazilian and North American cities relate to the spatial distribution of income groups. First, higher-income groups tend to be more centrally located in Brazil than in the United States. The dilapidated downtown, so common in the United States, was virtually absent in Brazil until recently. The cramped *cortiço*, which is located near noisy railroad tracks, was the exception. The American pattern has been explained by the demand by higher-income groups for greater space and new, high-quality housing, which can be obtained on relatively cheap suburban land and reached by relatively fast private transportation. The Brazilian pattern may be related to the superior availability of municipal services in the central area and the exceptionally high costs of commuting. The accelerated decay in recent years may be related to the spread of urban services toward newer, peripheral areas and the increasing pollution and congestion of the downtowns.

Second, residential segregation by social class in Brazilian cities appears considerably less than in North American cities, the epitome being the live-in *empregada* (Vetter *et al.*, 1979). The willingness of the Brazilian upper class to live near the lower class may trace to several factors: the irrelevancy of the "neighbor" as a basis for social interaction; the patrimonial norms of etiquette and deference in public spaces; and the privatization of schooling, recreation, and security (embodied in the ubiquitous *zelador*).

These characteristics facilitate the process of gentrification as dilapidated housing in well-situated neighborhoods is replaced by newer units. It is interesting to consider whether class segregation will increase as a result of social change. Is residential segregation more prominent in "open-class" cities like São Paulo than in "traditional" cities like Fortaleza, where symbols of class membership are clearer and more likely to be ascribed, rather than achieved through competition? Is increasing concern with crime affecting the willingness of the middle class to live near the poor and to use public transportation? The answer to these questions will have a profound impact on urban spatial structure.

Land use in Brazilian cities is relatively more diversified than in North American cities. The grocery store and the tailor shop below the proprietor's apartment can be found in many luxury neighborhoods. This pattern may be explained by the delegation of domestic purchasing functions to the *empregada*, who must perforce travel by foot. Related to this phenomenon is the itinerant street market, the *feira*. As automobile ownership spreads, homogenization of land use seems to be occurring. Commerce and services are concentrating in shopping centers, and *feiras* are consolidating in fewer and more permanent facilities. Will trends toward greater residential segregation and homogenization of land use deprive low-income persons of service jobs? Such changes of urban form may have important impacts on labor absorption.

In capitalistic societies, decisions about land use are made by millions of individual households and enterprises, which are influenced by governmental regulations, infrastructure, and services. Location decisions are based upon each household and enterprise weighing the benefits to themselves of alternative locations. In an urban setting, many of these decisions can impose costs on others, so-called external diseconomies. The major external diseconomies of urbanization include traffic congestion, pollution and environmental health, crime, and to a lesser extent slum settlement. If these potential externalities are not well managed, urban growth will only make them worse.

Urban Policymaking within Brazilian Fiscal Federalism

The fiscal and organizational environments in which Brazilian cities solve their problems are far different from those in North America, where traditions of self-government are stronger and where municipal bond markets are well developed. In Brazil, states undertake many functions (primary schooling, policing) which are considered local in the United States. Furthermore, the division of taxing powers is more complete in Brazil, where localities are permitted to rely only upon property taxes and states upon sales taxes. Revenue sharing, however, is well developed in Brazil, where 10 percent of income taxes and special excises are returned to municipalities. The earmarking of Federal grants for specific purposes has been criticized as unduly rigid. Pressures for greater budgetary flexibility, *desvinculaçao*, are increasing.

Intergovernmental coordination is less of a problem in Brazil than in North America, where there are far more units of local government. Metropolitan São Paulo, for example, has only about three score *municipios*, while metropolitan Chicago, with a similar population, has about 110 units of local government. Furthermore, the central *municipio* of a Brazilian metropolis usually contains a much higher percentage of metropolitan population than does its North American counterpart.

Under the post-1964 regime, urban managers devoted little effort to reconciling the interests of different citizen groups. Decisions could be made on a "technical" base. In fact, urban planning and management decisions have been made as if the technicians were biased in favor of maximizing the welfare of the upper and middle classes, who benefited from the clearance of eyesore slums and the erection of limited access highways for their private cars. This bias is not uncommon in cities of the developing world (Linn, 1983).

As the Brazilian political system has opened up, urban managers have become more sensitive to some of the same pressures that existed prior to 1964.

Urban planning and management

Brazilian urban managers have several instruments for shaping the structure and quality of life in their cities. First, how much and where municipalities invest in infrastructure can have a great impact on the development of urban form. Of particular importance are transportation thoroughfares, water and sewerage mains, and parks.

Second, cities can select the range and level of social services. In Brazil, the range of municipal functions is virtually limited to the operation of the physical infrastructure. Indeed, nearly half of the budgets of cities is traditionally devoted to the provision of water, sewerage, and sanitation (*Anuário Estatístico do Brasil*, various years). In the arena of transit, the municipality may opt to run its own bus lines or to contract them out, but virtually all other operating agencies are public monopolies. About one tenth of operating budgets is spent on transit systems. Cities spend about one fifth of their operating budgets on social services (health, education, and social work), and they would not be prohibited, for example, from expanding their activities into day-care operations.

Third, cities can select the method of financing the infrastructure and services they provide. Basically the choice boils down to a mix of property taxes, license fees, and user charges. Utilities and other municipal services, like buses, are generally priced below cost. In the period of 1945 to 1964, only about one quarter of the operating cost of water, sewerage, and sanitation was financed by user fees (*Anuário Estatístico do Brasil*, various years). Since 1964, greater reliance has been placed on user charges, and the pricing of urban services below their marginal cost has come under considerable criticism.[6]

Fourth, cities can regulate land use through zoning, subdivision control, environmental health codes, and public ownership of open space. The external diseconomies of unrestricted vertical development have come under criticism. The right to build additional stories on a high-rise structure can be viewed as the creation of land ("*solo criado*"). Critics suggest the public appropriation of all or a portion of the land values associated with development rights.[7]

The utilization of these instruments in an environment of rapid urban growth is undoubtedly difficult. In a rural setting, where little is invested in infrastructure and where congestion and pollution are less salient, the pressures created by moderate population growth on public managers can be relatively minor. In an urban setting, however, rapid population growth creates automatic pressures on public managers as the water supply becomes contaminated, garbage piles up on the street, and road traffic comes to a standstill. These pressures would seem proportional to the rate of population change rather than to the level of population and thus may be almost as acute in small cities as in large ones.

There are no obvious solutions to the managerial problems created by rapid urban population growth. While smaller cities may learn from the larger cities that have been there before, each city is a unique configuration of economic, political, and cultural forces. The prospect of rapid population change for the foreseeable future indicates the necessity for first-rate urban managers. This is a hope, not a prediction. Without relying entirely on a "great man" theory of urban development, innovations in municipal finance and governance can help.

Neither North American nor Brazilian cities have developed adequate mechanisms for recapturing increments in land values created by public investment. The growth of land values at any particular site is largely a function of forces beyond the control of the owner. These are the growth in metropolitan population and income, changes in the accessibility of the site to jobs, and investments in municipal infrastructure.

Vetter *et al.* (1981) performed a fascinating study of the effect of utility infrastructure on urban structure in Rio. They found that higher income groups were more likely to live in central neighborhoods which were well supplied with water and sewerage, and other amenities such as parks. The availability of water and sewerage had a positive impact on land values when access to the sea or the central business district was held constant. In the mid-1970s, the higher the proportion of upper- and middle-income families in a neighborhood, the greater would be the magnitude of investments in this infrastructure. Since water and sewer services were priced below cost and since effective property tax rates were lower in the favored neighborhoods, these investments had regressive income effects.

A betterment tax is an ingenious way of recapturing a portion of the capital gain to landowners whose properties adjoin the infrastructure investment. In terms of both efficiency and equity, such taxation is the least distortive of all. Taxing land as opposed to taxing improvements has the advantages of reducing the incentive for speculative holding of idle land and also reducing the disincentive to build. Betterment or site-value taxation is equitable because it lays the fiscal burden on landowners whose properties capitalize the benefits from municipal services and infrastructure. For the financially strapped municipalities, the ability to recapture land value increments due to municipal betterments can be appealing. Highly developed in Columbia and Taiwan, this instrument of urban management merits careful attention in Brazil (Linn, 1983, pp. 156–57).

Incremental site-value taxation is conducive to local democracy. If a neighborhood votes to accept a betterment-*cum*-tax, then the municipal government has an indication that the expected benefits exceed the expected costs. This tax thus appears both equitable and efficient in terms of allocating scarce public funds to those who can benefit most from them.

Traffic Congestion

In order to function, a city must solve the problems of transporting people back and forth from domiciles to work places and moving goods within the city as well as back and forth to the hinterland. All this movement occurs on public thoroughfares of limited capacity, and to which all vehicles and pedestrians have free access. The entry of an additional vehicle during rush hours, which in many cities can last virtually all day, increases the traveling time of other vehicles and pedestrians on the thoroughfare. Such congestion is a classic case of an external diseconomy. The growth of population and traffic only increases this diseconomy.

Though comprehensive data are lacking, the costs of urban transportation and the resulting congestion in big Brazilian cities are clearly large. In metropolitan São Paulo, the median commuting time to work was about 45 minutes each way (Prefeitura, 1968, vol. 1, p. 117). For low-income workers, the costs of commuting in time and money are even more significant. Slum dwellers resettled on the periphery of Rio spend an average of 15 percent of the minimum salary and as much as 25 percent, in addition to two to three hours daily (Fortuna, Villaça, and Couto *e* Silva, 1974; Perlman, 1976). Slum dwellers resettled on the outskirts of Brasilia spend as much as 40 percent of the minimum salary on commuting (CODEPLAN, 1971).

The regulations on bus service also can contribute to congestion. For example, the inability of buses in Rio to utilize tunnels and expressways slows down commuting for all classes, and requires excessive transfers (Barat, 1973). Because of price controls on fares, private bus firms tend to offer infrequent service in low-density routes where middle- and upper-income groups predominate. As a result these individuals may be encouraged to purchase a car, which contributes to congestion and increases the inconvenience on such individuals. A solution to this vicious cycle would be the removal of price controls and the encouragement of a high-tariff luxury bus service.[8]

A most interesting and practical approach is to restrict access to major thoroughfares or to lanes within those thoroughfares to mass transit vehicles or to small vehicles like motorbikes. Curitiba's former mayor, James Lerner, significantly improved the flow of bus traffic by the creation of special bus lanes (Barat, 1979). This approach is now being attempted in Rio and other large cities. A complementary strategy is the prohibition of on-street parking in the central business district and the setting of high fees in parking lots.

In addition to reducing demand, the supply of thoroughfares may have to expand in growing cities. The costs of expanding capacity are immense, as indicated by the $2 billion Rio–Niteroi bridge and the $8 billion dollar São Paulo subway (Andreazza, 1973). Financing these expensive investments is a major problem. Since it is impractical to finance all but a few facilities by tolls or user charges, taxation must be employed. General property taxation may be workable for expenditures whose benefits are widely dispersed, but may be inappropriate to investments whose benefits are highly concentrated. Again, betterment taxes are recommended.

Pollution and Environmental Health

In premodern rural societies, waste residuals from production and consumption activity are invariably recycled. Those effluents that are emitted into the air or discharged into the surface or groundwater are easily assimilated by the inherent self-cleansing capacity of the biosphere. In urbanized settings, not only is the density of such residuals much higher, but many of them are synthetics which are not easily biodegradable. Human and industrial waste may seep into the groundwater, which is the major drinking source, thus spreading infectious diseases. In 19th century Europe, for example, the mortality rate in cities exceeded those in the countryside.

Environmental health hazards in Brazilian cities are a far cry from those dingy European cities, however. If industrial pollution were a major influence on health, then life expectancy would be lower in the more industrialized cities and regions. In fact, just the opposite is the case: less industrialized cities and regions have lower life expectancy. Interestingly, within regions, the proportion of the population with caloric intake below World Health Organization standards is higher in the cities than in the countryside (Morley, 1981, table 5.4). There are, however, relatively minor urban-rural differences in life expectancy and infant mortality both nationally and within states (Merrick and Graham, 1979, table X-4; Merrick, 1985, table 4). Clearly, the superior income and housing opportunities provided in more industrialized regions offset any debilitation from environmental pollution and malnutrition among the poor.

Increasing segregation by income groups may have an indirect effect on environmental health. High-income families, to whom time is relatively valuable, tend to throw away rather than maintain or resell disposable articles.

Because of Brazil's highly unequal income distribution, large numbers of poor people find it profitable to collect and resell newspapers, bottles, and broken gadgets which can be repaired or cannibalized. As affluent neighborhoods become less accessible to the poor, less recycling is likely to occur and the logistics of garbage and trash disposal become more difficult. As the informal recycling system withers away, urban residents become increasingly subject to failures in the formal system of sanitation. Thus strikes of municipal workers or mechanical breakdowns may pose a greater health hazard in the future.

Studies of urban environmental quality and health in Brazil are just beginning. The palpably low quality of air in some Brazilian cities is likely to raise the incidence of respiratory and pulmonary disease in the future. Because many of these diseases may take 20 years for manifestation, the health costs of heavy industrialization since 1945 have yet to be realized.

A sanitary water supply becomes a more serious problem in cities than in the rural areas because of the contamination of ground and surface water by human and industrial wastes. Brazil has been making outstanding progress in extending water networks, especially since the 1960s. Only one home in six had running water in 1950; only one home in five in 1960; only one home in three in 1970. By 1980, over half of the homes enjoyed running water. In urban areas the share of homes with running water increased from 42 percent in 1960 to 55 percent in 1970, to 76 percent by 1980.[9] By the 1970s, nearly three quarters of the homes in cities with more than 50,000 inhabitants were served with running water; but only one third in cities with 2,000 to 20,000 inhabitants (*Anuário Estatístico do Brasil*, various years, tables 4.2.1.1-.2). In São Paulo, 83 percent of the homes were served by running water by the mid-1960s (Governo, 1968, vol. 3).

Progress in providing treated water to rural populations has been slower. In 1970, only 3 percent of the rural households were served by water networks, about 25 percent by wells, and the remainder by "other" or "undeclared" sources. By 1980, the percentage served by water networks had hardly risen at all, but those served by wells had increased dramatically to 62 percent.

The diffusion of central sewerage has lagged behind the diffusion of water supply. In 1970, only 22 percent of urban dwellings were served by sewerage; by 1980, nearly 50 percent. Virtually, no rural households were served by sewerage. Because septic tanks may be a workable alternative in rural areas and small towns, the urgency of sewerage investments in those areas is obviously less.

Because most urban infrastructure is developed from the center outward, areas not served by water and sanitation tend to be inhabited by the poorer residences with larger households. In São Paulo, the 85 percent of dwellings served by water housed only 55 percent of the inhabitants. Of families earning below the minimum salary in 1968 (Governo, 1968, vol. 3), only 60 percent were served by running water. By 1978, differential access to sanitary water remained pronounced (IPT, 1978, table 3.3). About 90 percent of neighborhoods with median income above the minimum salary (about 2800 NCr$ in 1978) enjoyed water; about 53 percent of neighborhoods with median incomes one half the minimum salary enjoyed water; and only 21 percent of neighborhoods with median income one third the minimum salary enjoyed water. Similarly, 59 percent of all homes were served by sanitary sewerage in 1968, but only 40 percent of households earning below the minimum salary were served by sanitary sewers. In contrast, refuse collection covers virtually the entire population—about 84 percent of the homes and 90 percent of the population (Governo, 1968, vols. 3 and 5).

These results can be generalized throughout Brazil: central portions of metropolitan areas are less likely to be served by running water than the periphery; larger cities are more likely to be served by running water than smaller cities (Merrick and Graham, 1979, table VIII-11 & -12). In contrast to the 55 percent of urban residents receiving piped water in Brazil in 1970, 88 percent receive water in Malaysia. Fully 40 percent of rural Malaysians received piped water in 1970 (Fisk and Osman-Rani, 1981, table 3.10), a figure yet to be reached in Brazil.

As noted, public utilities in Brazilian cities are only partially financed by user charges. Because they are relatively restricted to more affluent neighborhoods, income is regressively redistributed. This need not be the case. In Malaysia, for example, user charges fully cover the cost of water utilities in most cities. However, by pricing water on a block-increasing basis and on a regionally differentiated basis, the water system redistributes some income from urban to rural areas and from wealthier to poorer families. While not the most efficient form of income redistribution, the Malaysian pattern is progressive and merits consideration in Brazil (Katzman, 1978b).

Crime

One striking generalization from urban sociology is the degree to which crime increases with city size (Katzman, 1981). This phenomenon is explained as a result of (1) the increasing proportion of daily contacts among strangers, and as a result the diminution in personal obligations as a mechanism on constraint; and (2) the opportunities for enrichment of the poor offered by the juxtaposition of different income groups. The emerging literature on the rational criminal indicates that acts of property crime are expressions of a calculus in which the probability and severity of punishment are weighed against the expected value of the booty.

In patrimonial societies like rural Brazil, norms of social relations provide the upper-income groups with a protective social distance from victimization by the poor. In the absence of social mechanisms of achieving distance from the lower class, the North American middle class achieves such distance by housing segregation. Such segregation raises the "commuting costs" of potential larcenists. Thus the North American dream home can be built with an open architecture, surrounded by a picket fence that has aesthetic rather than security value.

The apparent increase in property crime in Brazilian cities is not difficult to understand. First, the norms of interclass etiquette from Brazil's patrimonial heritage wither away in the urban environment, and the poor no longer "know their place" in public spaces. Second, the increasing disparity of wealth between rich and poor increases the returns to criminal activities on the part of the poor. Third, a diminished perception of the fairness of the Brazilian system for distributing rewards reduces the legitimacy of norms.

Given the income distribution of Brazil, one should expect rewards to property crime to increase. The rich may respond by altering their housing patterns. Demand for single-family homes may decline while that for apartments, protected by *zeladors*, may increase. Thus the maldistribution of income in Brazil may shape its urban form.

Housing

Squatting and self-built housing by the poor has been a major aspect of Brazilian cities. Such dwellings accounted for nearly half of the construction in São Paulo during the 1960s (Prefeitura, 1969, vol. 3). Crowded jerry-built dwellings are the most permanent and photogenic characteristics of poverty. Slums generally horrify the middle class, both those who sympathize with the poor and those who fear the poor. Because of its visibility, poor housing has tended to define urban problems and policies throughout the world.

The first intra-urban problem recognized in national economic plans was inadequate housing. In 1964, the major instrument for urban policy in Brazil was established: the National Housing Bank (BNH), which channels the forced savings of employees into the housing market. Mandated to provide housing for the poorest urban classes, BNH encountered a contradiction between this goal and its necessity to remain self-financing. The bank found that few of the poorest families were willing or able to afford "standard" quality housing, even when amortization was spaced to reduce monthly payments to only 20 percent of income. Consequently, BNH has shifted its loan portfolio from the low-income market to the middle- and upper-income markets. In 1964 and 1965, 90 percent of the units and 80 percent of the loans were devoted to low-income housing, built by various state and local housing corporations (COHABS). In 1967, the share of units and loans destined for this market fell to 40 and 23 percent respectively. By 1974, after ten years of operation, only 20 percent of the units financed by BNH were in the low-income market.

BNH has played a major role in the clearance of slums. In many Brazilian cities, self-help housing in centrally located areas has been demolished and replaced by subsidized housing for the middle class. The poor are often relocated in subsidized housing on the periphery. Exhaustive research has indicated that many of the poor are unable to pay the rent and utilities in these subsidized dwellings (Perlman, 1976; Katzman, 1977, chap. 11; Portes, 1978). Moreover, relocated families lost cheap access to "marginal" employment in the center.

A burgeoning revisionist literature suggests that slum housing is less disturbing to the poor than the malnutrition, lack of income, and job insecurity that pervade their lives. In fact, many slum dwellers in Brazil view themselves as upwardly mobile, relative to their rural origins, and view their homes as a major capital asset to be nurtured (Leeds, 1973; Perlman, 1976).

On net, it is hard to escape the conclusion that Brazilian housing policy, especially the housing finance system, has been detrimental to the poor. While slums are no longer demolished, a system for establishing clear title to urban homesites and for financing small purchases of building materials has yet to be developed.

CONCLUSIONS

The rapid growth of urban populations since 1945 is seen as an epiphenomenon. As was correctly intuited by early national development plans, the rapidity of urbanization and the slow growth of industrial employment are understood as the spatial expressions of macroeconomic phenomena, conditioned by Brazilian institutions and policies. As urban minimum wages and rural wages converge, the rapidity of urban growth, poor industrial labor absorption, and the bloated service sectors are withering away as problems.

The analysis of urban problems in this chapter diverges from that conventionally employed by Brazilian policymakers and their critics in the following respects:

First, the historical pace of Brazilian urbanization was neither a technical requirement of industrialization nor an inevitable outcome of dependent authoritarian capitalism. Brazilian policymakers could have altered the urban-rural balance by improving the opportunities for the rural masses. Concrete steps include protecting squatters and smallholders in frontier settlement schemes, providing fair access to agricultural credit and extension services, and increasing accessibility to schooling, water, electricity, and hospitals. In recent years, impressive strides have been made in extending public services, but little has been done to establish a prosperous class of smallholders.

Second, in contrast to the perceptions of most Brazilian urbanists, the "hyperconcentration" of the urban population in São Paulo and Rio de Janeiro is viewed as a nonproblem. The urban population has been widely dispersed among the nation's cities and towns since 1940, and primacy has been decreasing or stable thereafter. Brazilian cities adhere to a rank-size distribution, but this phenomenon is viewed here as a devoid of normative content.

Third, all observers agree that Brazilian cities play an important role in facilitating industrial development. The establishment of growth poles based on large-scale capital-intensive enterprises, however, has led to a cul-de-sac. Needed are policies that maximize the opportunities for small-scale entrepreneurship and that stimulate the self-generating agglomeration of diversified small businesses. There is no formula for success, but current policies that provide differential access to credit and licenses for large capital-intensive firms is likely to be counterproductive in the long run.

Fourth, the role of cities as growth centers for rural development has been relatively neglected. Again, there is no magic formula for creating viable middle-sized and small industrial towns in rural areas. The ongoing expansion of rural electrification, secondary highways, paved farm-to-market roads, and workable telecommunications is encouraging. This infrastructure enables firms in middle-sized satellite cities to avoid the congestion of the metropolis, where land and labor are more costly, without forsaking the economies of agglomeration.

Fifth, the problems of urban management (congestion, pollution, and inadequate public utilities) that plagued Brazilian cities in the postwar period are viewed here as growing pains. These will diminish as urban managers acquire experience with what works and what does not.

Brazilian urban managers have had notable success in expanding the network of water and sewerage and in reducing traffic congestion. More efficient and equitable management of this infrastructure is achievable by employing instruments such as betterment taxes and progressive utility rates. The removal of authoritarian restraints, however, will increasingly politicize urban management decisions. Policies that favored the upper-income groups, clothed in the guise of technical verity, will come under enhanced scrutiny by lower-income pressure groups.

Finally, Brazilian cities will continue to play an important part in the modernization of popular attitudes. The urban Brazil of today has lower fertility rates, higher levels of education, and a greater degree of participation in civic life than the predominantly rural Brazil of 1945.

What is Brazil's urban future? Will Brazil become a nation where the vast majority of the population lives in giant metropolises? Does a projected population of 200 million by the year 2000 (Merrick and Graham, 1979, table XII–1) imply the unimaginable equivalent of building four or five more São Paulos?

A resource-rich nation like Brazil is unlikely to become totally metropolitan. A relevant standard may be the resource-rich United States, where the growth rates of urbanized and rural areas now balance, and where only 60 percent of the population lives in urbanized areas. With 52 percent of its inhabitants living in cities of over 20,000 population, Brazil has nearly completed its urban transition. As in the United States in recent decades, most urban growth is likely to occur in middle-sized cities and in those small towns which are within striking distance of an advanced metropolis. Brazil's urban future does not require the construction of five São Paulos, but rather hundreds of Piracicabas. This is no trivial challenge, but certainly not insuperable. Brazilian urban planners and policymakers can surely look forward to interesting times.

APPENDIX

Central Place Theory

Central Place Theory (Beavon, 1977) assumes that each agricultural region is polarized around an entrepôt that channels its trade with the rest of the world. Farm households are uniformly distributed within each region at a density which depends upon soil fertility and the nature of the staple crop. Households are assumed to demand a variety of goods and services which depend upon income and prices. Some of these commodities are consumer goods; others intermediate goods necessary for agricultural production, such as milling or marketing. Because these nonagricultural activities enjoy increasing returns to scale within the relevant range, they may be undertaken at a central place rather than at the household level if demand is sufficient.

The price a household pays for each commodity equals the factory price plus the transport cost from the factory to the farm site. Since real prices increase with distance between these two points, demand per household tends to decrease with distance.

For a given factory price, the demand facing nonagricultural enterprises can be represented by a cone, the height of which reflects the quantity demanded at any point; the radius, the distance between production and consumption points; and the volume, the total quantity demanded. By equalizing marginal costs and revenues, the enterprise selects that combination of price and quantity that maximizes profits, and which incidentally determines its market area.

NOTES

1. An urban settlement connotes an agglomeration of a nonagricultural population. In practice, governments classify settlements as urban vs. rural on the basis of population or function rather than by the occupation of their inhabitants. Brazil classifies seats of municipalities and districts as urban. The United States classifies as urban those settlements containing more than 2,000 inhabitants.

2. In 1870, when one fourth of all Americans lived in cities, nearly 60 percent of the urban workers in New England, the most industrialized region, were employed in manufactures (Williamson, 1965). In that same year, nearly 30 percent of the urban workers in the American South, the most backward region, were employed in manufacturing, a level higher than virtually any large Brazilian city, save São Paulo.

3. In 1971, the Secretariat of Planning of the State of São Paulo initiated a series of subregional studies in order to provide information to potential investors in the interior. Under the general title of Coordenaria de Ação Regional, *Diagnostico*, these descriptive studies are entirely devoid of analytic content.

4. The rank-size formula is $P_r = P_1/r^a$, where a equals unity. The coefficients of determination for this expression are .91, .95, and .96 for 1940, 1950, and 1960, respectively. The corresponding estimates for a are .84, .83, and .90, which are significantly less than unity.

5. Growth pole theory was first propounded in Francois Perroux, "Note sur la notion de 'pole de croissance,' " *Economie Appliquee*, 8 (Jan.–June 1953):307–20 and brought into the mainstream literature in Albert Hirschman, *The Strategy of Economic Development* (New Haven: Yale University Press, 1958). For discussions and assessments of this concept, see Antoni Kuklinksi (ed.), *Growth Poles and Growth Centers* (Hague: Mouton, 1972).

6. "Desenvolvimento urbano—Alguns considerações," *Conjuntura Econômica*, 30 (Julho 1976):103–5.

7. "Solo criado—uso e problema," *Conjuntura Econômica*, 31 (Julho 1977):81–3.

8. "Desenvolviment urbano," *loc. cit.*

9. Tabulações Avançados, Censos Demografico, Brasil, 1980, table 6.

REFERENCES

Adams, D.W. and Nehman, G.I., "Borrowing costs and the demand for rural credit," *Journal of Development Studies*, 15 (Spring 1979):165–176.

Andrade, Thompson A. and Lodder, Celsius A., *Sistema Urbano e Cidades Médias no Brasil*, IPEA, Relatorio de Pesquisa, No. 43, 1979.

Andreazza, Mario D., "A Ponte Rio–Niterói: Dados e previsões," *Revista de Administração Municipal*, 119 (Jul./Ag. 1973):55–65.

Bacha, Edmar, "Crescimento econômico, salários urbanos e rurais: O caso do Brasil," *Pesquisa e Planejamento Econômico*, 9 (1979):585–628.

Baer, Werner and Samuelson, Larry, "Toward a service-oriented growth strategy," *World Development*, 9 (1981):499–514.

Barat, Josef, "Transporte e ecologia," *Revista de Administração Municipal*, 119 (Jul./Ag. 1973):19–34.

Barat, Josef, "Passenger transportation in metropolitan areas," *Brazilian Economic Studies*, 5 (1979):163–190.

Beavon, K.S.O., *Central Place Theory: A Reinterpretation* (London: Longman, 1977).

Beckmann, Martin, "City hierarchies and the distribution of city size," *Economic Development and Cultural Change*, 6 (April 1958): 243–248.

Berquó, Elza S., *et al.*, "Níveles y variaciones de la fecundidad en São Paulo," *Millbank Memorial Fund Quarterly*, 46 (July 1968):185–205.

Boisier, Sergio, *et al.*, *Desenvolvimento Regional e Urbano: Diferenciais de Productividade e Salários Industriais*, IPEA, Relatório de Pesquisa, No. 15, 1973.

Camargo, C., Procópio, F., and Berquó, Elza S., *Diferenciais de Fertilidade*, CEBRAP, 1970.

Cardoso, Ruth C.L., "Movimentos sociais urbanos: Balanço crítico," in Bernard Sorj and Maria Herminia Taveres de Almeida (eds.), *Sociedade e Política no Brasil pós–64* (São Paulo: Brasiliense, 1983), pp.215–39.

Cline, William R., *Economic Consequences of Land Reform in Brazil* (Amsterdam: North-Holland Publishing Co., 1970).

CODEPLAN, Governo do Distrito Federal, *Diagnóstico do Setor Transporte do Distrito Federal*, 1971.

Costa, Manoel, "Urbanização brasileira: Visão quantitativa," IPEA, mimeo, 1970, table II.

Dean, Warren, "Latifundia and land policy in nineteenth century Brazil," *Hispanic American Historic Review*, 51 (Nov. 1971):606–25.

Epstein, David, *Brasília: The Plan and the Reality* (Berkeley: University of California Press, 1973).

Faria, Vilmar, "Desenvolvimento. urbanização, e mudanças na estrutura do emprego: A experiência brasileiro dos últimos trinta anos," in Bernard Sorj and Maria Herminia Taveres de Almeida (eds.), *Sociedade e Política no Brasil pós–64* (São Paulo: Brasiliense, 1983), pp. 118–63.

Faria, Vilmar, "Changes in the Composition of Employment and the Structure of Occupations" in this volume.

Fei, John C.H. and Ranis, Gustav, *Development of the Labor-Surplus Economy: Theory and Policy* (Homewood, IL: Richard D. Irwin, 1964).

Fei, John C.H.; Ranis, Gustav; and Kuo, Shirley. W.Y., *Growth with Equity: The Taiwan Case*, World Bank Research Publication (New York: Oxford University Press, 1979).

Ferreira, Carlos Maurício de C. "A study of identification and selection of development poles in the State of Minas Gerais," presented to Colóquio sobre Desigualdades Regionais do Desenvolvimento, União Geografica Internacional, Vitoria, Brasil, Abril 1971.

Fisk, E.K. and Osman-Rani, H. (eds.), *The Political Economy of Malaysia* (New York: Oxford University Press, 1982).

Flynn, Peter, *Brazil: A Political Analysis* (London: Ernest Benn and Boulder: Westview Press, 1978).

Forman, Shepard, *The Brazilian Peasantry* (New York: Columbia University Press, 1975).

Fortuna, Affonso; Villaça, Marcio; and Couto e Silva, Wilma, "Valores urbanos e habitação popular," *Revista de Administração Municipal*, 122 (Jan./Feb 1974):49–78.

Foweraker, Joe, *The Struggle for Land: A Political Economy of the Pioneer Frontier in Brazil from 1930 to the Present Day*, Cambridge Latin American Studies (London: Cambridge University Press, 1981).

Frank, Andre Gunder, *Capitalism and Underdevelopment in Latin America* (New York: Monthly Review Press, 1967).

Geiger, Pedro Pinchas, "Urbanização e industrialização na orla oriental de Baía de Guanabara," *Revista Brasileira de Geografia*, 18 (Out. 1956):495–525.

Goodman, David E., "The Brazilian economic 'miracle' and regional policy: Some evidence from the urban Northeast," *Journal of Latin American Studies*, 8 (1976): 1–27.

Goodman, David E., "Rural economy and society," this volume.

Governo do Estado de São Paulo, Secretaria da Economia e Planejamento, *Diagnóstico Definitivo: Análise Macroeconômica da Região de Grande São Paulo*, 3 vols, 1969.

Grupo Executivo da Região Metropolitana (GERM), Pôrto Alegre, Plano de Desenvolimento Metropolitana, 3 vols., 1973.

Harris, John M. and Todaro, Michael P., "Migration, unemployment and development: A two-sector analysis," *American Economic Review*, 60 (March 1970): 126–142.

Hoselitz, Bert, "Parasitic and generative cities," in *idem, Sociological Aspects of Economic Growth* (Glencoe, IL: Free Press, 1960).

Instituto Brasileiro de Geografia (IBGE), *Microregiões homogêneas*, 1968.

Instituto de Pesquisas Tecnológicas de Estado de São Paulo, S.A. (IPT), Contribuição para análise intraurbanos de São Paulo: Caracterização de mercado das imóveis, April 1978.

Katzman, Martin T., "Urbanização e concentração industrial: 1940/70," *Pesquisa e Planejamento Econômico*, 4 (Dez. 1974):475–532.

Katzman, Martin T., *Cities and Frontiers in Brazil: Regional Dimensions of Economic Development* (Cambridge: Harvard University Press, 1977).

Katzman, Martin T., "São Paulo and its hinterland: Evolving relationships and the rise of an industrial power," in John Wirth and Robert L. Jones (eds.), *Manchester and São Paulo: Problems of Rapid Urban Growth* (Stanford: Stanford University Press, 1978a), pp. 107–130.

Katzman, Martin T., "Progressive public utility rates as an income redistribution device in developing countries," in J.F.J. Toye (ed.), *Taxation and Development* (London: Frank Cass, 1978b), pp. 174–192.

Katzman, Martin T., "The supply of criminals: A geo-economic examination," in

Simon Hakim and George Rengert (eds.), *Crime Spillover* (Beverly Hills, CA: Sage Publications, 1981), chap. 9.

Keen, David J. and Townroe, Peter M., "Polarization reversal in the state of São Paulo, Brazil," The World Bank, Urban and Regional Report No. 81–16, 1981.

Keller, Elza C.S., "As funções regionais e a zona de influência de Campinas," *Revista Brasileira de Geografia*, 31 (Abril/Junho 1969):3–39.

Kelley, Allen C. and Williamson, Jeffrey G., *Lessons from Japanese Development* (Chicago: University of Chicago Press, 1974).

Kelley, Allen C. and Williamson, Jeffrey G., "A computable general equilibrium model of third-world urbanization and city growth: Preliminary comparative statics," in Allen C. Kelley, Warren C. Sanderson, and Jeffrey G. Williamson (eds.), *Modeling Growing Economies in Equilibrium and Disequilibrium* (Durham, N.C.: Duke Press Policy Studies, 1983), pp. 3–42.

Kutcher, Gary P. and Scandizzo, Pasquale, *The Agricultural Economy of Northeast Brazil*, World Bank Research Publication (Baltimore: Johns Hopkins University Press, 1981).

Lampard, Eric E., "The evolving system of cities in the United States," in Harvey S. Perloff and Lowdon Wingo, Jr. (eds.), *Issues in Urban Economics* (Baltimore: Johns Hopkins Press, 1968), pp.81–140.

Lasuen, Jose Ramon, "On growth poles," in Niles M. Hansen (ed.), *Growth Centers in Regional Economic Development* (New York: Free Press, 1972).

Leeds, Anthony, "Political, economic, and social effects of producer and consumer orientations toward housing in Brazil and Peru," in Francine Rabinovitz and Felicity Trueblood (eds.), *Latin American Urban Research* (Beverly Hills: Sage Publications, 1973), pp.181–215.

Leme, Rui Aguiar da Silva, Contribuições a Teoria da Localização Industrial, Faculdade de Ciências Econômicas e Administrativas, Universidade de São Paulo, *Boletim* No. 39, 1965.

Linn, Johannes F., *Cities in the Developing World: Policies for their Equitable and Efficient Growth*, World Bank Report (New York: Oxford University Press, 1983).

Margolis, Maxine L., *The Moving Frontier: Social and Economic Change in a Southern Brazilian Community*, Latin American Monographs, 2nd series, no. 11 (Gainesville: University of Florida, 1973).

Mason, Edward *et al.*, *The Economic and Social Modernization of the Republic of Korea* (Cambridge: Harvard University Press, 1980).

Meerman, Jacob, *Public Expenditure in Malaysia: Who Benefits and Why*, World Bank Research Publication (New York: Oxford University Press, 1979).

Merrick, Thomas W. and Graham, Douglas H., *Population and Economic Development in Brazil: 1800 to the Present* (Baltimore: Johns Hopkins University Press, 1979).

Merrick, Thomas W., "Brazil's population since 1945," this volume (1985).

Morley, Samuel A., *Labor Markets and Inequitable Growth: The Case of Authoritarian Capitalism in Brazil* (London, Cambridge University Press, 1982).

Morse, Richard, *From Community to Metropolis: A Biography of São Paulo*, Brazil (Gainesville: University of Florida Press, 1958).

Morse, Richard, "Recent research on Latin American urbanization," *Latin American Research Review*, 1 (Fall 1965):35–74.

Morse, Richard, "Trends and issues in Latin American urban research, 1965–1970," *Latin American Research Review*, 6 (Spring/Summer 1971):19–76.

Nelson, Joan, Urban Poverty and Instability in Developing Nations, Center for International Affairs, Harvard University, Occasional Papers, No.22, 1969.

Perlman, Janice E., *The Myth of Marginality: Urban Poverty and Politics in Rio de Janeiro* (Berkeley: University of California, 1976).

Portes, Alejandro, "Housing policy, urban poverty, and the state: The favelas of Rio de Janeiro, 1972–76," *Latin American Research Review*, 14. #2 (1977):3–24.

Prebisch, Raul, "Economic development in Latin America and its problems," United Nations (1950), reprinted in Economic Bulletin for Latin America, 7 (Feb. 1962):1–22.

Prefeitura de São Paulo, *Metrô: Sistema Integrado de Transporte Rápido Coletivo da Cidade de São Paulo*, 2 vols., Hochtief–Montreal–Deconsult, 1968.

Prefeitura de São Paulo, *Plano Urbanístico Básico*, 6 vols., Asplan–Leo A. Daly–Montreal–Wilbur Smith, 1969.

Rebouças, Osmundo, "Interregional effects of economic policies: Multi-sectoral general equilibrium estimates for Brazil," unpublished doctoral dissertation, Harvard University, 1974.

Ribeiro, Miguel Angelo Campos and de Almeida, Roberto Schmidt, "A estrutura de fluxos dos estabelecimentos industriais da Área Metropolitana de Recife," *Revista Brasileira de Geografia*, 42 (Abr./Jun. 1980):203–64.

Rios, Jose Artur, "The growth of cities and urban development," in John Saunders (ed.), *Modern Brazil* (Gainesville: University of Florida Press, 1971).

Sanders, John, "Mechanization and employment in Brazilian agriculture, 1950–1971," unpublished doctoral dissertation, University of Minnesota, 1973.

da Silva, Elisabeth de Gesu Vianna, "O Metropolitano e a renovação urbana do Catete," *Revista Brasileira de Geografia*, 43 (Jul./Set. 1981):359–81.

Singer, Paul, *Desenvolvimento Econômico e Evolução Urbana* (São Paulo: Editora Nacional, 1968).

Smolka, Martin O. and Lodder, Celsius A., "Concentração, tamanho urbano e estrutura industrial," *Pesquisa e Planejamento Econômico*, 3 (Junho 1973):447–68.

Sorj, Bernard and Wilkinson, John, "Processos sociais e formas de produção na agricultura brasileira," in Bernard Sorj and Maria Herminia Taveres de Almeida (eds.), *Sociedade e Política no Brasil pós-64* (Sao Paulo: Brasiliense, 1983), pp. 164–214.

Suarez-Villa, Luis, "Rank size distributions, city size hierarchies, and the Beckmann model: Some empirical results," *Journal of Regional Science*, 20 (Feb. 1980):91–7.

Taylor, Lance and Bacha, Edmar L., "The unequalizing spiral: A first growth model for Belindia," *Quarterly Journal of Economics*, 90 (May 1976):197–218.

Tolosa, Hamilton C., "Política nacional de desenvolvimento urbano: Uma visão economica," *Pesquisa e Planejamento Econômico*, 2 (Junho 1972a):143–55.

Tolosa, Hamilton C., "Pólos de Crescimento: Teoria e política econômica," in Paulo

Haddad (ed.), *Planejamento Regional: Métodos e aplicação ao caso brasileiro*, IPEA, Série monográfica, no. 8, 1972b, pp. 189–244.

Tolosa, Hamilton C., "Macroeconômica de urbanização brasileira," *Pesquisa e Planejamento Econômico*, 3 (Out. 1973):585–644.

Tolosa, Hamilton C. and Reiner, Thomas A., "The economic programming of a system of planned growth poles," *Economic Geography*, 46 (July 1970).

Vetter, David Michael, "A segregação de população economicamente ativa na Região Metropolitana de Rio De Janeiro," *Revista Brasileira de Geografia*, 43 (Out./Dez. 1981):587–603.

Vetter, David Michael; Massena, Rosa Maria Ramalho; and Rodrigues, Elza Freire, "Espaço, valor da terra e equidade dos investimentos em infra-estrutura do Município do Rio de Janeiro," *Revista Brasileira de Geografia*, 41 (Jan./Jun. 1979):32–71.

Wilheim, Jorge, *Urbanismo no Subdesenvolvimento* (Rio: N.P., 1969).

Wilkening, E.A.; Pinto, João Bosco; and Pastore, José, "The role of the extended family in migration and adaptation in Brazil," *Journal of Marriage and the Family* (Nov. 1968):689–95.

Williamson, Jeffrey G., "Urbanization in the American Northeast, 1820–1870," in Robert W. Fogel and Stanley L. Engerman (eds.), *The Reinterpretation of American Economic History* (New York: Harper and Row, 1971), chap. 32.

Williamson, Jeffrey G., *Late Nineteenth Century American Development: A General Equilibrium History* (London: Cambridge University Press, 1974).

World Bank, *World Development Report* (Washington, D.C.: International Bank for Reconstruction and Development, annual).

Yap, Lorene Y.L., "Internal migration and economic development in Brazil," *Quarterly Journal of Economics*, 90 (Feb. 1976):119–37.

4

Changes in the Composition of Employment and the Structure of Occupations

Vilmar Faria

INTRODUCTION

The aim of this essay is to examine the transformations that have taken place in the occupational structure of Brazil over the past thirty years. The examination of this aspect of the recent Brazilian process is a crucial point of reference in studying social change in the country because the structure of employment and of occupations constitutes an aspect of the socioeconomic organization of a society that best reflects its structural configuration.

Moreover, from a theoretical point of view, some of the most important controversies regarding the nature of the economic development process in areas located outside the hegemonic centers of the world economy concern the consequences—for the dynamics of the different sectors of the economy and, therefore, for employment—that result from the prevailing way in which these countries are integrated into the international social division of labor.

Finally, one of the crucial problems that must be continually addressed by government policies is the creation of new jobs that provide the opportunity for vast segments of the population to enter the labor market.

Though this study could be carried out from several points of view and at various levels of analysis, I will examine only three aspects here. First, the changes in the composition of employment sectors that occurred between 1950 and 1980. Second, I will describe some transformations that occurred in the spatial and social profile of the Brazilian occupational structure on the basis

141

of a comparative analysis of census data from 1950 and 1980. Third, I will deal with the impact of the recent crisis on employment, analyzing the problem of official unemployment and the aggravation of the processes of informalization and "undergrounding" of sectors of the urban economy of the country.[1]

Before discussing the transformations that have occurred in the structure of occupations and employment, it is useful to keep in mind the overall picture of the transformations that Brazil has undergone in the last thirty years.

THIRTY YEARS OF ECONOMIC GROWTH AND SOCIAL CHANGE

At the end of the immediate postwar decade, the expression "essentially agricultural country" could be used to characterize Brazil superficially, although it would be inadequate if we took more profound aspects into account, especially the nature and meaning of the process already under way. The data presented in Table 4.1 justify this.[2]

First, it should be noted that 62.8 percent of the total existing housing stock in the country in 1950 was classified as rural; 78.5 percent of the population lived in rural areas, small towns or in cities of less than 20,000 inhabitants, and the proportion of total occupations connected with agriculture and mining was 57.8 percent.

So far as the structure of the economy is concerned, it is sufficient to point out that coffee sales made up 60 percent of the total exports of the country; the agricultural Economically Active Population (EAP) represented 59.9 percent of total EAP (EAP in manufacturing was little more than 9 percent of the total), and the agricultural share of national income in 1949, at current prices was 24.9 percent (in comparison with the manufacturing share, which was 20 percent). Manufacturing, although important due to the industrialization efforts of the preceding thirty years, was still conspicuously connected with "traditional" production with nondurable consumer goods representing 72.8 percent of the total value of industrial production (in 1970 Cr$). Capital goods made up a dismal 2.5 percent of the total value of industrial output while durable consumer goods made just 4.3 percent.

Around 1950, the country showed patterns of demographic dynamics characteristic of the pretransitional period with high mortality and fertility rates; it was characterized by incipient integration, whether from the point of view of spatial interrelations or from the point of view of labor and consumer markets. Public services, especially public assistance and social security, had atrophied and were directed toward privileged corporate segments (maritime workers, railway workers, banking employees, etc.) (see Faria and Barros da Silva, 1983b). A high illiteracy rate (55% among adults over the age of 15) was combined with a completely rarefied presence of the mass media: television did not exist and radio could not reach the almost 80 percent of homes which were without electricity.

Thirty years later, the generation that had learned in primary school about the essentially agricultural nature of the country, lived in a country that had changed completely. In 1980, Brazil was one of the ten important industrial economies in the world in terms of the volume of industrial output, although the implications of this should be treated with care. This change is reflected by the indicators in Table 4.1.

First of all, in 1980, 68.9 percent of the existing housing stock in the country was classified as urban; 67.7 percent of the population lived in areas considered to be urban according to the criteria of the Demographic Census, and 45.7 percent lived in cities with 20,000 inhabitants or more. As I showed in an earlier study (Faria, 1982, 1983a), in 1980 there were thirty urban agglomerations in Brazil with more than 250,000 inhabitants each, in which more than 42 million people lived, representing 35 percent of the Brazilian population. This segment alone represented four times the urban population of the country in 1950!

Second, the contribution of coffee sales to total exports had fallen to 13.4 percent, while the share of manufactured products had reached 56.5 percent of the total value of exports. The share of EAP in the agricultural and mining sector, in turn, had fallen to 30 percent, while the share of EAP in the secondary sector as a whole had risen to 21 percent of total EAP. Likewise, occupations connected with agriculture and mining represented only 30 percent of all occupations—a drop of more than 25 percentage points in thirty years—while the percentage of technical, administrative and scientific occupations and those connected with manufacturing and civil construction doubled, representing altogether almost 20 percent of total occupations. In 1980, the manufacturing share of national income, in current prices, was 26.3 percent of the total, practically double the figure for the primary sector: 13.2 percent.

The structure of industrial production had changed profoundly. The proportion of nondurable consumer goods in the value of industrial production in 1970 Cr$ had fallen by half since 1950, and was at 34.4 percent. The proportion of durable consumer goods had risen considerably (to 13.5 percent) as had that of the capital goods industry (14.7 percent). The two together had increased from 6.8 percent in 1950 to 28.2 percent in 1980.

In 1980, although mortality and fertility rates were still high in comparative international terms and still showed marked regional and social variations, they had fallen considerably, indicating that a large part of the population had already made the demographic transition (see Merrick, in this collec-

Table 4.1
Structural Indicators of the Profile of
Brazilian Society (1950–1980)

Indicator	Year CIRCA 1950 %	CIRCA 1980 %
A. URBANIZATION		
1. Population living in cities of more than 20,000 habitants	21	46
2. Population living in cities (Criteria of the Census)	36	68
3. Households classified as urban	37	69
B. OCCUPATIONAL AND EMPLOYMENT STRUCTURE		
1. Participation of the EAP sectors in the Total EAP*		
(a) Primary Sector	60	30
(b) Secondary Sector (Manufacturing, civil construction and other industrial activities)	14	24
(b.1) Manufacturing	9.4	16
2. Structure of Occupations		
(a) Percentage of occupations tied to agriculture and mining	58	30
(b) Percentage of technical, administrative and allied occupations	10	19
(c) Percentage of occupations tied to manufacturing and civil construction	13	21
C. STRUCTURE OF DOMESTIC PRODUCT (current prices)		
(a) Agriculture	25	13
(b) Manufacturing	20	26
D. STRUCTURE OF INDUSTRIAL PRODUCTION (value of production in 1970 cruzeiros)		
(a) Non-durable consumer goods	73	34
(b) Durable consumer goods	2.5	14
(c) Capital goods	4.3	15
E. EXPORTATIONS		
(a) Coffee	60	13
(b) Industrial Products	—	57

Source: Serra, 1981 and Faria, 1981

*EAP = Economically Active Population

tion); marked spatial integration had occurred and the markets for labor and consumer goods showed a high degree of integration. Illiteracy had decreased (only 27 percent of adults 15 years old or over) and the mass media had experienced considerable expansion. Social security and welfare services had been universalized as social rights, although there were still difficulties in effectively reaching the lower levels of the population, and there were doubts about the level of quality.

These transformations, which had occurred over a short period of time, make Brazil, as Serra notes, "a kind of paradigm for a country with late industrialization where economic growth and the differentiation of the productive forces have shown extraordinary vitality" (Serra, 1981). In fact, between 1947 and 1980, the Brazilian Gross National Product (GNP) grew at an average rate of 7.1 percent annually, a rate which was above that of all the developed and underdeveloped capitalist countries, with the exception of the oil-producing countries.

This growth was dominated by the manufacturing industry, which grew overall at an average annual rate of 8.5 percent; in fact, Brazilian growth in the period was profoundly marked by the remarkable expansion of the durable consumer goods industry, which grew at an average rate of 15.3 percent annually, reaching growth rates of over 23 percent annually at the expansive moments of the cycles that occurred in the period (1955–62 and 1967–73). The intermediate goods and capital goods sector also grew at high average rates (10.5 and 12.8 percent yearly, respectively).

Growth of such magnitude occurring at such an accelerated rate at the periphery of the world capitalist economy could not take place without, on the one hand, profound quantitative and qualitative changes in the spatial, demographic and social structure of the country and, on the other hand, the aggravation of old sectorial, regional and social imbalances and the appearance of new ones. Moreover, these transformations do not seem to have led to the elimination of extreme poverty and market social exclusion. One of the explanations offered for this persistence lies precisely in the somewhat perverse nature of the changes in the structure of employment.

CHANGES IN THE COMPOSITION OF EMPLOYMENT

One of the social changes that have occurred in the past thirty years is the change in the structure of employment. From a structural point of view, one aspect of the Brazilian development process that has generated the most controversy concerns its capacity to generate new jobs. An influential group of analysts have argued that the occurrence of this dynamic insufficiency, under conditions of demographic pressure in urban areas, leads to hypertrophied growth of the services sector and especially, of the personal services and small business subsectors, which grow abnormally on precarious bases with low capital density, low profitability, inadequate levels of legal and institutional development, occupational instability, and low salaries.

For the analysts who resort to the theory of occupational marginality inherent in the development of dependent capitalism—such as Kowarick, for example—given the financial and technology dependency of Brazilian industry on foreign investment, even if there is manufacturing growth, each new industrial expansion takes place on more advanced technological and capital intensive bases, aggravating the problem of exclusion. In this view, the jobs created by the expansion are not sufficient to compensate for the jobs destroyed by the process of concentration and centralization inherent in the development of the oligopolized capitalist society, especially in a society with late, dependent development.[3]

The Brazilian economic growth of the postwar period was strongly conditioned by the performance of the industrial sector under conditions that intensified technological and financial dependence on foreign capital. In addition, the industrial growth occurred through cyclical expansions accompanied, as is to be expected, by centralization and concentration of capital. As Serra points out, in the postwar period, "the expansion of manufacturing output showed three more crucial variations, which conditioned similar variations in the growth of the GNP. The first of these variations occurred beginning in 1963 after a notable expansionist trajectory starting at the end of the war (9.7 percent annually) and especially in the five-year period of 1956–1961, in which the growth rate for industrial output reached an average of 11 percent annually. In the five-year period of 1962–67, this rate declined by more than four times its value, to an average of 2.6 percent annually. The second variation was observed as of mid-1967, beginning the expansive phase of the enonomic miracle, during which industrial output grew at almost 13 percent per year until 1973. After that, industry entered a deceleration phase, between 1973 and 1980, with output only half of that observed during the 'miracle,' although still not much below the historic tendency of the postwar period and still reasonably high in comparison with other countries" (Serra, 1981, p. 22).

Furthermore, in both periods, expansion occurred under the leadership of the durable consumer goods and capital goods industries—sectors in which financial and technological dependency existed from the beginning and which became aggravated in the course of time, with the resumption of the expansive cycle (Serra, 1981, Mello and Belluzzo, 1977).

For all these reasons, on the basis of hypotheses of the theory of occupational marginality, the performance of the secondary sector—especially manufacturing—in the creation of new jobs would not be expected to be particularly brilliant, since there were changes in the occupational structure due to the growth of the tertiary and the civil construction subsector on the one hand, and the contraction of employment in the agriculture sector on the other.

In order to evaluate the changes in the composition of employment and the performance of the various sectors in this regard, it would be useful to have emloyment data that would allow for the accompaniment of the cycle. Without this, there is the risk of comparing a peak year with a year from a phase of severe contraction, which would lead to inadequate inferences if we started from the assumption that under recession conditions employment in the most dynamic sectors tends to fall, leaving installed capacity idle. Thus, in spite of fact that the only information that exists for the period as a whole is census data, which allows only for the evaluation of employment variation by decades, taking the years 1950, 1960, 1970, and 1980 as points of reference, in Table 4.2 we present the annual average geometric growth rates for industrial output and civil construction. This can help us to evaluate the performance of these two sectors with regard to the evolution of output in the various decades analyzed here.

In purely indicative terms, when evaluating the creation of jobs in each decade, it is useful to keep in mind the following information that can be seen from Table 2: (1) during the 1950s there was an acceleration in the rhythm of growth, 1960 being a peak year of this cycle; (2) in the 1960s there was an initial moment of deceleration followed by a period of notable expansion and; (3) the 1970s start with a major growth and end with a deceleration, though less pronounced than the one that occurred between 1962 and 1967, the year 1980 being a point in this deceleration phase.

Although they are aspects of the same basic process, I will analyze the data on evolution of sectorial employment on the basis of the information on the economically active population ten years of age and older from three angles: the composition of EAP by sectors; the number of new jobs created; and the growth rates and the number of individuals employed in the other sectors per person employed in the secondary sector of the economy. In this way, I hope to better delineate the problem.

CHANGES IN THE COMPOSITION OF THE EMPLOYMENT OF THE ECONOMICALLY ACTIVE POPULATION

½ The data that allow for an evaluation of the changes in the structure of the economically active population (ten years of age and older) appear in Table 4.3. The change that is quantitatively most conspicuous is, without a doubt, the substantial decrease in the percentage of individuals employed in the primary sector. This decline is relatively small in the 1950s, when the primary

Table 4.2

Brazil—Average*** Annual Rates of the Growth
of Industrial Production and of Civil
Construction (1947–1980)

Periods	Civil Construction	Total of Industry	Industrial Production				
			Durable Goods	Capital Goods	Inter- mediate Goods	Non- Durable Goods
1947–1955	5.5(*)	9.0(*)	17.1	11.0	11.8	6.7
1955–1962	5.1	9.8	23.9	26.4	12.1	6.6
1962–1967	2.8	2.6	4.1	2.6	5.9	0.0
1967–1970	9.8	11.9	21.7	13.5	13.7	0.8
1970–1973	12.0	13.5	25.5	22.7	13.2	9.1
1973–1976	12.1	9.1	10.3	13.0	8.7	4.8
1976–1980	6.2	6.4	8.6	3.4	8.0	4.1
1947–1980	5.6(**)	8.5(**)	15.3	12.8	10.5	5.8

Source: Serra, 1981

(*)   Period 1949–1955
(**)   Period 1949–1980
(***) Geometric Mean

Table 4.3

Brazil—Distribution of the Economically Active Population (10 years or over)
by Sectors and Subsectors (1950–1980)

	1950		1960		1970		1980	
	Number	%	Number	%	Number	%	Number	%
Primary	10,252,839	59.9	12,276,908	54.0	13,087,521	44.3	13,109,415	29.9
Secondary	2,427,364	14.2	2,940,242	12.9	5,295,417	17.9	10,674,977	24.4
Manufacturing	1,608,309	9.4	1,954,187	8.6	3,241,861	11.0	6,858,598	15.7
Construction	584,644	3.4	781,247	3.4	1,719,714	5.8	3,151,094	7.2
Other Industrial Activities	234,411	1.4	204,808	0.9	333,852	1.1	665,285	1.5
Tertiary	4,437,159	25.9	7,532,878	33.1	11,174,276	37.8	20,012,371	45.7
Distribution (commerce and transport)	1,581,233	9.2	2,455,615	10.8	3,415,359	11.6	5,926,848	13.5
Personal Services	1,781,041	10.4	3,028,933	13.3	3,925,001	13.3	7,089,709	16.2
Public and Social Administration	911,317	5.3	1,467,947	6.4	2,683,904	9.0	4,857,061	11.1
Other Activities	163,568	1.0	580,383	2.6	1,150,012	2.9	2,138,753	4.3
Total	17,117,362	(100.0)	22,750,028	(100.0)	29,557,224	(100.0)	43,796,763	(100.0)

Source: Fundação IBGE. Advanced Tabulations from the Demographic Census of 1980.

sector share of EAP falls only from 59.9 percent in 1950 to 54.0 percent in 1960; the decline increases in the 1960s, dropping to 44.3 percent in 1970. It is further accentuated in the 1970s, when the primary sector share falls almost 15 percentage points to 29.9 percent in 1980.

The changes in the secondary sector share are also important. The share of the civil construction sector more than doubles between 1950 and 1980, going from 3.4 percent to 7.2 percent; manufacturing share goes from 9.4 percent to 15.7 percent, with the relative share of the other industrial activities remaining relatively stable for total EAP. It is worth noting, however, that the increase in these shares occurs as of 1960, there having been a modest decline in the manufacturing share between 1950 and 1960. If we observe the overall behavior of the secondary sector in the 1950–1980 period, two changes stand out: the modest drop in its share between 1950 and 1960, and the increase by more then 10 percentage points between 1960 and 1980.

Finally, the tertiary sector share increases regularly throughout the period, going from 25.9 percent in 1950 to 33.1 percent in 1960, reaching 37.8 percent in 1970, and contributing 45.7 percent to total EAP at the end of the period. With regard to the tertiary sector, two developments stand out: (1) the increase in the contribution of social activities and public administration to employment, which doubles in the period (5.3 percent in 1950 and 11.1 percent in 1980), and (2) the growth of the share under the heading "other activities," which goes from 1 percent to 4.9 percent, although it is difficult to evaluate the qualitative significance of this heading because it covers activities that are poorly specified, activities connected with the financial sector, and even includes individuals looking for work for the first time, in the case of the 1970 and 1980 censuses.

Thus, in thirty years, the EAP goes from being predominantly rural to being predominantly urban, with the secondary sector share representing almost a quarter of all employment, there being, in 1980, almost 7 million people employed in manufacturing (15.7 percent of total EAP).

Now let us try to analyze the contribution of the various sectors and subsectors to the new jobs created in each decade of the period.

THE CREATION OF NEW JOBS

The population 10 years of age and older, grew by more than 50 million people between 1950 and 1980, going from 36,557,990 individuals to 88,149,988—a population greater than that of many European countries. In this period, almost 27 million new jobs were created, since EAP went from 17,117,362 individuals to 43,796,763, as can be verified by the data in Table 4.4.

Table 4.4
Brazil—New Jobs Created (1950–1980)

Sectors and Subsectors	1950–1960 Number	1950–1960 %	1960–1970 Number	1960–1970 %	1970–1980 Number	1970–1980 %	1950–1980 Number	1950–1980 %
Primary	2,024,069	35.9	810,613	11.9	21,894	0.2	2,856,576	10.7
Secondary	512,878	9.1	2,355,185	34.6	5,379,550	37.8	8,247,613	30.9
Manufacturing	345,878	6.1	1,287,674	18.9	3,616,737	25.4	5,250,289	19.7
Construction	196,603	3.5	938,467	13.8	1,431,380	10.1	2,566,450	9.6
Other Industrial Activities	−29,603	−0.5	129,044	1.9	331,433	2.3	430,874	1.6
Tertiary	3,095,719	55.0	3,641,398	53.5	8,838,095	62.0	15,575,212	58.4
Distribution	874,382	15.5	959,744	14.1	2,511,489	17.6	4,345,615	16.3
Personal Services	1,247,892	22.2	896,068	13.2	3,164,708	22.2	5,308,668	19.9
Social Services	556,630	9.9	1,215,957	17.9	2,173,157	15.3	3,945,744	14.8
Other	416,815	7.4	569,629	8.3	988,741	6.9	1,975,185	7.4
TOTAL	5,632,666	(100.0)	6,807,196	(100.0)	14,239,539	(100.0)	26,679,401	(100.0)

Source: Table 4.3

So far as the contribution of the different sectors to the creation of new jobs in concerned, it is noteworthy, first of all, that the primary sector played a very modest role, creating just 2.8 million new jobs in the period, a little less than 10 percent of the total jobs created. It is also notable that more than 70 percent of these new jobs were created in the 1950s; between 1970 and 1980, only 22,000 new jobs were created in the primary sector. However, this result should not obscure other important transformations in agricultural sector employment (see Sorj, 1983). The contribution of the secondary sector was important as 8,247,613 new jobs were created in this period, more than 5.2 million in manufacturing and a little over 2.5 million in the civil construction sector. The secondary sector overall contributed more than 30 percent to the creation of new jobs (30.9 percent). In addition, the rather modest performance of the sector in the 1950s is clear because, of the total jobs created in the period, 93.8 percent were created in the last two decades. The contribution of the manufacturing industry to the creation of new jobs increased over the course of the three decades analyzed here. Its share went from 6.1 percent between 1950 and 1960 to 18.9 percent between 1960 and 1970, and reaching 25.4 percent in the 1980s. The contribution of civil construction was also important—almost 10 percent of all new jobs created in the 1950–1980 period—although this was more pronounced, in relative terms, in the 1960s.

Finally, the role of the tertiary sector in the creation of new jobs should also be noted, not only because of the size of its contribution—over 50 percent in all the decades—but also because of its regularity, especially so far as the distributive services (commerce, transportation and communications) are concerned, along with the heterogeneous leftover group called "other activities." Personal services, in turn, showed a more cyclical behavior, contributing about 22.2 percent in the decades at the beginning and end of the period, with this contribution falling to 13.2 percent in the 1960s. This variation could point to the hypertrophied growth of the tertiary sector mentioned in the hypothesis that we have used as a background reference. It is impossible, however, to judge the phenomenon on the basis of this data alone. The expansion of the so-called social services (social activities, administration, armed forces, etc.) was also quite important throughout the period, especially in the last two decades. Nevertheless, the expansion of these services cannot be considered to be of an exclusive nature, since these sectors are generally characterized by greater stability, adequate legal protection, and institutional solidity.

GROWTH RATES AND INTERSECTORIAL EMPLOYMENT RATIOS

In order to complete the study of economic performance in the period, so far as employment growth is concerned, it is necessary to do a comparative analysis of the rhythm of employment growth in the different sectors in com-

Table 4.5
Rate of Growth of the Total Population of 10 Years and Over, of Urban Population and of Employment in the Secondary and Tertiary Sectors (1950–1980)

Sectors	Annual Geometric Rates of Growth			
	1950–1960	1960–1970	1970–1980	1950–1980
POPULATION				
Total				2.86
10 Years and Over	2.94	3.04	2.96	2.98
Urban	6.31	5.77	4.83	5.64
Employment				
Total Employment	2.89	2.65	4.01	3.18
Secondary	1.93	6.06	7.26	5.06
Manufactures	1.98	5.19	7.78	4.95
TERTIARY	5.43	4.02	6.00	5.15
Personal Services	5.45	2.62	6.09	4.71
Social Services	4.88	6.22	6.11	5.74
TOTAL URBAN EMPLOYMENT	4.31	4.63	6.42	5.12

Source: Fundação, IBGE, Demografic Census of 1950, 1960, 1970 and 1980.

parison with the growth rates for urban and total population, as well as an analysis of the intersectorial employment ratios. In Table 4.5, rates are given for a few specific sectors and those for population, while Table 4.6 gives the growth rates in each of the decades and in the 1950–1980 period.

Comparing the rates of population growth and employment growth in the period studied, the following should be noted:

1. For the period as a whole, the rate of employment growth was greater than the growth rates for the population as a whole and for those 10 years of age and older.

2. This employment growth was basically due to the performance of the economy in the 1970s, since in the preceding period the growth rate for employment was lower than that for total population and for those 10 years of age and older.

3. The growth rate for urban employment—secondary and tertiary sectors— was lower than the growth rate for urban population in the period as a whole.

4. In the 1970s, urban employment grew at a higher rate (6.42 percent annually) than urban population (4.83 percent annually).

Table 4.6

Brazil—Rates of Growth of Employment by
Sectors (1950–1980)

Sectors	1950–1960	1960–1970	1970–1980	1950–1980
Primary	1.82	0.64	0.02	0.82
Secondary	1.93	6.06	7.26	5.06
Manufacturing	1.98	5.19	7.78	4.95
Civil Construction	2.94	8.21	6.24	5.78
Other Industrial Activities	−1.34	5.01	7.14	3.54
Tertiary	5.43	4.02	6.00	5.15
Distributive Services	4.50	3.35	5.67	4.50
Personal Services	5.45	2.62	6.09	4.71
Social Services	4.88	6.22	6.11	5.74
Other Activities	13.50	7.08	6.40	8.95
TOTAL	2.89	2.65	4.01	3.18

Source: Table 4.3.

5. The performance of the secondary sector, which had been mediocre in the 1950s, improved considerably in the course of the period, reaching a rate of 7.26 percent annually in the 1970s, which was well above the urban population growth rate in that decade as it had already been in the preceding decade. This was, in part, due to the good performance of civil construction in the 1960s.

6. The manufacturing industry increased its capacity to create jobs throughout the period. Growing just 1.98 percent annually during the 1950s, it increased to 5.19 percent in the 1960s, and reached 7.78 percent annually in the 1970s.

7. For the period as a whole, the tertiary sector grew overall at a rate of 5.15 percent annually, a percentage slightly above that of the secondary sector and that of manufacturing (5.06 percent and 4.95 percent respectively). In the 1970s, however, the tertiary sector (and each of its subgroups) grew at lower rates than those of the secondary sector and of the manufacturing industry.

8. Within the tertiary sector, the subsector of the so-called social services grew at higher rates than did the tertiary overall and more the personal services subsector, except in the 1950s, when the opposite occurred.

In summary, these observations lead to the conclusions that in the course of the period: (1) the dynamic capacity of the secondary sector and of the

Table 4.7

Brazil—Persons Employed in Each One of the
Sectors and Subsectors by Persons Employed
in Total Secondary Occupations (1950–1980)

Ratios	1950	1960	1970	1980
Primary/Secondary	4.22	4.18	2.47	0.95
Tertiary/Secondary	1.83	2.56	2.11	1.87
Marketing/Secondary	0.65	0.83	0.64	0.55
Personal Services/ Secondary	0.73	1.03	0.74	0.66
Social Services/ Secondary	0.37	0.50	0.51	0.45
Other Occupations/ Secondary	0.07	0.20	0.22	0.20

Source: Table 4.3.

manufacturing sector to create jobs vastly improved; and (2) the performance of the institutionalized tertiary sector was better than that of the so-called "marginal" tertiary sector. These conclusions are strengthened when we examine intersectorial employment ratios, taking the secondary sector and the manufacturing subsector as reference points.

Thus, although the number of individuals employed in the tertiary sector as a whole per person employed in the secondary sector increased quite a bit between 1950 and 1960, when the ratio goes from 1.83 to 2.56, this number starts to fall beginning in 1960, going down to 2.11 in 1970 and falling to 1.87 in 1980. The decline is even more pronounced in the existing ratios between employment in personal services and in the secondary sector, on the one hand, and between employment in distributive services and in the secondary sector, on the other. In fact, in 1980 there were fewer people employed in both tertiary subsectors per person employed in the secondary sector than in the figures for 1950. The proportion increased only in the case of social services and in the case of other tertiary sector occupations.

In summary, the main changes in the employment structure resulting from the developments of the past thirty years have been:

1. A significant decline in the relative importance of employment connected with the agricultural sector, although in absolute terms this contingent still represented more than 13 million people in 1980.

2. Growth in absolute numbers and in relative terms of the segment of the population connected with manufacturing and civil construction. If we

take this employment as indicative of the magnitude of the industrial urban force segments, it means that in thirty years, their number has increased almost fivefold. The fact that this type of employment—especially in manufacturing—has grown in a spatially concentrated form has important social and political consequences.

3. The growth, absolute as well as relative, of employment directly or indirectly related to governmental functions that are not directly productive, which also grew fivefold in these thirty years.

4. The notable growth, in absolute terms, of the employment classified as "other activities," which, because of its heterogeneity, shows the complexity of the Brazilian occupational structure and the narrowness of the classical trisectorial classification system. It is important, however, to remember that, beginning in 1970, the unemployed and those seeking first-time employment were included in this group.

In generic terms, what stands out most is the relative dynamism of the secondary sector, especially beginning in 1960, and the expansion of tertiary activities connected with the growth of social services provided by the state.

CHANGES IN THE SPATIAL DISTRIBUTION AND THE INTERNAL STRUCTURE OF THE SECTORS

Along with the changes in the sectorial structure of employment, various other transformations occurred, which helped to significantly alter the profile of Brazilian society in the past 30 years. In a country of continental proportions, marked by profound regional imbalances, occupational changes not only occurred differently in different regions, but above all, they changed spatial relations in the country. With regard to this, the increasing integration of the national labor market, the vigorous expansion of the frontier in the farthest lying regions, and especially the growing urbanization of the labor force should be noted. On the other hand, whether due to the magnitude of the volume of new jobs created or because of the process of social modernization, or even as a result of the constraints imposed on family income in the poorest homes, female participation in the labor market increased considerably. Finally, the growing differentiation and complexity of the occupational structure resulted in significant changes in the nature of occupations and in the labor force's level of skill.

The most important spatial change took the form of a growing urbanization of the labor force. Not only because the originally urban sectors—the tertiary and secondary sectors—grew at rates a good deal higher during the period (5.12 percent annually, in comparison with the primary sector, which grew at an average annual rate of 0.82 percent), but also because a significant

Table 4.8
Growth in the Economically Active Population
by Regions and Grouped Sectors (1950–1980)

Regions	Grouped Sectors of Economically Active Population (EAP)			
	A*(%)	B*(%)	C*(%)	(%)
North/Center-West	35	8	8	10
Other regions	65	92	92	90
Brazil	(2,291,111)	(8,091,494)	(15,735,745)	(26,118,350)

Source: Fundação IBGE, Demographic Census of 1930 and 1980.
    *A = Primary Sector
    *B = Manufacturing, Other Industrial Activities
    *C = Other Sectors

part of the economically active population employed in agriculture and mining moved to the cities (19 percent in 1980). Thus, in 1980, 70 percent of the EAP were living in urban areas as compared with 36.2 percent in 1950.

A second important aspect to be noted with regard to the changes in the spatial distribution of employment concerns the advance of agricultural frontiers in the areas of the Center-West and the North. As the data below in Table 4.8 show, these two regions of the country received 10.4 percent of the increase in total EAP during the period and 35.1 percent of the EAP employed in the primary sector.

A third aspect of the spatial redistribution of employment is concerned with the dynamics of spatial concentration of employment in the secondary sector of the economy in general, and in the manufacturing industry in particular. The data in Table 4.9 show that the Southeastern region as a whole lost a small amount of its relative share of secondary EAP as well as of manufacturing EAP (4.3 percent and 1.1 percent respectively) to other areas of the country. The state of São Paulo, however, increased its relative share, especially so far as manufacturing EAP is concerned, which went from 37.9 percent in 1950 to 44.2 percent in 1980.

Another change that occurred in the last 30 years and which merits particular attention is the growing participation of women in the economically active population. The number practically doubled in the period by growing at an average annual rate of 5.2 percent, and increasing from 14.6 percent in 1950 to 27.2 percent in 1980.

The growth rates for the EAP of both sexes and the growth rates for the female EAP in the major sectors of the economy appear in Table 4.10. A comparison indicates that the female EAP grew at higher rates in all the sec-

Table 4.9

Brazil—Concentration of the Economically
Active Population in Industry (1950–1980)

Region	1950		1980	
	N	%	N	%
Southeast				
Secondary Sector	1,494,004	64.7	6,506,801	60.4
Manufacturing	1,103,735	(65.4)	4,464,138	(64.3)
São Paulo				
Secondary Sector	813,031	35.2	3,998,642	37.1
Manufacturing	639,557	(37.9)	3,068,936	(44.2)
Brazil				
Secondary Sector	2,311,694		10,772,463	
Manufacturing	(1,688,798)		(6,939,421)	

Table 4.10

Annual Rate of Growth of the Total and Female
Population Economically Active, by Years of Activity
(1950–1980)

	Rates of Growth (Annual %)	
	EAP Total	Female EAP
Agriculture and Extractive Activities	0.8	2.7
Industrial Activities and Civil Construction	4.7	5.0
Marketing	4.9	8.8
Personal Services	4.9	5.0
Transport, Communication and Warehousing	3.2	5.4
Social Activities	6.0	7.4
Public Administration	4.1	7.3
Other Activities	7.1	10.2
Total	3.1	5.2

Source: Fundacão IBGE, Demographic Census of 1950 and 1980.

tors, with significant differences in agriculture and mining, merchandising, public administration, and in the "other activities" sector.

This resulted in a greater differentiation of female employment between 1950 and 1980, as can be established by analyzing the data presented in Table 4.11.

Table 4.11
Predominately Female Occupations (1950–1980)

Occupations	1950		1980	
	N	%	N	%
Paid Domestic Occupations	734,492	29.3	2,367,616	20.6
Other Personal Service Occupations	10,344	0.4	1,237,720	10.8
Bureaucratic or Secretarial functions	109,305	4.4	1,428,967	12.4
Professors and Allied Teaching Occupations	140,525	5.6	984,441	8.6
Commercial occupations and Allied Activities	54,994	2.2	921,187	8.0
Clothing Industry occupations	223,847	8.9	841,262	7.3
Textile Industry Occupations	221,516	8.8	187,924	1.6
Medicine, Dentistry and Allied Occupations	34,173	1.4	274,668	2.4
SUBTOTAL 1	1,529,196	61.0	8,243,785	71.6
Agricultural Workers	762,882	30.4	1,270,455	11.0
SUBTOTAL 2	2,292,078	91.4	9,514,240	82.6
Packers and Shippers of Merchandise	30,904	1.2	99,028	0.9
Social Scientists and other technical, scientific and allied occupations	—	—	51,911	0.4
Communication occupations	13,124	0.5	74,873	0.7
Directors and Heads of Departments in Public Administration	—	—	49,035	0.4
SUBTOTAL 3	2,336,106	93.1	9,789,037	85.0
Other Occupations	171,485	6.9	1,716,280	15.0
General total	2,507,564	100.0	11,505,367	100.0

Source: Fundação IBGE, Demographic Census of 1950 and 1980.

In 1950, women were concentrated in five occupational categories, four of which were predominantly female (paid domestic labor, teaching and other educational support personnel, occupations in the clothing industry, and occupations in the textile industry), and in farming and mining occupations, which all together made up 83 percent of the total female employment.

In 1980, the share of these five major categories had fallen to 49 percent while between 1950 and 1980, the proportion of occupations connected with education had increased (from 5.6 percent to 8.6 percent). This means that with the exclusion of the education category the share of the four other categories fell by more than 50 percent.

Also, the significant growth of female employment in the following areas should be noted: In personal service occupations (not including paid domestic labor), the share went from 0.4 percent in 1950 to 10.0 percent in 1980; in bureaucratic or office positions (4.4 percent to 12.4 percent); in occupations related to the social sciences, medicine and other technical or scientific occupations (the share went from 1.4 percent in 1950 to 2.8 percent in 1980). In spite of these changes, however, one should not lose sight of the fact that even in 1980 personal services, agriculture and social services still provided more than 50 percent of the female employment.

The process of economic development that took place in Brazil during the last 30 years significantly altered another dimension of the occupational structure of the country. This was the growth of non-manual occupations requiring higher skill levels.

Although it may be difficult to evaluate the magnitude of this change with precision solely on the basis of aggregate data, the information synthesized in Table 4.12 indicates the size of the phenomenon.

If we take administrative, managerial, technical, scientific and related occupations (as well as occupations connected with securities trading, credit institutions and insurance companies) as representative of more highly qualified non-manual occupations, we see that these increased from 1,845,689 in 1950 to 8,855,270 in 1980, increasing almost fivefold in 30 years and having grown at an annual rate of 5.4 percent. These occupations, which had represented only 10.8 percent of the EAP in 1950, represented 21.1 percent of the EAP in 1980, forming the basis of a salaried urban middle class whose economic and political importance could not be minimized, especially because of its strong presence within the governmental system.

In conclusion, two changes that occurred within the primary EAP should be noted, in addition to the already mentioned urbanization of part of this contingent. First of all, the growth of the group of individuals in this sector involved in cattle raising, whose share of the agricultural EAP went from 3.6 percent to 10.3 percent in 1950 and 1980 respectively. Secondly, the decline,

Table 4.12

Brazil — Skilled Non-Manual Occupations (1950–1980)

	1950		1980	
	N	%	N	%
Administrative Occupations	1,367,478	8.0	5,101,926	12.1
Men	1,197,228	7.0	3,369,773	8.0
Women	170,250	1.0	1,732,153	4.1
Scientific, Technical, & Allied Occupations	362,723	2.1	2,773,886	6.7
Men	177,291	1.0	1,188,369	2.8
Women	185,432	1.1	1,585,517	3.8
Real Estate, Banking, Credit, & Insurance Occupations	115,488	0.7	979,458	2.3
EPA Total	17,117,362	100.0	42,271,526	100.0

Source: Fundação, IBGE, Demographic Census of 1950 and 1980.

in absolute as well as relative terms, of *empregadores* and family members (largely unpaid workers). Between 1950 and 1980, this force fell from 3,020,777 to 2,352,343 and its share of the agricultural EAP fell from 30.6 percent to 18.5 percent!

To compensate for all this, the number of self-employed workers grew in absolute terms (increasing from 3,521,778 in 1950 to 5,435,203 in 1980) as well as in relative terms, since its share of the agricultural EAP grew from 35.6 percent to 42.9 percent. Part of this group is made up of small farm owner families who practice a reasonably captitalized and modern form of agriculture, especially in the Southwest. In terms of social structure, this means the development of a rural middle class, which adds complexity and differentiation to the Brazilian social structure.

On the other hand, the contingent of salaried workers also increased, going from 3,334,479 (33.7 percent of the agricultural EAP) in 1950 to 4,809,592 (38 percent of the agrarian EAP) in 1980. Although there are not enough data to allow for a more precise comparative analysis, because of classification differences between the two censuses, one should not fail to consider the probable increase within this group of salaried workers in general and of those among them known as migrant workers, who have urban residences (or at least live outside agricultural settlements). Together, these represent the development of a proletarianized segment in the Brazilian rural world, and one which can even participate intermittently in urban labor markets. This change is quite significant in terms of the characteristics of the social structure of the country.

All these transformations confirm that in the past 30 years the Brazilian occupational structure has become significantly more complex, modern and differentiated, and has also been characterized by high rates of both social and spatial mobility.[4] A structure of social groups and classes anchored in a nationally integrated market economy took shape through the extension and deepening of capitalist production relations in the country as well as in the city.

To this extent, from a structural point of view, leaving aside simplistic, doctrinaire inferences, complex and differentiated interests appear more clearly, and serve as a potential source for increased dissension within the political arena. However, three factors may have contributed to minimize the effects of this structural differentiation on the level of the multiplication of cross-conflicts.

First of all, the persistence over a long period, of political authoritarianism, which, if it did not completely impede the differentiated organization of these multiple complex interests, at least made such organization difficult. Secondly, the predominance and persistence of policies of salary restraints which produced the basic split between "the rich" and "the poor," between "the government" and "the people," also made the appearance of a clearer consciousness of occupational differentiation difficult.[5] Thirdly, there is the considerable expansion of the mass media. Their impact on the population is far from adequately known. I dare say, however, that, at least until quite recently, it must have been more in the sense of homogenizing (except so far as the split between "rich" and "poor" is concerned) than in the sense of expressing the pluralism and the structural differentiation of contemporary Brazilian society.

These factors have contributed to the existence of superficial, fluctuating consensuses typical of a mass society, such as the "I love you, my Brazil" movement; or the "miracle"; or the movement "for direct elections now"; or the "crisis." Although endowed with a structural base that might permit pluralism and differentiation, unfortunately Brazilian society is not, in my opinion, immune to political phenomena typical, theoretically, of societies influenced by the mass media.

However, when emphasizing the modernizing aspects of the Brazilian development process of the past 30 years, we should not forget certain characteristics of the Brazilian occupational structure that *are* connected with social exclusion. The recent crisis forces us to do so.

BRAZILIAN OCCUPATIONAL STRUCTURE AND THE RECENT CRISIS: THE PROBLEM OF UNEMPLOYMENT AND UNDEREMPLOYMENT

Although the employment growth of the last thirty years has been satisfactory enough in quantitative and aggregate terms, it is claimed, on the one hand, that this growth remained below the needs of populational growth and, on the other hand, that the general characteristics of this labor market are known in terms of the incidence of generalized situations of poverty, which I analyzed in another study (Faria, 1983).

An important controversy persists as to until what point did the growth, differentiation and complexity of the labor markets in Brazil contribute to the decline of the so-called informal or marginal sector of the economy or, alternatively, to what extent that growth provoked the expansion of the sector.

I tried to analyze the problem with the perspective given by the economic growth process of the first half of the 1970s (Faria, 1976) and concluded that if the capitalist expansion of the labor markets could at first sustain the expansion of an informalized sector of the economy—especially of the urban economy of regions not directly affected by industrial expansion at a local level—that at a later point in time this expansion would be limited, given the fact that the growing capitalist sector would increasingly avail itself of its economic opportunities. Corner stores would be displaced by supermarket chains, small shops by department store chains, neighborhood laundries and shoe repair shops by modern capitalized businesses.

If that was true, the expansion of the informal urban sector as a mechanism for mitigating structural or conditional crisis situations in the generation of employment would be increasingly called into question. In situations of that kind, official unemployment would therefore tend to increase. Thus, the appearance of official unemployment in situations where there was a decline in the growth rate, stagnation or recession would constitute, however tragically, an additional indicator of the modernization of the labor markets and of the occupational structure (Faria, 1976 pp. 270–82).

Following this line of reasoning, official unemployment would tend to occur with greater intensity and frequency in the areas of the country where the structure of urban–industrial employment was most advanced and where agricultural activities had already reached more developed levels in technical and entrepreneurial terms—that is, in the most important cities and metropolitan areas, and particularly in the regions of the Southeast and the South.

As is known, in 1976 the Brazilian economy began to experience difficulties in maintaining its high growth rates, and in 1981 these growth rates

began to be negative, thus creating a growing situation of profound economic crisis. The impact of that crisis on employment is one of the main questions that has preoccupied investigators and administrators, especially with
regard to the mechanisms which respond to this situation in terms of labor
markets. Given the persistence of great regional and sectorial heterogeneity in
the labor markets, which the recent development process did not dissolve,
along with the fact that it is a multifaceted question, becomes a question that
is not an easy one to answer.

It is possible, however, to examine the extent to which the mechanisms
that respond to the crisis—official unemployment and expansion of the informal sector—are combined. Because of the impossibility of examining this for
the country as a whole at this time, let us take the most developed regions of
the country as a test case: that is, the metropolitan areas of the country and
the state of São Paulo.

Unfortunately, historical series of official unemployment rates, even for
the metropolitan areas, are very incomplete and present various methodoligical
problems. If we analyze the existing quantitative data, however, as well as
some indications of a qualitative nature—for example, the space occupied in
the major media by the topic of unemployment—we will not be far from the
truth if we estimate the official unemployment rate in the metropolitan areas
of the country as affecting between 2 percent and 3 percent of the economically active population in the mid-1970s.

Early in 1983, as a result of the recession of the preceding years and its
intensification, the official unemployment rate began to fluctuate between
5.6 percent and 7.2 percent for the metropolitan areas as a whole, reaching
rates of almost 9 percent in January of 1984 in the Belo Horizonte metropolitan area and almost 8 percent in the São Paulo metropolitan area.

Although this data is imprecise and subject to question, it clearly shows
that the transformations in the employment structure that occurred in the
past 30 years have made the occupational structure more vulnerable to official unemployment than before. This obviously puts a new and difficult problem on the political agenda, alongside the permanent problem of policies
oriented toward the creation of new jobs: How to deal with conditions of
official unemployment, from the point of view of the state's responsiblities to
provide workers with social assistance.

Official unemployment as a response to stagnation or recession does not
mean, however, that occupational sectors characterized by high informality
and marginality ceased to exist. In spite of the fact that the formalization
process has gained ground in the labor market over the last 30 years, this
process occurred very unevenly in the different sectors of the economy and in
the different sectors of the country.

This heterogeneity can be confirmed even in the predominantly urban economic sectors and in the metropolitan regions of the country. Thus, taking the nine metropolitan regions of the country in 1982 and using the proportion of individuals in each economic sector that contributed to social security institutions as a rough indicator of formalization, we see that this figure varies between 23.3 percent (in the "Services" sector, in the Fortaleza metropolitan region) and 98.2 percent (in the "Other Industrial Activities" sector in Curitiba), as shown by the data in Table 4.13.

An analysis of the data in Table 4.13 also indicates *a*) that in all of the metropolitan regions the least formalized sectors are services, civil construction and commerce; *b*) that the São Paulo, Curitiba and Porto Alegre metropolitan areas show higher rates of formalization in all the urban economic sectors; *c*) that the formalization process attained lower levels than were to be expected in the Rio de Janeiro metropolitan area and higher levels in the metropolitan area of Salvador, a phenomenon indicative of the differing development patterns in these two areas in the last 30 years (*i,e.*, the decline of the industrial importance of Rio de Janeiro and the specialization in boom industries (petrochemicals) in Salvador). However, this is not the only aspect that merits special emphasis as far as the informal sector of the economy is concerned, even in a quick summary like the one offered here.

Although the Brazilian occupational structure and the labor markets of which it is composed have become more vulnerable to crises of official unemployment because of their complexity, increasing integration and modernization, informalization continues to exist as a response mechanism—a phenomenon which of course also occurs in developed economies.

For the purpose of illustration, we will examine one aspect of this problem in the metropolitan economies of Rio de Janeiro and São Paulo. For this, we will take a different indicator than the one used in the preceding table: The percentage of employed individuals who have a *carteira de trabalho* (official work papers) signed by their employer as a precarious indicator of the formalization of the work relationship, and we will see what happened between 1976 and 1983 in the various sectors of the urban economy.

As the data in Table 4.14 shows, the rate of formalization fell in the two metropolitan regions (declines of 5.4 percent and 8 percent respectively for Rio de Janeiro and São Paulo) and in practically all fields of activities (conspicuously in civil construction in both regions, and in the personal services sector in São Paulo, and in the commercial sales sector in Rio de Janeiro).

Thus the impact of the recent crisis on the Brazilian occupational structure reveals its heterogeneity: on the one hand, relatively high rates of official unemployment occurred, indicative of the presence of advanced capitalist produc-

Table 4.13

BRAZIL: Metropolitan Regions: Level of Formalization of Different Types of Activity* (1982)

	Fortaleza	Recife	Belém	R. de Janeiro	B. Horizonte	Salvador	São Paulo	Curitiba	P. Alegre
Personal Services	23.8	30.4	33.1	45.5	42.7	39.2	49.2	48.3	61.2
Civil Construction	54.2	59.3	59.8	63.4	71.3	72.5	60.5	73.0	79.3
Commerce	59.7	49.7	57.8	69.6	73.0	68.3	71.0	80.4	80.7
Services Related to Production	78.9	74.0	78.5	81.9	79.8	80.3	85.6	83.8	86.3
Other Activities	82.7	72.4	76.5	85.9	85.8	85.7	92.4	88.5	93.3
Transport & Communications	76.1	73.6	80.8	90.1	89.0	85.3	88.7	92.6	89.5
Manufacturing	71.9	85.2	78.5	84.6	87.9	89.4	93.1	92.2	92.7
Social Services	83.3	84.7	82.2	87.1	85.4	90.2	89.0	89.3	91.5
Other Industrial Activities	84.4	90.4	95.8	95.8	92.0	97.8	96.2	98.2	90.8

Source: PNAD.

(*) Percentage of persons who contribute to the Institutes of Social Security.

Table 4.14
Informalization of the Metropolitan Economy*
Metropolitan Areas of Rio de Janeiro And
São Paulo (1967–1983)

	Rio De Janeiro			São Paulo		
	a	b		c	d	
	1976	1983	(a-b)	1976	1983	(c-d)
Personal Services	52.6	49.9	2.7	56.6	47.7	8.9
Civil Construction	81.7	59.7	21.0	80.5	67.8	12.7
Commerce	84.7	75.1	8.6	81.8	78.6	3.2
Services related to production	84.7	81.3	2.4	89.6	83.4	3.2
Other activities	91.5	90.2	1.3	95.4	95.3	0.1
Transport and communication	90.3	91.0	−0.7	91.9	90.8	1.1
Manufacturing	90.6	82.8	7.8	94.4	91.7	2.7
Social Services	71.7	65.2	5.5	52.6	49.4	3.2
Other Industrial Activities	93.6	90.1	3.5	88.7	85.3	3.4
TOTAL**	73.8	66.4	5.4	82.9	74.9	8.0

Source: Fundação IBGE, PNAD 1976 and 1983.
(*)   Percentage of employed persons possessing work papers.
(**) Includes agriculture, mining, Public Administration.

tion relations and, on the other hand, the persistence of normal adaptation mechanisms, through the reniformalization of the urban economy.

CONCLUSIONS

In this study, I have attempted to provide a general structural view of the transformations that have occurred in employment and occupations in the past 30 years, on the basis of publicly available census information.

Whether in terms of the Latin American literature that examined the question of the relationship between industrialization and employment in the underdeveloped periphery in the 1960s or in terms of the predictions resulting from political analyses of the same period, the surprising thing about the changes we have just analyzed is the dynamism—in terms of creation of employment—of the Brazilian secondary sector, especially after 1960.

The explanation for these surprising results is largely due to the fact that the predictive analyses conducted in the 1960s, extrapolated from the experience of the 1950s, did not give sufficient consideration to the possibility that the new expansive impulse would occur on the basis of more advanced technology and, probably, savings in the labor force, and that this new impulse would scarcely affect already existing products and processes. Such losses as undoubtedly occurred were more than made up for by the creation of jobs in sectors that had existed before. The expansion is explained largely by the expansion of completely new industrial subsectors, where the introduction of new technology did not destroy jobs, because they simply did not exist.

From this point of view, it is illustrative to compare the performance of already existing sectors that were predominant in the immediate postwar period (textiles, leather, clothing, food and beverages, ceramics, glass and furniture) with those that would form the dynamic nucleus of the industrial economy, especially after 1960, as is shown by the data in Table 4.15.

The newer sectors (metallurgy and heavy machinery, chemicals, rubber, pharmaceuticals among others) within the industrial structure in expansion were responsible for about 65 percent of the new industrial jobs created. The automotive industry provides a typical and significant example.

Nor did the predictive analyses of the 1960s consider the dynamic role of civil construction. Industrial expansion on the basis of almost nonexistent sectors would require the development of a physical infrastructure capable of supporting expansion, whether in terms of new industrial plants or in terms of communications and energy infrastructures that the industrial boom would need. This explains to a large extent the significant contribution of civil construction to the growth of employment in the period.

The crisis of the early 1980s, on the other hand, clearly shows that it is not possible to extrapolate exclusively from the significant employment growth experience of the 1960s and 1970s. In the first half of the 1980s, industrial employment returned to a level of growth closer to the pattern in effect in the 1950s. All of this strengthens the suspicion that employment growth shows cyclical variations on the one hand, and that, on the other hand, the expansive possibilities of the subsequent cycle depend, among other things, on the degree of complexity and completeness achieved by the industrial structure.

For this reason, within the scope of this work, it is difficult to speculate on the prospects for the future. It is almost redundant to note that in order for employment to resume its growth, the economy must resume its expansion. That is not sufficient. The growth of industrial employment will depend not only on the technological configuration adopted, but, above all, on the sectors that lead this expansion.

In this sense, it is possible that a new expansion, whether on the basis of the internal market or on the basis of the external market, anchored in the

Table 4.15

Subsectors of Secondary Occupations	Participation in Employment (in percentage)		Contribution to New Jobs created	
	1950	1980	(N)	(%)
Textile, Clothing, Leather, and Food	54.1	31.2	1,558,551	23.7
Civil Construction	22.8	30.8	2,193,878	33,4
New Sectors (Chemical, Heavy Industry, etc.)	23.1	38.0	2,819,017	42.9
TOTAL	100.0	100.0	6,571,446	100.0

technological renewal of the existing sectors would not be sufficiently dynamic in terms of employment. However, a resumption of growth also supported by the appearance of new sectors and products could certainly show a high degree of dynamism, even if it were based on capital-intensive advanced technology.

NOTES

1. In this study, I use data and information analyzed in two earlier studies (1983a and 1983b) but which is presented and organized here in a different form.

2. In this first part, I used information from several studies to gain a better understanding of recent economic transformations. Among them, the following should be mentioned: Serra, 1981; Bonelli and Malan, 1976; Draibe, 1985; Belluzo and Mello, 1977; Faria, 1981.

3. There is abundant Brazilian and Latin American literature with regard to this. For a systematic review, see Faria 1976. See also Kowarick, 1976.

4. In this regard, see the study by Pastore, this volume.

5. Whether this policy of salary restraints persistently and continually aggravated the structure of income concentration is a matter of controversy. With regard to this, see the study by Helga Hoffman, this volume.

REFERENCES

Belluzzo, L.G. e Mello, J.M.C. "Reflexões sobre a crise atual". Revista Escrita/Ensaio, n.º 2, 1977.

Berquó, Elza. Algumas considerações sobre a dinâmica da população brasileira. São Paulo, CEBRAP, 1983. 10 p.

Bonelli, R. e Malan, P.S. "Os limites do possível: notas sobre balanço de pagamentos e indústria nos anos 70". *Pesquisa e Planejamento Econômico*, vol. 6, (2), 1976.

Cardoso, Fernando H. "Comentários sobre conceitos de superpopulação relativa e marginalidade". *Estudos CEBRAP* 1, 1971, pp. 99—130.

Castells, Manuel. "La Urbanización dependiente en América Latina". *In Imperialismo y Urbanización en América Latina*, p. 7—26; Manuel Castells e Patrício Velez. Barcelona, Editorial Gustavo Gili.

Draibe, Sonia, *Rumos e Metamorfoses*. Rio de Janeiro, Paz e Terra, 1985.

ECLA—Economic Commission for Latin America. *Development Problems in Latin America*. Austin, Texas, The University of Texas Press, 1970.

Faria, Vilmar E. "O sistema de estratificação social e a estrutura ocupacional de Salvador". *Caderno CEBRAP*. São Paulo. CEBRAP, 1975.

————. *Occupational Marginality, Employment and Poverty in Urban Brazil*. Cambridge, Massachusets, June 1976. Mimeo. Ph.D. dissertation, Harvard University.

————. "Urbanização e qualidade de vida no Brasil contemporâneo", trabalho apresentado no Simpósito "A Questão Migratória no Brasil—Migrações Internas e a Ação do Estado", do CNPq, Brasília, December 1981.

————. Desenvolvimento, urbanização e mudanças na estrutura do emprego: a experiência brasileira dos últimos trinta anos. *In* SORJ, Bernardo & Almeida, Maria Hermínia Tavares de, org. *Sociedade e política no Brasil pós 64*. São Paulo, Brazil, 1983, pp. 118–63.

Faria, Vilmar E. e Silva, Pedro Luiz Barros, "Transformações Estruturais, políticas sociais e dinâmica demográfica: a discussão de um caso—Brasil—1950/1980". São Paulo, p. 61 (Paper presented in the 1o Congresso Latino–Americano de População e Desenvolvimento, México, DF, 8–11 November 1983), November 1983b.

Kowarick, Lucio. *Capitalismo e marginalidade na América Latina*. Rio de Janeiro, Paz e Terra, 1976.

Oliveira, Francisco de. "A economia brasileira: crítica à razão dualista". In *Seleções CEBRAP 1* (Questionando a Economia Brasileira), pp. 5–78. São Paulo, Brazil.

Pastore, José. "Inequality and Social Mobility: Ten Years Later" essay in this volume.

Quijano, Annibal. "Redefinición de la Dependencia y Proceso de Marginalización en America Latina". In *Populismo, Marginalización y Dependencia*, pp. 171–329. Edited by F.C. Weffort and A. Quijano. San José, Costa Rica, Editorial Universitária Centroamericana.

Saboia, João L.M. *As causas da difusão da posse de bens de consumo duráveis no Brasil*. Rio de Janeiro, COPPE/UFRJ.

Serra, José. *Ciclos e mudancas estruturais na economia brasileira do após-guerra*. Paper presented at the Seminário sobre Políticas para el Desarollo Latinoamericano do CECADE, México, July 1981.

Sorj, Bernard, and Wilkinson, John. *Processos sociais e formas de produção na agricultura brasileira. In* Sorj, Bernard & Almeida, Maria Hermínia Tavares de, org. *Sociedade, política no Brasil pós 64*. São Paulo, Brazil 1983, pp. 164–90.

5

Inequality and Social Mobility

Ten Years Later

José Pastore

INTRODUCTION

Preliminary work for studies of social mobility in Brazil began in the mid-1950s with the development of the first scales of social prestige and socio-economic status (Hutchinson, 1957). Pioneering works relating the socio-economic status of individuals to that of their parents appeared shortly thereafter, but none of them went so far as to cover Brazilian society as a whole. Instead, they were limited to very specific groups, such as small samples of urban groupings (Havighurst, 1957), immigrants (Hutchinson, 1958), college students (Hutchinson, 1960), and urban migrants (Hutchinson, 1961). The first analysis of social mobility to include the whole of Brazilian society was carried out on the basis of the data of the 1973 National Household Sample Survey and was published in 1979 (Pastore, 1979).

That study was groundbreaking and controversial: groundbreaking because, for the first time, adequate data supported a rigorous analysis of social mobility in Brazil; controversial because the results showed an apparent paradox by indicating that this same Brazil of poor income distribution had experienced a strong current of upward social mobility throughout this century and particularly after 1950. Compared with ten other industrialized countries, Brazil showed the highest mobility rates (Pastore, 1979)[1]. How could Brazil have produced such upward mobility if the distribution of income was distorted to such an extent?

The paradox demanded explanation. Even in its title my book proposed to explain it: *Desigualdade e Mobilidade Social no Brasil* (Inequality and Social Mobility in Brazil). In short, the data indicated that in the course of the century almost all Brazilians had risen in the structure of occupational status when compared with their parents or with themselves at the beginning of their own careers. That meant the social mobility was all encompassing, occuring throughout the social structure.

The data revealed, however, that individuals of low status moved short distances while individuals of medium status covered enormous social distances. The final result was a distension of the social structure—that is, mobility accompanied by inequality—which was consistent with studies that had emphasized the aggravation of income distribution (Langoni, 1973).

When the determinants of mobility were analyzed, expansion of employment and the differentiation of occupations within the job market stood out as the clearest inducements of the social mobility that had occurred. Other significant forces were personal factors, in particular, education and social origin. In short, the bulk of the mobility was *structural*—due to transformations of the economy—and the rest was formed by *circular* mobility—due to changes of position because of competition among individuals in the job market.

Between 1973 and the present, however, Brazil underwent various shocks and transformations. The Brazilian economy continued to expand, with the latent crisis not manifesting itself on the employment level until 1981 when the recession became clear, provoking a strong contraction of job opportunities, especially in the more industrialized regions. What impact did the recession have on mobility and inequality?

In order to avoid making false claims, it is important to note that no specific data exist with regard to recession and social mobility in Brazil. Therefore, in exploring the topic, we have to be content with indirect data and a good deal of speculation. Furthermore, the analysis of mobility requires a temporal horizon of several decades in order to detect inter- and intragenerational movements with accuracy. As a result, the analysis presented here is precarious since, in addition to the insufficiency of the data, the scarcity of time (and a possible economic recovery) impede the formulation of definitive conclusions with regard to the immediate effects of the recent recession on mobility and inequality.

Therefore, in order to provide a broader view of the general pattern of social mobility in Brazil, this study is divided into two parts: The first part presents a summary of the long-term tendencies observed in the course of this century. The second part presents speculative considerations with regard to the period 1973 to 1983, with special emphasis on the recession years (1981–83) and the resumption of growth in 1984.

MOBILITY AND SOCIAL INEQUALITY: 1900–73

The study *Desigualdade e Mobilidade Social no Brasil* (Pastore, 1979 and 1982) was based on a comparison of occupation statuses. The basic variables consisted of the father's occupational status when the child first started working, the individual's occupational status at the beginning of his career, and his present occupational status (in 1973). These three statuses were measured according to a single scale of occupational social status (Silva, 1974) so as to permit comparison of the three moments in time. The scale combined occupation, education, and income, and consisted of a ranking of 259 occupational titles used in the 1970 demographic census. For purposes of analysis, the social positions were grouped and ranked in six occupational strata (see Table A5.1 in the Appendix).

In this sense, the measurement and analysis were of the type commonly used for sociological methodology in the field of stratification and social mobility. The data stemmed from a subsample of male heads of households, between 20 and 60 years of age, extracted from the National Household Sample Survey conducted in 1973 by the *Fundação IBGE* (PNAD/73). After exclusions due to inconsistencies of one kind or another, this subsample included 58,286 individuals[2]. The following sections present a summary of the results.

Panorama of Social Mobility in Brazil

Table 5.1 is an integrational mobility matrix. The percentages in the rows show how individuals from the same social background were distributed among the different final statuses. The total percentages at the ends of the rows and columns indicate respectively the proportion of individuals in each initial and final social status. In order to easier understand it, the reader should first observe the values of the main diagonal. Those values represent the situation of the individuals who are in the same social position that their fathers were in—that is, *immobile* individuals who neither ascended nor descended on the social scale. Next, we can proceed to a line by line reading. With the exception of the position on the diagonal, the others include *mobile* individuals— that is, those who ascended or descended on the social scale. For example, the second row indicates that 28.7% of the individuals remained immobile in comparison with their fathers, 15.2% descended one level (from status 2 to status 1) and 56.1% ascended one or two levels.

When we compare the present status of the family heads with that of their fathers, we see that in spite of a few points of immobility, Brazilian social structure was characterized by high rates of social mobility between the two

Table 5.1
Occupational Matrix of Intergenerational
Mobility (%)

	Status of the Individual in 1973							Total of Fathers
Status of the Father	1	2	3	4	5	6	Total	
1. High	29.8	22.5	27.4	12.5	5.0	3.1	100	2.0
2. Upper Middle	15.2	28.7	28.7	15.5	6.1	5.8	100	3.1
3. Middle Middle	8.6	14.3	36.2	18.9	10.5	11.5	100	13.8
4. Lower Middle	3.8	8.7	21.6	46.3	14.9	4.7	100	9.3
5. Upper Lower	3.2	7.4	20.7	35.4	23.8	9.5	100	6.9
6. Lower Lower	1.0	2.5	13.1	21.1	17.4	44.9	100	64.9
Total Number of Individuals N = 44,307	3.5	6.3	18.4	23.8	16.0	32.0	100	100

Source: Pastore, 1979 and PNAD/73
1. For more details on the methodology of the study, see Pastore, 1979.

generations, especially by upward social movement. In fact, almost 81% of the mobile individuals were upwardly mobile.[3]

A considerable amount of this upward social movement took place in the lower strata. About 55% of the individuals coming from the lower lower stratum ascended in the social structure. Among those from the upper lower stratum, the proportion was even higher—approximately 67%. This upward mobility is even more significant if we consider that the relative participation of these two strata in the total number of the individuals comes to almost 50%. On the other hand, it shows that a large part of the upwardly mobile individuals tended to stay in positions close to their starting point. So that of the 55% that ascended, approximately 39% went at most to the lower middle stratum. Out of the 67% of upper lower stratum origin that were upwardly mobile, about 56% moved no farther than to the lower middle and middle middle strata.

This concentration of short-distance upward mobility at the base of the social pyramid reflected social changes *and* the labor market. Migration, rapid expansion of employment and its redirection towards the tertiary sector all contributed to the opening up of new opportunities for the individuals of the lower strata, especially for those coming from rural areas. The final result was

Table 5.2
Matrix of Intragenerational Occupational
Mobility (%)

Initial Status	Status of Individual in 1973						Total	Total Initial Status
	1	2	3	4	5	6		
1. High	72.8	14.2	9.6	1.2	1.9	0.3	100	0.6
2. Upper Middle	24.9	47.3	19.4	6.3	1.3	0.8	100	0.7
3. Middle Middle	16.7	24.8	45.0	8.8	3.9	0.8	100	6.9
4. Lower Middle	2.8	7.3	17.1	59.5	10.3	3.0	100	7.3
5. Upper Lower	4.0	9.0	24.6	34.0	22.1	6.3	100	25.2
6. Lower Lower	0.7	2.6	13.4	18.7	17.0	47.6	100	59.2
Total Number in 1973								
N = 53,764	3.4	6.5	18.7	24.7	16.7	30.0	100	100

Source: Pastore, 1979 and PNAD/73

substantial upward mobility for the majority of Brazilians in comparison with their fathers.

Table 5.2 is an intragenerational mobility matrix. With it, we can ascertain what progress the individuals made between their starting position (initial status) and their current situation (status in 1973). This table also shows some signs of immobility (see diagonal), but in the case of intragenerational mobility, this in itself constitutes an indicator of attainment. As can be seen from the table, the proportion of individuals who descended in the social structure is also small. What stands out is the high proportion of upward mobility, which is in fact even more pronounced than in the case of intergenerational mobility: more than 93% of the total number of mobile individuals ascended in comparison with their initial statuses.[4]

Likewise, intergenerational mobility shows that for the most part upward mobility was concentrated in the lower strata—*i.e.*, among those who started their careers in the lower lower level, about 52% were upwardly mobile. For those who started in the upper level, about 73% were upwardly mobile. In addition, as in the case of intergenerational mobility, the majority of the upwardly mobile individuals shifted to strata close to their starting points.

The Role of Changes in the Labor Market

Social mobility occurs, in essence, by means of two mechanisms: In the first, individuals of a lower occupational origin take advantage of new job opportunities with a higher occupational status. The upward movement is related to a structural transformation of the job market that creates higher-status job opportunities—thus, the concept of *structural mobility*. In the second, individuals change positions by means of competition—*i.e.*, for one person to ascend, another has to descend—thus, the concept of *circular mobility*.

In Brazil, most of the social mobility which has taken place in the course of the century has been structural, reflecting the expansion and differentiation of new occupational statuses summarized below.

Table 5.3 shows several moments in the evolution of the job market of the period. Although the data must be considered with due caution because of its fragility, it does show that in the 1920s and 30s the generation of employment was largely concentrated in the agricultural sector (about 60% of the total). Even though primary sector activities lost ground in relative terms, they continued to have a role in the creation of jobs throughout the 1940s and 50s; of the 7.5 million new jobs generated in the period, 40% were still located in the agricultural sector.

In the 1960s and 70s, however, structural changes became pronounced, with the tertiary sector becoming the main source of opportunities in the job market. Of the almost 7 million new jobs generated, almost 53% occurred in the tertiary sector, 34% were in the secondary sector, and only 13% were in the primary sector. The redirecting of the rural work force to the secondary and, mainly, the tertiary sector opened up countless opportunities for upward social mobility to young migrants. In addition, the acceleration of industrialization and of all types of related employment introduced countless new higher-status occupations into the country, which also made mobility of greater distances possible for people coming from the middle strata.

For an adequate analysis of this effect, it is interesting to examine the occupational differentiation that occurred in the 1950 to 1970 period. Table 5.4 shows the distribution of the Brazilian Economically Active Population (EAP), taking into account an increase in occupations based on the relative homogeneity of the occupational strata. As in the case of Table 5.3, the data show a strong decline in the proportion of workers in the areas of services, manufacturing and civil construction.

Combining the expansion of employment in Table 5.3 with the sectorial changes in the occupation of the EAP in Table 5.4, we have an explanation of the reason why a large part of the social mobility in Brazil had its roots in the expansion and structural transformations of the labor market. In fact, the data regarding both intergenerational and intragenerational mobility show that almost 60% of the identified mobility was structural in nature—that is, upward social mobility was preceded by the utilization of new opportunities which had appeared in the job market. A smaller part of the mobility (about

Table 5.3
Number of New Jobs Created and Annual Rates of Growth of Employment (%)

	1920/1930		1940/1950		1950/1960		1960/1970	
	New Jobs	Annual Rate	New Jobs	Annual Rate	New Jobs	Annual Rate	New Jobs	Annual Rate
Primary	59.3	1.7	41.1	1.4	34.2	1.7	13.4	0.7
Secondary	6.3	1.0	27.9	4.7	9.6	2.0	33.8	6.0
Manufacturing	—	—	15.9	3.9	7.1	2.2	17.9	4.9
Construction	—	—	10.1	8.3	3.6	3.0	13.5	8.2
Others	—	—	1.9	3.1	-1.1	0.0	2.4	6.8
Tertiary	34.2	2.9	31.0	2.6	56.2	5.5	52.8	4.0
Distribution	12.2	2.7	15.5	3.3	20.1	5.0	15.2	3.1
Social	9.7	5.2	8.9	3.7	10.5	5.0	19.6	6.5
Others	12.3	2.3	6.6	1.3	25.6	6.4	18.0	3.4
TOTAL	100	1.9	100	2.1	100	2.9	100	2.7

Source: Faria, 1976. Faria, 1986

Table 5.4

Changes in the Economically Active Population
by Occupational Categories (%)*

Occupational Categories	Difference (1970–1950)
1. Personal Services	+2.5
2. Manufacturing and Construction	+2.4
3. Administrative and Office Workers	+2.2
4. Technical-Scientific, Artistic and Allied occupations	+1.9
5. Commerce and Allied Activities	+1.1
6. Transport and Communications	+0.8
7. Defense and Security	+0.4
8. Mining	−0.1
9. Agriculture and Allied Industries	−13.0

Source: Taken from the Demographic Censuses of Brazil, 1950 and 1970.
*Excluded are other and non-declared occupations (+2.0%).

40%) was circular, stemmed from competition and changes in position among individuals of hierarchically different occupational statuses (Pastore, 1979, Chapters 6 and 7) and was closely connected with education, as explained below.

The Role of Individual Resources

In late industrialized countries like Brazil, structural factors have a clear predominance in the conditioning of social mobility. Nevertheless, their influence does not occur unequivocally; it depends a good deal on the action of individual factors. In other words, if the development route followed by Brazil determined the extent and type of occupational opportunities available, it would be the individual resources that determined to a large extent how these opportunities were utilized.

In less developed societies like Brazil, however, entry into the job market tends to occur earlier because of the economically active role that many children assumed within the family. In fact, 70% of the family heads in the sample began to work at the age of 14 or less.[5]

Table 5.5 shows that the earlier the entry into the labor market, the lower the individual's initial status. Among those who started working at the age of 14 or below, 94% began in low-skilled occupations in the agricultural or

Table 5.5
Age of Entrance into the Labor Force and Initial Occupational Status (%)

Initial Occupation Status	Age of Entrance into the Labor Force					
	14 or less	15–17	18–20	21–26	26 or more	Total
High	0.0	0.1	1.2	10.7	30.8	0.6
Upper Middle	0.0	0.6	3.3	9.1	9.8	0.7
Middle Middle	1.3	11.2	34.0	38.3	21.9	7.0
Lower Middle	4.4	12.3	19.5	15.5	11.3	7.4
Upper Lower	22.3	39.1	29.7	19.0	19.0	25.8
Lower Lower	72.0	36.7	12.3	7.4	7.2	58.5
TOTAL	100	100	100	100	100	100
N = 55,801						

Source: Pastore, 1979.

Table 5.6
Age of Entrance into the Labor Force and Current Occupational Status (%)

Current Occupational status	14 or less	15–17	18–20	21–26	26 or more	Total
High	1.8	4.1	9.7	21.7	36.9	3.7
Upper Middle	4.5	8.5	14.8	19.8	11.8	6.7
Middle Middle	16.4	22.4	28.7	27.3	14.7	18.9
Lower Middle	23.6	29.2	26.2	19.1	13.6	24.6
Upper Lower	17.0	17.8	14.4	8.7	12.0	16.6
Lower Lower	36.7	18.0	6.2	3.4	5.0	29.5
TOTAL	100	100	100	100	100	100
N = 55,801						

Source: Pastore, 1979.

urban sector. What are the consequences of this phenomenon for social mobility?

Table 5.6 shows that there has been a lot of mobility between the initial status and the present status. Nevertheless, this has not completely compensated for the pernicious effect of early entry into the work force. A comparison of the two tables shows that the negative influence of early entry on the social destiny of the individuals is reflected more strongly in present status than in their initial status. In the first case, it is quite clear that the earlier the entry, the greater the probability that the individuals will occupy positions of low status and will remain there. Thus their early entry into the job market has had a doubly negative effect. On the one hand, it has led to a poor career beginning; on the other hand, it has made access to higher social positions difficult.

Early entry is closely connected with educational level and with future prospects. For many, it means the interruption of their schooling—that is, the downward leveling of an important individual resource for mobility. This becomes very clear when the opposite is considered—that is, the effect of education on those who had greater access to schooling. Table 5.7 shows that the higher the individual's level of schooling, the better his career beginning and the better his trajectory of mobility—that is, education counts for mobility.

But not every trajectory follows the sequence of school first and then work, since much of the professional preparation Brazilians receive is provided in the market itself. Schooling and work also coexist.[6] Whatever the case, the influence of education for the present status of individuals remains clear. Table 5.8 shows that higher educational levels tend to place individuals in a higher present status. On the other hand, only a small proportion of individuals with a high school degree (or higher educational level) are in low-status occupations. A large proportion of individuals without formal education or who have not completed primary school predominate in this stratum.

In short, although the relationship between education and upward social mobility is not perfect and isolated, there is no doubt that educational differences constitute important mechanisms for upward mobility, especially when combined with so many structural transformations.[7]

ECONOMIC CRISIS AND SOCIAL MOBILITY

Growth During the Crisis: 1973–80

In spite of the crisis that affected almost all the industrialized nations between 1973 and 1980, Brazil continued on its path of economic growth and generation of employment. In that period, the average annual growth rate was about 8% and per capita income increased from Cr$ 1,827 in 1973 to Cr$ 2,477 in 1980. Both industry and agriculture experienced very favorable development during the period. The average annual growth rate for the industrial sector was almost 10% and for the agricultural sector it was about 5.5%. In addition, the positive performance of the economy was greater than the growth in

Table 5.7
Education and Initial Occupational Status (%)

Level of Education		Initial Social Status					
	High	Upper Middle	Middle Middle	Lower Middle	Upper Lower	Lower Lower	Total
University	11.1	9.3	47.6	3.9	24.0	4.1	100
Junior High School	1.3	2.4	40.3	9.2	39.8	7.0	100
High School	0.3	1.2	18.0	15.6	48.0	16.9	100
Completed Primary	0.1	0.2	4.6	14.4	40.5	40.2	100
Incomplete Primary	0.0	0.1	0.9	5.7	20.3	73.0	100
No Schooling	0.0	0.0	0.2	1.3	9.8	88.7	100
TOTAL N = 56,909	0.6	0.7	7.0	7.8	25.6	58.3	100

Source: Pastore, 1979.

Table 5.8
Education and Current Occupational Status (%)

Levels of Education		Social Status of Individuals in 1973					
	High	Upper Middle	Middle Middle	Lower Middle	Upper Lower	Lower Lower	Total
University	42.6	33.7	21.8	1.2	0.5	0.2	100
Junior High School	12.7	26.8	47.4	8.7	4.1	0.3	100
High School	3.3	14.5	41.4	27.3	11.7	1.8	100
Completed Primary School	1.7	6.2	23.2	40.3	17.8	10.8	100
Incomplete Primary School	0.7	2.5	13.8	28.9	20.1	34.0	100
No Schooling	0.3	0.6	7.3	10.9	18.0	62.9	100
TOTAL N = 54,950	3.6	6.6	18.8	24.7	16.6	29.7	100

Source: Pastore, 1979

population and greater even than the growth of EAP. The economy grew 8% a year; the population, about 2.4%; EAP, less than 3%; and urban EAP, about 5.5%.

So far as the behavior of the labor market sector is concerned, the decade from 1970–80 further accentuated the importance of industry and services in the general formation of the employed EAP. The secondary sector generated about 5.3 million new jobs, with 3.6 million occurring in manufacturing. The tertiary sector continued to have the largest share, generating about 8.8 million new jobs in the decade (Table 5.9).

The decade from 1970–80 not only maintained the tendency described above but also further accentuated the annual growth rates for jobs in the sectors that show a high level of occupational differentiation (secondary and tertiary) and, therefore, greater opportunities for social mobility. Everything indicates that with the intensification of this tendency, the pattern of structural mobility identified above was also maintained. This leads us to speculate that even at the time of the international crisis, Brazil kept on growing and providing opportunities for upward social mobility to a good part of its work force.

Recession and Social Mobility: 1981–83

Nevertheless, the crisis remained dormant throughout the 1970s. However, inflation and the external debt became powerful time bombs that would explode in 1981. Indeed then reversing the employment picture in the more industrialized regions. The need to decrease public indebtedness, together with the monetary restraint that was part of the stabilization program, made investors apprehensive and brought a lack of incentive to invest, which, in turn, manifested itself in a decline in production and in employed manpower. Between 1981 and 1983, the job supply did not only stop growing, but what was more serious it also started to shrink, thus generating severe unemployment in the metropolitan areas. Let us now analyze the interaction between recession and employment in greater detail so that we can then speculate as to its effects on mobility.

Recession and Employment

Table 5.10 shows that in the recession period—except for one year—urban EAP grew at higher rates than employed urban EAP. That is, urban Brazil entered the deficit area as far as employment was concerned. The decline in job opportunities in itself constitutes an inhibitor of structural social mobility. Without jobs, and especially without new job opportunities, structural

Table 5.9
Number of New Jobs Created and Annual Rates
of Growth of Employment (1970/1980)

Sectors	New Jobs	%	Annual Rate
Primary	21,894	0.2	0.02
Secondary	5,379,550	37.8	7.3
Manufacturing	3,616,737	25.4	7.8
Construction	1,431,380	10.1	6.4
Others	331,433	2.3	7.1
Tertiary	8,838,095	62.0	6.0
Distribution	2,511,489	17.6	5.7
Social	2,173,157	15.3	6.1
Personnel	3,164,708	22.2	6.1
Others	988,741	6.9	6.4
TOTAL	14,239,539	100	4.0

Source: Faria, 1986

Table 5.10
Utilization of the Urban Labor Force

Categories	Millions of Persons				Percentage Change		
	1980	1981	1982	1983	81/80	82/81	83/82
EAP Urban	32.4	34.2	35.8	37.8	5.6	4.7	5.6
EAP Urban Occup.	30.9	32.2	33.8	35.4	4.2	5.0	4.7
Formal Sector	17.6	18.1	18.7	17.4	2.8	3.3	−7.0
Public/Private Employment	16.0	16.3	16.7	15.4	1.8	2.5	−7.8
Public Administration	1.6	1.8	2.0	2.0	12.5	11.1	0.0
Informal Sector	13.3	14.1	15.1	18.0	6.0	7.1	19.2

Source: SES/MTb, 1985, pp. 32 & 37. Adopted by the Author.

mobility is impossible. In addition, it is useful to examine the form that the contraction of the job supply took.

The same table shows that in 1981–83, employment in the formal (or organized sector) decreased at a rate of 2.8% annually. This means that during this period the sector lost almost 1 million jobs. The data show increased employment in public administration (5.1% yearly). But this sector is very small in comparison with the total labor market and does not change the final negative balance for the formal urban labor market during the period.

However, this is not enough to form a conclusion. A different picture emerges in the informal sector.[8] Here almost 4 million new jobs appeared in the 1981–83 period. This is generally interpreted as a natural reaction of Brazilian society which, because of not having any form of unemployment insurance at the time, was forced to accommodate a growing EAP with decreasing formal employment. This indeed happened, and informal employment increased. But the increase had little impact on social mobility. In fact, an earlier study (Pastore and Haller, 1982) showed that workers in the informal sector have only one third the chances for upward social mobility of workers in the formal sector. Therefore, on the whole, in terms of social mobility, it is very probable that in the metropolitan areas these 4 million new job opportunities did not manage to compensate for the loss of one million positions in the formal sector. If this scenario is accepted, it is plausible to accept a deceleration of upward social mobility in those regions.

Industrial Deceleration and Social Mobility

Corroborating the preceding hypothesis, the data indicate, in fact, a deceleration of industrial growth beginning in 1981 in the metropolitan areas with a perceptible reduction of the general job supply. Table 5.11 focuses on the reduction of the total job supply in three regions that formed the "employment paradise" of the 1970s—that is, Rio de Janeiro, São Paulo and Curitiba. During the period examined, the job supply in the formal sector of these areas declined by more than 15% while their EAP grew by more than 20%.

The data show particular aggravation of formal employment in manufacturing and civil construction. In the former area, São Paulo experienced a 25% reduction and Rio de Janeiro almost 30%. In the case of civil construction, the situation was even more alarming, since in Curitiba the job supply in that sector declined by almost 60%, and in São Paulo and Rio de Janeiro by almost 50%.[9]

To identify the effects of this reduction on the overall social mobility of the country, however, requires a more extensive treatment of the question, which is presented below.

Recession and Structural Mobility

The data from the PNAD/73 showed that much of the structural mobility that occurred after 1950 was closely associated with the increase in job oppor-

Table 5.11

Indice of Employment in Selected Metropolitan Regions

Month/Year	Rio de Janeiro			São Paulo			Curitiba		
	Total*	Industry	Civil Constr.	Total*	Industry	Civil Constr.	Total*	Industry	Civil Constr.
Aug/78	100	100	100	100	100	100	100	100	100
Dec/78	99.4	99.6	90.5	100.2	99.6	96.0	99.9	100.9	95.0
Dec/79	98.0	97.9	77.6	101.9	101.8	79.9	95.8	104.2	67.2
Dec/80	96.9	91.6	80.8	101.3	100.5	76.1	95.3	108.7	64.0
Dec/81	92.2	79.6	71.4	91.3	83.7	72.5	93.6	97.6	67.8
Dec/82	90.0	77.9	62.1	91.2	82.3	65.1	93.8	97.0	62.3
Dec/83	84.9	69.7	50.9	85.0	74.4	50.7	86.4	91.4	39.6

Source: CDI/SINE, Brasília, Ministério do Trabalho, 1984.
*The totals include industry, civil construction, commerce, and services.

tunities and the occupational differentiation of the industrial sector. Countless new higher status occupations were calling for workers and thus promoting inter- and intragenerational mobility. A perceptible amount of the long-distance upward social mobility was related to the emergence of a large spectrum of new jobs in industry in the area of production as well as in the areas of administration, finance and marketing. The industrial progress and the expansion of government-owned companies throughout the 1960s and 70s had a clear impact on the promotion of structural mobility (Pastore 1979, Chapter 4). Thus, the recent contraction of the job supply in the industrial sector, in manufacturing as well as in civil construction, leads us to accept the appearance of forces detrimental to structural mobility in the metropolitan areas.

Recession and Circular Mobility

What can be said about circular mobility in the same regions? By way of speculation, it should be mentioned that the 1981–83 period was characterized not only by the reduction of the job supply in the industrial sector but also by unemployment and rapid job turn over.

Unemployment tends to diminish upward social mobility. Reemployment tends to stimulate circular mobility. Official unemployment calculated for six metropolitan regions went from 6.5% in 1980 to almost 10% in 1981, only returning to the level of 7% in 1983. The large layoffs carried out by the industrial sector in 1981 affected first and foremost the least skilled manpower and, therefore the lower-status occupations. At the same time, most companies tried to keep the skilled professionals. In some cases, they were left for later layoffs. By all indications, during the years 1981 and 1982, it was difficult for the majority of those who had lost their jobs to find new employment in jobs of equal or higher status. This suggests that the unemployment in the industrial sector of the metropolitan areas must have provoked downward mobility.

Frequent job turnover has always been high in Brazil in general, including in the industrial sector. The data indicate that only 25% of the work force employed in that sector had been with the same company for more than 5 years (RAIS, 1982). It is reasonable to assume, therefore, that at times of unemployment and oversupply of manpower, the companies practiced rotation, seeking to minimize salaries and maximize qualifications. This did, in fact, occur. The experience of SINE (National Employment System) of the Ministry of Labor shows that in the 1981–83 period employers demanded increasingly higher qualifications to fill vacancies which they had themselves created through their rotation practice. So it is very probable that circular mobility had been increased in these cases, due to the change of less skilled workers for others who were better qualified for the same occupational position. There is a scarcity of data in this regard. However, 12 case studies conducted by the Technical Assistance Office of the Ministry of Labor in 1981 in the São Paulo ABC industrial district showed a systematic shift of less skilled manpower to lower positions in the social structure.

Civil Construction, Migratory Currents, and Mobility

Going back to civil construction, it is important to note that that sector offered countless opportunities for short-distance upward social mobility to young migrants who had recently arrived in the cities in the 1950–80 period. With the strong contraction of the formal job supply in this sector, what happened to the candidates for this type of mobility? Moreover, what happened to those who lost their jobs in the civil construction sector? By all indications, two effects must be considered: the frustrated upward movement of many and, in addition, the forced descent of others. Finally, the contraction of the job supply in civil construction also had the effect of discouraging rural-urban migration. What happened, then, with the nonmigrants—that is, with those who remained in the interior?

The data for the analysis of this segment of the labor market are precarious and scarce. It is important, however, to point out that the Brazil of the interior, the border, and the energy-producing (alcohol and coal) regions showed countless points of expansion in the above-mentioned period. So far as the border zone is concerned, the migratory flow toward Central and West Brazil had already intensified long before 1980, especially in Mato Grosso do Sul, Goiás, Rondônia, Acre, and even in Maranhão.

So far as energy is concerned, the expansion occurred after 1980 in response to the recession itself, especially in the case of alcohol. Table 5.12 presents estimates of the alcohol sector and shows that the production of alcohol in the interior of Brazil—especially in São Paulo, Minas Gerais, Rio Grande do Sul and Pernambuco—had already led directly to the employment of 400 thousand workers. Specific estimates for the sector indicate the generation of 1.2 million jobs indirectly.[10] That is, the sector generated more than 1.5 million new jobs in the period considered.[11]

Apart from alcohol, in the 1981–83 period the interior of Brazil also opened up new job opportunities in other energy and agricultural sectors. By Nogueria's estimates, charcoal and mineral coal created about 200 thousand jobs directly and indirectly; while mining created about 35,000, and hydroelectric power 80,000 (Nogueira, 1981).

At the same time, Brazil's expansion into new areas led to jobs in agricul-

Table 5.12
Estimate of the Number of Jobs Generated
by the Production of Alcohol

Harvest	Production Billions of Litres	No. of Jobs
1978/79	2.5	117,500
1979/80	3.4	159,800
1980/81	3.7	173,900
1981/82	4.2	197,400
1982/83	5.8	272,600
1983/84	7.9	371,300
1984/85	9.0	423,000

Source: CENAL—Comissão Executiva Nacional do Álcool, 1984.

ture and agroindustry. In Mato Grosso do Sul, in the period considered, the job supply increased by 15%; in Rondônia by 18%; in Acre by 14%. Those regions together directly created more than 200,000 new jobs (SINE/Mtb, 1984). In addition to this, there is a group of peripheral activities—such as jobs related to the development of local commerce, to administrative support for agroindustry and agriculture, and to expansion of community and government services—which, according to the estimates of SINE, created more than 300,000 new jobs.

All told, the energy sector in general, and the above-mentioned activities in particular, probably created about 2.5 million new positions in the interior of Brazil in the 1980–83 period. No doubt this helped to diminish the migratory flow to the major cities. On the other hand, this expansion of employment probably produced short-distance structural mobility in the interior since the great majority of the opportunities generated consist of low-skilled jobs.

Thus, the expansion in the interior combined with the contraction of civil construction in the metropolitan areas probably led to a redirectioning of youthful migration to the newer areas where there were better chances of finding employment and experiencing vertical mobility, although of short social distance.

It is quite probable, however, that this complex of positive changes was still not enough to foster the upward social mobility of all the workers located in the lower strata of the Brazilian social pyramid, since many of the unemployed civil construction workers in the metropolitan areas remained there (underemployed or unemployed) dramatically influencing the social picture of the major Brazilian cities. Few of them were in a position to return to their places of origin or to migrate to other areas. For these workers, the new times most likely provoked a serious regression in terms of social mobility.

In short, the combination of the contraction of manufacturing and civil construction and the expansion of new sectors in the interior probably provoked three phenomena: (a) downward social movement for a large number of workers in the major cities; (b) redirecting of migratory currents; (c) upward social movement for workers employed in the new labor markets of the interior of Brazil. In even more speculative numerical terms, it can be said that the situation of the urban labor market in the 1981–83 period behaved as follows: (a) the demand for new jobs increased by 4 million, (b) the supply of formal jobs declined by 1 million; (c) the supply of informal jobs increased by 4 million.

There are several ways to evaluate this picture. If the standard is the supply's capacity for accommodation, the development was reasonable. If the criterion is the capacity to respond to demand in the formal sector with a minimum of legal protection of labor, the performance of the urban labor market was dramatic: Instead of creating 4 million new jobs, there was a reduction of 1 million—that is, a negative balance of 5 million jobs. This second criterion has greater importance for the analysis of social mobility. With this drastic reduction of formal jobs, the prospects for upward social mobility must have diminished for the major portion of labor.

In the interior of the country, on the other hand, the picture was probably the reverse: (a) the demand for new positions of employment increased by about 3 million; (b) the supply in the interior, in the energy areas and border regions alone, increased by about 2.5 million new jobs. That movement probably created conditions not only for the accommodation of most of the new demand but also for upward social mobility. Therefore, in these regions the tendency toward structural mobility that had taken root in Brazil as a whole since 1950 was probably maintained. In other words, the recession changed not only the profile of production and geographic distribution but also the direction taken by the currents of structural mobility.

Recent Trends

In the year of 1984, however, signs of a recovery in urban employment appeared. In fact Brazil's industrial product started falling with less intensity as of September 1983, then it began to grow in 1984 and finished the year at the 7% mark. For this sector, the data show a growth of formal urban employment on the order of 1.5%—which meant the generation of almost 300 thousand jobs. Other sectors paralleled industry in this respect. Services, for example, showed an increase in employment of 1.7% compared with 1983—that is, 154 thousand new jobs.

These signs of recovery, although encouraging, are very far from the real needs of the metropolitan labor market. The impact of the recession on employment was severe, especially in those regions, and it can only be neutralized by a much more vigorous resumption of growth. Only then will the social structure as a whole once again show the same rhythm of general mobility as was recorded, with certainty, until 1973 and very probably until 1980.

However, both the three recession years and the recovery of employment in 1984 are short-term phenomena so far as the analysis of patterns of social mobility is concerned. More definitive effects can be detected only by specific data at the beginning of the next decade—that is, in 1993—when there will be a horizon of 20 years to compare with the PNAD/73.

CONCLUSION

The data for social mobility based on changes of occupational status reflect a considerable dynamism in Brazilian society throughout this century. Most of the Economically Active Population (EAP) achieved upward social mobility, which means that the social statuses of individuals are often higher than the statuses of their parents and higher than their own statuses at the start of their professional careers. Industrialization, the expansion of commerce and services in the course of the century, as well as urbanization and rural-urban migration contributed decisively to this mobility. That is—Brazil intensively experienced a process of structural mobility stemming from the opening up of new employment opportunities and higher-status occupations.

The recent period, affected by the recession beginning in 1981, seems to have reversed this process in the metropolitan areas. However, that period, besides being recent was also very brief, given the recovery that began in the second half of 1984—and this could result in a new acceleration of social mobility so as to resume the process and, who knows, even compensate for the suspected stagnation.

In this same period, new job opportunities continued to expand rapidly in the interior of the country, especially in the regions connected with the energy sector and in the border areas. This suggests a redirectioning of the focuses of structural mobility and an intensification of the short-distance movements that were already in the majority before 1980 and that are continuing in the new regions where new job opportunities are opening up.

In any case, what can be conjectured from this is that on the whole Brazil has maintained the dynamism of its largely structural social mobility up to the present time. It is worthwhile to discuss here the implications of this phenomenon for social equality, poverty, and the general welfare of the population.

For some reason, there is still a tendency to consider equality, decreasing poverty, and improvement of welfare as automatic consequences of social mobility. Nothing is further from the truth. Mobility can often lead to greater inequality, as has been the case in Brazil. However, this does not make it a detrimental phenomenon. It simply shows a pattern of growth and development in which some people rise more than others, while the majority of people rise only a little in the social structure.

It is important to point out that occupational mobility—no matter how insignificant it may be—always represents a modification of career prospects for the individual when he is young, and for future generations. The data for Brazil are unequivocal in this regard. There are no indications of significant occupational regression or even of stagnation in the Brazilian work force. Other changes in the areas of employment, industrialization profile, salary and greater access to property, could set mobility on the path toward equality.

Thus it is illusory to claim equality or even the explanation of social inequality on the basis of mobility studies. Mobility studies aim only at identifying the volume and direction of the movement that individuals make in relation to their parents and within the course of their own lives. That is all! It is inadequate to try to draw conclusions about income distribution, equality or social welfare on the basis of mobility studies. For those purposes, there are other dependent variables such as distribution of income, of salaries, or even the general way of life or standard of living of the populaion. In the study of social mobility, the dependent variable is neither differences of salary nor differences of income; nor even differences of standards of living or ways of life. It is simply the transition from one position to another. On this basis, the degree of fluidity (or rigidity) of the social structure is identified; the level of the social pyramid with the greatest permeability is determined; the extent to which fluidity and permeability lead to equalization or inequalities is investigated.

These studies are also insufficient to explain prosperity or poverty. In principle, the general well-being or poverty of a people is independent of the social flow. There are examples of rigid societies with a good level of general prosperity. In the case of Brazil, we see the opposite: substantial fluidity accompanied by the maintenance of certain pockets of poverty. In Brazil, the problem of poverty is chronic in spite of all the mobility recorded. The pockets of urban and rural poverty are going to require specific structural changes. This task has little to do with the occurrence of general social mobility in the society.

It is equally illusory to consider mobility as a panacea for a dissatisfied society or to believe that mobility is a mechanism for coopting classes and maintaining the social order. In fact, mobility is a progressive process that generates satisfaction and dissatisfaction. However, it is precisely the union of these forces that leads to the improved organization of institutions and social groups, of businessmen and workers, of the governing and the governed. In the Brazil of today, the participation of these groups is minimal, while the government has grown to enormous size in areas in which it is unnecessary and is missing from areas in which its compensatory role is absolutely indispensable. This reformulation of the institutional picture certainly has much more relevancy for questions of equality, poverty and well-being than mobility does.

But mobility studies contribute precisely in the characterization of what is happening to the social structure, to the dynamics of the society, and to the utilization of occupational opportunities. If Brazil is not a more homogeneous society, this cannot be attributed to a lack of dynamics in the social structure. There is activity, but the type of activity that it is leads us to the realization that it is moving the social structure as a whole toward ever greater inequality, in addition to being unable to eliminate the areas of greatest poverty. However, the ingredients of an active, lively society are there. Brazil is a society that is destined to grow. Brazilians respond to job opportunities with the desire to work. By working, the majority rise in the social structure. Today—in occupational terms and in terms of future prospects—is better than yesterday. For a few, it is much better, which on the whole makes Brazil a society with high rates of mobility and inequality. This is the empirical solution to the apparent paradox between mobility and inequality.

APPENDIX

TABLE A 5.1
SOCIAL STRATAS, AVERAGE VALUES AND ILLUSTRATIVE OCCUPATIONS*

Social Status	Mean Value**	Illustrative Occupations
High	63.71	Industrialists, large landowners, high bank functionaries, doctors, lawyers, engineers.
Upper-Middle	30.84	Public Service Administrators, fiscal agents, technical administrators, middle-size landowners, commercial representatives.
Middle-Middle	17.01	Designers, musicians, announcers, buyers, office workers, small landowners, master artisans.

Lower-Middle	9.47	Electricians, Masons, plumbers, carpenters, textile workers, bus drivers, barbers.
Upper-Lower	5.84	Urban Manual workers, delivery boys, shoeshine boys, washerwomen
Lower-Lower	4.70	Unskilled rural workers, fishermen, rubber gatherers

*The definition of status used here, as with any other schema, is somewhat arbitrary. An alternative categorization could be: High, Upper Middle, Lower Middle, Upper-Lower, Lower-Lower Urban and Lower-Lower rural. This classification has the utility of better describing the lower strata and the disadvantage of denying to the more skilled manual occupations a *status* of middle class, though of the lowest level.

**The average values indicate the arithmetic mean of the values of the components of each social strata. Each strata is made up of a group of values—one for each occupation. The average values are thus the average of the individual values of each strata.

NOTES

1. In the above-mentioned study, social mobility rates were compared for Brazil and the United States, England, Switzerland, Austria, West Germany, Italy, Yugoslavia, Argentina, and Indonesia (Pastore, 1979, Table 6.11).

2. For further details concerning the methodology of the study, see Pastore, 1979, chapter 3.

3. The total number of upwardly mobile individuals is given by the sum of the percentages showing upward mobility in each row of the matrix.

4. A large part of this rise, it is true, consisted in a simple process of recuperation due to the tendency of Brazilian workers to enter the job market precociously in occupations of low status.

5. This suggests that the great majority of Brazilian families have been unable to keep their children in school, with serious consequences for their careers later in life.

6. Countless studies identify large proportions of working students in Brazil. Fifteen years ago, about 30% of junior high school students studied at night and held full-time jobs during the day (Dias, 1967, pp. 141–43). This tendency has become even more pronounced recently and has also affected High School and university students. In 1983, the proportions were 41% and 62% respectively (Anuário Estatistico do Brasil, 1983).

7. For an analysis of the net effects of education on social mobility, see Pastore, 1979, chapter 10.

8. All workers who do not have contractual job relationships, and, therefore, are not covered by social welfare programs and other benefits, are considered part of the informal sector. Possession of a signed *carteira de trabalho* (work permit) is the main indicator of a formal contractual relationship. However, individuals, such as public officials, members of the armed forces, the liberal professions and the clergy, who receive social welfare benefits although they do not have signed working papers, are excluded from the informal sector.

9. The commerce and services sectors show positive results. Rio de Janeiro increased 22% in commerce and was stable in services; the figures for São Paulo were 4% and 14% respectively, and for Curitiba, 7% in both sectors (see Table 5.13 in the Appendix).

10. The estimates of indirect generation of employment were calculated by Nogueira, 1981.

11. Even considering the effect of crop substitution, the net effect of Proálcool on the generation of employment is frankly positive (Pereira, 1983).

REFERENCES

Dias, José A. *Ensino Médio e Estrutura Sócio-Econômica*. Rio de Janeiro, Fundação IBGE, 1967.

Faria, Vilmar E. "Occupational Marginality, Employment and Poverty in Urban Brazil." Cambridge, Harvard University, Ph. D. dissertation, 1976.

―――. "Changes in the Composition of Employment and the Structure of Occupations," in this volume.

Havighurst, Robert J. "Educacão, Mobilidade Social e Mudança Social em Quatro Sociedades," *in Educação e Ciências Sociais*, 2:114–219, 1957.

Hutchinson, Bertram. "The Social Grading of Occupation in Brazil," *in The British Journal of Sociology*, 3:176–89, 1957.

―――. "Structure and Exchange Mobility in the Assimiliation of Immigrants to Brazil," *in Population Studies*, 12:111–20, 1958.

―――. "Aspectos da Educação Universitária e *Status* Social," in Hutchinson, B. (ed). *Mobilidade e Trabalho*. Rio de Janeiro, Centro Brasileiro de Pesquisas Educacionais, 1960.

―――. "Fertility, Social Mobility and Urban Migration," in *Population Studies*, 14:182-9, 1961.

Langoni, Carlos G. *Distribuição de Renda e Desenvolvimento Econômico no Brasil*. Rio de Janeiro, Expressão e Cultura, 1973.

Nogueira, Uziel B. "Energia e Emprego." Brasília, Ministério do Trabalho, mimeo, 1981.

Pastore, José. *Desigualdade e Mobilidade Social no Brasil*. São Paulo, T.A. Queiroz, 1979.

————. *Inequality and Social Mobility in Brazil.* Madison, University of Wisconsin Press, 1982.

Pastore, J. and Haller, A.O. "Social Mobility under Labor Market Segmentation in Brazil," *in Social Structure and Behavior.* New York, Academic Press, 1982.

Pereira, Armand. "Producción de Etanal en Brasil: Consequencias para el Empleo," *in Revista Internacional del Trabajo*, Vol. 102, N.^{0}1, Jan.–March, 1983.

RAIS. *Relação Anual de Informações Sociais: Tabulações Especiais.* Brasília, Ministério do Trabalho, 1982.

SES/MTb. "Políticas de Estabilização e Emprego: O Caso do Brasil: 1980–84." Brasília, Secretaria de Emprego e Salário, Ministério do Trabalho, 1984.

Silva, Nelson V. "Posição Social nas Ocupações." Rio de Janeiro, IBGE, mimeo, 1984.

SINE/MTb. *Oferta Global de Emprego, Tabulações Especiais.* Brasília, SINE/MTb, 1984.

6

Poverty and Property in Brazil
What is Changing?

Helga Hoffman

1. INTRODUCTION

In the period of high rates of economic growth labeled the "Brazilian miracle," it was said that in order to "distribute the cake" it was necessary (and sufficient) to let it "grow."[1] The trickle-down of the benefits would either have to come spontaneously or would have to wait.[2] Gross National Product (GNP) growth and the battle against inflation were the priority goals of economic policy. But under this policy the "miracle" was soon tarnished.

In the 1980s foreign debt became the most notorious element and the central worry of public policy. The balance of payments deficit became once more a constraint to growth, and adjustment to the external shock gained priority even over and above growth and the fight against inflation. Again, there was no concern with distributional implications of the main policy decisions. Those who had had to bear the brunt of the burden in the recent period of economic hardship were not consulted, just as they had not been consulted about their share in the benefits of growth. Changes in distribution have been taking place nothwithstanding the absence of this issue among the main explicit concerns of government policy.

This chapter focuses on the changes in economic inequality, particulary income distribution; on absolute poverty in the longer run as well as in the last years; and on the challenges present levels of inequality and absolute poverty in Brazil pose for public policy.

197

The theory of distribution will not be discussed. The theoretical debate on equity and distribution is part of a more general one confronting different schools of economic thought with different views of the functioning of society. It has been very lively and is still open among neoclassicists, marxists, sraffians, neo-ricardians or institutionalists.[3] As a rule, studies on income distribution in Brazil have not approached the Brazilian case in the light of competing theories or tried to use it as a test for theory.[4] Even the interdependence between certain characteristics of the growth model followed in the country and its patterns of income distribution and consumption have often been examined without referring explicitly to any particular theory of distribution. "Human captial theory" is behind one of the well-known studies (Langoni, 1973), and various versions of it are part of the repertoire of justifications presented for Brazil's highly inegalitarian path, particularly during the "boom" period of 1968–1974.

Inequality in income distribution in Brazil seems to be one of the highest in the world. It is certainly far higher than in developed countries: while the Gini coefficient of the income distribution by households is 0.530 in Brazil in 1970, around the same year it is 0.407 in Japan, 0.404 in the United States, 0.382 in Canada, 0.346 in Sweden, 0.382 in France, 0.344 in the United Kingdom (Lecaillon *et al.*, 1984, p. 40).

The picture that emerges from this comparison with other developing countries is less clear. Sufficiently reliable data are available only for a limited number of developing countries. But these data are not homogeneous. The year in which the information was gathered is not the same for all countries. The source for some countries is the census; for others, it is household budget surveys; for others still, it is wage statistics. The chosen income recipient unit is also different. In some cases, it is the individual; in others, the family or the household; and in others, the economically active person. Moreover, the surveys use a variety of income concepts and sample designs, and their coverage is not always nationwide. Intertemporal data from comparable sources are even more scarce (Lecaillon *et al.*, 1984, p. 42). Thus, even with the best available estimates of income distribution for various countries, international comparisons can be made only with reservations.

Besides the statistical pitfalls for international comparisons of income distribution, the same inequality index may have different significance in different historical contexts. How much is it possible to infer from the fact that the Gini index of the income distribution among Economically Active Persons (EAP) in Brazil in 1980, which was 0.592, is the same as it was the in South Africa of fifteen years before?[5]

A recent survey by the International Labour Office (ILO) presented a new set of estimates of income inequality in developing countries. After screening various national sources, rejecting estimates derived from incomplete sources, and making some adjustments for the sake of comparison, the ILO set was limited to 39 countries for which existing data were considered reliable: of these, 15 were in Africa, 10 in Asia, and 14 in Latin America. For these countries the Gini coefficient of the income distribution by EAP and by households was estimated in years that vary between 1957 and 1976, depending on the country.

Within this set of estimates the position of Brazil is in the highest range of inequality. Only 12 countries have a higher Gini coefficient of the distribution of household incomes around the year 1970. Among them were Mexico (0.567), South Africa (0.563), Iran and Peru (both 0.561), and Turkey (0.549). The countries with a Gini coefficient lower than Brazil's 0.530 numbered 26: among them were the Philippines (0.490), Thailand (0.504), the Ivory Coast (0.487), and India (0.411 in 1961–64) (Lecaillon et al., 1984, p. 39).

The World Bank's World Development Report has been including a table on income distribution since 1983. The information is the share of household income by percentile groups of households. The World Bank warned, however, that this collection of data has only limited comparability. Brazil emerges from that table having the worse situation among 43 countries (27 developing economies and 16 industrial market economies). In the World Bank table, the share of 20% poorest families in total income in Brazil is lower than in any other country. Also, the share of the 40% poorest families is the lowest. And no country in the table has the share of the 10% and the 20% richest families as high as Brazil (World Bank, 1984, p. 272).

Brazil has been presented as the classic case of rapid growth with growing income concentration. The debate on income distribution in the country spread in the academic area in the beginning of the Seventies, when the results of the 1970 demographic census seemed to offer evidence of a sharp increase between 1960 and 1970 in the degree of income inequality. These data came out at the time when the country was experiencing the economic boom of the 1968–1974 period, and what was more often than not felt as a lack of parallelism in this coincident occurencies must have helped to spur the debate. The Seventies saw a mounting literature on the distribution of income in Brazil. The changes in the approach to development that were taking place in the World Bank at the beginning of the decade must have equally played some role. One should recall that in 1975 the Bank for the first time explicitly published project evaluation criteria including the effect on the income distribution of people affected by the project to be financed. A World Bank-sponsored publication of that time, *Redistribution with growth* (Chenery et al., 1974), was often quoted in the debate. Moreover, the administration that took over Brazilian government in 1974 had a somewhat changed attitude toward the growth-distribution relationship—at least in the rhetoric of the *II National Development Plan 1975–1979*: "In the option taken, the Government does not accept the formula of expecting that economic growth will in itself solve the problem of income distribution, *i.e.*, the theory of waiting for the cake to grow. In maintaining accelerated growth, there is need for redistributive policies 'while the cake grows.' The truth is, on the one hand, that growth might not solve the problem of an adequate income distribution if left to the mere evolution of market factors. And, on the other hand, the solution through growth alone might take much more time than the social conscience would permit, in what concerns the need of improving rapidly the level of welfare of wide layers of the population" (II PND, 1974, p. 61).

No attempt will be made to thoroughly review the debate on what happened to growth and equity in the Sixties.[6] The newly published data of the 1980 demographic census will be used here to include in the analysis the period of 1970–1980, and insofar as data permit, we will try to assess the effect of the recent recession on the level of poverty in Brazil. The trends in inequality in the last decades, regarding income and wealth, are analysed in Section 2. Section 3 examines changes in the levels of absolute poverty in Brazil. The corresponding policy issues for the Eighties are the main concern in Section 4.

2. TRENDS IN INEQUALITY 1960–80

Inequality is not only manifested in the distribution of incomes. These incomes are derived partly from labour, partly from property. Inequality arises also from the distribution of opportunities and the distribution of property or the stock of real and financial assets. But data on wealth distribution are difficult to come by in Brazil, except for data on land ownership from the agricultural censuses. We will come back to this issue later. The distribution of opportunities—such as as social mobility, education, employment—will be taken up by other participants in this discussion. This relates to the question of the incidence of the benefits from public spending for services such as education and culture, sanitation and health, housing, social welfare, environment— all of which are growing components in the population's well-being—on different income groups.

Personal income distribution

We will start with the changes in the patterns of income distribution, and in that we do not break away from the mainstream of the vast literature on the subject. The comparison has to start from 1960, when the demographic censuses began to collect information on incomes. Data on incomes from tax declarations exist for earlier periods, but they cannot be used for historical comparison since their coverage has varied considerably from one year to another, and, moreover, they include only the comparatively richer.

The story of the Sixties is widely known as a "model" case of income concentration. This is still so in the Seventies, but some qualification is necessary. Between 1970 and 1980 the increase in the degree of inequality of income distribution was much less than the one registered in the previous decade. Table 6.1 shows this deceleration. During the Seventies the income share of the poorer half of the population declined from 15.6% to 13.4% while that of the richest 10% grew from 46.7% to 49.7%. The Gini index went from 0.561 to 0.592, while in the previous decade, according to Langoni's (1973, p. 67) results, it had gone from 0.500 to 0.568.

Before proceeding with the comparison between the Sixties and the Seventies, a brief reminder on the empirical basis. The results in Table 6.1 cover the EAP with positive income according to their individual income. Inactive persons with income as well as persons who declared no income are excluded. The inequality coefficients are higher, when, for instance, the EAP with zero-income, like family workers without remuneration, are included. Most researchers do exclude zero income earners in their calculations. These individuals are mostly sharing in the income of their families and cannot all be considered poor. Their inclusion in the indicators would overestimate inequality. It should be remembered, though, that even this decision has been disputed. Some of the divergence on the interpretation of the Sixties is around this inclusion of zero income earners. Since their proportion declines over time, along with the shrinking of subsistence farming and the expansion of labour participation, their inclusion tends to show a less worrying performance of the concentration indicators between 1960 and 1970.[7] For the Seventies the dispute can be settled by examining the *income of families* (information that was not published in the 1960 Census).

We do not dwell on the problem of precision and reliability of the data. This has been scrutinized elsewhere (Fishlow and Mesook, 1972; Hoffmann, 1977, 1979 and 1984; Pfefferman and Webb, 1979; Hoffmann and Kageyama, 1984). It is acknowledged, however, that the census data used to estimate inequality present unavoidable limitations of a different nature. One is that the census underestimates the total income, probably due to underreporting of high incomes. Nonmonetary incomes of the higher levels of managerial staff have been spreading in the form of benefits, such as company car and driver, expense accounts, special medical insurance, etc. The census also underestimates the income of the poor, mainly nonmonetary income corresponding to own consumption by farm households. Another type of limitation relates

Table 6.1

Income Distribution of Economically Active Persons 10 years old and
above who received some income, in Brazil, *cf.* Demographic Censuses.

% of population	% of income			
	1960[a]	1970[a]	1970[b]	1980[b]
40	11.6	10.0	10.6	9.5
50	17.7	14.9	15.6	13.4
60	25.4	20.8	21.7	19.3
70	34.8	28.2	28.7	26.2
80	45.6	37.8	38.6	35.9
10	39.7	47.8	46.7	49.6
5	27.7	34.9	34.4	37.0
Gini coefficient	0.500	0.568	0.561	0.592

Source: (a) Langoni 1973, pp. 64–67. (b) Results obtained by Rodolfo Hoffmann based on the 1970 and 1980 Demographic Censuses and methodology described in Hoffmann and Kageyama, 1984.

to the way census data are published—for instance, the income strata, which among other things make necessary some assumptions on the distribution within the strata. A third type of problem, which affects the comparison between 1970 and 1980, is the change in the questionnaire, which was more detailed in 1980. Any corrections for these limitations imply assumptions with some degree of arbitrariness. A considerable portion of the debate has revolved around the accuracy of the available empirical information.

Views differ on the direction of the distortion and on the margin of uncertainty these data limitations impose on the distribution estimates, particularly for the trend comparisons. Such limitations, however, do not invalidate the analysis, they have to be included in the debate. By comparison, Brazil has plenty of fairly accurate information on income distribution,[8] so the debate can concentrate on its interpretation and on what can be expected of public policy to improve overall distribution and reduce poverty.

Improvement of the distribution among families

We will now examine further differences between the Sixties and the Seventies. As shown from the individual incomes of the (EAP) the increase in inequality was much sharper in the Sixties. Moreover, in the Sixties this increase in inequality can be detected from whatever unit used for the analysis, be it the family income, the income of individuals 10 years old and above, or the income of the EAP. In the Seventies, however, we observe a slight decrease in income concentration when we consider the families as an unit of analysis.

We are interested in income as a rough indicator of welfare. Therefore, in principle, it is the income of each individual that has to be taken into account. However, a process of income redistribution operates inside the family. In most cases, the declaration of "no income" either derives from conditions in which we have production for own consumption or in which the head of household declares the total income in his name and the other members of the household appear as having "zero income," although they participate in some way in receiving this income (and often also in generating it). A considerable number of these people cannot be considered poor, and their inclusion would tend to increase artificially the indicators of inequality and poverty.

On the other hand, families who declared zero income must be considered poor. Even when they are units producing for their own consumption, the monetary equivalent of this consumption probably would place those families in the poorest strata of population. Moreover, the proportion of families with zero income is far lower than the one of individuals without income, which affects less the measures of inequality. Thus, the Gini index of the income distribution among families in 1980 changes from 0.590 to 0.597 according to the exclusion or the inclusion of the families who declared zero income, while the comparable change is from 0.592 to 0.624 when we consider the EAP.

In comparing the income distribution among families in 1970 and 1980 (Table 6.2) we have included the families with zero income declaration. They amount to 3.7% of the total of 17,945,000 families in 1970 and 1.9% of the total of 26,575,000 families in 1980.

The main changes in the distribution of income among families between 1970 and 1980 are in the following directions:

a) There was a considerable increase in the average income, which tended to benefit to a lesser degree the richest region (Southeast), thus contributing to the reduction in regional disparities (see Tables 2.2 and 2.3).

b) For the country as a whole there was a decline in inequality although this seems to result basically from the decline verified in the Southeast region (see Table 6.3).

c) In the regions of more recent settlement, such as the North frontier and the Middle-West region, the trend has been toward increasing inequality (Table 6.3).

d) The Northeast continues to be the most critical area in the country, with the lowest levels of income and the highest degree of inequality.

The novelty is the reduction of inequality among families, while, as we

Table 6.2

Distribution of families according to family income, in Brazil,
cf. Demographic Census 1970 and 1980. Average and median family income,
both in multiples of the equivalent of the minimum wage of August 1980

	Average			Median		
Region	1970	1980	change (%)	1970	1980	change (%)
North	1.95	3.71	90	1.10	1.92	75
Northeast	1.31	2.61	99	0.65	1.21	86
Southeast	3.55	6.25	76	1.82	3.50	92
South	2.34	4.76	103	1.22	2.70	121
Middle-West	2.12	4.76	125	1.08	2.27	110
Brazil	2.56	4.83	89	1.17	2.45	109

Source: Hoffmann and Kageyama, 1984

Table 6.3

Distribution of families according to family income in Brazil, *cf.* Demographic
Census 1970 and 1980. Gini index and percentages of income
corresponding to the 50% poorest (50−), and to the 10% richest (10+)

	Gini		50−		10+	
Region	1970	1980	1970	1980	1970	1980
North	0.529	0.562	17.1	14.2	43.3	44.9
Northeast	0.593	0.614	14.1	11.9	49.7	50.0
Southeast	0.585	0.564	12.9	14.2	45.5	44.2
South	0.547	0.560	15.9	14.5	43.9	44.2
Middle-West	0.573	0.604	14.8	12.4	47.3	49.1
Brazil	0.608	0.597	12.1	12.2	48.3	47.1

Source: Hoffmann and Kageyama, 1984

have seen in the previous section, income inequality among the EAP continued to rise, despite the reduction in pace (compare Tables 6.1 and 6.3). The
explanation seems to be the rise in the number of income earners per family.[9]
Such rise also increases the possibility of different performances in inequality
among the EAP and their families. The rise in the number of income earners
per family does, *per se*, lead to a reduction in inequality when we move from
the "person" to the "family," provided there is a low correlation between the
"new" incomes and the ones which existed previously.

Table 6.4

Percentage of families according to the number of members with income, by percentile group in Brazil, 1970 and 1980

Percentile according to family income		0 or 1 person with income		2 persons with income		3 or more with income	
1970	1980	1970	1980	1970	1980	1970	1980
26–	22–	94.5	89.9	4.8	9.2	0.6	0.9
39–	44–	91.2	78.9	7.3	17.4	1.5	3.7
8+	10+	40.7	33.0	34.6	36.7	24.8	30.2
5+	3+	42.6	34.3	35.2	38.9	22.2	26.8
TOTAL		72.0	57.7	18.2	26.3	9.8	16.0

Source: Hoffmann and Kageyama, 1984

The proportion of families with no income earner or with only one income earner declined from approximately 72% in 1970 to approximately 58% in 1980, while the proportion of families with two income earners and especially with three or more income earners went up (see Table 6.4).

Besides the general reduction in inequality among families caused by the rise in the number of income-earning persons per family, it also was observed that this rise was not uniform among rich and poor families. Hoffmann and Kageyama (1984) have made the comparison which is in Table 6.4, taking more or less equivalent percentiles, because it is impossible to organize this information in totally compatible percentiles. Nevertheless, it is clear that during the Seventies the increase in the number of income earners per family was stronger among the poorest: the proportion of poorer fmailies with two income earners almost doubled, and the ones with three or more income earners increased 50%. For the richest families the relative increase is much less, particularly in the case of families with two income earners.

The main reason for the rise in the number of income earners per family seems to be the increasing labor participation of women. Their proportion in the economically active population in Brazil expanded from 17% in 1960 to 20.9% in 1970, and to 27.4% in 1980. Moreover, there was some change in the traditional pattern that women were in the labor market basically while they were single: the proportion of married women in the female economically active population was 35.7% in 1980, up from 25.8% in 1970[10]. The participation of children in the economically active population (10 to 14 years old) and of youth (15 to 19 years old) did not change much in the period, staying around 5% and 15% respectively, and therefore does not explain the increase in the number of income earners per family.

When we come to discuss distributional implications of economic policy, the findings reported in this section should be kept in mind. They underline the important role of all policy decisions that affect employment and, more than in the past, the employment of women.

Wealth distribution

Despite the mounting number of careful studies on income distribution in Brazil, researchers tended to leave aside the disaggregation by factor income. In fact it is impossible to depict clearly to what extent very high incomes in Brazil are derived from the property of capital or from the ownership of natural resources and land. From some of the studies one would almost think that labor is the only production factor. The importance of education has been given a large weight among the determinants of income inequality, implying an assumption which is naive, to say the least: That there is nothing beyond them that might be responsible for both income inequality and inequality in education[11]. The difference in wealth of the families sending their children to school could not be measured.

It has to be recognized that our statistics do not favor an analysis of the role of property relations in income distribution and in social inequality in general. The availability of data might be one of the reasons why so many of the studies on income distribution in Brazil have given such large weight to the spread of earnings from labor.

One difficulty in trying to distinguish between incomes from labor and incomes from the property of capital or land is a more general one—the impossibility of obtaining information about the highest incomes, whatever their origin. They are grouped in an open-ended upper-income class. No distinction is made between incomes above a certain level, and so the largest fortunes in the country appear together with other income recipients that are modest by comparison. The highest of the ten income strata of the economically active population in the 1980 Census groups all incomes above the equivalent to 20 minimum wages—an amount that could be the salary of a university professor, an economist, or an engineer. There is no basis for drawing any arbitrary line above which one could assume that the incomes could not possibly be derived from labor.

Methodological difficulties equally reduce the possiblity of using the functional distribution of income from the national accounts for the purpose of separating what is remuneration of labor from what is remuneration of capital and analyzing changes in their relative share over time. It is doubtful that what is presented as the sum of wages actually does indicate the share of labor in national income. The wage bill of any firm includes the remuneration of directors and higher executives. But what is at the origin of the remuneration of managers is the profit of enterprises, and not the cost of qualified labor.[12] Thus, their inclusion together with all the rest of the labor force blurs the distinction between what represents payment to labor and what in fact represents sharing in the remuneration of the capital invested. This is the main source of distortion in the data for the functional distribution of income, which groups the total urban income in "labor income" and "other incomes" (Fundação Getulio Vargas, 1977, p. 9). The same limitation is present in the information from IBGE surveys that provide information on value of production and wage bill in the manufacturing industry.

While some of the highest incomes appear as salaries; in the second grouping there are also people of very modest means who receive property incomes, as rent or interest. Income derived from non-labor assets is not necessarily associated to wealth.

It has been argued that the inclusion of the remuneration of management in the wage bill, which limits the significance of the functional distribution of income to measure the absolute value of the participation of labor, does not totally impair a comparison over time in the shares of labor income in total income (and, by exclusion, of other incomes, basically property incomes). The factors that hinder the measurement of its absolute value are present over time, and do not necessarily affect the direction of change, particularly if they represent a small proportion and/or if they change in the same direction as the share of labor income (Macedo, 1977, 54–5).

According to the study done by Macedo (1977), there is clear evidence that the share of labor income has been declining since 1950, not only in manufacturing as a whole, but also in practically all the branches into which it is divided. The share of labor in the value of total manufacturing production in Brazil was 0.283 in 1949, 0.261 in 1959 and 0.231 in 1969, according to data from the Industrial Censuses. If only the category of "workers directly linked to production" is taken, which corresponds roughly to blue collar workers as distinguished from administrative personnel, those shares are respectively 0.229, 0.185, and 0.171, revealing a steeper decline in the share earned by blue collar workers. Calculations on the basis of IBGE's yearly survey of the manufacturing industry (IBGE, Levantamentos Anuais sobre a Industria de Transformação) show the same trends. [13] In 1973 the share of labor had continued to decline, and was 0.233 for all labor and 0.152 for the category of "workers directly linked to production."[14] The functional distribution of urban income as published from the national accounts shows the same trend, though less pronounced: the share of labor income declined from 56.6% in 1949, to 55.5% in 1959, and to 52.0% in 1970, but after that remained relatively stable until 1975 (FGV, 1977, p. 9).

The changes in relative shares of labor income and other incomes do not tell us much about the distribution of wealth in Brazil. The relationship between the concentration of property and the concentration of income remains unclear. While data on the wage structure are available, the distribution of incomes derived from property cannot be assessed. The distribution of dividend incomes, interests and rents remains an uncharted field for researchers in Brazil.

The distribution of wealth is a relevant issue not only because it could help explain the distribution of income. There are more general questions of social equity, justice and the meaning of democracy involved, because the concentration of wealth among a few means also the concentration of economic power. And great inequalities in the distribution of economic power usually mean great inequality in the ability to influence the decision-making process in society.

Distribution of wealth is not officially measured in Brazil, except for land ownership. It is true that there must be some information on the value of urban residences, at least in the administrative units responsible for collecting taxes on real estate, but this information has not been put together from the municipal level. IBGE's (Instituto Brasileira de Geografia e Historia) sample survey PNAD (Pesquisa Nacional por Amostra de Domicílios) publishes several pieces of information about the homes—whether they are houses or flats, rented or owned, already paid or yet to pay, etc.—but nothing about their value. It tells us the proportion of families that own their dwellings, also by income strata, but from this we cannot tell anything about the distribution of home values. The proportion of families owning their dwellings does not change very much according to income strata. In fact, 62% of the families with incomes below one minimum wage declared they owned their dwellings in 1982. This is the same as the share of owner-occupied dwellings for all the families, and (PNAD 1982, Table 5.9) indicates only that many of the poorest families have their own "barracos" or "palhoças."[15]

Home values might have a cumulative influence in the process of wealth concentration, because houses and flats tend to increase in value more than proportionally in the periods of high inflation and low real interest in Brazil. They are an important item in wealth distribution from the standpoint of welfare distribution. But it can be argued that if the concern is economic power, home values should not be included in the measurement of the distribution of wealth, because they are not a source of wealth that can be used to control others (Thurow, 1984).

It would be much more important to know how the control over the non-residential private capital is distributed. How is the total of business investments assets distributed among individuals and families in Brazil? Very little research has been done on this subject in Brazil, but the indications are that the concentration of economic power is very high and that changes have been towards more concentration.

Studies on aggregate industrial concentration have used a list or a selection of biggest firms ordered by size, measured by their sales or their capital. They provide various indicators of the distribution of firms by size. Using data from the Brazilian federal revenue office on firms required to present financial statements and pay taxes accordingly, a recent study (Braga and Mascolo, 1982) assessed industrial concentration in Brazil. It is high indeed: 0.5% of firms—the top ones in a list of 77,185 industrial firms ordered by the value of their sales—are responsible for almost half (exactly 48.6%) of total sales and (47%) of the capital in industry in 1977. With the top 3% we cover approximately 70% of the sales and of the total capital. And this list excludes small firms that are not required to present a financial statement and do pay taxes on their presumed profits. They are a big number. Together with the firms that failed to present required financial statements they make up 46%

of the number of industrial firms, but only 1% of total sales (Braga and Mascolo, 1982, p. 412). Moreover, there is clear evidence that aggregate industrial concentration increased during the Seventies (*idem*, p. 420).

These indicators of aggregate industrial concentration, however, bypass the question of ownership and control of business capital. The sizes of the industrial establishments might be justified from the standpoint of efficiency and technology, or the size distribution might be less than adequate according to some chosen standard. At any rate, while drawing the attention to indexes of industrial concentration by the size of firms, we are far from suggesting that industry should be organized in smaller firms. That is beside the point here. Perhaps the greatest shortcoming in distribution or concentration indicators which ignore ownership is that they are unable to reflect crucial shifts between state ownership and private national and foreign ownership.

For the purpose of assessing the distribution of wealth and economic power a more meaningful approach was the one adopted in a research on economic groups in Brazil conducted in the early Sixties at the former Institute of Social Sciences of the Federal University of Rio de Janeiro. In identifying the economic groups, it took into account the linkages between firms through stock ownership, particularly voting capital, and interlocking directorates. A detailed study exists for 1962. For that year, 276 economic groups—*i.e.*, all the ones then controlling over 1 billion cruzeiros—were identified and analyzed (Vinhas de Queiroz, 1962 and 1965; Pessoa de Queiroz, 1965; Martins, 1965). From those, each of the biggest 55 economic groups were studied one by one, from their origins. Of these 55, 29 economic groups were controlled by foreign capital including a total number of 234 firms; 24 were national, encompassing 506 firms; and 2 economic groups were considered mixed, because while combining national and foreign capital, no clear decision center could be identified (Vinhas de Queiroz, 1972). What emerges is much more complex and obviously far less handy than any single aggregate concentration index. It would be fascinating to know what had happened to the 276 billionaire groups after two decades: where the success or survival; where the fusions, breakups, bankruptcies, divestures; where the shifts in ownership between nationals, foreigners and the state. Such an investigation would not be easy but it would tell a real story about the concentration of wealth.

As in other developing countries, land ownership in Brazil is better documented than other forms of property from which income can be derived. Concentration of land ownership in Brazil is very high and remarkably stable. Taking into account that in Brazil land is the main component of the capital of agricultural enterprises, we can say that concentration of wealth in the primary sector of the economy is very high. The overall degree of concentration of land ownership has not changed in the last six decades at least[16]. One

Table 6.5

Percentage of total area covered by the 5% largest agricultural establishments, in Brazil and its regions

	1960	1970	1975	1980
Brazil	67.9	67.0	68.7	69.3
North	90.1	64.5	72.8	68.6
Northeast	65.3	66.7	68.3	68.3
Southeast	55.2	53.0	52.7	53.9
South	56.6	56.3	57.0	57.9
Middle-West	64.6	67.4	66.7	65.3

Source: Agricultural censuses, cf. Hoffman, 1982

indicator of this concentration is in Table 6.5. The Gini index of the distribution of land ownership was 0.857 in 1980, according to data from the last agricultural census. An examination of data from the first agricultural census, in 1920, suggests that the level of inequality in the distribution of land ownership was not much different then. During the decades in between, the Gini index was around 0.84. This Gini index is of the distribution of agricultural establishments by size, *i.e.*, landless agricultural laborers are excluded. When the number of families without land (but for which agriculture is the main activity of the head of household) is included in the calculations, giving them land size equal to zero, the Gini index for the concentration of land ownership is approximately 0.90 (Hoffmann 1971 and 1982).

The stability of the concentration indexes verified for Brazil as a whole prevails also in the regions, despite some oscillations in the North and a slight increase in concentration in the Northeast and in the South.

The extreme concentration of land ownership is one of the factors in the Brazilian model of rapid growth with inequitable distribution. It will be impossible to follow here the complex relationship between the structures of land tenure and of income in the way it operated in Brazil's history. It is interesting to note, however, that the two states in Brazil with the least degree of concentration of agricultural property—Espírito Santo and Santa Catarina—are the two states where family-sized property was introduced earlier in their history through a colonization program by European immigrants. It is no coincidence that Santa Catarina, when compared to other states in Brazil with comparable average rural income, has a much lower degree of income concentration in the rural area (Hoffmann, 1983, p. 40).

The stability of the overall degree of ownership concentration in Brazil in all its regions does not negate vast changes taking place in the rural area.

And they are in the direction of more concentration of land ownership and property income. We have still an agricultural frontier in the country. The total area occupied by agricultural establishments continued to expand between 1960 and 1980 at an annual average rate of almost 2%, and more rapidly in the last decade. This expansion has been taking place mainly in the Middle-West during the Sixties, and mainly in the North during the Seventies, although the pace of expansion continued to be high in the Middle-West. The areas of new occupation, under tax incentive schemes of SUDAM and Polocentro, are also the ones with the highest average size of establishment. The incorporation of agricultural land is being done by very large establishments. In some of the areas of old occupation, the technological modernization was accompanied by concentration of ownership. Thus, the states of Espírito Santo and Paraná have been going through a process of reconcentration of land tenure since the Sixties. In the first caused by the expansion of cattle raising in former coffee areas and by reforestation programs for the production of cellulose; in the second by the expansion of soya for exports. The combined result for the country is that while the number of the smallest units (less than 10 hectares) is declining, the number of largest units of 10,000 hectares or more is growing fast, and the number of all largest, with area of 100,000 hectares or more, has the fastest rate of increase. In 1978, rural property units having 10,000 hectares or more controlled one quarter of the total area of the registered rural property units (Graziano da Silva and Hoffmann, 1980).

Modernization of Brazilian agriculture in the Sixties and particularly in the Seventies has been taking place in the export crops and in sugar cane. Those who studied the process recently[17] show convincingly that the increased use of modern technology in the given institutional setting did bring an increase in income inequality. The elements of this technology were mainly partial mechanization (particularly the use of tractors) affecting more intensively the stage of cultivation than the harvest, and the use of fertilizers and insecticides or other defensive chemicals. The result was a heightened seasonal swing in the use of labor, rapidly increasing the number of temporary wage laborers in agriculture. Many of these laborers now have urban domicile and are reflected in the urban poverty indicators.

3. ABSOLUTE POVERTY DURING THE LAST DECADES

Measures of inequality provide information about relative welfare and relative deprivation, but they are an incomplete approach to poverty. Inequality is fundamentally a different issue from poverty, though related to it. The literature on Brazilian growth and distribution has dedicated more attention to the analysis and interpretation of the concentration of personal incomes than to the extent of absolute poverty in the country. One might say that in the last instance the issue under discussion was in fact poverty, since the focus was very much on the effects of global economic growth on the relative share of the lower income groups and on whether they had participated in the benefits of growth. At the present moment some shift in attention is taking place, and a great deal more research and debate is being done on the levels of absolute poverty.[18]

Before attempting to measure poverty, some "poverty line" has to be specified, i.e., the level of income below which a family is considered to be poor. Ideally it should be physical minimum in the provision of needs, but there are practical limitations for such a procedure. The chosen level of income is supposed to represent the basket of goods and services considered essential. The definition of the poverty line, however, becomes more complicated when the purpose is to examine changes over time, since the composition of the basket of goods forming the accepted minimum does not remain always the same.

As we said above, income inequality and poverty, though not the same, are related. There is a relative component in poverty, and what is considered *poor* changes with overall conditions and with the general level of income. The choice of the poverty line might also have a broadly political aspect related to what each society at a certain moment views as the threshold of "tolerable" deprivation.[19]

The final tabulations of the 1980 demographic census became available recently, so that changes in absolute poverty between 1970 and 1980 can be assessed. We will summarize here some of the findings of a recent study of poverty in Brazil carried out by Rodolfo Hoffmann (1984)[20].

After identifying who will be counted as poor, a widely used way of measuring aggregate poverty is the ratio between the number of poor and the total number of people. This simple indicator of poverty appears in Tables 6.8 to 6.14 as H (for head count), and is the proportion of poor families in the total number of families. H varies from 0, if no one falls below the poverty line, to the maximum of 1 if the total number of families is below poverty. (To facilitate referral, we have grouped all the tables referring to poverty indicators at the end of this section.)

Our H, or proportion of poor families, is a rough measurement of aggregate poverty, but it has drawbacks. It does not take into account the extent of income shortfall of those who lie below the poverty line. It does not reflect at all whether someone is just below the line or very far below it, in acute misery and hunger. Also, it should be noted that a reduction in the incomes of all the poor will leave H unchanged.

The second poverty indicator which appeears under I in Tables 6.8 to 6.14 measures the aggregate income shortfall of the poor. The income shortfall of a person whose income is less than the poverty-line income can be called his "income gap." The sum of income gaps of all the poor from the specified poverty line is the aggregate income gap sometimes called "poverty gap." Thus, the measure I takes into account the aggregate income gap, expressing it as percentage shortfall of the average income of the poor from the poverty line. I varies from 0—which would imply the nonexistence of anyone with income below the poverty line—to a maximum of 1 if all the poor had income zero.

While H is insensitive to the income gap, I does not reflect the number of poor, and both are insensitive to inequality of income among the poor. Hence a combined measure has been proposed by Amartya Sen: the measure P, which is a function of H (reflecting the number of poor), I (reflecting the aggregate poverty gap), and of the Gini coefficient of the distribution of income among the poor (reflecting the degree of inequality below the poverty line and capturing the aspect of relative deprivation). If all the poor had the same income, Sen's poverty index P would be the product HI.[21]

The calculations for Brazil were made adopting for 1980 the legal minimum wage. The comparable poverty line for 1970, however, is not the legal minimum of that year, because the purchasing power (or real value) of the minimum wage decreed every year is not the same. It has been observed that the real value of the legal minimum in 1980 was lower than the one of 1970, even on the day of the decree. Both the 1970 and the 1980 Censuses do register the incomes received in the month of August. Using the cost of living index of DIEESE, we find that the value equivalent to the legal minimum wage of 1980 (Cr 4149.60) in August 1970 is Cr 161.84. This is lower than the highest legal minimum wage of 1970, which was Cr 187.20. Thus, using the legal minimum wage in 1970 we would obtain higher levels of poverty then and, by comparison, overestimate any improvement during the decade.

What changed in the Seventies? Real average income per family[22] increased almost 89% for the country as a whole. The highest increases were in the Middle-West (124%) and the lowest were in the Southeast, so that regional concentration of income declined slightly. But the Southeast continues to be the only region with average income above the national average. (Compare Tables 6.6 and 6.7.) As noted before, the reduction in the overall inequality index in the decade was due to a reduction in the Southeast region (which covers the states of S. Paulo, Rio de Janeiro, Minas Gerais and Espirito Santo). The Northeast continued to be the region with the lowest average income and the highest degree of inequality. From this combined information one would already expect the levels of absolute poverty to be the highest in this region.

Table 6.6

Distribution of families according to their monthly family income,
in Brazil, according to the Demographic Census of 1970.
The average income is in multiples of the equivalent to the minimum
wage of August 1980 and Gini index (G) of the distribution*

Regions	Families with income declaration no.(1000)%		Total income (%)	Average income	G
Brazil	17,945	100.0	100.0	2.56	0.608
North	613	3.4	2.6	1.95	0.529
Northeast	5,207	29.0	14.8	1.31	0.593
Southeast	8,022	44.7	62.1	3.55	0.585
South	3,176	17.7	16.2	2.34	0.547
Middle-West	927	5.2	4.3	2.12	0.573

*Since the published data do not include the value of the average income in the 12 strata (whose lower limits are 0.50, 100, 200, 250, 300, 400, 500, 1000, 1500 and 2000), these values were established as 33, 80, 128, 176, 225, 275, 348, 448, 730, 1210, 1700 and 4000 cruzeiros per family.

With the exception of the income-gap ratio (I) in the North region, all the poverty indicators declined in the Seventies. (Compare Tables 6.8 and 6.9.) The proportion of poor families (H) fell to almost half in the country as a whole. In 1980 it was less than half the proportion of 1970 in all the regions except the Northeast, where the decline was not so pronounced. The extension of poverty (H) varies more according to region than the intensity (I). The Northeast, more than 20 years after the creation of SUDENE, continues to be the area where poverty is more extensive (as measured by H) and more intensive (as measured by I). From a regional standpoint there is even a worsening in the decade, because in 1980 more than half (53.6%) of the poor families of the country were concentrated in the Northeast, while this proportion was lower in 1970. Also, the Northeast's proportion in the total national income gap increased. (Compare Tables 6.8 and 6.9, column 5.)

Poverty in Brazil is not only northeastern, but rural, The average rural income is nearly one third of the urban. All the poverty indicators are systematically higher in the rural area than in the urban (compare Tables 6.13 and 6.14). There might be some overestimation of rural poverty due to the characteristics of the data, which fail to capture non-monetary incomes. But the importance of non-cash incomes has been declining in Brazilian agriculture, parallel to the reduction of unpaid family workers, resident laborers and

Table 6.7

Distribution of families according to their monthly family income,
in Brazil, according to the Demographic Census of 1980.
Average family income is in multiples of the minimum
wage per family and Gini index (G)*

Regions and condition of domicile	Families with income declaration no.(1000)	%	Total income (%)	Average income	G
Brazil	26,575	100.0	100.0	4.83	0.597
North	1,140	4.3	3.3	3.71	0.562
Northeast	7,117	26.8	14.5	2.61	0.614
Southeast	12,290	46.2	59.9	6.25	0.564
South	4,400	16.6	16.3	4.76	0.560
Middle-West	1,628	6.1	6.0	4.76	0.604
Urban	18,732	70.5	86.8	5.94	0.572
Rural	7,843	29.5	13.2	2.16	0.543

*Since the published data do not include the value of the average income in the 8 strata whose lower limits are 0, 1/4, 1/2, 1, 2, 5, 10 and 20 minimum wages, these values are established as 0.165, 0.40, 0.77, 1.50, 3.38, 7.1, 14 and 40 minimum wages per family.

sharecroppers, and the soaring in the numbers of wage earners, particularly temporary wage earners. Still, according the 1980 Census, 60.9% of the families in the rural area were below the poverty line of one minimum wage. In 1980, 29.5% of all the families in Brazil were in the rural areas (Table 6.7), but 48% of the poor families below the two minimum wages line (Table 6.10). If a lower poverty line is chosen, the concentration of poverty in the Northeast and in the rural areas is even more marked (Table 6.9).

In certain aspects one can say that poverty did not change. From the 1960 Census, Fishlow (1972) had already shown the concentration of poverty in the Northeast and in the rural areas. He estimated that 60% of the poor families were rural in 1960. But in the meantime Brazil had become much more urbanized, and part of the "rural" poverty is now in the cities, with a greater expansion of temporary agricultural wage laborers living in the towns.

In general, the improvements in the poverty indicators from 1970 to 1980 have been significant. They are confirmed by other indicators in living conditions, such as the increase in the proportions of households with piped water, sewerage, and electric light (Table 6.11). Among these other indicators there

Table 6.8
Poverty among families in Brazil, considering the monthly income per family and a poverty line of Cr $161.84 (equivalent to 1 minimum wage of August 1980), cf. Demographic Census 1970

Region	H	I	P	Poor families (%)	Insufficiency of income (%)	% insuf. of income in total income
Brazil	0.422	0.466	0.265	100.0	100.0	7.7
North	0.453	0.373	0.237	3.7	2.9	8.7
Northeast	0.682	0.510	0.452	46.9	51.3	26.5
Southeast	0.271	0.451	0.169	28.7	27.8	3.4
South	0.359	0.403	0.202	15.1	13.0	6.2
Middle-West	0.462	0.404	0.257	5.7	4.9	8.8

Table 6.9
Poverty among families in Brazil, considering the monthly income per family and a poverty line equivalent to one minimum wage per family, cf. Demographic Census 1980

Region or condition of domicile	H	I	P	Poor families (%)	Insufficiency of income (%)	% insuf. of income in total income
Brazil	0.219	0.420	0.128	100.0	100.0	1.9
North	0.218	0.422	0.130	4.3	4.3	2.5
Northeast	0.439	0.431	0.260	53.6	55.0	7.3
Southeast	0.115	0.408	0.066	24.3	23.6	0.8
South	0.161	0.403	0.090	12.2	11.6	1.4
Middle-West	0.202	0.406	0.115	5.6	5.5	1.7
Urban	0.135	0.429	0.081	43.3	44.2	1.0
Rural	0.421	0.414	0.240	56.7	55.8	8.0

is perhaps a sign of the times and of the universalization of patterns of consumption: while the literacy rate changed only from 61% to 68%, the proportion of households with TV more than doubled in the decade (Table 6.11).

The importance of the changes is not to be denied. Nevertheless, the progress made is nothing to boast of. First, poverty in Brazil is still dismal by any

Table 6.10

Poverty among families in Brazil, considering the monthly income per
family and a poverty line equivalent to 2 minimum wages per family,
cf. Demographic Census 1980

Region or condition of domicile	H	I	P	Poor families (%)	Insufficiency of income (%)	% insuf. of income in total income
Brazil	0.444	0.477	0.281	100.0	100.0	8.8
North	0.517	0.444	0.310	5.0	4.7	12.4
Northeast	0.704	0.540	0.488	42.4	48.0	29.1
Southeast	0.300	0.424	0.173	31.2	27.8	4.1
South	0.401	0.431	0.233	24.9	13.5	7.3
Middle-West	0.465	0.447	0.279	6.4	6.0	8.7
Urban	0.327	0.441	0.195	51.9	48.0	4.9
Rural	0.724	0.516	0.483	48.1	52.0	34.5

indicators or criteria, while the country continues to have one of the highest
degrees of income concentration in the world. Second, we have to look at our
progress in the context of the very rapid economic growth of the country
during the period.

Gross Domestic Product (GDP) increased 127% in real terms between 1970
and 1980. Real GDP per capita went up 79%. The industrial product showed
an increase of 145%.[23] A really huge reconcentration process would have had
to occur for absolute poverty not to have improved. Moreover, there are indications that much of the improvement occurred in the first half of the decade
and then slowed down after the economic boom. At present it is reversing.
Hoffmann (1984a) calculated the poverty indicators from PNAD data between
1976 and 1982 (Tables 6.12 to 6.14). The poverty indicators remained more
or less constant in the period 1976–1981, but there is a clear worsening from
1981 to 1982, both in rural and in urban areas. The poverty line adopted in
these calculations is the legal minimum wage, and no adjustment was made
for its changes in value noted before. Since the purchasing power of the legal
minimum has been declining since 1978, the worsening situation in 1982 is
underestimated and also might have started earlier, when growth slowed down.
Real GDP per capita, which was growing at an annual average rate of 7.6%
in the period 1970–76, grew only at 3.6% per year in the period 1976–1980,
and began to decline in 1981. And with the recession came the reversal of the
improvements that were being achieved in the alleviation of poverty.

Table 6.11
Selected indicators of the quality of life in Brazil
in 1970 and 1980, in percentages

		Year	
Indicator	Area	1970	1980
Literacy of people 5 years old and	Urban	75.2	77.6
above (undeclared excluded)	Rural	41.9	47.3
	Total	60.9	68.0
Households with piped water	Urban	52.6	71.9
	Rural	6.2	18.1
	Total	33.3	56.0
Households with sewerage (public	Urban	44.2	58.1
(network or septic tank)	Rural	2.0	7.4
	Total	26.6	43.2
Households with electric light	Urban	75.6	88.2
	Rural	8.4	21.4
	Total	47.6	68.5
Households with radio	Urban	72.4	79.1
	Rural	40.1	69.2
	Total	58.9	76.2
Households with refrigerator	Urban	42.5	65.7
	Rural	3.2	13.6
	Total	26.1	50.4
Households with TV	Urban	40.2	73.0
	Rural	1.6	15.7
	Total	24.1	56.1
Households with car	Urban	13.7	28.2
	Rural	2.5	9.8
	Total	9.0	22.7

Source: Basic data from the Demographic Censuses of 1970 and 1980.

4. INEQUALIZING MECHANISMS AND POLICY ISSUES FOR THE 1980S

Any attempt to make specific recommendations for policies concerning or affecting income distribution is beyond the scope of this paper. We will simply draw attention to some of the issues that surface in the research of and in the debate on income distribution.

Some caution against too much hope for changes in the short run—or even

Table 6.12

Earnings and poverty of people 10 years old and above,
with positive income, in Brazil in the period 1976–82,
considering 1 minimum wage as the poverty line

Year and data source	Average (in multip. of the min. wage)	Median	% without earnings	G	H	I	P
PNAD 76	2.76	1.42	49.0	0.592	0.407	0.363	0.205
PNAD 77	2.64	1.33	47.3	0.593	0.422	0.371	0.217
PNAD 78	2.65	1.25	45.7	0.607	0.421	0.414	0.237
PNAD 79	2.76	1.35	46.5	0.593	0.382	0.409	0.213
Census 80	2.75	1.31	47.1	0.595	0.386	0.385	0.204
PNAD 81	2.73	1.39	45.6	0.583	0.371	0.428	0.212
PNAD 82	2.40	1.19	44.7	0.589	0.436	0.444	0.256

Table 6.13

Earnings and poverty of people 10 years old and above,
with positive income and urban domicile, in Brazil in the period 1976–82,
considering 1 minimum wage as the poverty line

Year and data source	Average (in multip. of the min. wage)	Median	% without earnings	G	H	I	P
PNAD 76	3.26	1.59	45.2	0.590	0.333	0.353	0.164
PNAD 77	3.11	1.56	43.9	0.590	0.343	0.357	0.171
PNAD 78	3.15	1.53	42.2	0.597	0.341	0.383	0.182
PNAD 79	3.27	1.63	43.0	0.586	0.311	0.390	0.168
Census 80	3.20	1.54	43.2	0.587	0.310	0.371	0.161
PNAD 81	3.15	1.64	42.6	0.575	0.307	0.415	0.173
PNAD 82	2.77	1.40	41.5	0.581	0.366	0.430	0.210

Table 6.14
Earnings and poverty of people 10 years old and above,
with positive income and rural domicile, in Brazil in the period 1976–82,
considering 1 minimum wage as the poverty line

Year and data source	Average (in multip. of the min. wage)	Median	% without earnings	G	H	I	P
PNAD 76	1.52	0.91	56.5	0.508	0.588	0.378	0.306
PNAD 77	1.47	0.89	54.2	0.520	0.620	0.390	0.332
PNAD 78	1.34	0.79	53.2	0.536	0.629	0.458	0.379
PNAD 79	1.37	0.88	54.2	0.500	0.578	0.437	0.335
Census 80	1.43	0.87	56.0	0.519	0.609	0.405	0.330
PNAD 81	1.38	0.83	53.4	0.507	0.581	0.450	0.336
PNAD 82	1.17	0.74	53.0	0.503	0.667	0.470	0.408

in the medium run—might be in order. The measurements of poverty presented in the previous section include one item, the "percentage of the income gap in total income" (last column in Tables 6.8 to 6.10), which can be read as the dimension of the income transfer necessary to eliminate poverty (as defined). That is, for the country as a whole, it would be necessary to put into operation mechanisms to transfer permanently to those below poverty line approximately 2% of total income in 1980 (see Table 6.9). This rough indicator of the transfer necessary, for the Northeast is 7.3% of the regional income, and less than 1% of the regional income in the Southeast. These percentages are obviously a function of the established poverty line and are considerably higher for a poverty line of two minimum wages per family (see Table 6.10).

These figures might give a wrong impression of the challenge: after all, 2% of total income does not seem to be much. However, besides the consideration that these percentages certainly increased after 1980, one should remember that it took ten years of exceptionally high economic growth rates to bring the percentage of the income insufficiency in total income from more or less 8% to 2% (see last columns in Tables 6.8 and 6.9). Even 1% of total income is very difficult to transfer. And if we consider what share of the government budget this insufficiency of income might be, a redistribution can hardly be expected to come into effect in the short run.

What priority these distributional concerns will have in the actual policy package is another issue. No amount of research can decide that. It is to be decided by the social praxis. But research and academic debate are part of that social praxis. In this respect, the results would be (at least for Brazil) that redistribution cannot be treated as a mere by-product in a policy package aiming to restore economic growth. No prediction about the performance of distribution as a by-product can be warranted, in any direction. The Brazilian experience is not to be explained by the Kuznets hypothesis about the relationship between income per head and the distribution of incomes (Bacha and Taylor, 1980). Neither does it validate an earlier ECLA (Economic Commission on Latin America) hypothesis that without redistribution there would be stagnation, because, for growth, mass markets that reach the bulk of the population are needed, and not diversified purchases of a small high-income group (Wells, 1974).[24] The reverse of this—the argument that income concentration is necessary for growth because of the greater propensity of higher-income groups to save—has not been confirmed for Brazil, either (Lopes, 1972). But to say that there is no automatism in the relationship between growth and income distribution gives more weight to the policy decisions. The distributional implications of the main economic policy decisions have to be evaluated and taken into account. Invisible market forces will not do the job for the social and political groups that will decide or have the decision made for them. The assumption that there is a dichotomy between economic policy, with higher ranking priorities, and a social policy depending on the first, is false, because the first will have social implications that imply a *de facto* social policy, even if by exclusion. If poverty increases as the result of priority given to a particular set of policies to face the balance of payments deficit, it cannot be said that social policies had to wait. That one *is* the social policy decision.

On another level, distributional policies have to distinguish between wealth distribution, or the property of real and financial assets, and income distribution derived partly from property and partly from labour. The importance of employment creation is stressed by the experience of the Seventies and the reversal in the Eighties. The convergence between employment policies and reduction in poverty and income distribution was established before (Mata, 1979). Wages and wage policy received the bulk of the attention in the debate on income distribution. It is clear that pay rates of the unskilled workers depend on the official minimum, but there are obvious limits to the extent in which wage policy can function as a redistribution mechanism. Recently, many voices have been raised against government intervention in the labor market and in favor of free bargaining. It is debatable that the elimination of the official minimum and the process of free bargaining will in itself bring an improvement in the distribution of incomes if trade unions are not strong. While the role of wages in the overall income distribution has been ascertained[25], little is known on the distribution of property incomes and their role in the overall distribution. The structure of land ownership and the way in which technological modernization is spreading in agriculture are clearly factors in the perpetuation of poverty and unequal distribution. The issue is not to restrain the introduction of technology, but how to restrain its negative effects linked to the institutional setting.

The attempt to enumerate all the policy areas that affect distribution is in vain, because it probably covers the complete possible set of policies. We have many open questions that will be answered by other groups. How, for instance, can the tax system be improved as a distributional tool in Brazil? This relates to both income and property distribution. How far does the system of transfer payments go in cushioning declines in earnings from retirement and disability? What is the degree of feasibility for introducing unemployment payments in the system of transfer payments? What is the differential effect of inflation upon the various income strata? Some studies have shown that the price of necessities has been rising faster than other prices, which would mean that inflation causes a stronger decline in the living standard for the lowest income. Where can the price mechanism be administered to reduce inequality? Can a decentralization of some of the decisions and budget resources to the municipal level take better care of basic needs of the population or will this disperse and waste scarce resources? The list is long.

With the deterioration of the general economic situation, the core of the controversy is no longer on growth and equity, on who benefited and who was bypassed by economic development, but on the social costs of the recession and adjustment to the external shock, on who are the main victims of reduced employment opportunities, inflation and cuts in public spending, or, as a summary, on how the recession affected the different income strata. It is no consolation that the average income is declining. Previously, some gained more than others, and some had no gain at all; and now some are losing more than others, and some may have no loss at all.

The special difficulty of the moment is that in times of retrenchment there is no way of improving the living conditions of the groups with the lowest incomes and of reducing absolute poverty without redistribution. The "automatism" seems to be one of less-than-proportionate trickle down of the goods, and more-than-proportionate trickle down of the bads. And if Hirschman (1973) is right in his "tunnel effect" hypothesis of development, the fact that most of society is worse off is even less a reason for postponing measures to reduce poverty and maldistribution. While many were improving in life, the ones who were not moving upward could cherish the hope that their turn would arrive. They were like the driver in a one-way, two-lane tunnel who is stuck in a lane that does not move, but whose spirits lift when the other lane starts moving, because he is content so long as he feels that soon he also will be on the move, and who will get desperate if after a while he does not move. Apart from the possibility of this kind of change in the degree of tolerance for economic inequality, there is certainly much hope being put on the prospects of a more democratic government committed to equity and improvement of the lot of the poorest.

5. POSTCRIPT 1987: SHIFTY EIGHTIES

When this paper was presented at the end of 1984, there were already signs that recession in the period 1981–1983 had brought about a worsening of poverty in Brazil. From the PNAD surveys published since then this worsening is clear (Table 6.15). At the end of three recession years, in September 1983 (month of the PNAD Survey) the share of poor families in the total number of families (H) was 26.5%, up from 21.9% in 1980. This is the extension of poverty below the line equivalent to one minimum wage of August 1980. If a poverty line of the equivalent of two minimum wages of August 1980 is taken, half of all the families at the end 1983 were poor, up from 44% in 1980. Poverty had also become more intensive (as measured by I). The combined poverty index (P) increased constantly, and the increase was more intense when recession deepened in 1983.

The average family income at the end of 1983 was more than 20% below the level of 1980. At the same time, the income distribution did not change much during the period 1980–1983. The Gini index (G) remained around 0.59. The share of the 50% poorest in total income remained near 13%, and the share of the 10% richest remained around 46% of total income. Such a development necessarily implies a worsening of the poverty levels. If average incomes are falling, there is no hope of any improvement for the poorest groups in the population without redistribution.

The reduction in family incomes and the extension and deepening of poverty in the period accompanied the shrinking of Brazil's Gross Domestic Product (GDP). Per capita GDP declined 5.7% in 1981, 1.5% in 1982 and 4.9% in 1983. The accumulated loss in per capita GDP from 1980 to 1983 was near 12%. The decline in per capita income was steeper, since it reflected a deterioration of almost 19% in terms of trade between 1980 and 1983, as well as net payments abroad on account of factor services (in these four years US$36.5 billion alone went for net interest payments on foreign debt).[26]

The year of 1984 marked the end of recession. GDP per capita went up by

Table 6.15
Evolution of poverty among families in Brazil, 1980–85, considering
as poverty line the equivalent to one minimum wage of August 1980

Year and data source	Average family income*	G	H	I	P	% insufficiency of income in total income
Census 80	4.83	0.597	0.219	0.420	0.128	1.9
PNAD 81	4.60	0.584	0.208	0.460	0.132	2.1
PNAD 82	4.68	0.587	0.211	0.454	0.133	2.0
PNAD 83	3.82	0.589	0.265	0.469	0.169	3.3
PNAD 84	4.04	0.588	0.243	0.460	0.153	2.8
PNAD 85	4.51	0.592	0.221	0.454	0.138	2.2

*In multiples of the equivalent to the minimum wage of August 1980.
Source: Hoffmann 1987

3% and by 5.6% in 1985. The general economic improvement is reflected in the indicators in Table 6.15: the average family income started to move upward in 1984, the Gini index continued to be remarkably stable around 0.59, and, accordingly, some reduction in the poverty indicators had to occur.

GDP growth continued in 1986 and was almost 6% in per capita terms. The year was marked by the launching of the economic policy package known as the Cruzado I, with the basic aim of fighting inflation. This is not the place for a full discussion of that controversial package, but reference has to be made to the strongly voiced claim that Cruzado I has helped to improve income distribution in Brazil.

A full assessment will have to wait for data referring to 1986. In the metropolitan area of São Paulo, the most industrialized part of the country, employment expanded by 8.8% in 1986, and the average earnings from employment went up 9.7%. Wage earners had an increase of 4.9% in average earnings compared to increases of 22.8% and 26.6% respectively obtained by employers and self-employed. Together, rises in employment and in average earnings brought an expansion of 19% in total earnings. For the metropolitan area of São Paulo, data available for 1986 indicate some improvement in income distribution among wage earners as well as among the total employed population.[27] This information covers only earnings from employment, and data about other incomes will have to be known for a more general evaluation of the trend in distribution. It is possible that, while it lasted and inflation could be held in check, the Cruzado I experiment had a favorable impact on the real incomes of the poorest. But, at best, this lasted only a few months. High inflation has come back, together with a strong deceleration in growth. It is evident that nothing permanent was achieved in 1986, and that the huge social debt to the poorest in Brazil remains to be paid.

NOTES

1. The opinions here presented are those of the author in her personal capacity and do not in any way involve the United Nations. In this paper I have drawn heavily on the work done by Rodolfo Hoffmann (ESALQ, University of S. Paulo), particularly his recent papers in collaboration with Angela A. Kageyama. I am indebted for comments to the participants of the Conference on "Social Change in Brazil since 1945," Columbia University, New York, 3–5 December 1984. I am also grateful to Andrzej Krassowski and Iqbal Haji for their helpful comments. My greatest debt, however, is certainly to Rodolfo Hoffmann, for without his help and advice this paper would not have been produced.

2. As expressed by Professor Antonio Delfim Netto in 1973 "in this context [of rapid expansion of the modern sectors] it does not make sense to take the increase in inequality as an indicator of decline in welfare. On the contrary, . . . accelerated growth is the most powerful instrument to redistribute opportunities." (Delfim Netto's Preface to Langoni, 1973)

3. The most interesting analysis focusing on institutions that regulate ownership and exchange is the "entitlement approach" of Sen (1981).

4. One of the exceptions is Lopes (1972).

5. For the Gini index for South Africa and 38 other developing countries, see Lecaillon et al., 1984.

6. For a review, see Bacha 1980; also Tolipan and Tinelli (org.), 1975; Pfefferman and Webb, 1979.

7. See debate Fishlow (1980)–Fields (1977 and 1980) in the *American Economic Review*.

8. Reviewing aspects of income distribution that affect, in particular, developing countries, a report prepared by the United Nations Secretariat noted: "Both research and policy are hampered by the still woefully inadequate data on distribution, particularly as to country coverage. Improvement in the data base on income distribution by size—that is, the percentage of income received by a given percentage of recipients, arranged in order of size of their income—remains a pressing need in most countries. Such information is available for only some 50 developing countries. Even then, the latest estimates for some countries are more than 20 years, and for many others more than 10 years, old; only about half the number of estimates refer to a year within the last 10 years." (United Nations Economic and Social Council, Doc. E/CN.5.1983/5)

9. It is worth noting that the reduction in the degree of income inequality among families verified from the census data is revealed as well if we compare the national

household sample survey PNAD of 1972 with the PNAD's of the end of the decade (1977, 1978 and 1979) (Hoffmann and Kageyama, 1984, p. 21).

10. In this respect—the rise of income earners per family and its influence on the improvement of income distribution among families—Brazil is moving in the same direction of developed country experience some 20 years earlier.

11. One of the few to draw attention to inequality arising from the property of real and financial assets was Malan (1979), in a conference at Escola Superior de Guerra in August 1978. See also the debate Langoni-Malan (respectively 1974 and 1973, 1974) and Fishlow (1973 and 1975).

12. In Brazil this difference in the nature of remuneration inside the hierarchical structure of the big enterprise has been examined by Bacha (1973).

13. There are caveats, as with almost any use of statistics: First, the ratio given is wage bill over value of production instead of value added, which was not available. Even when there are no changes in the physical proportion of raw materials in the process, the value of production might change due to fluctuations in the price of raw materials and not of the value added. Macedo (1977) took into account this and other limitations, as the difference in coverage between the census and the annual surveys and the influence of the business cycle in labor participation, but they do not invalidate the trend.

14. The characteristics of the data basis really do not warrant fine distinctions, but it is interesting to see that between 1969 and 1973 (the boom period) the share of blue collar workers did not fall more rapidly than the one of all labor.

15. IBGE has published a beautiful little book on the different types of rural dwellings in Brazil (Barbosa da Costa and Mesquita, 1978). Something analogous could be done for urban habitations.

16. In this respect, one could say Brazil is unique in an unexpected way. Land concentration seems to have increased almost everywhere in the world, despite land reform. Concentration indexes certainly declined where land reform was implemented, but subsequently the process of reconcentration did set in again.

17. Some of the recent studies are Graziano da Silva, 1981; Graziano da Silva and Hoffmann, 1980; Hoffmann and Kageyama, 1985; Pinsky (org.), 1979, Sayad, 1980; Graziano da Silva (org.), 1978; Homem de Melo, 1980.

18. We are only talking of a difference in emphasis. Certainly absolute poverty in Brazil was examined before. See for instance, Mata, 1979; Bacha, in PREALC, 1980; Pfefferman and Webb, 1983. The shift in favour of the preparation of poverty profiles seems to be common to other developing countries also. See United Nations, 1983.

19. Sen (1981) has a beautifully written and probably exhaustive discussion of the concepts of poverty.

20. We will mostly disregard here Hoffmann's careful discussion of the methodological and statistical problems involved in the measurement of poverty in Brazil, which are only in part the same as for income distribution estimates.

21. For a formal presentation, see Sen, 1981 and Hoffmann, 1984c.

22. We have argued that the family is a more meaningful unit of analysis. As before, families with no income were included among the poor.

23. Massive expansion in urban employment accompanied this growth. See Faria's article in this volume.

24. One example of this ECLA hypothesis is in United Nations, 1970.

25. Among the most recent studies: Camargo 1984 and 1984b.

26. Average family incomes declined more than per capita income given that from 1980 to 1983 the average number of members in the family went down from 4.4 to 4.2.

27. The Survey of Employment and Unemployment in the Great Metropolitan Area of São Paulo was carried out by SEADE/DIEESE—Fundação Sistema Estadual de Análise de Dados/Departamento Intersindical de Estatistica e Estudos Socio-Econômicos.

REFERENCES

Braga, Helson C. and Joao L. Mascolo, 1982, "Mensuração da concentração industrial no Brasil. *Pesquisa e Planejamento Economico* 12(2).

Bacha, Edmar, 1973, *Hierarquia e remuneração gerencial*. Textos para discussão no. 11. Departamento de Economia, Universidade de Brasilia. (Included in Tolipan and Tinelli, org. 1975).

————, 1980, *Essays on Brazilian Growth, Wages and Poverty*. International Labour Organization, Working Paper PREALC/188, July.

Bach, Edmar and Lance Taylor, 1980, Brazilian income distribution in the 1960s: "facts", model results and the controversy, in Taylor et al., 1980.

Camargo, Jose MARCIO, 1984a, *Minimum wage in Brazil: theory, policy and empirical evidence*. Texto para Discussão no. 67. Departamento de Economia, PUC, Rio de Janeiro.

————, 1984b, *Income distribution in Brazil 1960–1980*. Departamento de Economia, PUC, Rio de Janeiro.

Chenery, Hollis et al., 1974, *Redistribution with growth*. Oxford University Press.

Fields, Gary S., 1977, Who benefits from economic development? A re-examination of Brazilian growth in the 1960s. *American Economic Review*, Vol. 67.

————, 1980, Who benefits from economic development? Comment. *American Economic Review*, Vol. 70.

Fishlow, Albert, 1973. Distribuição da renda no Brasil: um novo exame. *Dados* 11.

————, 1975. A distribuição da renda no Brasil, in: Tolipan and Tinelli, org. (originally published in *American Economic Review*, Vol. 62, May 1972).

————, 1980. Who benefits from economic development? Comment. *American Economic Review*, Vol. 70.

Fundacao Getulio Vargas (FGV), 1977. *Contas nacionais: revisão e atualização 1949–1975*. Separata de *Conjuntura Econômica*, 31(7), Junho.

Graziano Da Silva, Jose F., coord., 1978. Estrutura agária e produção de subsistência na agricultura brasileira. Ed. Hucitec, S. Paulo.

Graziano Da Silva, Jose, 1981. *Progresso técnico e relacões de trabalho na agricultura*. Ed. Hucitec, S. Paulo.

Graziano Da Silva, Jose e Rodolfo Hoffmann, 1980. A reconcentração fundiária. *Reforma Agraria*, Vol. 10, no. 6.

Hirschman, Albert O., 1973. The changing tolerance for income inequality in the course of economic development. *The Quarterly Journal of Economics*, Vol. 87, No. 4, Nov.

Hoffmann, Rodolfo, 1971. *Contribuição à análise da distribuição da renda e da posse da terra no Brasil*. Tese de livre docência, ESALQ-USP, Piracicaba.

————, 1977. Informações necessárias para a análise da distribuição da renda no Brasil. *Estudos CEBRAP* 21, jul.–set.

————, 1979. Estimação da desigualdade dentro dos estratos no cálculo do índice de Gini e Redundância. *Pesquisa e Planejamento* 9(3).

————, 1982. Evolução da desigualdade da distribuição da posse da terra no Brazil no período 1960–1980. *Reforma Agrária*, vol. 12, no. 6.

————, 1983. Distribuição da renda no Brasil, en 1980, por unidades da Federação. *Revista de Economia Política*, vol. III, no. 1, jan.–mar.

————, 1984a. *Pobreza no Brasil*. Série Pesquisa no. 43. Departamento de Economia e Sociologia Rural, ESALQ-USP, Piracicaba, S. Paulo.

————, 1984b. Estimation of inequality and concentration measures from grouped observations. *Revista de Econometria*, 4(1).

————, 1984c. *A pobreza no Brasil: Análise dos dados dos Censos Demográficos de 1970*. (Paper presented to VI Encontro Brasileiro de Econometria, S. Paulo, 5–7 December 1984).

————, 1985. Distribuição da renda e pobreza entre as familias no Brasil, de 1980 a 1983. *Revista de Economia Politica*, 5(3).

Hoffmann, Rodolfo and J.C. Duarte, 1972. A distribuição da renda no Brasil, *Revista de Administração de Empresas*, 12(2).

Hoffmann, Rodolfo and Angela A Kageyama, 1984. *Distribuição da renda no Brasil entre familias e entre pessoas, em 1970 e 1980* (Paper presented to the XII ANPEC meeting, S. Paulo, 5–7 December 1984).

————, 1985, Modernizaçao da agricultura e distribuiçao de renda no Brasil, *Pesquisa e Planejamento Econômico*, 15(1).

————, 1987. *Distribuição da renda e pobreza entre as familias, no Brasil, de 1980 a 1985* (mimeo).

Homem De Melo, Fernando, 1980. A agricultura nos anos 80: perspectivas e conflitos entre objetivos de politica. *Estudos Econômicos*, vol. 10, no. 2. IPE-Universidade de S. Paulo.

Lopes, Francisco L. de P., 1972. *Inequality Planning in the Developing Economy*. Ph.D. Thesis, Harvard University, Cambridge, Massachusetts.

Langoni, Carlos, 1973. *Distribuiçao da Renda e Desenvolvimento Econômico do Brasil*. Editora Expressao e Cultura, Rio de Janeiro.

————, 1974. Distribuição de renda: uma versão para a minoria. *Pesquisa e Planejamento Econômico*, vol. 4, fevereiro.

Lecaillon, Jacques, Felix Paukert, Christian Morrison and Dimitri Germidis, 1984.

Income distribution and economic development: an analytical survey. International Labour Office, Geneva.

Macedo, Roberto B., 1977. *Distribuiçao funcional na indústria de transformação:* do trabalho (Tese de Livre Docêcia, FEA-USP), S. Paulo.

Malan, Pedro, and John Wells, 1973. Distribuição de Renda e Desenvolvimento Econômico no Brasil. *Pesquisa e Planejamento Economico*, vol. 3, no. 2, dez.

Malan, Pedro S., 1974. Ainda sobre a distribuição da renda. *Revista de Administração de Empresas*, Fundação Getúlio Vargas, S. Paulo, vol. 14, no. 2, abril.

Malan, Pedro, 1978. Distribuição de renda e desenvolvimento: novas evidências e uma tentativa de clarificação da controvérsia no Brasil. *Dados*, 21: 33–48.

Martins, Luciano, 1965. Os grupos bilionários estrangeiros. *Revista do Instituto de Ciencias Sociais*, vol. 2, no. 1. Universidade Federal do Rio de Janeiro.

Mata, Milton da, 1979. *Concentração de renda, desemprego e pobreza no Brasil* (Análise de uma amostra de municípios em 1970). IPEA, Relatório de Pesquisa no. 41, Rio de Janeiro.

Pessoa De Queiroz, Jose, 1965. Os grupos bilionários nacionais. *Revista do Instituto de Ciências Sociais*, vol. 2, no. 1, Universidade Federal do Rio de Janeiro.

Pfeffermann, Guy and Richard Webb, 1983. "Poverty and Income Distribution in Brazil". *The Review of Income and Wealth*, Series 29, no. 2, June.

————, 1979. *The Distribution of Income in Brazil*. World Bank Staff Working Paper no. 356.

Pinsky, Jaime, org., 1979. *Capital e trabalho no campo*. Ed. Hucitec, S. Paulo.

PNAD - *Pesquisa Nacional por Amostra de Domicilios*. Rio de Janeiro, FIBGE, various issues.

II PND, 1974. Projeto do II Plano Nacional de Desenvolvimento (1975–1979). Brasilia.

Sayad, João, 1980. *Crédito Rural no Brasil*, Série Relatório de Pesquisas no. 1, IPE-Universidade de S. Paulo.

Sen, Amartia, 1981. *Poverty and Famines: An Essay on Entitlement and Deprivation* (Study prepared for the International Labour Office) Oxford University Press.

Taylor, Lance, Edmar L. Bacha, Eliana A. Cardoso and Frank J. Lysy, 1980. *Models of Growth and Distribution for Brazil*. A World Bank Research Publication. Oxford University Press.

Thurow, Lester C. 1984. The leverage of our wealthiest 400. *The New York Times*, October 11.

United Nations, Economic Commission for Latin America, 1970. *Economic Survey of Latin America 1969*, New York (E/CN.12/851/Rev.1).

United Nations, 1983. Economic and Social Council, Commission for Social Development. *Socio-economic policies related to issues concerning the equitable distribution of national income and the process of institutional development. Preliminary conclusions of a project on income distribution.* (Note by the Secretary General). Doc. E/CN.5/1983/5, 14 December 1983.

Vinhas De Queiroz, Mauricio, 1962. Os grupos econômicos no Brasil, *Revista do*

Instituto de Ciências Sociais, vol. I, no. 2, jul.–dez. Universidade Federal do Rio de Janeiro.

————, 1965. Os groups multibilionários. *Revista do Instituto de Ciências Sociais*, vol. 2, no. 1, jan.–dez. Universidade Federal do Rio de Janeiro.

————, 1972. *Grupos econômicos e o modelo brasileiro*. Tese de doutorado, Departamento de Ciências Sociais da Faculdade de Filosofia, Letras e Ciências Humanas da Universidade de S. Paulo.

Wells, John, 1974. Distribution of Earnings, Growth and Structure of Demand in Brazil during the 1960s. *World Development* 2(1), Jan.

World Bank, 1984. *World Development Report 1984*. Oxford University Press.

7

Social Welfare

Maurício C. Coutinho and Cláudio Salm

INTRODUCTION

The social repercussions of economic development have traditionally been analyzed from three different angles: (1) employment and income distribution; (2) regulation of labor relations and access to the collective goods; and (3) services necessary for survival. In spite of the obvious overlapping that exists among these ways of viewing the question, the last of the three generally forms the field known as *Social Policy*.

Brazilian economic literature on the subject in the last two decades has favored study of the forms of insertion in the labor market. The crystallization of the concepts of *formal and informal labor markets* was a conspicuous point in this school of thought.[1] And, in fact, the paradigm constitutes a useful division for understanding the differences in the workers' standard of living. In Brazil, to have *carteira assinada* (working papers)—that is, to participate in production of a legally recognized contractual nature—would clearly be equivalent to a differentiated situation in relation to other workers.[2] Those who do not share in the advantages reserved for the formal labor market are largely agricultural workers, workers in very small businesses in general, domestic servants, and self-employed low-income workers. Although still important, the dividing line is no longer as clear as the categories *formal* and *informal* suggest.

This is true, first of all, because the organized sector itself is

233

heterogeneous. Minimum wages have deteriorated over time and the minimum guaranteed by law is far from representing a privilege. Second, because the explosive growth of the cities in the postwar period, and especially in the last decade, strongly contributed to lowering urban living standards. Rural poverty was transferred to the outlying urban areas, and from the point of view of the response to social demands, a downward leveling can be seen in the quality of life of those who depend on the formal and the informal market. Third, because the economic crisis that occurred beginning at the end of 1980 threw millions of workers formerly employed in the formal sector into poverty to an extent never before experienced in the country. The burden of the economic adjustment imposed by external restrictions fell hard on workers in the organized sector. By showing the ease with which mass firings take place in Brazil and the absence of adequate unemployment assistance programs, the crisis made clear the precariousness of the supposed privileges attributed to the formal sector of the labor market. In summary, *worker* is once again becoming a synonym for *poor*, without regard to the way in which the worker is intregrated in the labor market.

It is important to keep in mind that the performance of the labor market in Brazil over the last three decades, until the crisis, was quite reasonable.[3] On the average, organized employment grew at around 4% annually, so that until recently, the proportion of workers surviving on unstable forms of work did not increase, in spite of the accelerated urbanization. Now, as a result of the recession, industrial employment in São Paulo is at 1973 levels, and among analysts optimism does not prevail so far as the strength of the recuperation of employment is concerned, even in the event of a return to sustained positive growth rates.

Of course it can be pointed out that it was also the vigorous expansion of the formal labor market that provided the basis for the development of the financing system for social policy programs, since taxes based on payrolls pay the basic costs. With the exception of education, which is predominantly, although not exclusively, financed with fiscal resources, the other areas essentially depend on the level of employment and on salaries. In fact, in Brazil only a quarter of government spending in the social area is covered by taxes and a significant part of that is targeted for higher education. In other areas, outside of education, Treasury funds do not even cover 18% of expenditures. One might say that those resources do not take care of much more than the bureaucracy of the social programs.

The study of the question from a labor relations viewpoint is much more recent.[4] This interest was sparked by the outbreak of illegal strikes that occurred in 1978,[5] by the new salary policy introduced in 1979, and by the succesion of governmental decrees attempting to counter salary adjustments, starting with the agreements made with the International Monetary Fund (IMF).

This second focus on the social question will certainly pick up force in economic investigations in view of the obvious obsolescence of the labor laws, since they are inadequate for the very mechanisms that make up the latest salary decrees which broaden the scope of collective bargaining negotiations.

The existing labor laws date back to the 1940s and result from the linking of unions to the state during the Vargas dictatorship. This governmental guardianship imposed heavy restrictions on union activity, inhibiting unions in the assertion of their rights and turning them into a kind of agency collaborating with the authorities so far as social assistance for their members was concerned. The New Republic, interested in putting together what becomes known as the *social pact*, cannot fail to make concessions to the old claims of union autonomy and freedom. It should be noted that direct negotiations, often conducted *ao arpio* of the law, begin to increase, even with the consent of businessmen connected with the most profitable sectors. If the immobility of the government continues, the Consolidation of the Labor Laws (CLT) could become a dead issue, which, it should be emphasized, would mean a victory only for the most organized categories.

So far as the third focus is concerned, as we mentioned, it constitutes the field of Social Policy properly speaking. Social Policy is a matter linked like an umbilical cord to urbanized societies. In these societies, there is no way to defend the liberal maxim that "people have a right to liberty but not to survival," since it no longer depends so much on individual solutions—personal income—as on collective means which, in order to achieve an acceptable minimum of comprehensiveness, can only be organized by the government.

Therefore, the important questions that concern the evaluation of a system of social protection deal with its *coverage* and to its *financing*: Which segments have access to the services and what are the criteria for inclusion or exclusion? Who pays and who benefits from subsidized services?

In order to conduct an analysis of social policy properly it will therefore be necessary to reveal the composition and the political obligations of the government in each stage that is analyzed, as well as to examine the coherence with the dynamics of the economy. We are not trying to offer explanations here that would reveal these major dimensions. However, we do believe that we are making a positive contribution to the understanding of the question by focusing on several aspects of Social Security coverage and financing, although at times descriptively.

Social Security stands out in the context of Brazilian social policies both for the volume of resources involved and for the range of social services provided. The National System of Social Security and Assistance (SINPAS) has a budget greater than that of all the units of the Federation and surpassing half the federal budget. The proposed budget for SINPAS for 1985 was 57 trillion cruzeiros, while the federal government estimated a budget from the Treasury and other sources of 88.9 trillion and those of the largest state in the federation, São Paulo, were 2.2 trillion; in the same year, Social Security collected 6.7 trillion.

In the course of its existence, Brazilian Social Security has incorporated innumerable functions, so that today it includes a broad spectrum of social welfare programs of different kinds. Three distinct fields of action can be identified so far as the kind of services provided is concerned:

(a) programs properly concerned with social security, such as the provision of retirement income to people withdrawing from the work force and pensions to their dependents;

(b) individualized medical assistance: outpatient care and hospitalization;

(c) social assistance programs for the needy, especially minors and the aged.

These three areas, all included in the group of agencies that make up the SINPAS, unfold to make a broad list of services and benefits, the most important of which are:

retirement pensions for period of service and old age
disability pensions
sickness benefits
dependent benefits
outpatient medical care
medical tests and hospitalization
lifelong monthly allowances for the aged not receiving pensions
social services
occupational rehabilitation
assistance to needy minors

There is no question that there is a broad range of social services and benefits, which make up an almost complete social security system if we take countries with mature social security programs as our point of reference. Leaving aside for the moment an aspect that is as controversial as it is crucial—the quality of the services provided and the value of the benefits—and considering only the list of programs developed by the SINPAS, it would not be an exaggeration to claim that until recently in Brazil there was only one of the classical items of modern social security that we did not have: *i.e.*, unemployment insurance. If in the past the lack of broader financial protection measures for unemployed workers reflected our labor policy's conception of worker security, now it suggests the difficulties in protecting workers in situations where the "informal labor market" reaches excessive proportions and where underemployment, low salaries and high labor turnover are the dominant realities. If a broad program of unemployment insurance or some other minimum income program were instituted for those left out of the formal labor market, the demand for benefits would be almost inexhaustible.

The lack of a broad unemployment insurance program is still common to almost all the Latin American countries. And if we focus on the extent of coverage and the main types of benefits and services, we will see that Brazilian social security is comparable to those of the most developed countries of Latin America, such as Argentina, Mexico and Venezuela. Below is a brief outline of the most significant characteristics of the social security programs in these countries.[6]

BRAZIL

Services/benefits: old age, service and disability pensions; medical care and hospitalization; work injury.

Coverage: employees in industry and commerce, domestic servants, self-employed, employers, public employees and rural workers.

Sources of funds: salary and payroll deductions; government budget contribution. For public employees and rural workers, specific contribution systems. All the benefits are financed indiscriminately from the same source of funds.

Qualifying conditions: age 65 (men) and 60 (women) and 60 months of contribution; 35 (men) and 30 (women) years of service, independent of age. For survivor pensions, 12 months of contribution prior to death.

ARGENTINA

Services/benefits: old age and disability pensions; medical care and hospitalization; work injury; special insurance system for unemployment in civil construction.

Coverage: employed and self-employed persons. Separate systems for private employees, self-employed and public employees.

Sources of funds: contributions from earnings and proportional government appropriations (for retirement income and pensions); salary and payroll deductions (for medicine).

Qualifying conditions: age 60 (men) or 55 (women), with a minimum of 30 years of employment and 15 years of contribution.

MEXICO

Services/benefits: old age and disability pensions; medical care and hospitalization; work injury.

Coverage: employees, agricultural workers and small businesses, self-employed, domestic workers and family labor. Voluntary affiliation open to

all persons not covered. Special systems for public employees and petroleum workers.

Sources of funds: salary and payroll deductions, governmental appropriations
proportional to employers' contributions (for benefits and pensions); specific salary and payroll deductions and governmental contributions proportional to employers' contributions (for medical care).

Qualifying conditions: age 65 and 500 weeks of contribution (for benefits and
pensions); 4 weeks of contribution (for medical care).

VENEZUELA

Services/benefits: old age and disability pensions and benefits; medical care and
hospitalization; work injury.

Coverage: employees in public and private employment—in the latter, coverage
is being extended gradually to different regions. Excludes self-employed
and temporary or casual workers.

Sources of funds: salary and payroll deductions, governmental appropriations
(for benefits and pensions); salary and payroll deductions and governmental appropriations (for medical care and hospitalization).

Qualifying conditions: age 60 (men) and 55 (women) and 750 weeks of contribution (for benefits and pensions); no restrictions (for medical care).

From the above, it can be seen that Brazilian social security is equal to or
better than those of the principal Latin American countries in services and
range of coverage, having even greater flexibility as far as conditions of access
are concerned. Retirement income based on length of service is peculiar to
Brazil, as is the lack of discrimination among sources of financing for benefits
and health care.

At first glance—given the comprehensiveness and maturity of the Brazilian social security system—the succession of budget deficits could be considered a natural result of the economic recession. The narrowing of the tax base
(salary and payroll rates) resulting from the drop in employment and in the
average salary and accompanied by the continual increase in the number of
beneficiaries and of people seeking medical care causes the system to go into
crisis, as do all the social programs, especially those financed by payroll taxes.

While we are not denying the close relationship between the economic
crisis and the crisis in Social Security, in the text that follows we will defend
the idea that in addition to the general collapse of the welfare system, the
recent recurring deficits of Brazilian Social Security, combined with the poor
quality of the services provided and the low value of most of the benefits
offered, show the existence of a structural flaw in the insurance system. The
flaw results from the lack of definition of financing mechanisms that are in

agreement with the nature of the social policy put into effect. In other words, the range of services and benefits offered was gradually widened, as was its coverage of the population, but with no financing source other than that obtained through a simple increase in payroll taxes. At the times when the number of contributors increases, the system expands and carries out its functions satisfactorily, since the system is established on a tax basis, but when there is a downturn, the system faces serious financial pressures. The economic recession accelerated the emergence of the social security crisis, which, nevertheless, is a crisis of definition rather than a crisis related to the economic situation.

In order to learn the nature of the collapse of the social security system, it is necessary to go back to the historical roots of the Brazilian social security program and show how the financing mechanisms were set up, parallel to the expansion of the system. That is what we will do below, calling attention to the controversial points in the interpretation of the social security system.

ORIGINS AND EVOLUTION OF BRAZILIAN SOCIAL SECURITY

Legislative Decree 4862 of January 24, 1923, which created the Retirement Income and Pension Bank for railroad workers, is considered the starting point of Brazilian Social Security. The Elói Chaves law—known as such in memory of the representative from São Paulo who formulated the preliminary project—foresaw contributions from three sources (employees, companies, and government) and benefits including retirement income, pensions, and health care. The system of capitalization was adopted, with a structure of awards and benefits governed by insurance criteria, in accordance with the current state of the international social security practices of the time.

The system of retirement and pension funds expanded rapidly. In 1926, it was extended to longshoremen and maritime workers and after that to other areas. In 1937, there were 183 funds in existence, administered by governing bodies made up of employees and employers.

In the 1930s, the system of funds established by companies began to be revised in favor of a greater centralization of social welfare administration units. Several funds covering the same occupational categories were merged, and retirement and pension institutes appeared that were strictly organized by occupational categories: maritime workers (1933), banking (1934), commercial employees (1934), industrial workers (1938), and, finally, transportation and freight workers (1938). Until the end of the 1950s, the funds and institutes continued to coexist, but both were related to occupational categories, since the old funds merged and ceased to be related to individual companies.[7]

The most important institutional characteristics of Brazilian social security organization from then until now can be listed as follows:
—uniformization of the systems of benefits, financing, and management
for all the institutes (Organic Law for Social Security, 1960);
—institutional unification, with the creation of the National Institute for
Social Security (INPS) (1967);
—extension of social security to rural workers (1968–71);
—creation of the Ministry of Social Security (1974) and subsequent clear
division of functions within the National System of Social Security and
Assistance (SINPAS) around social security properly speaking (INPAS),
medical care (INAMPS), social welfare assistance (LBA and FUNABEM)
and social security administration (IAPAS).

Apparently, the institutional development of the Brazilian social security
system seems to form a coherent trajectory that goes from initial dispersion
to institutional unification. It starts with company funds, with various systems of benefits and financing, goes through a period of organization by occupational categories (the Institutes) and then finally social security is united
both with regard to financing criteria, benefits and services provided as well
as institutionally. Parallel to this, the expansion and universalization of the
clientele is followed in the 1970s by a specialization of functions that distinguishes between social security, medical care, and social welfare assistance,
and even opens up the possibility of the long-awaited goal of a total separation between social security and medical care, with the possible movement of
the latter to the sphere of the Ministry of Health. This version of continuity
and coherence is shared by countless analysts, particularly those in public
administration or identified with the social security bureaucracy. Nevertheless,
the coherence of the trajectory does not withstand careful analysis. An initial
query can lead us to question the supposed coherence and perhaps contribute
to the emphasis on several characteristics of the Brazilian social security system that can help in the clarification of its current status:

*What is the reason why, in over sixty years of existence, our social security system
has not managed to succeed either in attaining financial stability or providing quality
service?* The question is not farfetched. After all, countless countries have established efficient and comprehensive social security legislation within a short
period of time: England—a classic example—did so in half a century, by
revolutionizing social security and welfare legislation though the public obstacles to its establishment were by no means small; in Germany—another
classic example—encouraged by Bismarck, the social security system was
consolidated in five years, and in forty years even unemployment insurance
was instituted.

In responding to this question, we will find that our social security system is not a single evolving system, but that on the contrary we have had several social security systems in the past sixty years, judging from the standpoint of the political and administrative ups and downs that social security legislation and practice have undergone. Nevertheless, and strangely enough, certain traits of Brazilian social security are conspicuous throughout its development. With the brevity required by the limits of this text, we will examine what has stayed the same and what has changed in our social security system, by pointing out the characteristics that help to explain its current crisis. We will start from an evaluation of the basic aspects of the social security dilemma: political significance, economics and financing mechanisms, the problem of medical care; benefits and social welfare assistance programs.

POLITICAL SIGNIFICANCE, ECONOMICS AND FINANCING MECHANISMS

Malloy stands out among political analysts of Brazilian social security because of his insistence on the grantlike character of the social security legislation of 1923.[8] Basing his argument on a concept in which the distinction *conquest versus grant* occupies a major place, Malloy considers the development of social security to be characterized at its beginning as a concession on the part of the dominant classes. From this point of view, the Elói Chaves Law would have constituted an anticipation of future social pressures that would make themselves felt; on the other hand, it would be a response, in a moment of relative political calm, to the proletarian demands of the preceding decade, *i.e.*, a movement of anticipation, co-opting and demobilization of union and popular organizations.

Yet, according to Malloy, the choice of the railway, maritime and port sectors as the first centers for the establishment of Retirement and Pension Funds was not a matter of chance. It was probably a question of protecting the heart of the export system against possible movements in demand of workers' rights.

Even putting aside the distinction *conquest/grant*, this still seems to be a somewhat simplistic theoretical basis for the comprehension of the emergence of social policies. One cannot fail to acknowledge that the establishment of social security systems generally accompanies or constitutes the culmination of the processes of the formation of the urban proletariat and the development of social conflicts. Nevertheless, we will steer clear of these political arguments, and instead we would like to point out that social security mechanisms generally appear only after the formation of consolidated proletarian nuclei. Salaried employment and concentration of the work force—in short, defined, stable work relationships and a large number of contributors—are prerequisites for putting into effect an insurance system that leads to the beginnings of social security.

The Funds, like the Institutes later on, will be established where consolidated proletariate nuclei definitely exist—that is, in institutions or occupational sectors where salaried employment is the dominant work relationship and where there is a reasonable concentration of salaried workers and homogeneity in working conditions. In Brazil, the urban sectors observed to have social security protection are those where a clear and stable salary relationship appeared early.

The predominance of salaried employment is a necessary, but not a sufficient condition for the establishment of social security. Other factors must be taken into account, such as characteristics of union action, the composition of the work force, and the salary structure. The domestic industrial sector is characterized from the beginning by concentration in large units and by salaried employment; at the same time, it is an economic sector with strong union organization, with a proletariate that is very active at the beginning of the century in demonstrations demanding its rights. Nevertheless, this sector does not participate in social security until late, which perhaps can be attributed to the regional heterogeneity of the industrial base, the salaried employment of women and children in subhuman conditions; ultimately, to factors that either impede the actual functioning of the insurance mechanism, or put other matters in the forefront—health conditions, length of working hours, regulation of work by minors—that come before social security policies.

In any case, putting aside the attempt to characterize the political factors that preside over the establishment of social security, what we would like to emphasize is the relationship between urbanization, salaried employment, and social security. Social security is one of the basic institutions to govern social coexistence, once salaried employment has been established; on the other hand, the mechanics of social security require salaried employment and concentration (large contingents of beneficiaries) in order to be viable. Countless factors—union organization, predominance of impresarial structures, international example, pressure from bodies connected with the League of Nations—converge around these points to explain the origins of Brazilian social legislation.

Apart from its origin, Brazilian social security has been affected a good deal by the political and economic characteristics of the periods that followed the Revolution of 1930. As salaried urban populations become widespread in the 1930s and 40s, social security changed its political role. Now organized according to occupational categories, social security developed in the same political and institutional space as the corporatist unionism organized by Getúlio Vargas. This may be the source of the temptation to attribute social security legislation to the same pattern of grants generally accepted for "Estado Novo" labor and union legislation, established at a time of complete political and institutional repression.

Once again, more important than the distinction between grants and conquests is the study of the course taken by social security policy. Getúlio Vargas was deposed in 1945 without seeing the establishment of his project for the unification of Social Security in the Social Services Institute of Brazil, an autocracy the establishment of which—as had occurred earlier with the IAPI (Instituto de Aposentadoria e Pensões dos Industriários)—was preceded by a broad survey of the health needs of the population and of the resources to be mobilized for medical and social welfare assistance. Since the unification was blocked, the scattered social security administration assumed a dominant role in the so-called "populist pact" during the following democratic interval and until 1964.

Starting in 1945, social security is, in fact, viewed as an arm of the Brazilian union organization. The union bureaucracies take over the boards of the respective Institutes, if not the presidency, and social security practice is adapted to union practices, embracing the relationship between the working masses, the executive power, and the union structure that characterize the "populist republic" and the alliance between the Social Democratic Party (PSD) and the Brazilian Workers Party (PTB).[9]

In this context, the unification of the financing and benefit systems, although not of the institutional social security apparatus itself, is hindered by union interests for various reasons ranging from the fear that the level of health care would be lowered (the typical case of the IAPB—Instituto de Aposentadoria e Pensões de Bancários) to the rejection of the loss of powerful political bargaining tool in relation to both the working masses and the executive branch. It was a silent struggle between the dominant union bureaucracy and certain administrators of the modern social security technocracy, especially those from the IAPI, who wanted to give the social security system a higher degree of administrative efficiency and coherence. At the same time, bills that would lead to the unification of the social security system crept through Congress without obtaining approval; characteristically—and suggestively—the struggle for nationalization of social security was headed by the representative Aluísio Alves, then a young exponent of the National Democratic Union (UDN) opposition. Of course, in this movement, the UDN was trying to gain support among the urban population by its attempts to make the system more efficient, while at the same time undermining the bureaucratic social security machinery that was one of the bases of the government coalition.

Finally, in 1960, the Organic Law Concerning Social Security, was approved. Although it unified the systems of benefits and financing, it did not unify Brazilian social security as an institution. The fight for unification would be

won only after 1964, when all the mechanisms for political action characteristic of the post-Estado Novo period—and social security was one of them—
were dismantled.

It does not seem an exaggeration to claim that the unique role played by
social security during the democratic period hindered what would have been
a natural movement towards unification, following a very segmented and partial origin and significant development. The unification and the reorganiza-
tion toward greater efficiency—an expected corollary of the Brazilian social
security experience—were delayed twenty years, until another period tended
toward complete centralization.

The year of 1964 marked another important break in the course followed
by social security. All of the union system's interference was eliminated, but
it was not replaced by any other form of expression or representation of the
interests of the clientele in management. The eradication of the political conditioning that had existed for two decades impeding administrative centralization and homogenization of the benefits and services provided opened up
the possibility of a broad institutional reform, which does not mean there is a
change of attitude as far as the basic premises of social security policy are
concerned.

The merging of the Institutes organized according to economic categories
into a single National Institute for Social Security in 1967 was a logical corollary of the centralizing tendency that had already partially made itself felt
through the approval of the Organic Law Concerning Social Security in 1960.
Similarly, the expansion of contributors and beneficiaries that had already
begun with the inclusion of employers and self-employed workers as individuals subject to compulsory insurance (Organic Law) continued with the incorporation of domestic servants and rural workers. Thus, all individuals
participating in remunerated activities became subject in principle to the protection of social security.

This is, perhaps, the great historical challenge successfully faced by social
security after 1964. It was no longer a question of granting social security
coverage to certain companies or occupational categories, no matter how broad
they might be. It was a question of universalizing social security, and the
results are unmistakable, as we can see in Table 7.1.

During the 1970s there was significant growth in the number of contributors, and also of the ratio of contributors to total population, which stabi-
lized at around 20% in the final years of the decade (Table 7.2).

The ratio of contributors to Economically Active Population (EAP) rose
substantially, from 29.4% in 1970 to 54.3% in 1980. There was a vigorous
expansion of the group of contributors, both in absolute terms and in proportion to the population. On the other hand, the factors generating expendi-

Table 7.1

Number of Contributors to Social Security

1930	142,464	1970	8,700,000
1940	1,912,972	1975	16,347,000
1950	2,857,356	1980	23,782,000
1960	4,058,000		

Sources: Rezende and Mahar, *Saúde e Providência Social*, IPEA, RP21, 1974; Barros Silva, "Atenção à Saúde como Política Governmental", thesis UNICAMP, 1984; Possas, *Saúde e Trabalho*, Graal, 1981.

Table 7.2

Contributors to Social Security—Absolute
Number and Proportions of Total Population—1970–1980

Ano	Contributors	% total pop.	Ano	Contributors	% total pop.
1970	8,700,000	9.37	1976	18,595,367	17.41
1971	9,690,583	10.21	1977	21,006,000	19.18
1972	10,436,000	10.75	1978	21,166,088	18.83
1973	11,963,000	12.05	1979	22,436,053	19.44
1974	14,973,024	14.73	1980	23,782,216	20.05
1975	16,347,382	15.69			

Source: Barros Silva, Atenção à Saúde como Política Governmental, Thesis UNICAMP, 1984.

tures increased, whether because of the generalization of medical and hospital care to almost all of the population or because of the growth in the number of beneficiaries.

The number of nonworking insured individuals more than tripled in a decade, as can be seen in Table 7.3. So far as the expansion of medical care is concerned, the increase in the number of outpatient consultations and the number of hospitalizations (Table 7.4) is quite illustrative of the widening degree of coverage provided by the system. There are some discrepancies depending on the source used, but once again the numbers indicate a tripling of medical assistance, judging simply from the number of hospitalizations and outpatient consultations of the social security complex.

The data given here is sufficient to show that at the same time the post-1964 period changed the organizational structure and the political-administrative role of social security, it revolutionized the economic significance. Economic growth and urbanization themselves significantly increased the base of regis-

Table 7.3

Non-Working Individuals Insured by Social
Security—Urban and Rural Clientele—Estimated*
Brazil—1971–1980

Year	Urban	Rural	Total	Indice (1971 = 100)
1971	2,268,129	—	2,268,129	—
1972	2,481,870	—	2,481,870	109.4
1973	2,682,691	833,613	3,516,304	155.0
1974	2,941,237	1,064,309	4,005,546	176.6
1975	3,469,799	1,477,148	4,946,947	218.1
1976	4,269,930	1,811,982	6,081,912	268.1
1977	3,520,232	1,897,274	6,417,506	282.9
1978	4,968,334	2,150,685	7,119,019	313.8
1979	5,230,818	2,356,579	7,587,397	334.5
1980	5,312,706	2,496,523	7,809,229	344.3

*Estimate taken from the number of subsistence benefits as equivalent to the number of inactive persons insured.
Source: Barros Silva, Atenção à Saùde como Política Governmental, Thesis UNICAMP, 1984

Table 7.4

Inpatient Care and Outpatient Consultations
for Social Security—Brazil—1971–1980

Year	Inpatient Care	Outpatient Consultations
1971	2,931,589	44,688,476
1972	4,448,712	52,686,858
1973	4,718,528	53,899,843
1974	5,194,394	59,618,443
1975	6,649,136	92,333,187
1976	8,356,067	118,647,964
1977	8,617,431	132,502,898
1978	9,658,055	145,411,612
1979	10,571,214	154,535,578
1980	11,753,451	179,751,174

Source: Barros Silva, Atenção à Saùde como Política Governmental Thesis, UNICAMP.

tered salaried workers; in addition, there is a voluntary movement of expansion of the base of contributors by means of the inclusion of previously excluded categories. Between 1971 and 1981, the ratio of contributors to urban population grew from 17.8% to 30.1%. If we consider that the same ratio was 14.8% in 1940 and just 12.6% in 1960, we will see not only the strength of the expansion of the social security system in the 1970s but also its weakness throughout the pre-1964 period—an example also of the well-known idea that the populist pact was upheld by maintaining social exclusion.

Although it was freed from direct pressure on the part of the clientele and was institutionally reorganized, Brazilian social security did not promote fundamental changes in the conception of its financing system. Resources continued to come from percentages withheld from company payrolls and workers' salaries, and, in a much smaller proportion, from governmental contributions. This created an imbalance: while the financing criteria were preserved, the scope of the social security system was altered by the expansion of the social welfare assistance provided and by the effective incorporation of medical assistance as a basic function. Individualized medical attention, which had always been an appendage accommodated with difficulty in the old Funds and Institutes, now constituted an active element in the social security complex which even became the main agent of Brazilian health policy. The growth of the mass of contributors hindered the emergence of a financial imbalance that did not appear until the moment in which the economy entered a prolonged crisis. The apparent solvency of the system could not hide an incompatibility between social policy (the "supply" of services and benefits) and its financing criteria. This incompatibility, however, is just one more added to a long series of disagreements and lack of determinateness in the financing of our chief social policy, as can be seen in a rapid historical overview.

The first Retirement Funds were created under the aegis of insurance norms current in international social security practice. The resources stemmed from the contributions of beneficiaries, employers and the public domain, and the contributions-benefits relationship was governed by the capitalization system. The tripartite responsibility in financing guarantees the public payment and the social character of an insurance contract; capitalization, in turn, aims at giving autonomy to the social welfare funds and simultaneously at establishing a link between contributions and benefits. Unlike the relationship between the individual and the government that results from normal taxation—taxes do not allow the contributor to establish any individualized collection of public services, nor do they generate any expectation or even right to individualized compensation in benefits or services—the capitalization system links the premium to future benefits. The contributor "has a right" to retirement income or to a pension, with the state acting as a guarantor in the final instance in this type of contract.

The Elói Chaves Law sanctioned a curious form of tripartite contribution: the employees contributed 3% of their earnings, the employer contributed an amount equivalent to 1% of the company's gross annual income (with an absolute minimum value equivalent to the contribution of the individual employees) and the state contributed resources stemming from "Social Security quotas" added to the prices of goods sold, generally public services, in addition to amounts allocated in the federal budget.

With the proliferation of Funds and Institutes, both the benefit plans and the contribution rates began to differ. Many of the new institutions did not have the right to charge "Social Security quotas"—a fact that leads the IAPI, for example, to show a lack of resources for medical assistance. Thus, we can see that the federal government shied away from a broader tax reform that would have enabled it to meet the rising social security responsibilities—that it also promoted the emergence of differences in contribution plans and, as a result, in benefits.

The prediction that social security would function under a system of capitalization of resources soon proved to be unrealistic, although only much later did it adhere explicitly to the simple distribution system. Due to the increase in the number of contributors and to the youth of the social security system, the reserves (surplus of taxes collected over costs) obtained in the 1930s and 40s, soon faced an inflationary reality that did not provide the social security administration with adequate assets for long-term capitalization.

According to Rezende da Silva e Mahar,[10] the surplus of current receipts over current expenditures (social security "savings") was significant in the 1940s and 50s. In 1947, 48 and 49 the "savings" represented, respectively, 44%, 35% and 46% of current receipts; in 1954, 55 and 56, respectively, 4%, 10% and 13%. Throughout the 1930s and 40s, the generation of surpluses (total receipts less total expenditures) was significant. Built up year after year, by 1945 total reserves corresponded to three times annual social security receipts.

These reserves formed during the first few decades of the existence of the social security system, supposedly the supports of the capitalization system, soon encountered two obstacles, however. On the one hand, the elevation of expenditures as a proportion of total receipts during the 1950s and 60s is noteworthy; on the other hand, the Brazilian financial system never had long-term securities with the degree of reliability and valorization required in order to make the capitalization of reserves operational.

Part of the reserves was employed in suburban land and real estate, and these investments were said to guarantee to a large extent the endowment of social security; another part was designated for governmental programs with little or no return. Social security funds financed the Volta Redonda ironworks and the hydroelectric system; until recently there were controversies regarding eventual new allocations of social security resources to Itaipu. Furthermore, some Institutes, especially the IAPI, financed construction of residential blocks for their contributors.

Both cases—residential financing and infrastructure projects—were harmful to social security capitalization, although they have different economic characteristics from the point of view of their suitability to the nature of the system. In principle, real estate financing is not an activity that is incompabible with the capitalization of reserves; on the contrary, provided that the real interest rate obtained is positive, the buyer of the real estate and the reserve fund benefit. However, Brazilian financial legislation did not anticipate mechanisms capable of ensuring positive real interest rates, and the concrete result of this was that the properties were greatly subsidized by the buyers, thus harming the reserve fund and therefore also the contributors. The attempt to decrease the housing shortage at the expense of social security reserves only showed the difficulty of the coexistence between inflation and the system of housing financing—that is, between the exercise of a social policy and the need to capitalize funds whose long-term usage is linked to a passive nature.

The use of social security reserves in infrastructure projects is even more controversial. Unless we were to allow for an eventual purchase of stock in government-owned companies by retirement and pension funds—in which case we would have high risk capitalization with variable income bonds—the simple transfer of funds to other governmental agencies constituted a misappropriation of the reserves. We could allow for this misapplication of funds to create a counterpart—for example, the federal government would accept responsibility for benefits whenever there was a social security shortfall, in order to compensate for the earlier social security aid. Then we would already have abandoned the logic of capitalization for the unexpected logic of intertemporal social pacts.

The purpose of these arguments is not so much to discuss investment alternatives for the reserves as to show the difficulty—or even impossibility—of capitalizing social security funds in unstable inflationary economies without financial securities that guarantee a long-term positive remuneration. Add to this the lack of standards in the use of social security reserves, and you have a picture in which the dominant tone was that of the nonexistence of an adequate employment of the surpluses inherent in social security systems in the formation phase.

Moreover, the lack of standards requires additional commentary. It implies both a certain servility or lack of autonomy for the social security administration in relation to the central authority or to the dominant political pact, and a utilization of social security resources in social policies not necessarily of a social security nature. In both cases, the result is the same: the erosion of social security finances. The funds collected by social security are viewed as money available to the Executive Branch, an indistinguishable part of the income of the union, that can be applied to economic infrastructure programs or to any other sector short of resources.

This question is important and leads to a central point in the financing of social policies in Brazil. The new demands for public services that accompany urbanization are being met within the financial framework of the social security system. The same thing happened with financing for housing; until the creation of the *BNH* (Banco Nacional da Habitação), the Institutes were the great financers of privately owned housing in the country in spite of the complete inadequacy of resources of a social security nature and long-term loans with returns eroded (and therefore subsidized) by inflation. The same is also true in the most notable case of a social program introduced into social security without the necessary corresponding resources—*i.e.*, medical and hospital assistance. With the lack of a specific program for providing individualized medical attention to the populace, the problem is being handed over to the unions and to social security.

It is highly debatable whether medical care and social security resources are compatible. Most economists believe that universal medicine goes along with resources of a completely tributary nature and expenditures by current budget means. In Brazil, not only does this not exist, but there is no specific provision of resources within social security receipts for each item among the countless social programs developed.

As a result of this failure to specify the financing channels for the different social programs, the attitude of the federal government is to meet financing difficulties by raising rates, but always within the same pattern of payroll and salary taxes. The contribution rate for companies and employees has grown progressively until it reaches 8% of payroll. The federal government's share, which was no longer described as obligatory in the 1946 Constitution, comes from social security rates and various taxes (on exceptional profits, lottery ticket sales, horse-racing bets) authorized in the Organic Law Concerning Social Security.

Once the capitalization funds had been exhausted and the government had excused itself from further responsibility so far as its contribution was concerned, social security's success in ensuring the financial solvency of the system—which beginning in the 1960s was seriously overburdened by the extension of medical services—can only be explained by the dynamism of the economy and by the permanent incorporation of new batches of contributors into the tax-collecting net.

The financial crisis in social security that emerges in the 1980s at the same time as the payroll debacle and also because of it, is met once again with the typical response—an increase in rates. The basic financing mechanism remains untouched despite the enormous importance of the medical and welfare programs it includes. Social security, which changed so much on the political, institutional and economic levels, did not carry out the only reform actually necessary for the fulfillment of its functions—the adjustment of financing standards to the social programs that had been developed.

SOCIAL SECURITY HEALTH CARE

Social security health care has been one of the most controversial topics in the social policy area. With medical assistance expanding in such a way that the agency in charge of its execution—INAMPS (Instituto Nacional de Assistencia Medica e Providência Social)—becomes the chief instrument of Brazilian health policy, to discuss it means to question the whole national health services structure. This implies the analysis of matters so important and controversial as the priorities of public health expenditures (preventive medicine *versus* outpatient-inpatient care), the relationship between public services and private medicine, the remuneration pattern for medical personnel and medical services, the location of institutions that is most suitable for health care (Social Security Ministry or Health Ministry), and so on.

It is clear that public health specialists are needed to put such varied topics into proper perspective. Even so, opinions would be extremely diverse because, ultimately, questions such as the concept of health, health and economic development, and public health in a privatist structure will be considered; after all, these are questions that do not have a single answer. Without even pretending to deal with this extremely delicate topic on that level, our objective right now is simply to point out some controversial points in the concept of financing for preventive medicine.

First of all, contrary to popular opinion, we believe that health assistance has never been a substantive part of Brazilian social security plans from their origins. While it may be true, as countless authors affirm, that the legislation governing the establishment of Funds and Institutes had specified medical assistance as one of the components of the social security complex, there have always been strict limitations on expenditures in this sector.[11] Administrative norms and directions were concerned with setting maximum resource amounts to be allocated for health, specifically in order to maintain retirement incomes and pensions—that is, to maintain the benefits that were essentially of an insurance nature. The amounts budgeted for medical assistance were always considered—as they are today—leftovers in the total social security pot. In conclusion, to make medicine a priority in a social security system would be merely a formal gesture unless adequate sources of funds or allocations were specified at the same time and explicitly reserved for this social policy.

Secondly, and once again in contrast to popular opinion or at least without endorsing it, we do not believe that social security has been the agent par excellence for dealing with curative medical practices, which are associated with a privatist medical system under capitalist organization, to the detriment of preventive medicine.[12] On the contrary, it seems to us that these are two distinct areas, although not unassociated, of two clear social needs. On the one hand, there is a lot of room for public health, the institution of generalized preventive measures, sanitary campaigns, and even for the extension of basic outpatient care; on the other hand, there will always be a demand for hospitalization, laboratory tests, and certain medicines. Social security did not let the former atrophy in favor of the latter; it barely paid attention to individualized medical assistance, while collective health programs had ceased to develop due to a lack of specific policy for their development.

The lack of basic medical and sanitary assistance to the population—thus, the small importance of the Ministry of Health—must be added to the other social deficiencies: low salary levels, inefficient education pattern, housing deficiencies for the poor, nutritional deficiencies, etc. The federal budget has not been the ideal place for social policies, and only resources of a general budgetary nature can satisfy this type of demand. A medical system financed through the generosity of social security tends to be individualized, due to systemic and financial reasons.

It is estimated that medical care and hospitalization was responsible for 13% of public health spending in 1949, and for 85% in 1982; expenditures for collective measures in the same years represented 87% and 15% of health spending.[13] This information can be interpreted as an indication of a loss of importance for collective medicine in the country, and that is the usual interpretation. However, it can be indicative of the lack of a public medical and hospital system prior to the expansion of the social security medical system.

In the context of social security medicine there is certainly room for a discussion and a qualitative option for the prevailing type of medical structure: operating social security medical facilities *versus* third party services; salaries *versus* accreditation; analysis of the apparently exaggerated number of hospitalizations; consequences of the various modes of payment (including payment for units of service). Social security may perhaps not support the most appropriate medical practices in the context of individualized assistance, but its role as an effective creator of mass medical assistance in the country should not be minimized. Although there is no data available, we know that the previous medical system never took care of more than a small proportion of the population. Giving individual medical assistance the status of social policy was the work of social security. In fact, as Table 7.4 shows, making medicine a broadly based system was one of the tasks undertaken by post-1964 social security, with unparalleled quantitative success.

A third point of controversy concerns the role played by social security medicine in the SINPAS financial crisis. Economic policy authorities have often magnified this role and attributed an image approaching budgetary unruliness to the current INAMPS; there is no way to plan for expenses in social security medicine, since the demand for assistance is inexhaustible. There is some truth to this point of view, but there are also many doubtful aspects.

There are countless indications contrary to the position that in the case of the INAMPS, expenses are uncontrollable. First, the evidence of the facts themselves. For 1985, the Ministry of Social Security projected a ratio of health care costs to receipts from contributions of around 25%, less than the average found in the last ten years. In addition, after a peak period (1976, 77, 78), INAMPS's expenditures declined in proportion to receipts from contributions, with values below the 30% level typical in the previous decade. Furthermore, INAMPS's expenditures in constant prices underwent little variation from 1976 to 1983 (around Cr$ 4.5 trillion at 1984 values), with the exception of the years 1977 and 78 (Table 7.5).

Apparently beginning in 1981, the year in which the depth of the social security financial crisis became clear, the Ministry of Social Security and Assistance successfully adopted cost control measures such as an increase in hospitalizations and examinations in its own hospitals, frequent checking of accounts, and a decrease in referral amounts for payment of services provided by accredited professionals. Thus, it is easy to see that there are countless actions that make it possible to control medical assistance costs. In an intensely inflationary economy, the actions that are the most far-reaching and the easiest to implement are decreasing the real salaries of employed officials and the real cost of Service Units, or by decreasing other forms of remuneration for services contracted outside social security hospitals. In the final analysis, social security can impose inpatient quotas at associated hospitals that function as cost ceilings. In that case, the insured is left either to search for an institution that has not exhausted its quota or simply to do without assistance.

The cost squeeze for medical assistance ends up by lowering the assistance pattern even more under the pretext of cutting the abuses and fraud found in the relationship between hospitals and the INAMPS. There are indications (although not verified) that the importance of parallel health assistance plans— such as individual health insurance plans, agreements between companies and firms or cooperatives providing medical services—tends to increase. The tendency is for the INAMPS to be left to assist those who are excluded from

Table 7.5

INAMPS' Expenditures as a Percentage of

Receipts from Contributions to Social Security

Year	INAMPS' Expenditures/ Contributions to Social Security (%)	Year	INAMPS' Expenditures/ Contributions to Social Security (%)
1971	32.12	1977	33.80
1972	28.99	1978	33.73
1973	27.98	1979	29.68
1974	27.32	1980	27.32
1975	31.29	1981	30.20
1976	36.37	1982	24.39

Source: Oliveira and Azevedo, "Previdência Social", IPEA, 1983.

nonsocial security health systems—in general, individuals with lower income levels—and to provide certain types of medical services that because of their high costs are not included in private assistance contracts.

The truth of the governmental arguments stems from the lack of definition of specific financing channels for medical assistance in social policy terms. Medicine is a residual expense in the social security budget because there is no clear determination of resources or rates specifically placed at their disposal. Thus, the growth of the proportion of medical assistance expenditures out of total contribution receipts seems like a pressure on resources primarily earmarked for benefit payments. The payment of benefits derives from the law; therefore, it is obligatory, coercive, independent of the volume of resources of the Social Security and Assistance Fund. Medical assistance is one of social security's responsibilities; nevertheless, the extent and quality of services will always depend on the availability of resources, once benefits have been paid.

Brazilian social security goes from a ratio level of medical assistance expenditures to receipts from contributions of below 10% in the 1920s, 30s, and 40s, and levels a little below 20% in the 1950s and early 60s to around (and above) 30% from the end of the 1960s. This can be interpreted both as a pressure on social security resources and as a failure to allocate alternative resources to health care, in a situation in which the task of broadening access to medical assistance in the country is assigned to a social security system that has been institutionally transformed, but is still based on the same inadequate financing mechanisms.

BENEFITS AND SOCIAL ASSISTANCE

Much of the national debate over social security has focused on health care. Thus, questions about fraud, the poor quality of services, and the participation of this service in the overall deficit of the system stand out. Curiously enough, the problem of benefits—retirement income and pensions—and of social welfare assistance is left on the fringes of the discussion despite the fact that these costs dominate the budget and that it is here that the major difficulty of the social security complex, as executor of social policies, lies.

Throughout the 1960s social security benefits surpassed 70% of receipts from contributions. On the average, this ratio was 78% between 1960 and 1970, excluding expenditures for family allowances and work-related injuries. In the 1970s, and until 1982, this ratio was maintained at about the same level, if we take INPS expenditures as corresponding to benefits in the SINPAS complex after 1977 (Table 7.6).

The importance of the benefits-social assistance segment within the Brazilian social security system is not solely a question of its impact on receipts from contributions. Apart from its magnitude, there are serious problems that should be discussed, problems regarding the adequacy of financing and efficiency so far as the social policy objectives are concerned.

Historically, just as health care costs continued to grow without the establishment of new sources of financing, the social assistance component was also signed without the necessary specification. However, we are referring here only to programs for the protection of needy youths and the elderly, developed by two specific institutions in the social security complex—the Brazilian Assistance Legion (LBA) and the National Foundation for the Welfare of Minors (FUNABEM)—which, although important, have not absorbed more than 2% of receipts from contributions. We are thinking of the programs that are typically or partially assistential and that are among the continuous payment benefits—the main one being the lifelong monthly income (½ minimum salary) meant for noninsured individuals over the age of 70 or for noncontributing invalids of whatever age. In recent years, these benefits have represented more than 15% of all beneficiaries in the area of continuous payment benefits, and have absorbed around 6% (from 6.71% in 1979 to 5.10% in 1982) of their value. The dividing line between social security and social welfare assistance is quite tenuous nowadays, leaving room for commentary in this regard, since the growth of the extra-social security components is frequently alleged to be the cause of the current crisis in the system.

The strict concept of social security as social insurance is only supported so long as the system of capitalization is in force. In that case, as in private insurance, the capitalized monthly payments from the contributors guaran-

Table 7.6

Expenditures in Benefits and Social Assistance
in Proportion to Receipts from Contributions—1971–1982*

Period	Benefits & Social Assistance/ Receipts from Contributions (%)	Period	Benefits & Social Assistance/Receipts from Contributions (%)
1971	75.5	1977	71.8
1972	74.7	1978	74.5
1973	70.6	1979	74.0
1974	70.2	1980	79.7
1975	69.7	1981	84.6
1976	71.8	1982	75.6

*Exclusive to Social Assistance provided by CBA and FUNABEM
Source: Oliveira and Azevedo, "Previdência Social", IPEA, 1983.

tee the future retirement income or pensions. There is a strict relationship between the values of premiums and benefits, stipulated by actuarial calculations; the presence of the state and its possible financing of the system represent the only protection and an official political and economic seal guaranteeing solvency in the final analysis.

In Brazil the simple distribution system is in force. In this system, the contributions are a kind of tax collection, and their value, like that of the benefits, depends on political decisions. The loss of the insurance nature of social security separates the benefits from a possible contribution fund formed by the capitalization of the resources collected from the beneficiaries themselves.

Abandoning the concept of the system of capitalization and all its implications, the state excessively expanded the range of benefits. The above-mentioned lifelong monthly pension and other benefits as well "do not have financial coverage" whether because they are typical components of social welfare assistance (family allowance, maternity benefits), or because they are retirement income or pensions which, given the short period of need required by social security (60 months), can mean expenditures not covered by past contributions.

In summary, apart from the system of capitalization, one can hardly speak of "financial coverage" for the benefits paid. Most of the benefit programs have a social assistance component, whether the activities concerned are considered as extra-insurance activities or as not covered by past contributions. Even so, it is not unreasonable to think that given the lack of a relationship between the value of contributions and the value of benefits, the extreme growth in the number of contributors and in social security receipts in the 1960s and 70s facilitated the expansion of social security social policies.

As was seen in Table 7.2, the number of contributors virtually triples between 1970 and 1980. As of 1977, the ratio of contributors to urban population is about 0.3, an indication that the possibility of increasing revenues through the absorption of insured individuals at a rate much greater than that of population growth seems to have been exhausted.

Despite the immense incorporation of contributors, the growth rate for the number of nonemployed is never much lower. The ratio of nonemployed to employed was a little above $\frac{1}{5}$ at the end of the 1950s, declined at the beginning of the 1970s, only to increase again dangerously at the end of that decade, reaching $\frac{1}{2.7}$ in 1982. This ratio, an indication of the burden of the average number of nonemployed individuals who are dependent on the contributions of employed individuals, is not completely frightening financially because a significant proportion of the increase in nonemployed individuals was due to the extension of social security to rural workers and to social security coverage for the elderly and for invalids, whose monetary benefits were of little value.

The small value of the benefits shows that Brazilian social security, successful so far as the expansion of the coverage of services and benefits is concerned, did not work out the problem of quality and even of the social significance of the benefits granted in a reasonable manner. Contrary to what happens in the case of health care, where quantitative goals do not always mean efficient services, here quantity and value are characteristics that fully define the efficiency of the social policy. In this case, the extremely low value of some types of benefits introduces an imbalance between distribution numbers and distribution amounts, in a clear demonstration of the inadequacy of social security coverage.

This occurs both with the relationship between rural and urban benefits—urban benefits represent $\frac{2}{3}$ of the total number of continuous payment benefits, but they absorb 85% of the value of these benefits; rural benefits represent $\frac{1}{3}$ of the number and 15% of the value—and in the area of urban benefits (Tables 7.7 and 7.8).

Even retirement pensions, benefits of a greater average unit value, admit situations of extreme differentiation between allocations of number and of value. Retirement pensions based on the period of service absorbed more than half the resources earmarked for pensions, with an average unit value of 3.8 minimum salaries (in November of 1982). The lifelong monthly income corresponds to a set value of $\frac{1}{2}$ minimum salary, and old age and disability pensions had an average value of 1.78 and 1.26 minimum salaries (November of 1982). Even considering the reduced value of rural retirement income

Table 7.7
Urban Social Security—Main Types of Continuous Payment Benefits—
Participation in Number of Benefits and in Value—1979–82

Type of Benefit	1979		1980		1981		1982	
	% benef.	% value	% benef.	% value	% benef.	% value	% benef.	% value
Retirement	38.73	60.54	39.61	61.04	40.36	62.37	41.24	63.89
Pensions	25.55	17.81	25.89	18.80	25.54	18.35	25.55	17.65
Monthly life Annuities	18.21	6.71	17.10	6.21	16.15	5.67	15.11	5.10
Assistance	14.77	13.02	14.86	12.21	15.29	12.03	15.53	11.77
Others	2.74	1.92	2.54	1.74	1.26	11.58	2.19	1.59
Total	100	100	100	100	100	100	100	100

Source: Oliveira and Azevedo, "Previdência Social", IPEA, 1983.

Table 7.8

Urban Social Security—Main Types of Pensions—Participation by Number of Benefits and by Value—1979–82

Type of Benefit	1979		1980		1981		1982	
	% benef.	% value	% benef.	% value	% benef.	% value	% benef.	% value
Accident	52.35	29.21	51.72	29.15	50.38	28.62	49.21	28.28
Retirement	30.78	53.68	30.86	53.49	31.39	53.37	36.64	53.19
Old Age	12.06	9.52	12.58	10.15	13.44	10.77	14.29	11.24
Special	4.32	6.85	4.43	6.91	4.45	6.55	4.57	7.10
Others	0.49	0.34	0.41	0.30	0.34	0.24	0.29	0.19
Total	100	100	100	100	100	100	100	100

Source: Oliveira and Azevedo, "Previdência Social", IPEA, 1983.

(½ minimum wage), we can affirm that a very significant proportion of the benefits has a low average value.

The general picture of a social welfare benefit system like that of Brazilian social security is one of very broad coverage, with low benefit values. Social security goes into crisis without having constituted an effective mechanism for granting survival conditions to the nonemployed. In the list of proposals that emerge as solutions for the crisis—apart from the resumption of economic growth, of employment and of the average salary—the reform of the structure of retirement income, with emphasis on the elimination of the criterion of length of service as a determinant for access to benefits, stands out. While the financial impact of this measure cannot be specified, it should be pointed out that less than ⅓ of urban pensions are given under these conditions, although they represent more than half the expenditures for urban pensions and approximately 30% of the value of urban continuous payment benefits.

There are countless arguments in favor of the abolition of pensions based on length of service—among them the weight of international experience and the evidence that while the life expectancy of Brazilians is low at birth, it is not all that low for those who have already passed the threat of infant mortality and entered the EAP. Without dismissing the validity of these arguments, one should remember that there are other problems of equal importance on the social welfare agenda.

The strangulation of social security finances was due, even before the emergence of the negative impact of the economic crisis, to a crisis of conception. Taking advantage of a natural explosion in available resources due to the incorporation of new populational contingents, the government neglected to provide resources of another nature for the expansion of a series of social programs that were added onto the social security system. Financing on the basis of salary and payroll taxes today forms a narrow base for the support of social programs of such size.

CONCLUSIONS

Throughout the crisis of the early 1980s, unemployment and salary constraints made the mass of salaries fall, while federal tax collection fell less due to increased fiscal capacity. However, the government's improved fiscal capacity was not used to compensate for the decline in social security receipts, in view of the priority given to taking care of the financial obligations of the Central Bank (internal debt obligations, subsidies, etc.). In other words, fiscal resources were heavily used as an instrument to cover financial deficits. And that occurred at a time when it was becoming more necessary to expand and reinforce the programs entrusted to social security.

The inadequacy and the narrowing of the financial base has different repercussions in the various social areas. While the educational deficits scarcely have a direct effect on the millions excluded from the educational system, in the case of social security, as well as in that of Housing and Sanitation,[14] the difficulties also cause serious financial imbalances.

The roots of the financial problems faced by these areas are still the subject of controversy, as are the means proposed to heal them. In the case of social security, its costs should be covered by contributions and some government transfers, since the costs basically depend on the value and extent of the monetary benefits distributed and on what is spent on health care. The cumulative debt today is on the order of US$ 1 billion. How it should be met will depend on political decisions which will certainly be made soon, since it is no longer possible to continue bearing the burden.

It is unparalleled that social security should suffer the pernicious effects of the crisis that has battered the country since 1980. And no matter how much people call for "political solutions," these can only become viable through the resumption of economic growth—an absolutely necessary condition for any innovative project in the social area, including the restoration of government spending capacity.

Therefore, the resumption of growth is now considered the greatest national aspiration. However, given the preceding considerations, it will certainly not be a sufficient condition. No matter how favorable the effects of an eventual prolonged expansion of the economy may be on overall salaries, this will be a precarious basis on which to face the deficit accumulated by social security.

As we have seen, the country does not have significant segments to be incorporated as social security contributors. The rates are at high levels now and the beneficiaries tend to continue increasing at an accelerated rate independently of economic performance. It is therefore necessary to rethink the financing system, given the significant and growing participation of fiscal resources in social security expenditures.

NOTES

1. P.R. Souza. *Emprego, Salários e Pobreza*. São Paulo, HUCITEC/FUNCAMP, 1980.

2. See the concept of Regulated Citizenship, in W.G. dos Santos, *Cidadania e Justiça*, Ed. Campus.

3. With regard to this, consult the study by Vilmar Faria in this volume.

4. In 1982, the FIPE/USP began a systematic study of collective bargaining and the DIEESE has been going over its records in the same area.

5. In Brazil, *illegal strike* is almost a redundancy, since it is practically impossible to conduct a legal strike.

6. According to the report "Social Security Programs Throughout the World—1983", *Research Report* n.º 59, U.S. Department of Health and Human Services.

7. Several texts describe the development of Brazilian Social Security, among them: Celso Barroso Leite, and Luiz P. Velloso, *Previdência Social*, Rio de Janeiro, Zahar, 1963, and J. Malloy, *The Politics of Social Security in Brazil*, Univ. of Pittsburgh Press, 1979.

8. This point of view is present in countless texts by Malloy. A specific development of the topic can be found in J. Malloy, "The Politics of Social Security in Brazil", *op. cit.*, and J. Malloy, "Previdência Social e classe operária no Brasil", in *Estudos CEBRAP*, 15, pp. 115–31, June-March, 1976.

9. This stage of Brazilian social security development is very well documented and analyzed in Amélia Cohn, *Previdência Social e Processo Político no Brasil*, São Paulo, Moderna, 1981.

10. F. Rezende da Silva and D. Mahar, *Saúde e Previdência Social-uma análise econômica*, Rio de Janeiro, IPEA, RP 21, 1974.

11. This is the opinion of the following authors, among others: H. Alqueres; Gentile de Mello; Vespasiano Ramos, "Assistência Médica". In Celso B. Leite, Org. *Um Século de Previdência Social-balanços e perspectivas no Brasil e no mundo*, Rio de Janeiro, Zahar, 1983; and C. Possas, *Saúde e Trabalho: a crise da pervidência social*, Rio de Janeiro, Graal, 1981.

12. This point of view is supported by J.C.S. Braga, and S. Goes de Paula, *Saúde e Previdência-estudos de política social* São Paulo, Cebes-Hucitec, 1981, among others.

13. This information is found in André Médici, "A saúde no Brasil pós-76: crise e alternativas", the preliminary version of a report produced for the Pan American Health Organization, 1984.

14. In the case of the Financing System for Housing, factors of a strictly financial nature are more important, given the fact that the system is completely based on tax funds, which requires that the allocations made be *profitable*. In addition, this aspect of the SFH leads one to question its *social* policy nature, that is, to what extent does it differ from normal business practices?

8

What Is Happening In Brazilian Education

Cláudio de Moura Castro

INTRODUCTION

The Brazilian educational system has undergone profound change in the last three decades.[1] It has displayed very high growth rates, though tension and conflict have been present throughout. Yet it is to be noted that the problems of any one level bear little similarity to those of other education levels.

In this chapter the main issue to be faced at each level of education is reviewed. The first section deals with current deficiencies in elementary education. The second examines certain ambiguities in the role of secondary education. The third discusses the very serious crisis of higher education. Finally, the last section deals with the development of a science community around the nation's graduate schools.

ELEMENTARY EDUCATION: PERSISTENT FAILURES AND FUTURE PROSPECTS FOR DECENTRALIZATION

This section provides an overview of recent trends in Brazilian elementary education. Attention is devoted to the interplay of factors that have been responsible for the success or failure of primary education policies—including the availability of resources, the nature of political commitment, and the quality of administrative personnel. From the administrative offices of Brasília to the nation's classrooms, the distances are formidable. The current sentiment is that centralizing solutions have failed, and that the new gospel should be decentralization. This provides yet another factor to be considered.

1. Too little, too late: the growth of elementary education

Brazil is a latecomer to educational development, even when compared with other Latin American countries that have achieved relatively little in terms of educational performance. However, the general situation has changed dramatically in Brazil during the last three decades, with enrollment growth rates becoming quite impressive.

Again, when compared to the more affluent Latin American countries, Brazil was an underachiever until three decades ago, but the situation has reversed thereafter. Education has grown and changed much faster than, say, in Chile, Argentina, or Uruguay. Yet, on the whole, Brazilian schools are neither better nor significantly different from the mediocre school systems of the average Latin American country.

The experience of industrialized countries suggests that after a certain degree of saturation is obtained at one level of the education system, growth rates at this level will then tend to decline, while growth at the next higher level of instruction will begin to accelerate.[2] This pattern does not apply to Brazil. During the 1970s, the higher enrollment growth rates were obtained in graduate education (31%), followed by undergraduate (12%) and then secondary education (11%). The level with the slowed enrollment growth was found in elementary education, which increased only 4% during the period (Table 8.1). It seems evident that this growth was especially inadequate at both the primary and secondary levels. Such a distorted pattern of growth appears to be related to the fact that those who politically demand education are overwhelmingly members of an educated elite. The saturation hypothesis does not apply. Yet this hypothesis does seem apt in a different way, if we consider only those who are willing to politically fight for education, namely, the elites and the middle class. Having been eventually satisfied in their demands for elementary and, subsequently, secondary education, this educated elite becomes an advocate of undergraduate and ultimately graduate education. Therefore, the top expanded before sufficient coverage was attained at the lower level.

It is my contention that the basic weakness in Brazilian education lies in the early elementary grades. Many students never enter school; of those who do enroll, many drop out before meaningful learning could take place. Thus, while Brazil has become a significant producer of science, as compared to the most advanced Third World countries, its achievements in basic education have been meager, even as compared to the poorer Latin American countries (say, Paraguay and Bolivia).

Table 8.1

Enrollment and Percent Growth at the Graduate, Undergraduate, Secondary, and Elementary Levels in Brazil, 1970–80.

Year	Graduate	% Change	Under-Graduate	% Change	Secondary	% Change	Elementary	% Change	Population
1970	3,068		456,134		1,007,600		15,904,627		93,193,000
1971	5,690	85	575,010	26	1,153,768	14	17,137,439	8	95,513,506
1972	8,960	57	709,316	23	1,299,937	15	18,370,252	8	98,690,200
1973	10,887	22	820,493	16	1,490,831	15	18,828,431	2	101,147,586
1974	15,212	40	897,220	9	1,681,728	14	19,286,611	3	102,767,940
1975	22,245	46	967,000	8	1,935,903	15	19,549,249	1	105,326,806
1976	26,255	18	1,042,472	8	2,212,749	14	19,523,058	0	107,949,490
1977	31,532	20	1,137,070	9	2,437,701	10	20,368,436	4	110,637,430
1978	33,631	7	1,267,599	11	2,519,122	6	21,473,100	5	113,392,300
1979	36,608	9	1,298,331	2	2,667,359	6	22,025,449	3	116,215,760
1980	38,609	5	1,345,000	4	2,812,416	5	22,522,756*	2	119,070,865
AVERAGE RATE OF GROWTH		30.9		11.6		11.4		3.6	

Sources: —Fundação Instituto Brasileiro de Geografia e Estatística, Crescimento e Distribuição de População Brasileira: 1940–1980 (Rio de Janeiro, 1980)

—*Id.*, Anuário Estatístico do Brasil, 1980.

—MEC–CAPES, Situação Atual de Pós–Graduação do Brasil–75 (Brasília, 1976).

—*Id.*, 1980, unpublished.

—MEC–SESu, Boletim Informativo SESu (Brasília, March, 1981).

Table 8.2

Literacy Rates among Persons Ten Years of Age and Older in Brazil, by Sex (1940, 1950, 1960, 1970, and 1980).

	Percent					Percentage Points Gained During Period			
SEX	1940	1950	1960	1970	1980	1940–50	1950–60	1960–70	1970–80
Male	48.2	52.6	64.0	68.9	75.6	4.4	11.4	4.9	6.7
Female	38.0	44.2	57.3	64.4	73.5	6.2	13.1	7.1	9.1
Total	43.0	48.4	60.6	66.6	74.5	5.4	12.2	6.0	7.9

Source: Fundação Instituto Brasileiro de Geografia e Estatística, Indicadores Sociais (Rio de Janeiro, 1977), Tables 1 and 1.a., p. 209
Ibid., Tabulações Avançadas do Censo Demográfico—1980 (Rio de Janeiro, 1981), Table 3.1, p. 42.

Considerable success has been achieved in extending the initial coverage of Brazilian elementary schools (Table 8.2). In fact, in the more developed regions, something in excess of 90% of a generation eventually enroll in the primary school system. Yet a significant number drop out before reaching second grade (Table 8.3). This can be inferred by examining enrollment rates for the population 7 to 9 years of age. Moreover, recent evidence suggests that a generation currently receives something in excess of 7.5 *years* of primary education. However, due to high rates of repetition that eventually arrest progress through the system, recently educated generations complete only four *grades* of instruction. Students remain in the primary school system for many years, but progress through the grade sequence at a very slow rate. Only 58% of those who complete the first grade go beyond the fourth grade and only 16% of the same group go on to secondary education.

Enrollment rates, quality of instruction and related expenditures per enrollment vary markedly from one part of the country to another. The correlation between state per capita income and education expenditures per capita is fully 0.80.[3] Which is to be expected, since richer states want more education and pay dearer for it. Wheras poorer regions have lower enrollment rates and spend proportionately less money on their students. Thus, in the less developed North and Northeast regions, expenditures per enrollment are only 65% of the national average. Remarkable differences exist even within cities. In the city of Rio de Janeiro school system, operating under a single unified budget, expenditures per enrollment in the affluent southern areas of the city are three times higher than those in the poorer districts.[4]

The quality of elementary instruction is extremely varied, and since the weaker schools predominate, average educational quality is remarkably low. Academic achievement varies accordingly. Reading comprehension and science achievement tests applied in Brasília and its satellite cities, as well as in the remote *município* of Barra do Corda in Maranhão produced results that are illustrative (see Table 8.4). Middle- and upper-class students residing in the central district of Brasília (Plano Piloto) obtained test results roughly equivalent to those attained in Buenos Aires. Also, as expected, lower-class students residing in the satallite cities of Distrito Federal did much worse than their more affluent students in the central areas of Brasília. But the really surprising result was to find that the lower-class students of Brasília did almost as well as Buenos Aires students from the same origins. Buenos Aires is a rich city which has displayed close to 100% literacy for several generations. By contrast, the poor students from Brasília were the sons of workers who had recently migrated from the poorer and most backward regions of the country. This anomaly can be attributed to the unusually high level of expenditure and uniform quality of elementary education administered in the Distrito

Table 8.3
Highest Schooling Attained by the Literate Members of
the Population (percent).

Highest	1970			1976		
Schooling	Total	Urban	Rural	Total	Urban	Rural
Elementary	91.1	87.8	98.7	84.3	80.4	96.8
(1–4)	74.3	66.3	93.2	57.2	49.2	82.7
(5–8)	16.8	21.5	5.5	27.1	31.2	14.1
Secondary (8–11)	6.0	8.1	1.0	10.8	13.4	2.7
Higher	2.9	4.1	0.3	4.9	6.2	0.5

Source: Fundação Instituto Brasileiro de Geografia e Estatística, Indicadores Sociais (Rio de Janeiro, 1979) Table 4, p. 111.

Federal. By contrast, students in Barra do Corda produced test results that scarcely differed from scores that would be obtained with random answers.

These test results are consistent with current knowledge of the relationships linking socioeconomic status, education quality, and academic achievement. Those who are poor and who live in more isolated areas receive less expensive education of deficient quality. Disparities in the quality of instruction interact with the educational prospects of students coming from different socioeconomic backgrounds and thus tend to amplify the already existing heterogeneity of Brazilian society. By contrast, the Distrito Federal provides an example demonstrating the potential for improvement that could be achieved with uniform high-quality instruction offered to less-affluent students.

2. The growing awareness of an elementary education crisis

The goal of equity has acquired much greater prominence in Brazil during the last decade. After first being charmed with the appeal of higher education during these last two decades, the country has finally turned its attention to the crisis in Brazilian elementary education. Nevertheless, this new interest is bound to encounter strong resistance. For instance, university student and faculty protest in the 1960s, as well as the inherent bureaucratic resistance of university administrations, made it difficult to control higher education expenditures.

Yet it is at the lower levels of the education system that critical decisions

Table 8.4

Reading Comprehension and Science Test Scores by Region and Grade Level

	Brazil				Argentina				Barra do Corda (Maranhão)	
	BRASÍLIA									
	PLANO PILOTO		SATELLITE TOWNS		Urban		Rural		Urban/Rural	
Grade	Reading	Science	Reading	Science	Reading	Science	Reading	Science	Reading	Science
4th	19.7	16.5	16.5	13.7	13.2	11.6	10.7	8.7	12.3	9.3
6th	20.4	16.9	16.3	14.8	15.6	14.4	—	—	11.7	10.9
11th	15.2	11.8	16.2	11.6	21.7	16.0	—	—	12.0	9.2

Source: C. M. Castro, J. A. Sanguinetty et al., *Determinantes de la Educación en America Latina: Acesso, Desempeño y Equidad* (Rio de Janeiro: Programa ECIEL/FGV, 1984).

Source: F. Spagnolo, *A Escola Rural em Barra do Corda: Perspectivas e Realidada* (Dissertation in Teacher Education, Rio de Janeiro. PUC/RJ, 1979, mimeo).

need to be made. Should greater emphasis be placed on expanding primary enrollments, leaving the quality of instruction much as it is today, or should present enrollment levels be maintained and greater emphasis be given to improving the quality of instruction among those already enrolled? The trade-off between quantity and quality is necessarily a very critical issue. It is doubtful that such questions will ever be publicly debated by the government, but the real tragedy is that they are not even the subject of private discussions within the Ministry of Education.[5] In that particular matter, utopias and dogmas prevail.

From the point of view of efficiency, improving the quality of existing schools would appear to be the preferred alternative. Concentrating such improvements in the industrialized regions would also appear to make economic sense. However, from an equity point of view, resources should be concentrated in the more isolated areas, *i.e.*, areas that remain deficient both in terms of the number of enrollments and the quality of instruction.

School improvements are apt to imply different things in almost every case. The basic issue is how to avoid a precipitous fall in quality as one moves away from the very best schools in the central districts. This implies developing suitable classroom strategies and curriculum materials that correct the shortcomings, and more adequately serve the needs of disadvantaged students. In the most deficient areas, a bare minimum would imply providing a *modicum* of equipment for each classroom, including a blackboard, chalk, chairs, and at least one textbook per student.

Evidence of deteriorating quality among elementary school teachers has been lamented by all concerned. The predicament in teacher recruitment is that outside of isolated rural areas, current wages attract more formally qualified candidates than there are vacancies in the elementary school system. Only a small proportion of normal-school graduates ever enter the teaching profession, and for every vacant position, many formally qualified candidates apply. Yet, prevailing wage rates discourage talented individuals from applying for admission to the normal schools and encourage the students to take other jobs after graduation. In other words, current wages attract too many people with formal credentials and hardly anyone with the requisite skills and talent. The concern with only quantitative goals has contributed to the deteriorating quality among teachers due to the limited availability of funds.

Preschool is yet another issue that has recently come to the forefront in Brazilian education. As it now stands, preschool education is practically nonexistent. The Ministry of Education had demonstrated its willingness to give wholehearted support to preschool programs. Yet in so doing, it has ignored a number of caveats. These include reticent evaluations given to such extravagant programs as Project Talent and Project Headstart, whose results have not even been considered. Furthermore, the first grade of elementary school already includes an implicit first year of preschool education for the majority of low socioeconomic status students, who are often found to be unprepared to begin literacy instruction. Essentially, teachers track students, promoting some after only one year of study, while requiring others to repeat the first grade after a year of improvised preschool training. This clandestine preschool instruction is inadequate because appropriate teaching aids and formal orientation are nonexistent. Thus, in a way, preschool education already exists for a large, but still undertermined, number of students. Should it be left where it is? Or should it precede first-grade instruction as a separate program?

Brazil being very large geographically, on the average poor, and extremely heterogeneous in composition, the problems of educational disparities can find no easy answers. In the more advanced states, better science education, computer literacy and "hands on" experience with technological innovations are pressing educational needs. Although experience with comprehensive high schools and technical industrial schools demonstrates that many problems are encountered upon implementation, the need for skilled manpower should not be underestimated. To fulfill such needs realistically implies widening the gap between rich and poor regions.

Perhaps the most mystifying of all these problems concerns rural education. Chances are that the nation's administrators and policy-makers have heard more about New York City schools than about Brazilian rural schools. What should these rural schools teach? Who should teach? In what ways should they differ from urban schools or should they be different at all? There is much argument about the purposes of rural school. Should it be urban in the sense that emphasis is on the three R's? Or, instead, should they equip children for rural life, whatever that be? Has anyone ever found a core curriculum for rural schools that is both meaningful and really different from that taught in urban schools? The concern with rural education has ignored enormous differences existing within the rural sector. Research on the meaning and benefits of a rural education makes little sense unless we understand the specific context of this education. Are we talking about rich soybean farmlands, export crop plantations, Nisei orchards, or economically stagnant regions? Quite apart from the need for a political commitment to develop rural education, purely conceptual problems in this area remain the least understood and the most perplexing of all education issues.

3. Feasibility: money, cadres, and political commitment

Thus far, we have raised issues; some of these are commonly perceived as such, while others remain themes of scholarly inquiry. This section is to be devoted to an exploration of the practical feasibility of a number of alternative paths for the development of education policy. Any significant change in the orientation of education policy requires at least these three supporting factors: Only the most naive reformer would ignore the need for *financial resources*. Nevertheless, *political will* and the requisite *cadres for new initiatives* are all too often taken for granted. It is as if only a good idea backed with plenty of cash were enough.

It is instructive to review past experience. What has the Ministry of Education really been trying to do? During the late 1950s and throughout the 1960s, it promoted technical secondary education. Although this policy resulted in schools that were later criticized for being excessively elitist, the effort was in general remarkably successful. A significant network of shophisticated, well-equipped and well-run technical high schools was created and still survives today.

During the 1970s, higher education became the new priority. With the help of a number of agencies, the second largest graduate training capacity in the Third World was developed and the country achieved impressive strides in science and technology. University enrollment growth was spectacular, and great success was achieved in developing fairly respectable universities away from the Río de Janeiro–São Paulo axis.

The 1980s had promise to become the decade of elementary education. It appeared that the Ministry of Education would like to move in this direction. However, this possibility required additional consideration. When technical schooling was promoted, the Ministry of Education was very clearly committed to this objective, and the political will existed during the prevailing "developmentalism" of the period. Higher education, in turn, became a major issue as a result of the political activism of prominent intellectuals and much of the middle class. In the 1980s, the conspicuous crisis in elementary education has become widely recognized as an affront to national pride. There is growing awareness that the trend of deterioration at this level needs reversal. Thus, political will—resulting from the confluence of public opinion and technocratic commitment—has been evident in all three of these cases.

Does anything stand in the way of repeating the educational successes of earlier periods? I believe such obstacles do exist. When technical education was being developed, the effort was led by a young and aggressive group possessing some of the best education minds in the country. During the 1970s, the Department of University Affairs (DAU) was similarly staffed with some of the most qualified personnel found in the Ministry of Education. The qualifications of those concerned with graduate education, science and technology—some from within but most from outside the Ministry—were even more impressive.

It is a fact that no comparatively qualified group has been formed to deal with elementary education. Five years of elementary education rhetoric have scarcely altered the mediocre level of personnel involved in this area. It is not a matter of diplomas and degrees—in fact, there are plenty of Master's degree holders and a few Ph.D.s in the ministry now. Rather, it has to do with leadership, assertiveness, decision-making . These abilities are hard to define, but we do know when they are present or missing.

Budgetary allocations for primary education projects all too frequently fail to materialize as effective action. Bureaucratic activism has proven itself to be the real determinant of educational expenditures. Ministerial projects have deadlines and review boards. Education projects that are slow to develop produce loose money in the form of unused allocations that are often grabbed by projects that promise sound and fast results. High-level administrators are all too willing to accommodate attractively presented and appealing new projects at the expenses of slow-moving or messed-up projects—never mind how important they may be. Thus, lack of imagination, deficient proposals, and inefficient administration in the use of funds have often reduced the effectiveness of primary education programs sponsored by the ministry. Many times, initial allocations have severely overestimated actual expenditures in timidly or ineptly managed areas.

4. Decentralization imposed from above

Whenever the Minister of Education wants to implement a policy, the first task is to set the federal bureaucratic machinery in motion. Whatever actions ultimately emerge from Brasília encounter equally ponderous but probably less competent bureaucracies at the state level. From there, policies have to be communicated to the schools, often by way of the municipal secretaries of education. The effect of all this on the classroom is not entirely clear. Despite the oppressive glut of legislation and regulations, teachers ultimately manage their classrooms with enormous freedom, virtual impunity, and utter lack of connection with educational policy.

At all levels of society, there is growing awareness of the plight of centralized rule that intends to do so much, but is virtually impotent in terms of results. It has become increasingly clear that without greater initiative, participation and responsibility at the local level, close to where educational services are rendered, all other efforts will remain largely inconsequential. From Golbery to Couto e Silva, one of the most astute of regime conservatives, to the most naive and romantic left-wing groups, the new gospel is decentralization. This is the new dimension in education policy. Resources, political commitment and qualified personnel are obvious requirements for successful policy implementation. But much more is needed.

Overwhelming support for decentralization has developed in the last few years for two reasons. First, centralization in the social areas has become widely recognized as a miserable failure. Second, decentralization has a broad appeal because thus far it can mean different things to different people. Any move away from the center of power represents *ipso facto* decentralization. It can imply greater power for lower echelon bureaucrats in Brasília, extend the authority of state secretaries, increase the discretion of municipal governments, and even extend down the line to school principals, teachers, voluntary associations, and individual users of social services.

If the concept were provided with greater specification, the consensus of support for decentralization would probably dwindle. At the political level, it implies renegotiating the distribution of political power. In government administration, some bureaucrats, notorious defenders of their prerogatives and authority, would likely lose much of their power in the process. Certainly, one of the most obvious possibilities of decentralization would be the strengthening of local state governments. Some observers, myself included, fear that this would merely represent "recentralization", re-creating an intrinsically dysfunctional centralizing solution in as many places as there are states. Are we sure that they are any more competent and, in the final analysis, any closer to the ultimate user of social services? It may take another decade to learn that this is the wrong solution.

By contrast, change requires an arduous and laborious process of developing local initiative and competence to bring forth desired results. People will have to cooperate and control the delivery of social services. Leadership will have to identify with the new goals and targets, and do everything within its power to see that these are attained. All of this will take time. Since excessive centralization has been a real impediment to the development of the lower levels of the education system, no one can deny that it is a major problem that needs to be squarely faced. Yet, to the extent that education policy becomes decentralizing policy, it is a new problem in its own right. Administrators and researchers not only have to consider education goals and strategies but also learn to translate them into decentralizing solutions as well. This additional difficulty has at least retarded, if not paralyzed, the formulation and implementation of recent education policies.

Who should be responsible for the allocation of funds, and who should receive them? Who should take control, and who should hold them accountable? The answers to such questions remain unclear. To give one example, who should take responsibility for deciding the menus for the school lunch programs? Today, school principals make such decisions in the state of Rio de Janeiro, mayors or their appointees in São Paulo, state education secretaries in a few other states, and the Ministry of Education in Brasília for the vast majority of states.

Again, the nature of current political support for decentralization is undoubtedly its most enigmatic feature. Many countries have experienced pendular swings involving greater centralization and decentralization, reflecting a constant struggle between central authorities and the bases of local power. However, this has not been the case in Brazil, where long-standing patrimonial authority reflects an enduring Iberian imperial tradition. The social periphery of this state has never been strongly organized. It is not that local autonomy and participation has been repressed by central power; it simply has never existed.

No one can deny the serious nature and real existence of the present movement towards decentralization. Yet the origins and impetus of this movement are not to be found in the periphery among groups that identify with the movement as their cause. Intellectuals and bureacrats at the center are doing all the preaching; it is here that it finds its roots. Brasília, Rio de Janeiro and São Paulo, the nerve centers of the country, are leading the movement towards decentralization. A prominent set of cases is provided by people who have been extensively exposed to the intellectual and bureaucratic atmosphere of Brasília and later return home, where they become outspoken champions of decentralization.

By way of recapitulation, there is widespread agreement that a crisis in elementary education exists today. There is evidence of political commitment to alleviate the problem. To date, there has been much discussion, but little agreement on what should be done. Administrative personnel are in short supply, rendering action slow and ineffective. Growing awareness of the failures of centralization have given the movement toward decentralization much sympathy, but its true nature remains equivocal. Emanating from bureaucrats at the center rather than as a consequence of a political demand from the periphery, it has been preached more than practiced. This notwithstanding, it seems essential to move the focus of decision-making closer to the end users of education services. This may be a slow process, but it may prove to be the most effective. But be that as it may, educational policy today is also and necessarily decentralization policy, since it cannot avoid the issue.

CONFUSING ROLES AND THE QUIET DECADENCE OF THE SECONDARY SCHOOLS

Brazilian secondary schools have lost their once comfortable role of preparing elites for a higher education. An enormous number of less qualified students now enter these schools, lowering academic standards and completing their studies with the hopes of entering the university. Their number, of course, exceeds the capacity of higher education institutions, and consequently much effort has been expended attempting to render secondary schools adequate as a terminal level of instruction. This attempt has been largely unsuccessful. Its failure is now widely recognized. Unfortunately, new objectives for this level of schooling have not been forthcoming. Consequently, Brazilian secondary education has been recently losing ground in the competition for funds. It is presently experiencing a period of quiet decadence.

1. Changing roles: from college preparatory to containment

Brazilian secondary education has pursued a course of development resembling that of several other countries. As the number of students increased, several schemes were proposed to provide a curriculum suitable for a terminal level of instruction. The children of affluent families have long enjoyed opportunities beyond the elementary education level. Academic barriers prevented less affluent children from reaching secondary education. Consequently, these were traditionally very selective schools.

In the past, most secondary schools were private schools, in clear contrast with the elementary level where public initiative has been more energetic. Not only did they cater to the elites but they also established a broad network of proprietary and religious schools which responded to the needs of the several layers of society who could afford the tuition and, above all, who managed to finish elementary education.

Some Brazilian secondary schools catered to those who were academically more ambitious. Girls' schools offered the necessary finishing without unduly burdening their students with science and mathematics training. Some private secondary schools were run by outstanding teachers who imprinted on them their personal styles. Although the scene was dominated by private schools, a few public secondary institutions, including the Colégio Pedro II in Rio de Janeiro and the military high schools, were highly competitive and also possessed outstanding teachers. One may say that public schools were few in number but they were as good if not better than the very best private institutions.

As in other parts of the world, following World War II, a rapid expansion in enrollments took place. Brazilian secondary enrollments grew from 60 thousand in 1950 to 2.8 million in 1980, representing annual growth rates in excess of 13.5%. Since Brazilian secondary schools already enrolled most of the middle-and upper-class children, new growth implied extension of new educational opportunities to the lower middle class and to privileged sectors of the working class.

This growth took place mostly at the public side. Many thousands of secondary schools were built, spreading from wealthy areas to progressively lower-class districts. The share of private schools went down from 45% in 1970 to 37% in 1983. Private schools now play a dual role. They offer the very best education—while public high schools have unduly suffered at the upper end of the scale—and they fill voids left by the public system. Usually this has meant geographical areas not covered by public schools or a market for very easy education, with lax standards and few requirements.

Providing qualified teachers for all the new students would have been a major challenge in even the best of circumstances. However, during the same period, higher education enrollments experienced explosive growth, attracting the best teachers to positions of higher rank. Since possession of formal credentials often bears little relation to the quality of instruction, it is difficult to document the subsequent deterioration in the quality of Brazilian secondary education. However, qualified observers willingly acknowledge that a significant deterioration in the quality and leadership of secondary teachers did occur.

Higher education not only siphoned off the best secondary teachers but also, a great many traditional high schools moved into higher education as well. As a consequence, high schools lost their once preeminent and privileged position in Brazilian education. Naturally, the very best private schools refused to move into higher education and continued a tradition of excellence, but in terms of total secondary enrollments this mattered very little.

2. Containment with comprehensive schooling

The impossibility of accommodating all secondary school graduates at the higher education level is quite obvious. Since there are only half as many vacancies at the freshman year as there are high school graduates, this would require the doubling of university level enrollment. This possibility is clearly unfeasible and probably unwise as an education policy in the present context. Even so, ever since the late 1960s, almost all high school students expressed their intention to go on to university and thought that they would "realistically succeed."[6] In these circumstances, the education system was bound to frustrate half of its students; namely, those who were unable to fulfill their dream of a university education over sold by government policy. Their frustrations found political expression in the student and intellectual protests of the late 1960s.

The government sought to contain these pressures, finding inspiration in its own highly successful technical schools and the model provided by American comprehensive high schools.[7] As a consequence, in 1970, a very radical education reform law (no.7044) was enacted, requiring all Brazilian secondary schools to offer vocational training for all their students. Every student was to be provided with a profession, even those who would later pursue studies in higher education. Naturally, this law was highly unrealistic.

The better secondary schools catering to upper-class students had the means and know-how to offer respectable vocational courses. However, even less affluent students attending these secondary schools expressed little interest in the vocational curricula. Less than one percent of these students expected to seek employment in the vocational areas of their training. By contrast, research showed that more than 98% of the students continued to aspire to a university education. Students never took their vocational training seriously, giving it only the perfunctory attention necessary in order to satisfy their legal obligations. The secondary schools were all too aware of their students' real interests and accordingly diluted the vocational component of their programs.[8]

High school represents a moment of disequilibrium in the career plans of students. Elementary education constitutes a formidable hurdle for Brazilian students. Even today, more than two thirds of the first-year students drop out before entering the secondary level. It seems as if those who are fortunate enough to enter secondary schools believe that they have succeeded in overcoming the most difficult stages, and that from now on everything will be smooth sailing. It is irrelevant, from the point of view of our argument, whether or not this is a realistic appraisal. What matters is that students do no take seriously a program that they intend to abandon once they begin their university studies.

Three additional considerations deserve mention. First, the usual version of a comprehensive school conveys a very light and superficial notion of what is meant by acquiring a profession. There is the question of immersion in the ethos and values of a profession that extend beyond the instrumental use of information to include numerous beliefs and values almost resembling a religion.[9] By contrast, the watered-down environment of a comprehensive school can only offer meaningful indoctrination in the academic areas.

Second, the dogmas of our time require that all such programs offer the equivalent of a high school diploma permitting access to higher education. The formal equivalence of high school diplomas reflects an egalitarian impulse to avoid the once despised distinction that discriminated elite and popular schools. The irony of the egalitarian impulse is that students who are unable to pursue a higher education—and they are fully half of the total—are left with virtually no meaningful trade skills. The practical consequences hardly imply a gain in equity. This, of course, represents a true dilemma since tracking is now considered morally and pedagogically unacceptable, even in countries like Brazil.

Third and finally, although thousands of experiments with vocational curricula were conducted in the 1970s, no effort was made to take advantage of those that were successful or even, for that matter, to preserve them. Unfortunately, less affluent students having the greatest need to acquire a profession were enrolled in schools lacking both the means and know-how necessary to develop meaningful programs. However, in between these schools and schools catering to an elite, many ingenious experiments were developed. Ultimately, some of these may have been successful, but nothing was done to make systematic use of them.

Secondary education is a level in which foreign influences have played a major role. Agencies like UNESCO and the World Bank have influenced perceptions and educational fashion, as much as their funds brought in entire school systems, importing solutions regardless of the existence of the problem. As dual systems were eliminated from Europe, Brazilian educators, mimicking their European counterparts, execrated the duality of the Brazilian schools—which actually resembled pre-World War II Europe rather than the present scene which generated the new equalitarian policies. When in Europe comprehensive schools were pegged to high school level, Brazilian educators were eager to move them up from junior high school. That, of course, was totally incompatible with the realities of the Brazilian labor market.

The main reason most of these changes had only minor consequences for society is that a very large and consistently high-quality vocational system has been in existence for forty years, totally outside the formal system. SENAC (Servico Nacional de Aprendizagem Comercial) have been providing training for a number that is presently close to a million people a year.

The contrast is quite stark. While the country's academic high schools have been prey to a continuous sequence of foreign fads and fashions, playing havoc with its programs, SENAI (Servico Nacional de Aprendizagem Industrial) has given Brazil a leading position in technical-vocational training. In fact, some of the solutions have been copied in several Latin American and African countries. [10]

By way of recapitulation, the attempt to provide all students with professional training by means of comprehensive schools met with failure. Students showed little interest, and the schools responded with strictly perfunctory programs. The entire enterprise accomplished little in altering student aspirations for a university degree.

3. Neither good ideas nor fresh money: the quiet decadence of secondary education

In 1981, the law prescribing mandatory professional training for all secondary students was revoked. The law had proved unwise. It had created no provisions to assist schools in enforcing it, and had done little to promote its objectives. Obviously, one cannot legislate and then fail to provide the means and technical solutions necessary for adequate implementation. Nor can one legislate against the will of students where there are no means of enforcement. Eliminating the law was no immediate loss. However, the grave consequence of this funeral was the vacuum of meaning and purpose it left at the secondary education level. The legal recognition of the practical nonviability of the vocational intention of Brazilian secondary education amounted to nothing more than a final requiem and was hardly a master plan for the reform of secondary education.

No new ideas replaced this attempt at wholesale professionalization. This is ominous, since inspiration seems to be essential to the drive of educators and administrators. The education scene is constantly animated by ideas and plans that are going to rescue it from disaster or mediocrity. With plentiful ideas existing at other levels, the attention of educators moved away from secondary education.

An awareness of the catastrophic situation in elementary education has led administrators to improve funding at this level. Higher education has been able to maintain its share of the education budget. Since additional money is not available, funds have to be subtracted from other uses. That leaves secondary education as the only important area that can be siphoned. Consequently, the federal budget for secondary education declined by 25% in real terms between 1977 and 1982.

The new predicament of secondary education is that it has silently slipped into a period of quiet decadence. Between the conflagrations of the universities and the dire poverty of basic education lies secondary education. Financially squeezed, forgotten and disinherited in the realm of ideas, it lacks attention and prominence on the agenda of administrators.

However, behind the oscillations of education fads and fashions lie some enduring and challenging questions. Preparing students for higher education is a very demanding task. Yet, at the conceptual level, it is easy and straightforward. University curricula are clearly defined, and it is simply a matter of designing high school programs that will meet the entrance requirements for these courses. The major challenge is that at least half the students will terminate their studies upon high school graduation. What should they learn?

The prescription of offering a general education hides more than it reveals.

The meaning of general education can be quite misleading. It is said that such an education will impart an ability to act intelligently under a wide variety of circumstances and to learn from experience. However, this end result tells us very little about how such goals are to be achieved. In the case of curriculum, we are unsure whether geography is considered to be general and typing specific, or vice versa. Since often those who pursued specialized courses turn out to be better equipped in a wide variety of circumstances, the best general education may turn out to be the best specialized education. [11]

Furthermore, general education for what? Is it not that *BASIC* is general education in a technological society? And maybe Latin is a very specialized education in this same society?

One may ask under what circumstances education should be tailored to meet the needs of specific jobs. The only thing that can be said with certainty is that no single simple prescription is in order.

Quite aside from the utilitarian concerns, secondary education coincides with the age of individual assertion and value definition. Many important aspects of citizenship are shaped during this same period. Obviously, schools cannot be passive factors in such issues but ought to rather assume an active stance in defining and promoting the social roles of individuals.

To sum up, secondary schools have fallen victim to a vacuum of ideas. Almost imperceptibly, they have become a forgotten problem. Perhaps, as a consequence, money is siphoned off, further aggravating their condition. Nevertheless, major problems exist and involve the very conception and role of secondary education. But instead of progress, we are witnessing a period of quiet decadence. It is no coincidence that this crisis is to some extent also emerging in other countries. Indeed, this is probably the area in which foreign influences have been less filtered and critically reviewed.

IDENTITY CRISIS AND CONFLICT IN BRAZILIAN HIGHER EDUCATION

Institutions of higher education face unprecedented dilemmas. Their conventional roles in society have been questioned; their legitimacy—both internal and external—has been challenged; and their financial conditions have been eroded. The present essay discusses recent changes and predicaments experienced in Brazilian higher education. The roots of these problems lie in past events, related to the artificial nature of Brazilian universities. Their consideration provides a convenient point of departure.

1. Universities by decree and not by nature

Brazil is a latecomer to higher education, even by Latin American standards. While the universities of Peru and Mexico were founded in the seventeenth century, Brazilian universities were first established little more than fifty years ago. Thus, the University of Rio de Janeiro began its existence in 1920, and the University of São Paulo only in 1934.

However, it is not only the recent origin of these institutions but the organizational history of Brazilian universities that sets them apart from institutions of higher learning in other countries. Brazilian institutions of higher education were first established in the early decades of the nineteenth century, and their number has steadily increased ever since. In almost every case, Brazilian universities have been formed through the consolidation of already existing institutions established during different periods, serving different socioeconomic roles and reflecting different levels of academic excellence. With the exception of the universities of Campinas and Brasília, even the most recently established universities have been created through the merger of already existing schools. Moreover, during their subsequent course of development, Brazilian universities have often assimilated still other schools of higher learning.

Consequently, Brazilian universities have relatively little internal coherence in terms of their organizational goals, standards and loyalties. Contact among different disciplines has been minimal, hardly stimulating the communion of ideas that would further the purposes of a university. Lawyers do not accept the leadership of physicians, nor vice versa. Thus, growth through merger has severely limited the authority of each school without necessarily providing an alternative set of university ideals and loyalties.

In recent decades, government centralization has increased federal control of the universities.[12] The university is no exception to a national penchant for abundant legislation and elaborate bureaucratic control. University administrations have lost their flexibility, and the autonomy once possessed by isolated schools has been severely restricted. But, predictably, faculty compliance with federal guidelines has been less than satisfactory.

In many ways, this is the worst of two worlds. Individual departments that would rather be left alone to pursue their own goals, whatever these might be, confront compulsory, inflexible bureaucratic rules imposed on extremely heterogeneous institutions. Centralism more often than not has curbed experimentation and alternative lines of development, while limiting individual interests. At the same time, this has not rescued education quality, engendered personal responsibility or even prevented faculty absenteeism. Despite the best of intentions, the attempt to create universities out of isolated schools and the growing pervasiveness of federal control of Brazilian universities have created institutions whose formal external coherence belies fundamentally divergent internal interests pursued by a variety of heterogeneous groups.

Traditionally, Brazilian universities have emulated their French counterparts. Following a 1967 reform law, a new departmental structure was imposed on Brazilian universities, along with a number of other innovations clearly of North American inspiration.[13] Subsequently the research university has become the only officially recognized model. A research orientation is now considered to be an essential component of Brazilian university instruction, with the marriage of research and teaching officially endorsed for all institutions of higher learning. Brazilian universities now emulate the dogmas of research universities, even if the results are little more than mimicry.

The new system, with all its appurtenances—the basic instructional cycle, the credit system, collegiate decision-making, etc.—has been imposed upon an older structure. Predictably, Brazilian universities have assimilated the new orientation in form, although often without the necessary modification in spirit. Autocratic rule has not, in fact, been relinquished, while loyalties and a sense of purpose remain largely what they were before. An important exception to the general rule concerns the network of graduate schools created since the reform. These schools have benefited from the large numbers of Brazilian graduate students trained at American universities, who naturally identify with the objectives of the new university legislation.

Paradoxically, most of the recent expansion in Brazilian higher education bears little relation to the new legislation. The most dynamic growth has occurred in private higher education, a sector which operates predominantly small colleges and offers training in only a limited number of professions. Section 9 deals with the question of private education.

2. The reward system of Brazilian higher education

Despite the official orientation found in legislation, Brazilian universities serve a number of different roles. To illustrate these, several ideal types will be proposed in order to discuss the incentive system peculiar to each type. *These models are not meant to be mutually exclusive descriptions of existing institutions.* Instead, they must be understood as *different tendencies that might coexist within a single institution.* An institution may lean more toward one model, but again it may also have features of another. Furthermore, large institutions have different segments that are better described by different models.

(*a*). *The research university model.* In these universities, research is valued as a legitimate goal in its own right and for the number of important fringe benefits that accompany the research endeavor. The quality and quantity of research publications are the main concerns in these institutions, along with the attendant personnel, laboratories, and travel grants that are obtained through the competition for research funds. Prestige and status are the welcome consequences of this eminently competitive and meritocratic system. In most cases, teaching is regarded as a necessary evil. This ideal type is best represented by a number of important graduate schools that find little company among other university institutions.

(*b*). *The teaching universities model*. Here, excellence in teaching is the dominant goal. In the tradition of the French *grandes écoles*, these institutions compete for the best students, offer theatrical and thoroughly convincing lectures, and provide an education that will foster significant professional careers among alumni. The social prestige, power and resources of these schools are clearly related to the success of their graduates. Traditional law, engineering and medical schools in Brazil follow this model.

(*c*). *The certification factory model*. As long as diplomas have market value, it makes sense for students to try and obtain them with the least possible effort. Since more learning implies greater effort not only among students but also on the part of teachers, both sides can be well served when only a minimal amount of learning takes place. Provided this implicit covenant remains discreet, this strategy produces benefits for both parties. Many of the weaker institutions in Brazilian higher education operate as if this were the rationale for their behavior.

(*d*). *The country club model*. Many Brazilian institutions of higher education offer a pleasant atmosphere and splendid facilities, especially the federal universities. Like the best country clubs, they cater to a select clientele and invariably socialize their members to adopt middle- and upper-class values and social manners. By frequenting their premises, but not necessarily their classes, one can find congenial company, spouses and future business connections. Above all, these institutions confer social status.

Brazilian universities are a complex concoction of all these different models. Consequently, they respond imperfectly to changes in only one dimension of the incentive system. Thus, when official rhetoric promotes the research university model as its major objective, it ignores much of the internal logic guiding the system. Ironically, the fastest growing institutions in Brazilian higher education these last few decades are little more than diploma factories. For these institutions, research is little more than a mythical god to whom homage is paid, and certainly not something to be undertaken or even seriously attempted. Graduating the largest possible number of students provides the real agenda.

3. The de-professionalization of professional careers

Between 1970 and 1975, when the national labor force at best grew only 16% (3% a year), total higher education enrollments increased 152% and private higher education 209%. Thus, during the same period, the number of graduates with higher education degrees grew at least five times as fast as the national labor force. Obviously, a national effort to increase enrollments in Brazilian higher education had been a spectacular success. As long as a backlog in demand for highly skilled personnel persisted, new graduates would continue to find the employment opportunities they expected. Nevertheless, after several years of extraordinary enrollment growth, these positions would be filled, and graduates would have to be satisfied with lower status jobs and less pay, since highly skilled jobs could not be expected to grow much faster than the labor force as a whole.

In these circumstances, it was unavoidable that university programs tailored for specific occupations progressively became a kind of general education for people moving into a larger variety of jobs. The available jobs required less specialized knowledge, were simpler to perform, and in most cases were bureaucratic or clerical in nature. This de-professionalization process as a natural and spontaneous outcome of market forces has been observed all over the world and is essentially unavoidable. Nevertheless, school programs tend to maintain the professional curriculum and orientation of their courses, even if much of this preparation will no longer be used in corresponding professions. It is not known if abandoning this professional orientation at the curricula level is a good idea.

But students find devastating the experience of not finding a job clearly connected to their curricula. The dream of instant upward mobility has been shattered. Worse, the significance of a higher education tends to be underestimated, since mobility is often a long-run consequence of particular career paths, rather than the instant reward of a first job. Naturally, students and their families do not search for an explanation of their frustrated expectations in such simple arithmetic. Instead, they blame the universities, the national economic administration, and the political system.

The adjustment of university graduates to the new occupational profile of the labor force represents a painful political liability for the universities. Ultimately, the glut of diplomas on the labor market erodes university prestige and challenges the institution's sense of identity. After all, if jobs are unavailable, why should universities promote their courses as important career opportunities. After all, what are universities *for?* Obviously, universities are not immune to this type of a loss in self-efficacy. If they no longer respond to the student's career expectations, one very important source of meaning and identity is lost.

4. An eroding financial position

Most Brazilian public universities are sponsored by the federal government. Their growth from 1960 to 1984 has placed an extraordinary financial burden on the Ministry of Education and Culture. Since the federal government is directly responsible for funding only a part of the other levels of education, higher education currently consumes 70% of the federal education budget. The research objectives of Brazilian universities have resulted in an increase in the proportion of full-time faculty, and as a consequence university expenditures have risen more rapidly than growth in enrollments. A national economic crisis, clearly visible from 1980 on, has put an end to budget increases. For every US$1 received in 1980, the federal universities obtained only 42 cents in 1984, leading inevitably to a deterioration in the services of these institutions.

Firing faculty or administrative personnel goes against the grain of the Brazilian civil service. Policies designed to reduce personnel are politically unfeasible. Deans and department heads could conceivably reduce superfluous personnel, but the incentives are lacking. Funds saved in this instance cannot be transferred to support other activities. The only available alternative has been to issue directives prohibiting the hiring of new personnel. This has damaged efforts to train qualified researchers, since their prospects for university employment are nil. It has also strained programs in situations where the skills of existing personnel were found to be inadequate for the development of departmental programs.

Most of the financial losses were absorbed through lower wages for faculties and curtailment of purchases. Pay scales were compressed, with senior faculty making the greatest sacrifices, thereby reducing incentives for those who could be expected to be more productive. Maintenance and laboratory expenditures were also cut, which especially affected serious scholars and researchers who are more dependent on specialized services and equipment. All of this points to a serious financial crisis facing Brazilian universities. Faculty have seen their living standards deteriorate substantially, and effective research capacity has been severely limited.

5. The visible inefficiency

Public bureaucracies are not known as efficient and parsimonious institutions. Universities are no exception. Educational accountability remains a difficult subject. There are no obvious standards for gauging university achievement. However, even some very rough calculations suggest that Brazilian universities are immensely inefficient. For instance, at the Universidade Nacional de Brasília in the nation's capital, on the average only about 10% of a professor's time is spent on teaching. Assuming that twice this amount of time is dedicated to class preparation, committee meetings and other administrative responsibilities, then something like 70% of the remaining time must be, *ipso facto*, officially dedicated to research. Considering national research output, as measured by the number of research publications and articles, and subtracting the work of professors associated with graduate schools, we find that an enormous amount of money is being spent on research that simply does not materialize.

Per capita productivity of graduate schools faculty is 0.87 which is a relatively low figure by international standards. Yet it is still an acceptable level. The problem is with nongraduate school faculty. They are more numerous by a factor of 2.8 to 1 in the typical federal university. Computing the overall scientific productivity—*i.e.*, including graduate and undergraduate professors— we find an average of 0.3 publications per year. In one particular federal university, on the average a professor will publish one article every 100 years! Surely, we have to question this publications imperative as a rule to be applied across the board. But at the same time, since extension hardly exists, what are all these faculty members doing while receiving a salary borne by the taxpayers?

The student-faculty ratios of Brazilian federal universities are unreasonably low when compared, for example, with American universities. In Brazil, there are only 7.69 students for every member of the faculty. Brazilian university administrations are cumbersome, inefficient and excessively rigid. Too many people are employed in university bureaucracies, as evidenced by a student-administrative personel ratio of only 5.6:1. It is doubtful if Brazilian universities are less efficient than other public bureaucracies, yet the inefficiency of universities is only too conspicuous. It is clearly perceived by public opinion and decision-making cadres. Almost anyone who matters in the administration has relatives who attend the universities and report the extravagant wastage, lack of excellence in standards, the absence of desire for real achievement, the high incidence of cheating among students, and the absenteeism among faculty. Brazilian universities are not only inefficient; they cannot even hide it.

6. From hero to villain: the loss of legitimacy

Brazilian universities have become visibly inefficient producers of an education that finds little reward in the labor market. It is as if the universities were losing their ecological niche in society. Public opinion has become less complacent toward the universities' occasional pecadillos and increasingly harsher in the judgment of their persistent failures. Perhaps the saddest aspect of the recent university faculty strike for higher salaries was the fact that the protest did not even make the front page of the nation's newspapers, even though this was the longest university strike in the nation's history. Political activism, designed to restore university budget cuts, is showing little consequence. The public does not seem to care and is not even very supportive.

The legitimacy of Brazilian universities among the general population is at an all-time low. Public opinion, with the aid of the press, readily identifies the obvious weakness and dysfunctionality of Brazilian universities. No one comes to their rescue when the press turns its guns on frequent cases of university corruption, disorganization, and the chronic state of crisis. Yet despite the pertinence of much of this criticism, it engenders a distorted view of Brazilian higher education by emphasizing its negative aspects. As stated previously, Brazilian higher education is an extremely heterogeneous system where the good and the bad coexist not only among institutions but often within institutions as well. An outstanding graduate school and a deplorable undergraduate program in the same discipline may thus share the very same building. It is not the patient and quiet labor of serious groups, but the turbulence, accidents and disasters of university life that attract press attention. Hence the earnest and industrious among the university community are getting a bad reputation that is undeserved.

The loss of the universities' legitimacy among the general public affects the internal operation of these institutions. Not only are universities sensitive to the same factors that corrode their external image but the same loss of prestige is reflected within. The faculty is perplexed by the devaluation of university credentials. They feel they are the victims of a financial squeeze and they are no longer certain of the goals for higher education. Hence, in many ways they share the uncertanties of public opinion concerning Brazilian higher education. Even though they resent harsh judgments directed at them from outside the university community, their insecurity renders them especially vulnerable to criticism. Thus a deterioration in the public image of higher education is paralleled by a loss of self-esteem on the part of university faculties and administrations.

7. *Faculty politicalization and the new egalitarian imperative*

Although Latin America has avidly imitated northern intellectual styles, the region has often been an innovative protagonist of student activism. Students have participated in educational and broader political issues for many decades, as is manifested in the numerous protest demonstrations and even riots. This is not the place to gauge the political impact of this participation. Whatever its effect might have once been, it bears little relation to events in the recent past. University students still protest and strike, and in some areas, such as charging tuition at public universities, they continue to be consistent victors. In other areas, however, their recent actions have accomplished little.

The really new development in university politics concerns the advent of faculty political participation. Repression of protest and free speech within the universities reached a peak in the late Sixties, followed during the second half of the Seventies by a slow process of liberalization. This process accelerated during the administration of President Figueiredo, following concession of a broad political amnesty and the politicalization of university professors. The arrival of Eduardo Portella, a liberal Minister of Education, paradoxically created a more radical confrontation.

Previous years had witnessed the discreet complaints and weak dialogue provided by the respected and conservative scholars. The most respected among them were the least suspect in terms of loyalty and consequently all the more willing to voice their criticism. The Portella period sharply inverted this pattern. It was as if middle-of-the-road faculty were content with knowing that they could speak out if they so desired, but in practice infrequently took advantage of the opportunity. This left the floor to irate radicals who wanted to redress the mistakes of past years and blame them on the present incumbents.

Portella brought open, frank and critical discourse to the Ministry. In many ways, this was representative of the opinions and perceptions of a moderate majority. It was a far cry from the thick, nondescript, technocratic jargon of his predecessors in the Ministry, but altogether not very different from that presented *sotto voce* by critical intellectuals during the previous period. However, the new official line left radical critics without a platform. To the extent that the government moved to the left, the Left had to go even farther. Nothing could be more embarrassing to this irate group than to use clumsy slogans to repeat what Portella had already stated masterfully in his own crisp and colorful style.

Organized faculty groups disparaged Portella's intentions and his words as they became increasingly more radical. This may explain the development of political platforms among faculty organizations that were far more radical and extremist than the opinions of average faculty members, including the most eminent scholars. The new activism did not originate among the outstanding scientists and members of the *intelligentsia* who had led the protests of the previous era, but from among the younger faculty with lesser academic distinction—although there were a few exceptions.

Within hours of his inauguration, Rubem Ludwig, the new Minister of

Education replacing Portella, summarily resolved a national faculty strike with a new decree that among more important changes led to the automatic hiring of the *colaboradores* (teaching assistants) as new assistant professors. [14] Many of these new professors lacked the usual credentials and experience normally required for such positions. Thus, the new professors were quick to learn the value of political activism. Although the recently established faculty associations (*associações docentes*) are usually led by faculty of demonstrated scholarly excellence, the new assistant professors are the most active members of these associations and seem to control their agendas. Their activism controls the political scene within Brazilian universities today. Ostensibly they fight for more funds and free tuition for students. However, the really ponderous issue on the agenda is more diffuse and rarely stated explicity. This concerns a certain kind of "egalitarianism."

Meritocracy and the new egalitarianism have considerable difficulty in coexisting. Egalitarianism collides head on with the belief that in the search for excellence, incentives have to be created, achievement recognized, and competition legitimized. Moreover, in a university setting of extraordinary diversity, governed by principles that are extremely divergent, and where current standards of excellence in scholarship can scarcely be accommodated within the same institution, egalitarianism can only mean acceptance of the lowest common denominator.

Egalitarianism is of course bound up with the notion of equality of opportunity affecting the different groups operating within the academic community. There is little agreement about the nature of equality of opportunity. On the one hand, it suggests the need for a competitive system regulating the distribution of research funds, although this may tend to confirm existing inequalities. At the other extreme, it suggests dividing research funds in equal parcels to be distributed without regard for a minimum threshold of competence. This can be wasteful and is probably beyond the financial horizons of present-day budgets. The tone of current political activism appears to endorse this second version.

The perverse side of this unionism concerns the implicit protection provided to dysfunctional behavior inimical to the long-run operation of these institutions. The pervasive absenteism, lack of punctuality, inadequate preparation of course work and lax standards for students are all very hard to curb under these circumstances. These groups claim that university professors are poorly paid and that this is the prinicipal reason for their inability to produce better results. This proposition is questionable. The faculties of federal universities once earned twice what they are now paid in real terms. Observers of the university scene believe that less dedicated professors did not respond any better then with higher salaries, although it may be true that some of the best faculty are less motivated today due to their involvement in consulting and other supplementary jobs. In any event, the new egalitarian mood would require pay increases across the board, and the financial implications of restoring lost incentives would be staggering if applied to all—in fact, nearly doubling university budgets.

It may be useful to conceive of the power structure of Brazilian universities as composed of three groups. The oldest of these is composed of a professorial aristocracy allied with members of an entrenched bureaucracy. We may call them the *bureaucratic oligarchies*. They consititute the older layers of universities, which, at best, are dedicated to teaching and, at worst, are given to issuing diplomas with the least sacrifice to all concerned, so long as the implicit covenant of such rites is not openly questioned. Since the best of the old-timers either move on to other careers or lose their identity with this group, the worst seem to prevail. As a group, they are not outwardly belligerent, but strong survival instincts and mastery of bureaucratic machinery assure them a place of prominence in university politics.

The second group is composed of the young Turks trained during the 1970s, who wield their PhDs as weapons in their quest for political power in Brazilian universities. If they could have it their way, Brazilian universities would resemble their *alma mater*—more than likely somewhere back in the United States. Meritocracy would be the rule, competition the means, and research the main goal. This group has fought fiercely to establish its power, while succeeding in establishing its own relatively protected territory in the nation's graduate schools. The group has made inroads in university administration, but at the cost of compromise with the older group.

To further complicate an already complex situation plagued by numerous internal cleavages, the new wave of politicalization has brought the *irate egalitarians* to the scene. Unprepared to advance through the ranks by means of academic achievement, they aspire to power through direct political confrontation. Their comparative advantage lies in public rallies and the different forms of participatory decision-making. In contesting the middle-age generation of young Turks, they are often able to summon support among the old rank and file, who share their common rejection of the competitive, meritocratic university model. So far, students have been their loyal supporters.

Ultimately, the future of Brazilian universities hangs in the balance awaiting the result of the power struggle among these three groups. It is perhaps worth noting that a recent faculty strike lasting more than a month was carried out by a tacit alliance among all three of these groups. This was a most critical event that deserves greater attention since it brought together in a common cause groups that are inherently antagonistic.

8. The dilemmas of Brazilian universities

This is a very difficult moment in Brazilian higher education. A number of circumstances have created something of a vicious circle. The universities have become poorer—with lower pay levels and a meager allotment of supplies eroding the motivation and commitment of many. The universities have always been inefficient and wasteful, but now it is common knowledge. The once heroic and prestigious role of the universities in preparing young people for the highest positions in society is considerably diminshed. Today, their graduates no longer find the expected jobs. The university is rapidly becoming a villain. The loss of external legitimacy bears its own financial liabilities. The longest university strike in the nation's history brought neither more money nor even front-page coverage.

An internal loss of identity and motivation has hurt morale and efficacy. Less money has the greatest effect among those from whom more should be expected. Being relatively few, it would take relatively little to restore their financial incentives. Yet the new egalitarian imperative makes it more difficult to reestablish such internal distinctions. The funds required to improve the status of everyone would be very large indeed, and therefore all the more difficult to obtain politically.

What are the options? Although this is beyond the scope of the present essay, it may be worthwhile to explore some alternatives. From their inception, Brazilian universities have been something of an artificial concoction. Despite official rhetoric, the real agenda was to maximize the size of enrollments and increase the number of graduates. The attempt to merge a heterogeneous variety of schools and administer them under one set of rules may have been a bad idea. What should the new agenda be?

Hundreds of thousands of Brazilian university students enrolled today lack the competence usually acquired at the high-school level. To them, a higher education is little more than secondary level education with a new name. Improving the scholastic attainment of incoming students would require a dramatic improvement in the quality of instruction offered to millions of students now enrolled in elementary and secondary education. This is not something that is going to happen very quickly, even under the most optimistic scenarios. Hence, for these students it is either a higher education with little more than high-school standards or nothing at all. To deny them higher education enrollment is politically unfeasible and not necessarily wise. Nothing suggests that spending four years reading, writing and thinking about the usual topics of university instruction is lacking in value, either professionally, personally, or in terms of citizenship. Personal gains may not be as dramatic as they once were when there was better screening of university entrants nor opportunities as spectacular as they were when there was an open job market, but there are good reasons to believe that such gains exist, nevertheless.

Services of university extension have been mentioned in official statements as an appropriate role for Brazilian universities. Hardly anything has developed along these lines, however. Though some institutions may legitimately want to move in this direction, it does not appear to offer special promise for avoiding present dilemmas.

Still another alternative concerns the development of a university for a more limited elite. Brazilian society still requires highly trained personnel. People will still have to take positions of important responsibility, and they had better be well prepared. Still others will have to be watchdogs, and they had better be no less prepared. In addition, advancing the frontiers of knowledge remains one of the noblest of roles for a university. Scientific pursuits and the development of technology are tasks well suited for a university environment. Brazilian universities have progressed considerably along these lines and have acquired the technical and social expertise necessary to move even further.

The predicament is that the roles of an elite university are ill suited for the present structures. In order to meet the imperative of quantity, university staffs have been inflated with people who do not have the profile for the dispassionate search for truth or the pursuit of scientific endeavors found at a real research university. Moreover, the few who do share these objectives— and they will be few in any country—cannot possibly operate in an environment that is hostile to such activities. The logistics of support for the development of science and technology require the maintenance of libraries, complex machinery, chemicals, laboratory animals, and so forth, that can hardly tolerate the derelict condition of physical facilities.

Unpopular as it may be, there is a social niche for an elite university. To state that intellectual elitism is desirable even though social elitism should be execrated helps little in this moment of egalitarianism *à outrance*. An elite university system would obviously be expensive, but on a limited scale, however, its costs would be more than bearable.

Parallel to that would coexist a large university structure that handles many more students, but operates on a leaner budget. Its main goal should be to teach adequately and adjust levels of difficulty and curriculum materials to better suit the variety of students in attendance. Internal efficiency should be pursued earnestly, since the total amount of resources involved would be immense. Research need not be an unattainable shiboleth, it can be given up altogether in many cases.

From what has been said about diploma factories, the goal of greater efficiency would seem like an impossible objective, a major inconvenience for all concerned. However, this is much less the case today, bearing in mind that the job market rewards diplomas with increasingly smaller benefits. The acquirement of any diploma once brought monopoly rents to its owner, but this is no longer the case. With mounting competition among graduates, true learning may become increasingly important. Learning, per se, will be sought after and diplomas from different institutions will, in each instance, be recognized on this basis.

All of this is at present nothing more than a vision. In order to move in this direction, very significant changes would have to take place, and I have very few suggestions as to how to bring them about. My inclination is to think that such a strategy should begin with an attempt to break the myth of the Brazilian university. Public opinion and those involved in higher education must come to realize the harm perpetrated by pretending that there is such a thing as one Brazilian university. However one may want to conceive of them, there is not one but practically as many models as there are institutions of higher learning. And, very often, heterogeneity within institutions may even be greater than between. This being so, rules of administration should allow flexibility among and within institutions by dramatically increasing their autonomy to use resources and to hire, fire and pay their personnel as they deem appropriate. Brazilian universities need to define their own roles and pursue their development along separate paths. The function of central authorities is not to replace local initiative, but to allocate resources according to how well the institutions do whatever it is they are trying to do.

Balkanizing the image of the Brazilian university should be the first step, thus making it easier for all concerned to distinguish the good guys from the bad guys and to act appropriately on this basis. Presently, the best people are suffering more than anyone else because of the deplorable behavior of a few. Some are forced to pretend they do research when they should instead be concentrating on becoming excellent teachers. Forcing them to do research makes serious research all the more difficult for others. We would also learn what forms of teaching can be conducted less expensively while others could be seen being inherently costly. Taking the long view, the faculty should see that their collective class action is ultimately artificial and harmful to all concerned.

9. The new paths of higher education

Federal universities comprise a small share of Brazilian higher education. But the remaining part has received little attention and has been treated as a bastard offspring. Yet, close to one million students are enrolled in private and proprietary institutions of higher education. Maybe these institutions are also under a crisis. But it must be a crisis of a different nature and depth.

Furthermore, a significant number of schools are quietly becoming stronger and are creating a new pattern of higher education with very interesting and innovative features.

It is worth considering that enrollment in higher education showed 44% of students in private institutions during the year of 1960. This share went up to 50% in 1970 and reached 65% in 1980. In 1983, among 868 institutions of higher learning, only 67 were officially permited to be called universities. There are 20 private institutions in this group. Among the remaining institutions 744 are the so-called isolated private schools, and 57 are diversified institutions without a university charter.

Today we are facing a group of several pedigreed federal universities which are confronting a crisis together with an enormous private system of mongrel origins, a significant number of which seem to be moving in the right directions.

Despite the favorable conditions, few public universities have escaped the fate of being cheap imitations of the research university model. What could we then expect of the poor isolated colleges that have no funds available and only a few faculty members with graduate diplomas? Ultimately, they will end up imitating the imitations of the research university. This is the image of private higher education: Second-rate education for second-rate students, since the academically better-endowed, higher-class students are able to secure most of the enrollment in the tuition-free public universities.

But we have to look at this more carefully. It seems that most people have overlooked the recent developments. From the broad universe of private education, as a result of a Darwinian evolution, many institutions have learned through hardship and crisis. They have progressively become financially stronger and academically sounder, and have added the traditionally expensive high-status courses (medicine, engineering, etc). They have acquired a decent reputation in their regions, and in some cases are competing on equal grounds—in fact, sometimes even disputing the market with the big federal universities.

But these are local institutions originating from local initiatives. As private institutions, their imperative need to operate in the black breeds a tradition of sound management. Administration tends to be stringent. The control over teachers is very tight. Absenteeism is not tolerated, class preparation is expected, as well as other details along the same direction. Since they have grown through their own leadership, management is always present and effective. By contrast with public universities, they have evolved with greater institutional organicity. In that sense, they are more flexible and manageable. After many years of quiet and insecure growth they are becoming more assertive and demanding the right to control their destiny and trajectory. While confessional institutions had a higher rate of growth in the past, lay institutions are now developing faster. Some of these are truly community institutions, others were created under poorly disguised profit motives.

Even so, it is instructive to observe that some of the most eager fly-by-night operators are now facing a sorcerer's apprentice situation. Their institutions have acquired, independently of their will, sounder educational standards and demand more positive public images and nobler goals. One can identify several of these owners of proprietary colleges who are being unwillingly co-opted by the institutions they created.

One of the more important issues is the search for a model of the local college. Despite the government rhetoric in favor of the research university as the model for all, there is finally the begining of a search for their own model. The solutions, clearly, have to do with down-to-earth rather than rarefied styles. It is the tight fit between solution and problem and sensitivity to local needs that seem to set the tone for such experiments. One must emphasize, however, that these are teaching institutions. And in teaching, one can expect from them competence and dedication rather than brilliant performance.

Research may be present, but under different conditions. It tends to be infrequent and deliberately undertaken. Two main features can be identified. First, it is detached from teaching. When one wants research, a researcher is hired and put to work, preferably without being disturbed by students. Second, this research is perceived as a service being rendered with the deliberate purpose of increasing the revenues of the institution. There is, indeed, a growing concern with paid extension work and the sale of services. In fact, some institutions are obtaining 40 to 50% of their revenues by sources other than tuition.

It makes sense to think that their entrepreneurial styles fit better with the needs of business. Hence one may imagine that they have greater vocation for providing firms with lowbrow technological development while public universities will do basic research better. According to their practices, full time regime for faculty is not meant for teaching but for the performance of very specific tasks, aiming at increasing their revenues. Research may be included under this category. Curiously, the institutions that stand out are not located in the largest cities, but in the medium-sized towns of the Center-South— Rio Grande do Sul, Santa Catarina, São Paulo and Minas Gerais are where most of them are located.

Today the modal student of the private institutions is a mature person about thirty years old, who took his entrance examination after getting a stable job. He attends courses in the evening and tends to remain in the same job after graduation. Altogether, this is a profile very different from that attached to students of the prestigious public universities. One may think of this as a "tropical" version of the so-called permanent education. This seems to be the new higher education! We do not know it properly, but we suspect that instead of the crisis which public universities are going through, the private system is experiencing a most interesting period, as it searches for its own identity.

Realizing that they would be unable to cover too much ground, these private institutions are trying to specialize in some activity in which they think they have a comparative advantage. Deliberately, they attempt to choose some activity that could project a favorable image of the institution. But they are not very clear, as of yet, on how to project and manage this image.

To illustrate ongoing tendencies, one could classify the new experiments under several models. The rationale underlying all of them is that association teaching with other activities would impart to this teaching greater usefulness or sense. Extension work seems to be the keynote of several such institutions. They would include radio programs about rural cooperativism, agricultural columns in local newspapers, vocational courses for industrial workers, etc. The college becomes the home not only of students but of cooperatives and union leaders as well. Sale of services, extension work, social assistance and cooperativism are the main features of this model.

Several small institutions were high schools and teachers high schools before coming teachers colleges. Their model, therefore, tends to be pedagogical research, assistance to schools, refresher courses for teachers, and editing books and journals of pedagogical content. By contrast, several colleges, usually of greater sophistication, try to adopt a model of political mobilization. This may lead to political activism or "engagé" social research. For instance, the Catholic University of São Paulo conducts activities of "social promotion" in the periphery of Greater São Paulo, attempting to commit students and faculty to social work. Other confessional institutions attempt to follow, in their colleges, activities that are similar to those typically carried out by their original confessional or congregational styles.

Given the chronic scarcity of resources that can be obtained from tuition charged not-so-affluent students, several institutions have been progressively learning to find other sources of funds. The most usual situation is the delivery of paid services, as consulting contracts, quality control tests, and in some more ambitious cases, technological developments.

In the rendering of such services, the logistical services of the institution play a major role. These would include the data processing unit, the printing shop, laboratories, speciality shops, clinics and hospitals. Some of the most interesting cases refer to institutions that have developed new products or processes and are beginning to produce them at industrial level (Examples include dentistry equipment, dehydrated bananas, oats, soybeans, lightweight bricks, etc.).

The analysis above indicates that something is beginning to happen in private education, with some institutions looking for new and different identities and roles. It is probably too early to gauge the weight and consequences of what they are doing. It may very well be that some of this is no more than a will-of-the-wisp, with a transient existence. Yet, there are signs that Brazilian private education is displaying some imagination and energy in finding new paths.

SCIENTIFIC GROWTH, AMATEURISH DABBLINGS IN TECHNOLOGY, AND THE ETHOS OF UNIVERSITY RESEARCH

A serious effort to train scientists abroad began in Brazil during the late 1950s. Upon their return home, a large number of graduate schools were established with their assistance during the late 1960s. Their participation was encouraged by new requirements for master's and doctoral degrees in higher-level teaching positions. The growth of these graduate schools marks the institutionalization of Brazilian science. Earlier scientific endeavors had occasionally been successful, but had had limited cumulative effect.

However, the financial resources of these graduate schools originated outside the universities. Government agencies provided not only the funds but also most of the motivation and leadership responsible for scientific development. Consequently, from their inception the new graduate schools acquired a semi-independent status within the universities. Despite some economic hardship, research developed and the number of scientific publications grew rapidly, making Brazil the second largest producer of scientific reports in the Third World.[15] On the whole, and particularly by comparison with other types of education, this was largely a successful endeavor.

Nevertheless, serious problems remain evident. The recent economic crisis has made these programs more vulnerable due to their excessive dependency on outside sources of financing. Another source of trouble is that the university crisis has infiltrated the graduate schools, producing undesirable effects on morale and working conditions. The coexistence worked out between graduate schools and the universities is strained and unstable. Between the chronic insecurity generated by outside financing and the existential crisis of the universities, Brazilian graduate schools are being threatened just as they reach maturity.

While Brazilian scientific research has benefited from this process of institutionalization, technological innovation remains largely a promise of the future. Previous efforts failed to produce technological innovations, possibly as a consequence of an inadequate scientific research capability. Only very recently has technological research and development begun to take shape.

1. The life cycle of university science

With few exceptions, Brazilian institutions of higher learning have shown little interest in research until very recently. Founded in 1876, the Ouro Preto School of Mines (Escola de Minas de Ouro Preto) was a distinguished exception, along with the University of São Paulo, established in 1934, which later became a significant and innovative research center. Apart from these exceptions, research played no role in higher learning, even at the largest universities. Consequently, most of the country's research effort took place at a series of specialized research institutes in the biomedical areas, for example the prominent role of the Instituto Oswaldo Cruz in the study of endemic diseases.

These institutes often produced remarkable results, satisfying the expectations that had accompanied their founding and in some cases attaining the highest international standards. Many such efforts, however, were pursued in isolation without producing larger consequences. In particular, they failed to develop as a network of institutes or to promote the development of a national research community. Each institute followed its own life cycle, and only a few with consistently high levels of achievement have survived down to the present day. Consequently, the major shortcoming of these institutes concerns the lack of cumulativeness in their efforts.

The development of a national research community began with the establishment of graduate schools, which coincided with the convergence of research and teaching in the same institutions. This does not necessarily imply that such responsibilities need to develop together, but that in the Brazilian case historical circumstance and a few deliberate policies made this occur. The turning point took place some time after World War II. The establishment of CAPES (Coordenação do Aperfeiçoamento de Pessoal de Nível Superior) and the CNPq (Conselho Nacional De Pesquisa) in 1952 provides a suitable reference point by ushering in, as it did, the first stage in the life cycle of Brazilian graduate education.

This period was characterized by recruitment and training, which in the circumstances required training abroad. The Rockefeller and Ford Foundations were deeply involved in this effort, particularly from the late 1950s onward. USAID (United States Administration for International Development) became involved somewhat later, providing substantial resources to sponsor graduate degrees in the United States. The formula followed was simple; namely, select the best candidates and send them to the best institutions. On the whole, this was a well-managed and successful undertaking.

For example, among the top five American universities chosen by the trainees in agriculture three are among the five most prestigious institutions in the field. [16]

The second cycle began in the late 1960s with the return of the first crop of Masters and PhD students when the first graduate level programs were established. The rationale for this development appears sufficiently clear. Young PhD's returned home imbued with research ideals, but with little inclination for the drudgery of undergraduate teaching. Copying the model of graduate education they had experienced abroad was a very natural path to follow. Between 1966 and 1970, graduate education became legally recognized and administered with federal regulations. At the same time, it became mandatory for assistant and associate professors at federal universities to have masters and doctoral degrees.

Also of major importance were specific policies pursued by a number of federal government agencies, designed to promote the development of research. In addition to CNPq and CAPES, FINEP (Financiadora de Estudos e Projetos) was established to administer the resources of the FNDCT (Fundo Nacional do Desenvolvimento Científico e Tecnológico). These agencies not only administered substantial resources but also did much to encourage the formation of new programs. FNDCT alone, during peak years, administered more than 1.1% of the entire federal budget. Between 1969 and 1981, the number of graduate programs grew from 228 to 1,021. The number of students increased from 1,352 to 38,748, while the number of graduates leaped from 423 in 1973 to 4,675 in 1980.

By the early 1980s, more than a thousand new graduate programs were in operation. Considering the speed with which these had been established, it is not surprising to find that an extraordinary heterogeneity of programs representing different levels of quality resulted. The distortions that resulted are shown by the fact that only 10 percent of the programs held 82% of the fellowships, conducted 86% of the published research, and produced 89% of the graduates. In terms of quality and productivity, these programs were producing at international levels. However, others ranged from fly-by-night operations to programs that are now approaching maturity. The diploma factories and week-end programs found at the undergraduate level are by no means absent at the graduate level.

By the end of the 1970s, the rate of resource growth began to abate and enrollments leveled off. The heady enthusiasm of the previous decade had given way to critical reflection. Thus, the third stage in this life cycle appears to involve a period of maturation and adjustment. The new agenda is concerned with the productivity, quality and heterogeneity of these programs.

2. Grafting science onto the traditional universities

The idea of creating research universities in Brazil took shape in the 1960s. Humboldtian ideals were exhumed, and it became official policy to promote teaching and research activities pursued simultaneously at the same time and place. Moreover, the new orthodoxy was prescribed for all institutions of higher learning virtually without distinction. This came on the eve of the return of a new generation of Master's and PhD students trained abroad. Federal agencies had almost more money than they could spend, and they made their grants contingent on the establishment of graduate schools. New university faculty statutes required possession of Master's and PhD degrees, thus providing an enormous incentive for enrollment in the new graduate schools. All of these factors encouraged the development of graduate schools.

While a new research effort eventually materialized, the research university did not. The universities were not much affected by the presence of a new corps of researchers. Older faculty resented the upstart researchers, and in fact both sides avoided each other. The young Turks failed to dominate the older structures. At best, they moved into a few key administrative positions, but had an insufficient degree of freedom to provoke significant change. Uncomfortable with older faculty, they were unsatisfied with what the university could offer them in terms of material conditions.

In many ways, the 1970 university reform can be interpreted as an attempted *coup d' état* by the younger group, designed to alter the distribution of power in their favor. Indeed, the demise of the *catedrático*, with his lifetime tenure rights over his discipline, was a very significant victory. Also, the establishment of a departmental system and the institution of collegiate decision-making struck yet another blow at the old power structure. However, in the end, these reforms proved to be only cosmetic, leaving the old system much as it had been before. Thus began a strategic retreat.

Most graduate schools deliberately attempted to set up their own administrative structures, sheltering them from the oppressive weight of university power structures and administrative bureaucracies. Thus, graduate schools defined an independent territory within the university campus. Professors received regular university pay, but sought to procure other funds to complement their salaries. Funds were raised outside the university for laboratories, special equipment, research projects, and travel grants. Entire buildings were negotiated and built by the graduate schools without interference from university administrations, and in a few cases buildings were erected without the knowledge or permission of the universities.

Responsibilities to the university involved undergraduate teaching and service on committees, drudgery that had to be minimized at almost any cost. The most prestigious professors were reluctant to teach undergraduate courses. Also, there was the drain of the best faculty, who moved up to teach graduate schools or to enroll as their students. The university resented the development of a privileged graduate faculty, yet on the whole graduate schools were mostly ignored. Deans were said to not even know of the presence of graduate programs on campus. They constituted an enclave that obtained funds from outside, bore little weight in university budgets, and created few problems for university administrators.

Agencies such as CAPES went to great lengths to reduce this distance, insisting that assistant deans for graduate instruction and research be appointed in all universities. In the final analysis, the influence of these appointees tended to be inversely proportional to the strength of the graduate programs. They had little say at universities with strong research programs.

Although it is risky to generalize, it appears that with time the distance between graduate schools and the universities has been somewhat reduced. While in principle this movement is highly desirable, the new wave of egalitarianism may create formidable problems for the graduate schools. They may fall victims to a political momentum eroding the legitimacy of the large differences between effective researchers and others belonging to an impoverished university system. The relative affluence of senior graduate faculty no longer goes unchallenged in the new political mood. Their privileged status has not been eliminated—as indeed they are supported by outside funds—but their privileges are becoming less legitimate, thus putting graduate school faculties on the defensive.

Graduate school faculties have fewer reasons to question their legitimacy. After all, their role in conducting scientific inquiry and in training an intellectual elite is as secure as ever, and the good programs have acquired a very respectable record in their fields. Nevertheless, their proximity to the university makes them vulnerable to the overall identity crisis affecting Brazilian universities. Their dilemma is that while they still retain a high degree of administrative and financial independence, they are part of the university and increasingly recognize this by narrowing the distance that separates them from the rest. This comes at a time when university life has turned sour, overtaken with pessimism and an egalitarian ideology antithetical to the competitive system in which graduate schools thrive. There lies the dilemma. Either to retreat back into isolation, with the alienated overtones that this implies, or to share the dire mood of the universities, with much to lose in terms of their social role in producing research, critical thought and well-trained elites.

3. External funds, external incentives, and external vulnerability

Today's thriving system of graduate schools resulted from sound internal leadership and initiative, supported by a number of outside government agencies. It seems evident that neither the administrative regulations nor the internal resources of the universities would have permitted the number of programs in existence today. Hardly any encouragement and definitely no significant funds were provided by university administrations during the establishment of these programs. By contrast, since the early 1950s, CAPES and CNPq provided scholarships initially for study abroad and later for study in Brazil, as the new graduate schools expanded their enrollments.

Recently, domestic scholarships outnumber grants for study abroad by a ratio of 10 to 1. These scholarships are responsible for about one fourth of total graduate school enrollments. Bearing in mind that the weaker programs, less qualified students, part-time students and paid faculty on leave cannot qualify, these scholarships represent a strategic and numerically important part of graduate education.[17] The PICD (Programa de Incentivo á Capitação Docente) program, providing scholarships for university professors who want to pursue further training, normally operates with greater supply than demand. For these reasons, chairmen of the prestigious graduate schools are for the most part satisfied with their quota of fellowships.

CNPq traditionally has offered small research grants on a project-by-project basis. It also provided individual support on a continuing basis for several hundred outstanding scholars. More recently, it has expanded support for a multitude of new programs, large and small, covering research and development in many areas.

However, the really big money had to await the arrival of FNDCT. When FINEP was established to administer the fund, it grew beyond the initial 0.5% of the entire federal budget. Throughout the 1970s, it seemed that there was more money available than bona fide research could use. For this reason, among others, the agency chose to move from individual project funding into institutional support. Although data are unavailable, it seems certain that FINEP-sponsored groups account for a staggering portion of Brazilian scientific research. Not that all these scientists directly receive FINEP financing, but rather that nearly all of their associated programs are supported with FINEP contracts.

Quite apart from the direct financing, these agencies provided other no less essential support. They financed the "invisible college" by means of conferences, travel grants, support for journals, technical consulting, and so forth. The development of an intellectual and academic network for a new class of scientists would have been impossible without this support. The agencies also supplied the encouragement of an incentive system that rewarded institution-building and publication activities. Researchers benefited from an alliance with the staff of these agencies, many of whom shared the same academic values and research backgrounds. Often these alliances boosted the influence of researchers on their own university campuses. Treading on territory inhospitable to the logistics of research, these agencies often had to protect and lobby for graduate programs within the universities. Ultimately, the money and other support of these agencies gave graduate programs an independence to pursue their own goals.

Outside agencies have set up an incentive system that rewards results. Quality and productivity are built into the mechanics of funding. In this context, these agencies provide an incentive to pursue excellence that is otherwise largely absent within universities. It is difficult to imagine that universities could have created such a vigorous program of scientific research, even if they had had the money, since a differential reward system that provides financial recognition of excellence goes against the university grain.

Very few groups depend on outside funds for more than half of their resources. Nevertheless, there are literally hundreds of programs that receive these outside funds and are ultimately dependent on them for their scientific work. Many groups receive scholarships (CAPES and CNPq), funds for research, laboratory assistants, other supporting personnel and equipment (CNPq and FINEP), library allowances (FINEP), chemicals and supplies (FINEP), and so forth. In addition, these programs have research contracts with other private and public organizations. Such programs would collapse in a matter of days without these outside sources of support.

Faced with mounting pressure from the agencies to support their best research groups, university administrators have come to accept the role of researchers and to treat them better. Researchers, in turn, still find enough people in public funding agencies who enjoy their confidence and provide support. However, there is evidence of deterioration in the honeymoon relationship bona fide graduate programs once enjoyed with the agencies. Two related factors appear to account for this: the recent shortage of funds and an increase in the number of qualified researchers applying for their use.

Since 1975, the FNDCT has seen its share of the federal budget reduced from 1.1% to 0.2% in 1984.[18] The consequence of this reduction for the nation's graduate schools is difficult to assess since the fund is used for a number of other purposes. Nevertheless, it seems reasonable to assume that a significant reduction in the overall funds for research and development allotted to the nation's graduate schools has occurred. The new scarcity of funds breeds mistrust between the agencies and their clients, and also aggravates inter-agency rivalries. This point deserves attention since one of the engines of activism within agencies was the fierce competition among them. In the early Eighties, the spice of competition gave way to a bitter and time-consuming warfare.

Perhaps at least as important is the mounting competition for funds among research groups. This has not produced a supposedly beneficial competition among better qualified research proposals but a struggle between the "haves" and "have-nots" of the scientific community. Established scientific groups are being challenged by emerging groups who claim that their reduced scientific output results from the limited funds that remain once the established groups have taken the major share. While there is certainly a grain of truth in this argument, established groups counter that any alternative arrangement would destroy the patient labor of three decades of effort and create very little in its place. The fact of the matter is that: (1) the most productive groups are too dependent on outside money, (2) there is less money available and more qualified candidates to receive it, and (3) this outside vulnerability has been made all the more acute and uncomfortable as the result of a breakdown in trust among all concerned.

By way of summary, Brazil has made considerable progress in developing and institutionalizing a productive research establishment. This is no minor achievement. A few decades ago, research was a heroic and all but random occurrence. Today, this effort is surpassed only by India among Third World countries. It is difficult to find another country with the same exhilarating rate of growth in research activities. Financing schemes and support institutions have played a prominent and largely successful role in this development.

Notwithstanding, there are dark clouds on the horizon. Overdependence on outside funds, mistrust within the scientific community, and the inevitable trauma produced through the competition for funds are creating imminent danger as these funds begin to shrink. Greater identification of graduate schools with their universities is welcome, but this may prove to be the wrong moment, since Brazilian universities are undergoing a serious existential crisis of their own, and the new egalitarian wave jeopardizes the distribution of resources to the strongest research programs.

Lo and behold, in spite of all this, the scientific establishment is still holding its own. Academic production has not been reduced; there is no solid indication of a deterioration in quality and no significant group has broken up. There is danger on the horizon but no record of disaster.

4. Professional scientists or amateur technologists?

It is difficult to understand the motives behind the Brazilian decision to make such a generous effort to develop a scientific capability. Did the nation really want that many scientists, graduate schools, and research reports? Did they really believe that science would produce immediate, practical results? Were they misled to finance pure scientific inquiry when what they really had in mind was technological development? Was there a clear understanding of the objectives or just enough slack in the system to permit a few activist technocrats to have their way?

Unfortunately, I do not have the answer. But looking not so much at intentions as at results, it is quite clear that an enormous expansion in scientific capability occurred. In fact, this spawned a scientific community governed by its own logic and rules. At the same time, however, it failed to generate technological innovations or, more precisely, to establish an industry of technological research and development. These observations raise two questions: Why did all of this occur? And could it have developed technology in addition to or instead of a science capability?

The second question falls in the limbo of contrafactual conditionals. One can only speculate. The progressive development of technology on the factory floor by people in charge of the production process has not been absent from Brazilian industry. However, a more ambitious and systematic attempt to produce technological progress in laboratories through the development of prototypes and things of this sort is something entirely different. It is exceedingly unlikely that such an endeavor can precede or be pursued in parallel with the development of a basic scientific capability. This is because the logistics of technological research and development can become even more complicated than those of scientific development.

Scientists produce for other scientists. That is to say, the "relevant public" of scientific inquiry is composed of other scientists that form a closed circuit. The logic of scientific production is internal to this community and the timing of events highly elastic. By contrast, in technological development, decisions have to be made in reference to an external community and proceed according to a critical sequence. An entrepreneur has to decide that it makes sound economic sense to have technology developed; research groups have to agree on its feasibility; and, eventually, consumers have to be in a position to purchase a product incorporating the new technology. All of this may be too complicated for a country that has not mastered the routine and technique of basic scientific inquiry. Thus, it seems that among other elements, a sound scientific community is a precondition for the development of technological research.

If those who desired technological innovations expected immediate results, they certainly must have been frustrated. The course of the last decades gave scientific inquiry a privileged emphasis and led to few achievements in technology. Indeed, I believe that it could not have been otherwise. FINEP was originally established to foster technological development. However, little was accomplished along these lines, and it moved instead to support scientific inquiry. The few technological projects it managed to support led nowhere. By contrast, science thrived. It is as if their own experience demonstrated that science must precede technology. Projects with firms and an attempt to develop their own in-house technology moved only slowly, while university research programs blossomed.

Although several technological areas were provided with support—for example, engineering and computer science—they were treated and behaved much like areas of pure scientific inquiry. This produced a professional group that wrote papers and frequently attended conferences in order to present their results, but contact with entrepreneurs was minimal. Projects were conceived, financed and their results published. Their eventual prototypes were shelved because they did not respond to a concrete demand. Only recently has technological research and development begun to take a different shape.

There is now a pool of researchers which can be deployed into more practical endeavors, and the experience of conducting such projects has now been mastered to a certain degree. A few of their results are now in evidence, including those that are usually cited in the computer, airplane and weapons industries.[19] Each of these cases demonstrates a clear pattern. Experience is first acquired by university groups working on rather idle and diffuse endeavors. When conditions are ripe, these groups normally detach themselves from their universities and are deployed among projects. This transition is far from smooth. Requirements are different, often more stringent, and timetables have to be respected. Scientists have to learn to deal with businessmen and vice versa. The entire process entails learning on both sides. A few positive results show that technological research and development is now a real possibility. However, the general picture remains unclear.

A major question deserves additional consideration. Through trial and error, public agencies have learned how to encourage the development of scientific inquiry. This has essentially involved providing incentives for researchers to develop good scientific research practices. Up until now the tendency has been to extend these same programs and incentives into the area of technological research and development. However, these arrangements are descendants of previous experience with university research groups. Businessmen have shown themselves to be far less willing to endure the red tape and delays commonly associated with these public programs.[20] Even so, this is not the main problem.

In most cases, research and development personnel are not the dynamic element in the production of new technologies. The key element is a decision on the part of an entrepreneur to develop technology locally instead of purchasing it abroad. Given relatively free access to foreign technology, Brazilian research and development institutions in most cases are unable to compete with the inexpensive, proven and reliable imports of foreign technology. In science, it is sufficient to reward scientists for good work; however, technology needs to be treated like an infant industry, requiring a period of protection before it can face competition from abroad.

This protection should be understood in the broadest possible sense. It may imply a market reserve, such as we now have in the computer industry, or it may require a fully explicit procurement system, much like that developed by the military when purchasing a weapons system, or it may simply be a god-given protection, as with development of an alcohol engine, since sugar cane does not exist in the advanced industrialized countries. It is also necessary to decide what not to protect and when to drop protective barriers. As elsewhere, protection can be expensive to the consumer and produce economic distortions. Obviously, the country cannot afford to develop new technologies in all areas simultaneously.

To sum up, the relative success achieved in developing a Brazilian capacity for scientific inquiry has created the preconditions necessary for technological research and development. However, the mechanisms that worked well in the case of scientific development are not necessarily applicable in the area of technology. Much effort to provide direct support for technological development was wasted. The slow machinery of government offered relatively little incentive for the development of technology. Here, by contrast, we are dealing with an industrial product that has to be clearly perceived as desirable by businessmen, and for this to occur, domestically produced technologies must compare favorably with foreign alternatives. Technological research and development must be treated as an infant industry requiring an initial period of protection in order to survive. The lessons of experience are obvious. Unprotected areas have been quickly dominated by foreign technology, while the few existing examples of effectively protected Brazilian research and development have produced promising results.

NOTES

1. The views presented here are the full responsibility of the author and should not be attributed to CNRH.

2. This saturation implies greater difficulty in finding new candidates with acceptable levels of qualification.

3. A. Mello e Souza, *Financiamento da Educação e Acesso à Escola no Brasil* (Rio de Janeiro: IPEA, 1979), p. 55.

4. C.M. Castro e Gaudêncio Frigotto, *La Educación en America Latina: um estudio comparativo de costos y eficiencia* (Rio: ECIEL/FGV, 1980) cap. V e VI.

5. This is my own perception as a former Education Ministry officer.

6. C.M. Castro *et al, Ensino Técnico: Desempenho e Custo* (Rio: IPEA, 1973), cap. X.

7. L. Antonio Cunha, *Educação e Desenvolvimento Social no Brasil* (Rio: Francisco Alves, 1975), cap. V.

8. Early arguments demonstrating the fundamental weaknesses of this policy can be found in Cláudio de Moura Castro, *et al.*, *Ensino Técnico, Desempenho e Custos* (Rio: ECIEL, 1972), cap. X. Several different pieces of research indicate above 95% expectations for post-secondary degrees. See review of studies in C.M. Castro and A. Mello e Souza, *Mão de Obra Industrial* (Rio de Janeiro: IPEA, 1974), p. 67.

9. C.M. Castro, "O ethos da Formação Profissional" (São Paulo: SENAI/SP, 1978).

10. See C.M. Castro, "L'enseignement professionnel et la formation de la main-d' oeuvre industrielle au Brésil" in *Revue Internationale du Travail*, vol. 118, n⁰ 5, 1979, pp. 645–54.

11. C.M. Castro, "Academic Education Is General Education" in *Educational Alternatives in Latin America*, edited by T. LaBelle (Los Angeles): (University of California, 1975).

12. Only São Paulo possesses a strong state system of universities. While public universities provide the best and most prestigious education in Brazil, more than two thirds of the students in higher education attend private nonuniversity institutions.

13. "The Impact of European and American Influences on Brazilian Higher Education," *European Journal of Education*, vol. 18, n°.4 (1983).

14. Having been sworn in a Minister just a few hours before, it is very unlikely that Ludwig was cognizant of the new decree's details.

15. C.M. Castro, "Há Produção Científica no Brasil?," *Ciencia e Cultura* (July, 1985).

16. C.M. Castro and Fernando Spagnolo, "Science and Scientists in Agriculture: The Brazilian Case" (AJIJIC–MEXICO: IASEI 1982).

17. There are above 10,000 graduate students with scholarships and close to 40,000 students.

18. See H.M. Nussenweig, "O PADCT e a Sobrevivência da pesquisa," *Educação Hoje* (julho-agosto 1984).

19. See C.M. Castro, "É possível uma tecnologia 'Made in Brazil'?" *Pesquisa e Planejamento Econômico* (December, 1984).

20. O'Keefe, "Pesquisa—instrumento-chave para R&D: uma revisão crítica," *Revista Brasileira de Tecnologia*, v. 12:1–88, n.2, (abril/junho, 1981).

9

Health and Health Care Since the 1940s

William Paul McGreevey
Sérgio Piola
Solon Magalhães Vianna

In the years since the end of World War II, Brazil's health-care system has come to resemble the systems of the developed countries.[1] By the mid-1970s, Brazil was the world's seventh largest importer of medical and diagnostic equipment and also had domestic capacity to produce many devices used in medicine. The bill for health care in 1982 may have exceeded US$10 billion, more than 5% of GDP (Gross Domestic Product), about equal to the United Kingdom at 5.2 percent though still well below the United States at 11 percent (see Table 9.1). The government bill for health care was more than US$6 billion in 1982; households spent directly an additional US$3–4 billion on medicines and the services of private physicians. Health-care expenditures rose most rapidly in the 1970s, by rates exceeding 20 percent per annum, when private-sector medicine was encouraged at the expense of preventive public care.

Payment by a third party (INAMPS—Instituto Nacional de Assistencia Médica e Previdência Social) covers virtually the entire health system and all persons, on an emergency basis at least. Health's share of national expenditure has risen from only 1 or 2 percent of GDP in the 1950s to its present level of 5 percent. Brazil retains the option of taking the low-cost (UK) or high-cost (USA) path for future health-system development. This choice is a major focus for health policy and public-sector investment in health. That

311

Table 9.1
Trends in Total Health-Care Spending As Percent of Gross National Product

				West Germany	Italy	Netherlands	Sweden	Switzerland	United Kingdom	United States	Brazil
	Australia[a]	Canada	France								
1950		4.0	(3.4)				3.4		3.9	4.5	1.0
1955		4.3	(4.5)				4.1		3.4	4.4	
1960	(5.0)	5.6	(4.7)			(4.0)	4.7		3.8	5.3	
1965	(5.2)	6.1	(5.3)		(5.0)	(4.5)	5.6	(3.8)	3.9	6.2	
1970	5.5	7.1	6.4	6.4	(8.1)[b]	6.3	7.4		4.3	7.6	
1975	7.0	7.1	7.9	9.4	7.1	8.1	8.5	6.9	5.5	8.6	3.6
1977	(7.9)	7.1	7.9	9.2	6.4	8.2	9.8	6.9	5.2	8.9	
1978	8.0		8.2	9.2					5.2	8.9	
1979			8.4						5.2	9.0	
1981										9.8	4.0
1983										11.0	5.6

Source: Table 3-3, Maxwell (1981), 35; Brazil from McGreevey, *et al.* (1984), 8; Kravis, *et al.* (1982), and Vieira (1984).
Note: Figures in brackets are approximate, not derived from primary sources.
[a]Fiscal years to 30 June for Australia.
[b]1971.

choice can usefully be informed by analysis of how expenditures in this sector have changed over the past forty years, and how such factors as the public-private balance, the role of public finance, and externally generated medical technology all promoted an expansion of curative medical care.

Spending For Health Care

Perhaps in no other way is Brazilian health care so much like the developed countries as in the tendency for the national health bill to grow. Just a few years ago Brazil's public-sector expenditure on health services was estimated to be a significantly lower 1 percent of GDP (1949), rising to 2.5 percent of GDP by 1976 (Knight and Moran 1981, p. 40). Combined public and private expenditures were 3.8 percent of GDP in 1975 (Kravis et al., 1982, p. 169) and reached 5.6 percent of GDP by 1982 (Vieira, 1984). By way of comparison, the health-care spending share doubled over thirty years in the United States and more than doubled in a slightly shorter period in Sweden and the Netherlands. Spending grew much less rapidly in the United Kingdom, Canada, Australia, and Italy. Thus, although the spending share on health rose in all countries, the rate of increase varied from more than doubling in some countries to increasing by only about 50 percent in some others.[2]

Higher incomes and a larger share of GNP devoted to health care do not necessarily buy better health. Comparisons across both developed and developing countries show that there is no correlation between mortality indicators and health or medical expenditures (Maxwell, 1981, p. 40). Good health and low mortality depend on many things other than medical expenditures; thus it is not surprising that no correlation is found between these two variables (cf. Fuchs, 1974).

Brazil, though spending a significant share of GDP on health, still spends a small amount per capita when compared to the developed countries, or even to Spain, Venezuela and Portugal. By 1982 combined public and private expenditures on health in Brazil had risen to about US$80 per capita; while North Americans spent about 15 times as much as Brazilians, the British 5 times as much.

When Brazil's government spent only 1 percent of GDP on health in 1950, almost all of that expenditure flowed through a preventive-medicine, public-health program. Since that time an individual-curative health subsystem financed through a federal payroll tax has grown up separate from, and independent of, the public-health program of the Ministry of Health and state secretariats of health. Over the past 40 years, the collective-preventive subsystem has lagged increasingly behind the individual-curative subsystem. Table

Table 9.2
Preventive and Curative Shares of Brazilian
Health Expenditures, Percent Distribution
in Selected Years, 1949–82

Year	Medical-Hospital or Curative %	Primary or Preventive %
1949	12.9	87.1
1965	35.8	64.1
1969	59.2	40.8
1975	70.2	29.7
1978	81.3	18.7
1979	81.9	18.1
1980	84.5	15.5
1981	82.2	17.8
1982 (budget estimate)	84.6	15.4

Source: McGreevey, et al. (1984), p. 14.

9.2 shows that the former's share of total public health expenditure fell from 87 percent in 1949 to about 30 percent in 1975. (If all investment expenditures on water supply and sanitation under the national sanitation plan were included, the 1975 figure would rise to 39 percent.) The clear trend has been the progressive marginalization of the Ministry of Health, whose budgetary allocation actually declined in real terms over the period 1965–75 and again in the early 1980s. One plausible explanation for this phenomenon is the generally low priority accorded to preventive health care observed in postwar plans and budgets. The primary care portion of the health budget declined from above three fifths in 1965 to below one fifth in 1980.[3] The impoverishment of primary health care had gone so far by 1985 that a new post-military regime placed considerable initial emphasis on enhancing support for this sector.

SUCAM (Superintendência de Campanhas de Saúde Pública, or Superintendency for Public Health Campaigns), a major operational program of the Ministry of Health which normally has spent one quarter to one third of the ministry budget, saw its expenditures cut by 20 percent between 1978 and 1982. The depressed condition of the Brazilian economy in the early 1980s, along with the need to reduce federal government expenditures in light of reduce revenues, accounted for a significant part of the reduction in budgetary support for preventive health programs. Nonetheless, the burden of essential budget reductions fell more heavily on preventive health than on the federal budget as a whole. The recession period was thus a repetition of a longstanding decline in emphasis on primary and preventive health care. Partly to reverse that trend the government established FINSOCIAL in 1982 to finance social expenditures.

The year 1982 may thus be said to mark a termination point for the long-term and massive shift of resources from primary care to the curative hospital model. Policy changes, in addition to FINSOCIAL financial support, also mark that year as the beginning of a process of reversing the growing privatization of costly medical-hospital care. The private medical complex had its day from the 1950s until 1982. Even while preventive health care declined, the medical-hospital system was a major growth industry. The federal government helped finance that growth in two ways: (1) By making third-party payments for health care out of its payroll tax collections, and (2) by financing private hospital construction with highly subsidized loans. INAMPS is a part of SINPAS (Sistema Nacional da Previdência e Assistência Social) which collects payroll taxes to pay for employee retirement and disability pensions, job-related illness or accidents, and medical care. In a series of administrative rearrangements and consolidations beginning in the 1920s, the management of the revenues and expenditures of this system of social security for workers and their families has gradually been extended, refined and consolidated until over 90 percent of all Brazilians are now, in some sense, covered. About two thirds of expenditures pay retirement and related benefits, a quarter is used for medical and hospital care and one tenth goes for administration of the system (MPAS, DATAPREV 1980, 45). FAS (Fundo de Apoio ao Desenvolvimento Social, or Fund for Support to Social Development), created in 1974, had funded construction of more than 30,000 hospital beds by mid-1978, three quarters of them in the private sector (Gentile de Mello 1981, pp. 104–6). INAMPS in turn exercised some control over private physicians and facilities by its system of credentials which defined those eligible for reimbursement when offering treatment to workers and their families. FAS (Fundo de Apoio Social) activities proved to be particularly controversial because loans and loan guarantees to private hospitals were offered on very favorable terms often involving negative real rates of interest.

In the 1970s and early 80s, INAMPS used about one quarter of the payroll tax revenues, which was slightly more than 4 percent of the total wage bill. Such a sum would be sufficient to finance primary and preventive public health care; however, most of it was used for medical-hospital care for which demand considerably exceeds that level of financing. Perhaps for that reason in part, private expenditures for health purposes were substantial. For example, in 1974 private expenditures ran from a low 3 percent of total household expenditures in the Northeast to over 5 percent of expenditures in the South (Cordeiro, 1980, p. 181). Families in rural areas spent a larger share of their income on health than did those in urban areas, presumably because of the lack of public health facilities (Musgrove, 1983). A national survey conducted by IBGE (Instituto Brasileiro de Geografia e Estadística) in October–November 1981, known as PNAD81 (Pesquisa Nacional por Amostra de Domicilios), shows that over half the households which had any health expenditures spent 5 percent or more of that month's income on health goods and services. Thus, health-care expenditures in the private sector rose in the period of 1974–81, as a share of income despite the expansion of free-to-the-patient medical-hospital services (IBGE, 1983). The president of INAMPS revealed in a press interview that only 740,000 hospitalizations per month, half of these in the state of São Paulo, were programmed for the nation as a whole. This level of service provided 0.07 hospitalizations per person per annum—a figure well below the WHO (World Health Organization) norms accepted by the Brazilian government (*Senhor*, 1985, p. 5). These facts point both to the growing demand for health care and simultaneously to a possible misdirection of funds to curative services which yield few tangible social improvements.

Throughout the period since the 1940s, the two health subsystems were not effectively coordinated. The Ministry of Health struggled with limited budget resources from general government revenues and often with but limited success to deal with major public health problems, particularly endemic diseases. The Ministry of Social Security and INAMPS, meanwhile, saw their earmarked funds grow at high rates and with ample assurance of continued expansion. Public health specialists led a battle in the late 1970s to devote more resources to primary health care; their effort, which was formulated in the PIASS (Programa de Interorização de Ações de Saúde e Saniamento) and PREVSAUDE (Programa de Saude Preventiva) programs, was successfully opposed by medical and hospital interests. Thus, in 1981, only about 1 percent of INAMPS funds was spent on basic health services.

By the early 1980s a geographic distance had grown up between the two functional ministries—with the Ministry of Health specializing in the health problems of the rural Northeast and Amazon, the poorest regions of the country; and the Ministry of Social Security specializing in the affluent Southeast, South and Center-West regions. In the years 1979–81, INAMPS spent twice as much per capita in the Southeast (São Paulo, Rio de Janeiro, Minas Gerais and Espirito Santo) as it did in the nine poorer states of the Northeast (McGreevey et al., 1984, p. 24). This inequality of expenditure is exactly the reverse of the health conditions: health status is worst in the Northeast, where the least money per capita was spent (Merrick and Graham, 1979, pp. 251–78; FIBGE 1984).

Table 9.3
Percentage Distribution in Five Major Regions.*

Region	Federal Revenues %	SINPAS Revenues %	Nonmedical Ben., Paid, 1979 %	INAMPS Expenditures %
North	1.5	1.9	2.0	2.4
Northeast	6.2	9.0	16.4	17.2
Southeast	62.7	62.6	63.0	52.6
South	9.7	14.2	15.8	18.8
Center-West	19.9	4.1	2.5	6.0
Other	0.0	8.2	0.3	3.0

*Percentages are from 1981 except as indicated.
Sources: SEPLAN (1982); MPAS, DATAPREV 1981.

Redistribution Through INAMPS

A notable feature of the curative health system in Brazil is that it effects some redistribution of resources from rich to poorer areas. This can be shown most readily by comparing, for 1981, the percentage distributions, by regions, of federal tax revenues, revenues from SINPAS through the payroll tax, total nonmedical social security disbursements, and INAMPS expenditures (see Table 9.3). In the poorest region, the Northeast, the federal government collected 6.2 percent of its tax take, and the payroll tax collected 9 percent of its total. The social security system spent 16.4 percent of nonmedical benefits in that region and INAMPS spent 17.2 percent of its resources there. In contrast, about 63 percent of tax resources were gathered in the Southeast, which includes the states of São Paulo, Rio de Janeiro, Minas Gerais and Espírito Santo. Nonmedical benefits were about an equal share of the national total, as were the receipts. However, medical expenditures in that region (52.6 percent) were a considerably smaller share of the total. The INAMPS system, more than other components of social security, transfers resources from richer to poorer areas of Brazil. From another perspective, however, in 1975 the per capita amounts of federal expenditures on health were twice as high in the Southeast as in the Northeast (see Table 9.4). The difference was similar in 1981 when INAMPS spent twice as much per capita in the South and Southeast as it did in the North and Northeast (McGreevey et al., 1984, p. 24). The point remains, nonetheless, that INAMPS spends proportionately more than is collected for it in many of the poorer states.

One mechanism by which this redistribution takes place is through INAMPS

Table 9.4
1975 Federal Direct Expenditures Per Capita,
by Function

Function	Region		
	Frontier	Northeast	Southeast
Transportation	Cr$ 164	Cr$ 53	Cr$ 327
Education	61	55	65
Housing and Urban Services	2	0	0
Health	84	55	116
Total (selected functions)	310	163	510
Official transfers	239	153	134
Total (direct expenditures plus official transfers)	549	317	644

Source: Fundaçao Getulio Vargas/Centro de Estudos Fiscais, Regionalização das Transações do Setor Publico—1975 (Rio de Janeiro, 1980), cited in Mahar et al., Financing state and local government in Brazil, some recent trends and issues (1982), p. 75.

cooperative agreements with PIASS (Programa para Interiorização de Ações em Saúde e Saneamento), and with state and municipal health services. These agreements constitute the mechanism through which INAMPS executes its obligation to provide health care to rural and sparsely populated areas where there are few physicians and service facilities. Of the 4,000 *municipios* in Brazil, nearly half had no resident physician in 1973; the majority of these were in the North and Northeast regions. Surprisingly, however, 175 *municipios* of the state of São Paulo out of a total of 570 *municipios* in the state—i.e., 31 percent of them—had no physician present (Gentile, 1981, p. 34). Not surprisingly, there is a closer positive correlation between income and physicians ($r = +0.78$) than between population and physicians ($r = +0.45$) when comparing the percentage distributions of these variables by regions (Gentile, 1981, p. 33). Physicians tend to go where there are financial resources to purchase their services; the PIASS programs are designed to go where there is need regardless of ability to pay. Basic health care was placed firmly on the national agenda around 1975, but the interests of physicians and hospitals specializing in curative care successfully resisted it (Gentile 1981, Landmann 1984). More recently, there has again been an effort in the public-health community to shift emphasis to primary care in the poorer regions. With the change of government in March of 1985, prospects for success now appear better.

Many indicators can be used to demonstrate the gap between the health status of the richer and poorer regions of Brazil. One of these is life expectancy. In the Northeast, male life expectancy was 48 years at the time of the 1970 Census; while female life expectancy, as is common in most populations, was higher at 52 years. In the richer Southeast, which includes the states of São Paulo, Rio de Janeiro, Minas Gerais, and Espírito Santo, male and female life expectancy was 60 and 64 years respectively (IBGE, 1981, p. 114).

These data can be combined with the results of international studies of causes of death to demonstrate differences in health problems between the two regions. Table 9.5 shows, for males and females in the two regions, the expected gain in average length of life from eliminating various causes of death or combinations of causes. These estimates are not based directly on Brazilian data on recorded causes of death, but are based instead on an international cross section (Preston, 1972). Primary health care programs could help eliminate such causes of death as tuberculosis, other infectious and parasitic diseases, influenza, pneumonia, bronchitis, diarrheal diseases, and maternal mortality; they could thus lengthen life by about fourteen years in Northeast Brazil and by about six years in Southeast Brazil. Even in the more developed Southeast, the causes of death which can be particularly addressed by a primary health care program predominate over neoplasms and cardiovascular disease as sources of gain in life expectancy from the reduction in health impairments.

Equalizing health expenditures

INAMPS has provided funds to support PIASS programs which include some 6,344 health posts, of which 14 percent are in the North, 51 percent in the Northeast, 26 percent in the Southeast, and 9 percent in the Center-West (SEPLAN, 1982, p. 247). In recent years, INAMPS has spent about the same amount per ambulatory patient visit in all regions of the country. However, expenditures per capita by region have differed considerably because consultations per capita vary substantially between regions. For example, the Northeast with a 1980 population of 34.9 million generated 32 million medical consultations in that year—slightly less than one per person. The Southeast, with a population of 51.7 million generated 88 million medical consultations—about 1.7 visits per capita (FIBGE, 1984).

To equalize expenditures per capita and yet remain within the budget ceiling of 1982 total expenditures, INAMPS would have to achieve a redeployment of resources along lines indicated in Table 9.6. Total expenditures in the Southeast would have to decline by one fifth, whereas expenditures in the

Table 9.5

Expected Gain in Average Length of Life from Eliminating Various Causes
of Death or Combinations of Causes, Males and Females, Northeast and
Southeast Brazil, 1970, in Years

Causes of Death or Combinations of Causes	Northeast		Southeast	
	Male	Female	Male	Female
1. Respiratory tuberculosis	2.25	2.22	1.27	1.10
2. Other infectious and parasitic diseases	3.20	2.99	1.38	1.22
3. Neoplasms	0.53	1.04	1.53	1.92
4. Cardiovascular disease	2.09	2.54	4.68	5.70
5. Influenza, pneumonia, bronchitis	4.45	4.00	2.07	1.82
6. Diarrheal diseases	2.70	2.56	1.33	1.17
7. Diabetes, cirrhosis of liver, nephritis, stomach ulcer	0.72	0.73	0.79	0.74
8. Maternal mortality	0.00	0.49	0.00	0.28
9. Certain diseases of infancy	2.27	1.91	1.74	1.39
10. Violence	1.67	0.54	1.89	0.65
11. All other and unknown causes	6.92	7.10	4.57	4.59
12. (1)+(2)+(5)+(6)+(8)	14.52	13.89	6.39	5.86
13. Life expectancy by eliminating all causes in no. 12 plus ascribed infectious diseases	69.60	72.56	70.40	74.20

Source: Life expectancy estimates from IBGE (1981), 114; expected gains by life-expectancy group from Preston (1976). Mortality patterns in national populations, with special reference to recorded causes of death; cited, with detailed life-expectancy gains, in Golladay and Liese (1980), p. 24.

Northeast would increase by three fifths, and those in the North would nearly double. The reorientation of financial resources would have to be complemented by a shift to primary health care to address the health impairments that are most important in the Northeast as outlined in Table 9.5. A redeployment of resources along these lines could raise life expectancy in the Northeast by reducing the incidence of the "diseases of underdevelopment."

Table 9.6
INAMPS Expenditures by Region (1982), Percent Distribution of
Population by Region (1980 Census), and Expenditures by Region
Which Would Equalize INAMPS Expenditures Per Capita

Region	INAMPS expenditures (1982) (billions of cruzeiros)	Population share	Expenditures to equalize per capita expenditures (billions of cruzeiros)
North	Cr$ 14.5	4.9%	Cr$ 27.1
Northeast	103.6	29.3	162.1
Southeast	304.0	43.5	240.7
South	97.6	16.0	88.5
Center-West	33.6	6.3	34.9
General Administration and Other	50.8	0.0	50.8
Total	604.1	100.0%	604.1

Source: MPAS, INAMPS (1982); FIBGE (1981).

Table 9.7
INAMPS Paid Hospitalizations in Thousands,
and Percent Distribution, 1981

Service Provider	Hospitalizations (000)	Percentage Distribution
Private contract hospitals	9,202	85.4
INAMPS' own facilities	215	2.0
Federal, state and municipal	565	5.2
University hospitals	179	1.7
Union and company facilities	509	4.7
Other	108	1.0
Total	10,778	100.0

Source: MPAS, INAMPS, 1982.

Three interesting questions cannot be given definitive answers here. First, were health status and health services already unequal in the 1940s so that the inequality observable in 1980 is due to prewar, or perhaps even colonial, causes? Second, if inequality did grow during the past forty years, was its expansion even greater during the military period (1964–85) than it was before? Finally, a question suggested by the work of McNeill, *Plagues and peoples*, is: Can one "properly think of most human lives as caught in a precarious equilibrium between the microparasitism of disease organisms and the macroparasitism of large-bodied predators, chief among which have been other human beings"? (McNeill 1976, 5). Northeast Brazil has suffered from both kinds of parasitism; McNeill believes they work together. To explain how that might have occurred, if it did, would require a separate essay.

THE MEDICAL-HOSPITAL SUBSYSTEM

The medical-hospital system is the largest component of Brazilian health-care services. It includes a number of public hospitals (those of INAMPS, the states, the municipalities, the universities and the public medical schools), private nonprofit hospitals, and private for-profit hospitals. The relative importance of these systems is shown by the share of total hospital admissions paid for by INAMPS in 1981, by class of service (see Table 9.7). Notice that private facilities were used for 85 percent of hospitalizations.

About 56 percent of total INAMPS expenditures in 1981 went to private contract hospitals and ancillary service organizations, *e.g.*, laboratories which conduct tests and give X-ray and other examinations. The next largest components of INAMPS expenditure are for services in INAMPS facilities (18.5 percent of the total) and for administration (5.4 percent). Smaller amounts were paid for services under agreements with state and municipal facilities (4.7 percent); university and teaching hospitals (2.2 percent); philanthropic institutions (3.4 percent); enterprises which provided their own health services (3.5 percent); and other classes of payment (6.3 percent) (McGreevey *et al.*, 1984). These data show that the predominant form of delivery of medical-hospital services is through the private sector with reimbursement of expenses by the government through INAMPS. These data do not, of course, encompass the direct payments of private individuals or private insurance schemes for hospital services. (Golden Cross, the largest private health insurance company, serves less than 2 percent of total population.)

High Costs In The Health System

Costs in Brazil's medical-hospital system deserve special discussion. Both systematic and anecdotal information shows that costs are often higher than in developed countries. The few tangible facts available provide some initial guidance on how to identify areas of excessive costs; less clear is how the structure of costs developed. Both the policies to encourage the private sector to build hospitals and the payments system for physicians are important. But, as in more developed countries, the role of the physician rather than the income he receives is the key to why costs are high.

The Physician's Role

A major cause of high costs in the health system is what Brazilians refer to as "a dupla militancia," or conflict of interest, which riddles the system. The majority of Brazilian physicians, particularly those in the larger cities, work as part-time employees at several jobs, some on salary, and some on a fee-for-service basis. São Paulo has the largest number of MDs of any city, urban area or state; physicians on average have 3.5 separate employments (Donnangelo, 1982). Virtually every MD works for at least one public health facility, such as a municipal clinic or hospital, a state clinic, a university hospital or a facility of INAMPS. Many of them, referred to commonly as "taxi doctors," move about the city each day to different places of employment.

In addition to his work in public clinics, each MD normally works with some private facility. Typically they use their employment in public clinics as a means to recruit patients into a private facility, in which, from the doctor's point of view, he can offer better-quality service on a fee-for-service basis, and in which the client can enjoy more personal attention. The physician can also control service delivery and profit therefrom in the private facility. Thus government-sponsored facilities (INAMPS, states, municipalities and universities) were, in 1981, responsible for 43 percent of medical and dental consultations, but for only 10 percent of hospital admissions. Private physicians, dentists and hospitals handled 30 percent of medical and dental consultations and 86 percent of hospital admissions, assuming the inclusion of admissions of rural INAMPS clients listed under other agreements (MPAS, DATAPREV 1981, Tables 76, 77).

The total of INAMPS facilities in the country (8,000 beds in 36 facilities) was only slightly larger in 1982 than it had been 20 years earlier (Landmann, 1982, pp. 104–6). Furthermore, anecdotal evidence, drawing on newspaper reports from 1981 and early 1982, reveals underutilization of public facilities in major cities. One of the five INAMPS hospitals in São Paulo remained closed a year after its completion. The Darci Vargas pediatric hospital in Morumbi, a São Paulo suburb, had only one third of its beds occupied in May 1982. The INAMPS Heliopolis hospital was less than 50 percent occupied at the same time. The INAMPS maternity hospital Leonor Mendes de

Barros in the Tatuape neighborhood of São Paulo was also less than half full (Nitrini, 1982). Mercy Hospital in Santos, a nonprofit but private facility, had 72 patients occupying its 1,400 beds; similar underutilization of these nonprofit facilities was occurring throughout the country; in part because the buildings are outmoded and inefficient but also because their regulated agreements with INAMPS leave them with much lower remuneration than is received by profit-making private hospitals (Veja, 1982). Note also that the physician plays a major role in advising the patient on which facility the patient should enter for hospital treatment.

The majority of initial consultations occur in public facilities, but there is excess capacity in public hospitals. The conflict of interest between the public- and private-sector roles of the physicians, who in fact dominate the referral decision, may be responsible for the under-use of public facilities. The overhead cost of maintaining these underutilized facilities falls entirely on the public sector.

A factor which exacerbates the physician's conflict of interest is the fee structure (Cf. Abel-Smith, 1976, pp. 58–74). This structure was in a process of slow evolution from the 1960s onward. That evolution has been influenced by such factors as changing medical technology, procedures followed in other countries (especially the United States), and the desire of many physicians to continue to maintain a private relationship with their patients in spite of the growing role of third-party payments by INAMPS.

By 1981, all medical services paid for by INAMPS to private contractors, hospitals or physicians were reimbursed at rates expressed in terms of numbers of service units, or Unidades de Serviço (US). An initial office or clinic consultation was worth 8 US which in mid-1982 was equivalent to US$2.80; an electrocardiogram was worth 18 US, while a dynamic two-channel electrocardiogram was worth 300 US. Psychological testing was worth 70 US, and a psychotherapy session only 10 US. The value of the US is, along with many other prices, indexed to adjust for inflation in the value of the Brazilian cruzeiro.

A normal birth procedure is paid 90 US, whereas a caesarean birth is paid at the same rate of 90 US to the attending physician, but with an additional payment of 60 US for the services of an anesthesiologist. Obstetrics accounts for one quarter of all hospital admissions (MPAS, DATAPREV 1980, Table 70). By adding a hysterectomy to the caesarean birth the total payment by INAMPS rises from 150 US to 270 US. This fee schedule is drawn from the INAMPS publication in 1979 of medical, dental and hospital fees (MPAS, INAMPS, 1979). The rates for birth assistance were changed in 1982 to equalize payments for caesarean and normal deliveries.

One public health specialist in Brazil concluded that the high rate of caesarean deliveries resulted in an estimated 186,000 unnecessary surgical procedures in 1979 at a cost to INAMPS of Cr$920 million (Gentile, 1981). That amount is equal to 1 percent of the INAMPS expenditures in that year, hardly a major financial problem. Nearly a third of all births in Brazil paid for by INAMPS in June 1980 were by caesarean section (MPAS, DATAPREV 1980, Table 70). Data from a 1981 survey show even higher rates of surgical births among private patients than those paid for by INAMPS. In São Paulo the share of all births delivered by caesarean section is highest among educated and high-income groups, reaching above 70 percent for those at the top of the income-education class (Merrick, 1984). Half the births which patients paid for out of their own resources, *i.e.*, not involving any public-sector payments, at the Catholic University Hospital Santa Lucinda in São Paulo in 1977, were by caesarean section—a rate even higher than prevailed for INAMPS beneficiaries (Gentile, 1981, p. 181). The analyst thus cannot readily conclude that such excessive surgical services are foisted on the client population of INAMPS; rather, individual recipients of medical services accept medical guidance for what, by international standards, must be excessive use of a surgical procedure.

The fee-for-service system can enhance physician income by the addition of services beyond the initial consultation. Moreover, the physician is likely to have recruited the client at a public facility, which is paid 8 US by INAMPS, and then to have offered additional services in a private hospital setting. There, he can admit the patient to a hospital bed and deluge *him* (more likely *her*) with tests and services. International standards provide on average 25 complementary examinations for each 100 patient consultations, whereas the private hospitals contracted by INAMPS provided, in 1981, 130 exams per hundred patient consultations—a rate five times the norm (O Estado de São Paulo, 14 May 1982, p. 15). The public and private systems taken together provided 95 exams per hundred consultations (McGreevey, *et al.*, 1984, p. 46). As much as 80 percent of all these examinations may be unnecessary (Cf. Landmann, 1981). The growing revelations of fraud among hospitals and medical laboratories in São Paulo during 1985 seem to have proved beyond any doubt that the services charged to INAMPS were excessive. The outgoing minister suggested that the cost of such fraud to the government would approach Cr$2 trillion, about 20 percent of the 1985 INAMPS budget.

By international standards, Brazilian physicians earn high incomes even though public-sector salaries are low. A physician working for the state health service in São Paulo earned about five minimum salaries in 1981, *i.e.*, about US$385 monthly for four hours of work per day (Echeverri, 1981, p. 6). He could make up for this low salary by working fewer than scheduled hours, by

Table 9.8
Doctor's Income in Relation to GDP Per Capita
and Earned Income, Mostly 1974

Country	Ratio of Doctors' Income to		
	GDP per Capita	Compensation of Employees per Employee	Average Production Worker's Gross Earnings
Belgium			
Physicians and dentists	6.3	3.7	5.2
Pharmacists	6.0	3.6	4.9
Canada	6.8	5.0	4.8
Denmark (1973)	5.7	4.0	3.8
Finland (1970)	5.2	5.0	4.2
France	7.0	4.3	7.0
Germany (1973)	8.5	5.6	6.1
Ireland (1973)	7.6	3.7	3.5
Italy (1973)	9.5	4.3	6.8
Netherlands (1973)	10.2[a]	5.0	6.3
New Zealand			
Physicians	6.2	(4.0)	3.9
Dentists	4.9	(3.1)	3.1
Norway	3.4	2.4	2.4
Sweden	4.6	3.3	3.5
United Kingdom (1973)	4.5	3.3	2.7
United States			
Physicians	6.7	4.5	5.6
Dentists (1972)	5.6	3.3	4.1
Dispersion[b]	1.7	.8	1.4
Average[c]	6.2	3.9	4.4

Source: Organization for Economic Cooperation and Development, Public Expenditure on Health (July 1977), p. 24, table 9. See also p. 25, the passage concerning definitions and the problems of international comparisons. Reprinted with permission.
[a]If GDP per person employed were used as the basis for this comparison, this apparent difference from other countries would be considerably reduced.
[b]Measured by standard deviation.
[c]Geometric mean.

holding several public-sector jobs and by maintaining a half-time private clinic or practice.

Rapid inflation, imperfect information about real incomes, and lack of comparability of indicators make any international comparisons of physician incomes controversial. One set of indicators developed by Maxwell on the basis of his international studies of health costs appears useful (see Table 9.8). He compares, for fourteen developed countries, the ratios of MDs' income to GDP per capita (mean = 6.2), to compensation of employees per employee (mean = 4.4). Thus mean physician income in the countries studied exceeded per capita product, average compensation and factory workers' earnings by the indicated ratios, on average. A study by Cecilia Donnangelo (1982) of a sample of 795 São Paulo physicians found that half of them earned 15 minimum salaries or more. In November 1981 the prevailing level of the minimum salary was Cr$11,928 and the U.S. dollar was worth Cr$115.86, yielding a presumptive minimum salary of about US$103 per month. Thus median physician income at 15 times the minimum salary was about US$1,545 per month, or US$18,540 per annum. GDP per capita was estimated by the World Bank to be US$2,050 (World Bank Atlas, 1981). By this estimate the ratio of physician income to per capita GDP was 9.0, a ratio nearly 50 percent greater than that for the composite of fourteen developed countries.

Not only are median salaries of Brazilian physicians high but also the incomes are unequal among MDs. A few earn very large incomes originating in substantial part from ownership of medical enterprises. A medical "middle class" of physicians old enough to have a decade or more of experience, but who do not own large hospitals or clinics, may also earn large incomes from fee-for-service practices combining part-time employment in the public sector. A significant number of young doctors just starting their careers earn considerably less and form the cadres who have led strikes in São Paulo and Rio de Janeiro against public facilities in an effort to improve working conditions and raise their incomes (Landmann, 1982, pp. 139–170).

There is alleged to be substantial unemployment among physicians in Brazil. The Donnangelo survey, conducted with the cooperation and financial support of the São Paulo Medical Association, found only 2 MDs of 795 interviewed who considered themselves unemployed. More than 40 percent of physicians interviewed work in excess of 50 hours per week, and 27 percent work more than 60 hours weekly. Fewer than 20 percent were employed for less than 20 hours weekly.

There has been a striking increase in the number of physician graduates in recent years so that now between 8,000 and 10,000 enter the labor market each year (McGreevey et al., 1984, p. 52). Each of these new entrants hopes for the income and prestige of the top income earners in a profession which counts among its numbers plastic surgeons and cardiologists commanding world-class income and status. Naturally, many are disappointed. Some have become ardent supporters of health-care reform; *e.g.*, Elio Fiszbejn, president of the São Paulo medical union.

Leaders of the health sector are concerned that only half the new graduates can be absorbed in productive medical employment. When the São Paulo office of INAMPS advertised 910 available medical positions in 1981, 6,810 physicians applied for them. A former Minister of Social Security stated at a conference in August 1980 that there were 33,000 doctors unemployed or underemployed in Brazil (Jornal do Brasil, 23 Aug. 1980; quoted in Echeverri 1981, pp. 5–6). The Donnangelo survey evidence is not consistent with this assertion. It may be that graduate MDs have unrealistic expectations of their income-earning potential; moreover, they demonstrate an unwillingness to leave large cities, where they are in oversupply.

Labor market conditions for physicians in Brazil yielded high relative incomes for this group when compared with other countries in the early 1980s. Relative incomes of the middle class fell with the recession after 1982. Physician services may have been in short rather than plentiful supply, but they believed their incomes should be higher because they compared themselves with colleagues in developed countries where the overall standard of living is several times higher than it is in Brazil. For 1983 and after, physician incomes are probably much lower than they were earlier.

In 1982 the INAMPS fee schedule provided that an initial consultation would be paid Cr$480 (less than US$3), an amount too low to compensate for the real cost of a physician's time. As Landmann points out, the most cost-effective stage of a physician's services is at the initial interview or physical examination, and that additional tests rarely contribute to change or improve the diagnosis made at that time (Landmann, 1982, p. 96). By underpaying for the most valuable service, the INAMPS payment system encouraged overuse of services, tests, facilities and operations that might have been avoided were it not for the physician's incentive to prescribe the additional things in order to enhance his own income.

In a peculiar way, high physician incomes are less a problem for medical costs than is the ample supply of physicians. As Maxwell notes,

> The direct costs of physicians, about one sixth of total health costs [in developed countries] at present, do not pose the problem. . . . The economic threat lies more in the discretionary work generated by each physician, since decisions on what services patients should have depend very largely on the judgment of the physician whom they consult. It is therefore highly probable, without assuming any malign conspiracy, that if the number of physicians at work increas-

es, total health-services activity and expenditure will also rise, although not necessarily in direct proportion. Of course, the change in activity may come in the mix of work, rather than in the quantity as measured by number of physician visits or inpatient days. (Maxwell, 1981, p. 76)

The Brazilian system, in other words, may not be very different from the developed countries in which costs for ancillary services have accelerated with the growth of the population of MDs (cf. Abel-Smith, 1976, pp. 45–7). One mechanism by which this cost expansion occurs in Brazil, and the other countries as well, is through the inordinate expansion of medical services, particularly in conjunction with the high technology of medicine prescribed and administered by physicians.

High technology in medicine

The growth of the medical system in Brazil since the early 1970s has been fueled particularly by expansion of high-technology medical equipment. Total medical consultations, taking 1970 as a base of 100, climbed to 565 by 1981 (McGreevey et al., 1984, pp. 48, 49). Hospitalizations expanded somewhat less (469) and total laboratory examinations somewhat more (551). But X-ray examinations expanded to a much higher level (1036), and other complementary examinations even more (1530). About 40 million X-ray examinations, most of them having no diagnostic value and many of them possibly leading to iatrogenic disease, were given to Brazilians in 1979. When the Rio de Janeiro state university hospital cut the number of X-rays by 40 percent, there was no loss in diagnostic efficiency. A publication by Guimaraes in 1977 revealed that chest X-rays, which in 1974 accounted for 42.3 percent of all X-ray examinations, found no diagnostically significant abnormalities among patients 0–19 years of age, 5.6 percent abnormalities among those 20–50, and 11.8 percent among those over age 50 (Guimaraes, 1977, cited in Landmann, 1982, pp. 89–90). Many of these X-rays were required for reasons unrelated to suspected illness, e.g., for participation in sports or required of job applicants. The dangers of excessive exposure to X-rays are better known today in developed countries, but the medical system in Brazil continues to permit overuse of these tests. Most X-rays and the cost associated with them could be eliminated with no real loss of diagnostic accuracy. As McClenahan wrote in 1970, "It is easier to ask for an X-ray than it is to think" (cited in Landmann, 1982, p. 88).

Studies show that better doctors ask for fewer tests, and vice versa (Daniel and Schroeder, 1977; cited in Landmann, 1982, p. 92). However, there now exists in Brazil a sizeable medical-industrial complex which sells the film and related products to the health system and thus has reason to resist change. Besides X-rays, INAMPS paid for 1.7 million electrocardiograms, 0.7 million electroencephalograms, and more than 10 million other laboratory exams, in 1979; virtually all these tests could have been avoided without interfering with treatment. Between 1979 and 1981, the last year for which data are available, the total of complementary examinations increased by 22 percent each year, *i.e.*, at a rate comparable to previous years even while INAMPS was reducing expenditures over all (McGreevey *et al.*, 1984, p. 49). Most of these services have no curative or pain-relieving value; their role is to assist diagnosis prior to treatment. Studies in the United States (Neuhauser and Lewicki, 1975), Canada (Henderson and Gardner, 1981) and the United Kingdom (*British Medical Journal*, 1981) demonstrate the inefficacy of many tests in diagnosis. The overuse of such tests in Brazil is thus similar to other countries, but more pernicious because the country can ill afford such waste.

Overprescription of drugs, particularly antibiotics, observed elsewhere in the world, is probably common in Brazil (Landmann, 1982, pp. 31–51). At the INAMPS Hospital de Ipanema in Rio de Janeiro, a study which began in 1973 found that 32.8 doses of antibiotics per patient were being prescribed by the medical staff. One third of the patients were being given 2 different antibiotics, and 12 percent were being given 4 or more different drugs simultaneously. As a result of a special educational program for the medical staff, the number of doses per patient treated was reduced to 16.75 in 1974 and 9.6 in 1975, *i.e.*, to less than a third of the level which prevailed before the start of the education program. A positive side-effect, probably attributable to the reduction in excessive prescription of the drugs, was a marked reduction in the rate of patient infections from 6.8 percent in 1973 to 4.9 percent in 1975 (Aguiar, 1977; cited in Landmann, 1982, pp. 43–44).

Brazilians can much more easily self-prescribe and obtain drugs such as antibiotics or birth control pills than can laymen in developed countries where access to the pharmacopeia is limited by the medical profession and the government. Thus overuse and even abuse of drugs is a common phenomenon. The extent of private use of drugs without physician consultation was the subject of a special study in Nova Iguaçu, an urban *municipio* near Rio de Janeiro. More than a third of antibiotics taken were consumed without a doctor's prescription; two thirds of contraceptive pills taken were without a prescription. Only in cases of hypertension and chest pains that persons thought related to suspected myocardial infarctions were most drugs taken under prescription (Cordeiro, 1980, p. 189).

In the 1974 ENDEF survey, expenditures on health varied from 3.4 percent of income in the poorer states of the Northeast to 4.3 percent in Rio de Janeiro and 5.3 percent in the richer states south of São Paulo (Cordeiro, 1980, p. 182). The share of expenditures on patent medicines varied inversely with the income share devoted to health: the poor Northeast spent most of its small health budget on such medicines (57 percent), the Rio sample spent 34 percent, and the Southern states, 37.6 percent on patent medicines (Cordeiro, 1980, p. 181).

Brazil is the world's eighth largest consumer of pharmaceuticals (after the U.S., Japan, West Germany, France, Italy, Spain and Great Britain, but ahead of Mexico and Canada) though consumption per capita is but one third the level of Canada and one sixth the level of France (James, 1977, cited in Cordeiro, 1980, p. 6). Brazil was also in 1971, the number eight producer of drugs (Possas, 1981, p. 282). Brazil is a particularly heavy user of antibiotics, which constitute 13 percent of all drugs used in the world as a whole but 18 percent of drugs sold in Brazil in 1973 (Cordeiro, 1980, p. 8).

Much of Brazilian drug purchase and use occurs outside the control or influence of the medical profession: Physicians are not entirely responsible for excessive drug use. The government, however, does not do enough to inform people of the dangers of overuse of antibiotics and X-rays, or the misuse of other common drugs and the possible uselessness of many patent medicines.

Behavior And Health Costs

For a time in the late 1970s, the Brazilian government promoted cigarette smoking; an unnamed minister was quoted in the press as saying, "If Brazilians stop smoking, the country will go broke" (Rosemberg, 1981, p. 297). Between 33 and 55 percent of a sales tax levied on manufactured products was generated by tobacco sales in the years 1970 through 1979. Government thus came to be a major beneficiary of the annual 8 percent increase in tobacco consumption in the early 1970s (Rosenberg, 1981, p. 296). Tobacco consumption in Brazil continued to grow at 4.1 percent each year in the late 1970s, after consumption had begun to decline in the UK and was growing very little in the United States. One Brazilian physician thus suggests that lung cancer may eventually join the list of the diseases of underdevelopment (Landmann, 1984, p. 33).

An effective health policy would at least prevent the government from promoting behavior injurious to health. Brazilian use of social drugs such as caffeine, alcohol, and tobacco seems to be at high enough levels to be potentially unhealthy. The use of these drugs, accompanied in the case of coffee by high intake of sugar, can certainly pose a health hazard and impose very large costs on the curative health system. Dr. G. B. Patino, editor of the *Revista brasileira de odontologia*, is quoted as saying, "The excessive amount of sugar consumption is a major factor contributing to dental caries and gum disease" (Emert, 1982, p. 1). For the poorer regions of the country, particularly the Northeast, poverty discourages behavioral changes—such as improved diet and abandonment of high sugar-content alcoholic beverages—which can lead to better health. In the more affluent South and Southeast, however, much more could be done to change behavior, improve health and lower curative services costs.

In the United States, cancer, coronary heart disease, stroke and motor vehicle injuries cost US$57.8 billion in health-care expenditures in 1975 (Hartunian, Smart and Thompson, 1981, p. 366). U.S. GNP that year totaled US$1,533 billion; thus the cost of just four health impairments was equal to 3.8 percent of GNP. All four sources of impairment are subject to substantial reduction by preventive measures involving behavioral change. In Brazil, as well as in the United States, it is easier to identify the remedies (stop smoking, change diet, reduce stress, wear seat belts) than to induce people to change their behavior. Because the Brazilian government pays so large a share of the national health bill, it has a large stake in healthful behavior.

Victor Fuchs showed in his book, *Who shall live? health, economics and social choice* (1974), the striking differences in mortality and life expectancy between the populations of Utah and Nevada in the United States, despite similar age structure, health-service availability and other presumably important mortality and morbidity differences. The main variable explaining the difference in mortality experience for the two states was personal behavior with respect to consumption of food and social drugs, particularly alcohol and tobacco; stress in work, and related social characteristics differentiating the Mormon population of Utah from the more secular population in Nevada. These choices may be as important for health status in Brazil as they have been shown to be in the developed countries. As Bryan Abel-Smith notes, "Action to prevent ill-health extends far beyond the health field" (1976, p. 129).

Choice Of Services

The Brazilian medical-hospital system offers a number of services which require extremely high costs for a few patients. These include renal dialysis, coronary bypass operations and intensive-care units.

In 1978 there were about 12 patients per million inhabitants (1,428 in total) on renal dialysis being cared for at the expense of INAMPS. The number had risen to about 3,000 total, or nearly 25 per million inhabitants, by May 1981—a level above East European countries but still well below the 120 patients per million inhabitants in the United States. As Figure 9.1 shows, Brazil is not very different from other countries, relative to per capita product, in the extent of use of renal dialysis. The total cost to maintain these 3,000 patients is estimated by Landmann to be about Cr$12 billion in 1981, or the equivalent of 4 percent of the total INAMPS budget (1982, 77).

In 1976 INAMPS spent 1 percent of its budget on heart bypass operations

Figure 9.1
Renal Patients per Million Inhabitants, Fifteen
Developed Countries (1975), and Brazil (1981),
in Relation to GDP per Capita

Renal patients (alive on dialysis or with a
functioning transplant) per million population

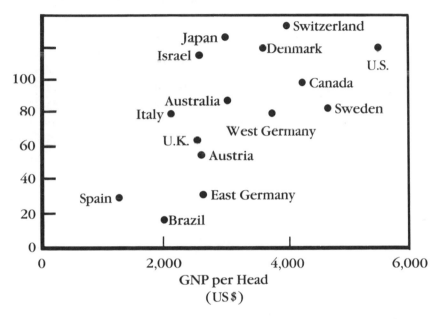

Source: A. J. Wing, "Prospects for the Treatment of Renal Diseases," *British Medical Journal,* 1 October 1977. Reprinted with permission. Cited in Maxwell (1981), p. 95; and Landmann (1982), p. 74.

and has probably spent an even larger share in recent years (Landmann, 1982, p. 70). A single private hospital in São Paulo performs more heart bypass operations than are performed in Holland, a country with low mortality and a population somewhat larger (13.8 million) than Greater São Paulo (12.5 million), yet which made a specific policy decision to limit such operations on grounds that they are ineffective and costly (Crook, 1978; cited in Landmann, 1982, p. 71). The Brazilian government decided in 1982 to limit many high-cost medical procedures to public-sector facilities.

Relatively useless intensive-care units (home care has been shown to be at least as effective medically) have expanded considerably in Brazilian private hospitals and cost on average six times as much as other hospital bed-days.

Angiograms, electrocardiograms and CAT scans are all in substantial use at great cost and with marginal real health benefit in Brazil (Solon and Vitor, 1981, p. 24; Landmann, 1982, pp. 57–65).

The use of these high-technology services in private hospitals at public expense diverts health-care resources to a tiny fraction of the population, instead of serving a potentially much larger group with basic health care. There were 3,000 renal dialysis patients and at most 9,000 patients treated with coronary bypass operations and in related intensive-care units. These patients are estimated to have used about 6 percent of the INAMPS budget or about Cr$22 billion in 1981. In that same year the budget for basic health services and communicable disease control totaled Cr$19 billion (McGreevey et al., 1984, p. 29). Those programs are aimed chiefly to benefit, through primary and preventive health care, the 41 million people living in North and Northeast Brazil. Thus, incredible as it may seem, Brazil's government spent more in 1981 on some 12,000 high-cost patients than on the sum of basic health services and disease control meant to serve 40 million or more people.

The choice between high technology for a few, and low technology for many, is not one that individual physicians would feel qualified to make. And in the health field, as Maxwell writes,

> The principal decisions about utilization are not made by consumers but by providers. Once we have asked a doctor for help, it is chiefly doctors who decide what services we require; they are therefore among the prime determinants of how resources are used in the whole health sector. The quantity and quality of medical services tend to rise to the point where, in the judgment of providers, the marginal benefit of further services is zero. Put more simply, when doctors and hospitals are paid for each item of service, they no doubt ask themselves whether an additional item will benefit their patient, but they do not ask whether he (or the organization paying the bill on his behalf) would prefer to spend the money in some other way. (Maxwell, 1981, pp. 49–50) Physicians are asked to deal with a specific patient and to offer such help as medical science can provide, no matter what the cost. There is little point in blaming the individual physician for choosing technologies which seem effective. What is essential is to create a system, or environment of choice for the physician, which can encourage a more socially efficient use of health resources.

The creation of such a system requires a more effective use of prices as signals to the physicians who are the decisionmakers. There have been few restraints and some outright encouragement to the use of high technology. If an office consultation is underpaid but a coronary bypass is amply rewarded, the physician will accept the pricing signal and act accordingly by doing his consultations in public clinics and his operations, in numbers beyond those which a second opinion might consider essential, in a private hospital with an intensive-care unit.

The physician normally does not make choices between patients but offers such services as he can to the patients with whom he deals. An exception occurs when, at particular moments, there is excess demand on the physician's time and talent, *e.g.*, in an emergency room after a major accident or with battlefield casualties. A triage system maximizes survival by giving up on some patients to save others.

HEALTH POLICY

The choice to eschew high technology is a form of triage. It limits resources devoted to one use in order to allocate those resources to save more lives. The choice is not one that individual physicians can make. The Hippocratic Oath virtually requires what Maxwell refers to as the application of resources until the marginal benefit is zero. That decision rule is directly counter to the social objectives of applying resources to a given patient only up to the point where the marginal benefit is no less than in the application of resources to all other patients. The physician cannot take these larger considerations into account, given his special doctor-patient relationship. He can, however, understand the principles of triage, and he can be brought to act in a manner consistent with those principles through a more effective system of pricing signals. Health policy can thus be seen, not as a program of poorly observed government regulations and decrees, but as a possibly rational and potentially effective branch of government price policy.

Change Within INAMPS

Four important changes in INAMPS policy occurred between late 1981 and February 1982: (1) a new payment system for university hospitals that rewards them more fairly for services rendered to INAMPS-financed patients; (2) restrictions on elective hospitalizations in private hospitals; (3) priority given to INAMPS and university hospitals, over private ones, for conducting sophisticated, costly and difficult examinations; and (4) initiation of studies for the abolition of the fee-for-service system of payment (Landmann, 1982, p. 9). Citing these significant changes, and the start of a process of further change, helps underline how fluid the policy situation is today in Brazil. The specific orders for change were issued by CONASP (Conselho Consultivo da Administração de Saúde Previdenciaria) on December 14, 1981, and signed by the Minister of Social Security on January 6, 1982. The INAMPS system made considerable progress in cutting expenses in 1981 below the 1980 level; further changes now under study could lead to even greater efficiencies.

To control cost INAMPS is experimenting with several reforms in private contracts, including restrictions on emergency visits, requirements for more detailed reporting of costs, and alternative payment arrangements. Commencing with 1981, INAMPS attempted to limit emergency visits to 15 percent of ambulatory visits to private contract institutions; this new action appeared to reduce emergency visits to about 35 percent of total visits for the first six months of 1981 (Barnum, 1981, p. 41).

The Curitiba Plan

Curitiba is the capital of the state of Paraná, a prosperous coffee-growing region just south of São Paulo. On January 8, 1981, the state superintendency of INAMPS began a pilot program to deal with such problems as high-cost treatment in private hospitals, long lines at INAMPS facilities and ineffective attention to primary health care needs of the Curitiba population. The plan provides for a triage at INAMPS and other public (state and municipal) facilities in which each walk-in patient is examined by a physician-auditor and either treated there or referred to higher-level service as necessary. It also alters the fee system by paying a fixed amount for a given procedure as prescribed at the public facility, rather than paying for all items as charged by the secondary-level facility (usually private) to which the patients are referred. This system differs from past practice in ways which affect overall system costs. Walk-in patients may not go directly to private facilities which may be unnecessarily specialized, or inappropriately specialized, in the light of patient need. This change could reduce the number of patients treated as emergencies. In the past many walk-in patients were treated by private hospitals as emergency cases which receive substantially higher fee-for-service allotments from INAMPS. The Curitiba system could reduce the number of walk-in patients who, as a result of consultation, are admitted to a hospital bed. About 85 percent of ambulatory patients had their cases resolved without referral to another level of service and without having to return to any long waiting line. Hospitalizations were reduced to 5 percent of initial consultations, somewhat below the Brazilian average of 6.5 percent in 1981. Public-sector hospitals were said to be absorbing 60 percent to 65 percent of persons referred for in-patient service (*O Estado de São Paulo*, 16 May 1982, p. 3).

By mid-1982 INAMPS management considered that the plan had already demonstrated a reduction by 30 percent in the number of hospital admissions; presumably all these were walk-ins who in fact did not need hospitalization. A preliminary evaluation in September 1981 did show conclusively that the service had improved in the users eyes: 78 percent said service was better and 93 percent had interviews with a physician within 15 minutes of arriving at the clinics studied (INAMPS, Sup. Reg., Paraná 1981).

This aspect of the Curitiba plan seems similar to the British National Health Service, which is marked by the pattern of general practice and the convention of referral from primary and secondary to tertiary care. More than 80 percent of episodes of illness reaching the National Health Service are dealt with from start to finish by general practitioners who account, with associated prescribing costs, for well under 20 percent of total expenditure (Maxwell, 1981, p. 87). In the British system, less than 2 percent of cases of recognized illness actually require hospitalization (see Figure 9.2). Because the United Kingdom has among the lowest levels of expenditures on health as a share of GNP among the developed countries, it is a positive sign that the Curitiba experiment has characteristics like those of the British system.

The other principal difference of the Curitiba plan with past practice is the alteration in the fee-for-service system to permit a lump-sum payment to private providers for an identified procedure. The triage system in the clinics puts the decision about appropriate treatment in the hands of the INAMPS physician-auditor rather than those of the private hospital and physician to which the patient is referred. The physician-auditor fills out a form, *Atestado de Internação Hospitalar* (AIH), establishing the diagnostically related group and hence the fee for the internment. By specifying treatment in accord with diagnosis, the INAMPS system can then specify, on the basis of past experience with costs for a given procedure, a fair number of *unidades de serviço* (US) for the payment to the private hospital. Then, if the private hospital incurs additional costs, it must absorb them out of profit; similarly, if the private hospital can effectively perform the procedure at less cost, it can enhance its profit. The system of reimbursement, unlike the previous method of paying for each test, exam, medication and service offered, encourages the private hospitals to economize on materials and services. If many tests, exams and services are not really useful, this new system of payment could reduce costs while maintaining quality of service.

At the mid-point of 1982, there was as yet no evidence that costs to INAMPS for hospital care were distinctly lower with the Curitiba plan. The first year of operations saw a reduction in the number of admissions in Paraná, but there was also a proportional increase in treatment costs. The net effect was a one-year growth in expenditures that was only slightly below that of the rest of the nation (Choyoshi, 1983). Preliminary analyses were unable to determine the causes of the higher cost per admission. One possibility is an undesirable "diagnostic-related group creep," a tendency to substitute costly for cheap diagnoses such as is occurring in the United States (Woodward, 1984,

Figure 9.2
Thresholds of Awareness and Consultation (Episodes of Illness
During Period of Study per 1,000 Patients at Risk)

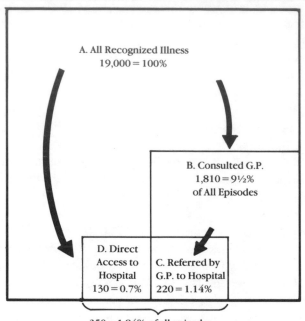

A. All Recognized Illness
19,000 = 100%

B. Consulted G.P.
1,810 = 9½%
of All Episodes

D. Direct
Access to
Hospital
130 = 0.7%

C. Referred by
G.P. to Hospital
220 = 1.14%

350 = 1.84% of all episodes
(18 percent of what reaches the Health Service)

Source: D. Crombie, "Changes in Patterns of Recorded Morbidity," in *Benefits and Risks in Medical Care,* edited by D. Taylor, p. 24, figure 1 (London: Office of Health Economics, 1974). Crombie's calculation is based on the Second National Morbidity Survey, 1970–1971 and (for total episodes) on M.E.J. Wadsworth, W.J.H. Butterfield, and R. Blaney, *Health and Sickness: The Choice of Treatment* (London: Tavistock, 1971). Reprinted with permission. Cited in Maxwell (1981), p. 89.

p. 376). Another possibility is that initial payment rates had to be set somewhat high in order to avoid resistance to the new scheme.

The Curitiba plan was started initially in six clinics in that city. Subsequently, it was extended to other parts of the state of Paraná. In mid-1982 the management of INAMPS was considering further extension of the plan to other cities and states. São Mateus borough in the Greater São Paulo area was identified as one pilot area for the plan which would be executed under terms of a cooperative agreement involving INAMPS, the São Paulo state health secretariat and the prefecture of the municipality of São Paulo. The latter organizations already had in place in São Mateus clinics and health posts which could serve as the first line of entry for potential clients into the health system. INAMPS management indicated in June 1982 that plans for extension to other states were under active discussion.

Shortly before leaving the presidency of INAMPS, Dr. Aloisio Salles strongly defended the new payment plan (*Senhor*, March 1985). Its efficacy has, nonetheless, not yet been proven, and it arrived on the scene in the midst of scandals and fraud which further undermined public confidence in the system.

Federal Health Policy

In December 1981 CONASP had already issued orders to reduce the inordinately high costs of renal dialysis, cardiovascular surgery, organ transplants, chemotherapy, CAT scanning, nuclear medicine, physiotherapy and outpatient treatment (CONASP 1982, Annex 2). In the first half of 1982 CONASP took up the analysis of overall objectives for the health sector and stated as one key objective, among others, "the search for lower unit costs and greater budgetary foresight, by means of a gradual reversal of the prevailing health model based on fee for service, and by instituting a payment schedule based on population coverage (prepayment), thus making possible the introduction of actuarial calculations for health costs" (CONASP 1982, 4). The May 1982 report of CONASP, said by its members in June 1982 to represent the likely future path of health policy, included these important points:

(*1*) Priority to be given to full coverage of the population through basic health services and primary health care.

(*2*) The criteria of *regionalization* and *hierarchization*, words used to describe the Curitiba plan, to be used to create a network of levels and complexity reserved to specialized services.

(*3*) Decentralization and deregulation of administrative, financial and accounting systems.

(*4*) Joint determination by state, municipal, federal and private institutions in budget planning and overall public responsibility for health policy and programs.

(*5*) Public-sector responsibility for ambulatory patients, private-sector responsibility for hospital patients, predominantly.

(*6*) Functional articulation of public and private health networks of referral.

(*7*) Priority utilization of existing public-sector facilities.

(*8*) Client access to the health system through the basic health services network, except in cases of emergency.

(*9*) Use of the system of agreements with private enterprises for coverage of specific population groups (CONASP 1982, 5–6).

In the short term the report calls for the installation of the Curitiba plan throughout Brazil (CONASP 1982, 15). In the medium term, a new health-assistance model is proposed, based on a system of prepayment which is justified, above all, by the fact that it permits more accurate anticipation of the total medical bill than does the current fee-for-service system.

Using established health parameters, *e.g.*, eight hospitalizations per hundred population per annum, specific hospital payments will be authorized to designated private providers serving an identified population group. An audit system can then concentrate on cases which exceed norms, analyze why excess service use occurred and rule on the acceptability of resulting charges. In the longer run it will presumably be possible to establish prepayment rates for health services so that it would no longer be necessary to use the medium-period system of paying private hospitals for maintenance of a set number of bed-days for an area's population. At that stage the health system will have achieved its objective of being a true health-insurance program financed out of the sum of individual contributions (CONASP 1982, 17). Finally, at an "opportune moment" it would prove useful to effect a consolidation of INAMPS and the Ministerio da Saúde (CONASP 1982, 31). The future functioning of CIPLAN, the Interministerial Commission for Planning and Coordination, and of CONASP, would presumably aid such streamlining of the health-sector organization chart.

Brazilian officials recognize excessive centralization of decisionmaking and adoption for fee-for-service, *unidade de serviço*, as the system of payment as systemic flaws which have created incentives among bureaucrats to overregulate and among private physicians to overcharge and overprescribe. It will not be easy to change these characteristics of the system. Each has powerful interests which will be undermined by adoption of the plans put forward by CONASP.

Some remaining health problems

Improvements in health and health care in Brazil over the past forty years nonetheless leave a significant residue of problems:

(*1*) Inequalities in the availability of health services between regions and income groups.

(*2*) Reliance on a social insurance scheme for health financing which leads to excessive demand for services among those who have access.

(*3*) Absence of personnel planning, particularly for physicians, which could lead to better geographic distribution of health resources and appropriate expansion of physician numbers.

(*4*) Lack of a program of health research and education designed to change behavior to improve health status.

(5) Inadequate analysis of the manufacture and importation of pharmaceuticals and medical instruments as they may affect medical practice.

(6) Insufficient planning for the expansion of basic health services and food and nutrition programs.

These issues need to be addressed in the policymaking process. The achievements of better health for many in Brazil are significant; the extent to which a large share of the population still suffers from ill health and has no effective access to basic health services demonstrates that there is much unfinished business in this sector.

NOTES

1. The views presented are those of the authors and do not necessarily represent those of the World Bank or of the Government of Brazil. This paper was prepared at the request of the organizers of a seminar on "Social Change in Brazil Since World War II." The seminar was held at Columbia University in December 1984 and organized by Professors Edmar Bacha and Herbert Klein. This work draws on an earlier paper prepared by the authors in collaboration with Vitor Gomes Pinto and Lucia Pontes de Miranda (1984).

2. Data on health-care expenditures are far from accurate. The ENDEF (Estudo Nacional de Despesa Familiar) survey in 1974 gathered some pertinent data and PNAD81 included questions on health spending. There remain problems of interpretation, particularly with respect to the question of what items should be considered as spending for health. As expected, the results of PNAD81 point to an increase in private spending for health care above the level presumed to obtain before the survey.

3. The dichotomy between preventive and curative services is drawn in Table 9.2 between medical-hospital services (curative) of the Ministerio de Previdência e Assistência Social (MPAS) and all other services. However, many medical procedures—even some employing high levels of technical sophistication, *e.g.*, coronary bypass operations for heart attack victims—can be viewed as preventive medical measures. MPAS does assist some primary health care through the Program for Grassroots Health and Sanitation Actions in the Northeast (PIASS). About 1.1% of MPAS funds in 1981 were spent on basic health services. In contrast, about 4% of the health ministry budget supports cancer and tuberculosis programs. Maternal and child health services and family planning are often delivered by the medical-hospital system and are essentially preventive measures meant to avoid health risks. A more relevant differentiation of services for policy purposes would identify services of low unit cost per beneficiary yet with high individual and social returns as preventive or primary health care, and high per unit cost services in specialized settings with high individual but low social returns as curative or secondary/tertiary health care. Brazilian data are not prepared with this distinction in mind.

REFERENCES

Abel-Smith, Brian. 1976. *Value for money in health services, a comparative study*. London: Heinemann.

Brazil. CONASP. 1982. Plano de reorientação da assistência à saúde no ámbito da Previdência Social. Mimeo. Rio: INAMPS.

Brazil. FIBGE. 1981, 1984. *Anuario estatístico do Brasil*. Rio: FIBGE.

Brazil. FIBGE. 1983. *Pesquisa nacional de amostra por domicilio, PNAD, 1981*. Rio: FIBGE.

Brazil. MPAS, DATAPREV. 1980. *A previdência social brasileira*. Brasilia: Industrias Graficas.

Brazil. MPAS, INAMPS. 1979. *Tabela de honorários*. Rio: INAMPS.

Brazil. MPAS, INAMPS. 1982. *INAMPS em dados*. Rio: INAMPS.

Brazil. MPAS, INAMPS, Superintendencia Regional de Paraná. 1981. Regionalização e hierarquização da assistência Médica ambulatorial em Curitiba. Mimeo. Rio: INAMPS.

Brazil. SEPLAN. 1982. *Consolidação plurianual de programas de govêrno*. Mimeo. Brasilia: IPEA.

Choyoshi, F.Y. Análise do impacto do nova plano de contas sobre as despesas. Mimeo. Rio: INAMPS.

Cordeiro, Hesio. 1980. *A industria da saúde no Brasil*. Rio: Ediçoes Graal.

Donnangelo, Cecilia. 1982. Modalidade de exercicio profissional de medicina na grande São Paulo. Mimeo. São Paulo: Departamento de Medicina Preventiva, Universidade de São Paulo.

Echeverri, Oscar. 1981. Human resources in the Brazil urban health sector with special reference to São Paulo. Mimeo. Washington, DC: World Bank.

Emert, Harold. 1982. Dr. Patiño and the state of Brazilian dentistry. *Brazil Herald*, June 2, 1.

Fuchs, Victor. 1974. *Who shall live? Health, economics and social choice*. New York: Basic Books.

Gentile de Mello, Carlos. 1981. *O sistema de saúde em crise*. São Paulo: HUCITEC.

Golladay, Frederick, and Bernhard Liese. 1980. Health problems and policies in the developing countries. *World Bank staff working paper 412*. Washington, DC: World Bank.

Guimarâes, R.F. 1977. A eficácia de exame telerradiográfico de tórax como técnica de screening em população hospitalar. *Revista de saúde pública 11*, 1, 97–109. São Paulo.

Hartunian, Nelson, *et al.* 1981. *The incidence and economic costs of major health impairments*. Lexington, MA: Lexington Books.

Knight, Peter, and Ricardo Moran. 1981. *Brazil: Poverty and basic needs series*. Washington, DC: World Bank.

Kravis, Irving, *et al.* 1982. *World product and income*. Baltimore, MD: Johns Hopkins University Press.

Landmann, Jayme. 1982. *Evitando a saúde e promovendo a doença*. Rio: Achamé.

Landmann, Jayme. 1983. *Medicina não é saúde*. Rio: Editora Nova Fronteira.

Landmann, Jayme. 1984. *A outra face da medicina*. Rio: Editora Salamandra.

Maxwell, Robert J. 1981. *Health and wealth, an international study of health care spending*. Lexington, MA: Lexington Books.

McGreevey, William, Lúcia Pontes de Miranda Baptista, Vitor Gomes Pinto, Sérgio Francisco Piola, and Solon Magalhâes Vianna. 1984. Política e financiameno do sistema de saúde brasileiro, uma perspectiva internacional. *IPEA estudos para o planejamento 26*. Brasilia: IPEA/SEPLAN.

McNeill, William. 1976. *Plagues and peoples*. New York: Doubleday.

Merrick, Thomas. 1984. Financial implications of Brazil's high rate of caesarian section deliveries. Mimeo. Washington, DC. World Bank.

Merrick, Thomas, and Douglas Graham. 1979. *Population and economic development in Brazil, 1800 to the present*. Baltimore, MD: Johns Hopkins University Press.

Musgrove, Philip. 1983. Family health care spending in Latin America. *Journal of health economics 2*, 245–57.

Nitrini, Dario. 1982. Médicos denuncian ociosidade nos hospitais da Previdência. *Folha de São Paulo*. May 9.

Possas, Cristina. 1981. *Saúde e trabalho, a crise da Previdência Social*. Rio: Edições Graal.

Preston, Samuel. 1972. *Causes of death: life tables for national populations*. New York: Academic Press.

Rosemberg, José. 1981. *Tabagismo, sério problema de saúde pública*. São Paulo: Editora Universidade de São Paulo.

Senhor (Joao Carlos Leal). 1985. O administrador de fraudes, entrevista com o Dr. Aloisio Salles. *Senhor*. Rio. March 6, 3–8.

Vianna, Solon Magalhães, and Vitor Gomes Pinto. 1981. A assistência médica da Previdência Social. Mimeo. Brasilia: IPEA/CNRH.

Vieira, Cesar. 1984. Financiamento do setor de saúde no Brasil. Mimeo. Brasilia: PAHO.

Woodward, Robert S. 1984. Brazilian health care delivery during a recession. *PAHO bulletin 18*, 4, 371–78.

NOTE ON CONTRIBUTORS

Edmar L. Bacha is an economist, president of the Brazilian Institute of Geography and Statistics, a former high government official, and professor of economics at the Catholic Pontifical University in Rio de Janeiro.

Herbert S. Klein is professor of history at Columbia University.

Thomas J. Merrick is director of the Population Reference Bureau in Washington, D.C.

David Goodman is professor of economics at University College, London, as well as on the faculty of the Latin American Institute at the University of London.

Martin T. Katzman is an economist in the Department of Environmental Science at the University of Texas at Dallas.

Vilmar Faria is a sociologist with CEBRAP and a professor in the Department of Social Sciences at the University of Campinas.

José Pastore is a sociologist and a professor in the Department of Economics and Administration at the University of São Paulo.

Helga Hoffmann is an economist with the United Nations in New York.

Maurício C. Coutinho is an economist and professor at the University of Campinas.

Cláudio Salm is an economist, head of the population section of the Brazilian Institute of Geography and Statistics, and professor of economics at the Federal University of Rio de Janeiro.

Cláudio de Moura Castro is an economist affiliated with the International Labor Office in Geneva.

William P. McGreevey is an economist and senior financial analyst with The World Bank.

345

Sérgio Piola is a public health professional affiliated with the Institute of Economic and Social Development.

Solon Magalhães Vianna is a public health physician with the Institute of Economic and Social Development.

41 · 61